Research in Corporate Sustainability

The Evolving Theory and Practice of
Organizations in the Natural Environment

Edited by

Sanjay Sharma
Wilfrid Laurier University

Mark Starik
George Washington University

Edward Elgar
Cheltenham, UK • Northampton, MA, USA

© Sanjay Sharma and Mark Starik 2002

Call

Published by
Edward Elgar Publishing Limited
Glensanda House
Montpellier Parade
Cheltenham
Glos GL50 1UA
UK

Edward Elgar Publishing, Inc.
136 West Street
Suite 202
Northampton
Massachusetts 01060
USA

A catalogue record for this book
is available from the British Library

Library of Congress Cataloguing in Publication Data
Research in corporate sustainability: the evolving theory and practice of organizations in the natural environment/ edited by Sanjay Sharma, Mark Starik.
   p. cm.
Includes bibliographical references and index.
  1. Sustainable development. 2. Environmental economics—Research. 3. Economic development—Environmental aspects. 4. Corporations—Environmental aspects—Case studies. I. Sharma, Sanjay. II. Starik, Mark, 1951-

HC79.E5 R457 2003
338.9'27—dc21
                                                            2002072157

ISBN 1 84064 906 2

Printed and bound in Great Britain by MPG Books Ltd, Bodmin, Cornwall

Contents

List of figures

List of tables

List of boxes

List of contributors

Linda C. Angell is a Senior Lecturer in Operations Management at the School of Business and Public Management of Victoria University of Wellington, New Zealand. In this capacity, she teaches quality, services, operations and environmental management in the undergraduate, graduate and executive education programs. Her research interests include environmental operations management, quality management practices, and work team performance. She publishes in the *Journal of Operations Management, International Journal of Operations and Production Management (IJOPM), Production and Operations Management, Organization Studies, Case Studies in Operations Management* and Germany's *Zeitschrift für Planung.* She guest-edited a special issue of *IJOPM* focusing on environmental issues in operations management (Vol. 20, No. 2, 2000). Dr Angell holds a DBA from Boston University, an MBA High Distinction from Babson College and a BA *summa cum laude* from the University of Massachusetts in Amherst.

Oana Branzei is a doctoral student in the Organizational Behaviour and Human Resources Division in the Faculty of Commerce at the University of British Columbia. She holds an MBA from the University of Nebraska and a Bachelor of Science in International Relations and Foreign Trade from 'Al. I. Cuza' University in Romania. Her research interests include international strategy, strategic processes, managerial cognition, learning and knowledge management. Her research work has focused on the cross-cultural similarities and differences in the corporate approaches to eco-sustainability, the antecedents of environmental innovation and the cognitive frames of CEOs and environmental specialists in Canada, China and Japan. Several of her papers have appeared in the Best Paper Proceedings of the Academy of Management (Organizations and the Natural Environment Interest Group, 2000), the Best Paper Proceedings of the Administrative Sciences Association of Canada (Best Student Paper, International Business Division, 2001), and the *International Journal of Cross-Cultural Management.*

Mark Cordano is an Assistant Professor of Management at Ithaca College. He received his PhD from the University of Pittsburgh. His research investigates the influence of managers' attitudes on their decisions and interactions. His research has been published in journals such as the *Academy of Management Journal,* the *International Journal of Management*, the *Journal of Social Psychology*, and *Women in Management Review.*

Nicole Darnall is a faculty member of North Carolina State University's Department of Political Science and Public Administration. She is completing her doctorate in public policy at the University of North Carolina at Chapel Hill (UNC), and holds an MS in Policy Development and Program Evaluation from Vanderbilt University and an MA in Economics from the University of Texas. Prior to her current appointment, she was a researcher at UNC's National Database on Environmental Management Systems and at Resources for the Future in Washington DC. She worked as an economist for the US Forest Service.

Kanwalroop K. Dhanda is an Assistant Professor in Operations Management at the University of Portland. She applies mathematical modeling to environmental issues and public policy. Her research has appeared in journals such as *Operations Research, Journal of Environmental Economics and Management, Energy Economics, Journal of Public Policy and Marketing*, and *Journal of Computational Economics*. Dr Dhanda is the author of *Environmental Networks: A Framework for Economic Decision-Making and Policy Analysis,* a volume in the New Horizons in Environmental Economics series (Edward Elgar Publishing Limited, 1999). She has received the Pamplin Fellowship for research for two consecutive years and has been awarded the Outstanding Graduate Professor Award at University of Portland.

Carolyn P. Egri, PhD, is an Associate Professor of Management and Organization Studies in the Faculty of Business Administration at Simon Fraser University. Dr Egri has published extensively on the topics of environmental issues, leadership, organizational change, innovation and organizational power and politics. She is on the executive of the Organizations and Natural Environment Interest Group of the Academy of Management, and has been a director in the Organizational Behavior Teaching Society and the Vancouver Folk Music Festival Society. She has extensive experience as a human resource management professional, and has worked as a consultant in this field.

Kimberly M. Ellis earned her PhD degree in strategic management from Florida State University and is currently an Assistant Professor at Michigan State University. Her research interests include the integration process associated with M&As of related and similar-sized firms, corporate environmental management strategies and the role of corporate governance in organizational change efforts.

Dale E. Fitzgibbons, PhD, is an Associate Professor of Management at Illinois State University. His current research interests include the integration of spirituality and management, social and environmental management, philosophy of science, alternatives to capitalism, scholarship of teaching/learning, critical theory and feminism. His publications have appeared in *Organizational Behavior and Human Decision Processes, Journal of Organizational Change Management, Journal of Occupational Psychology, Journal of Management Education* and the *Journal of Leisure Research,* and he has contributed scholarly chapters to several edited volumes. He is currently the editor of the *Journal of Management Education.*

Irene Hanson Frieze is a Professor of Psychology and Business Administration at the University of Pittsburgh. Her research related to this chapter concerns information processing and motivation. She is also interested in career planning, both in the United States and other countries.

Trudy Heller is President of Executive Education for the Environment. She has served on the faculties of the School of Management at New Jersey Institute of Technology and Franklin and Marshall College. She currently teaches courses on business and the natural environment at the University of Pennsylvania and Drexel University. Her research on innovation and new technology development has been published in *Organization Science, Entrepreneurship: Theory and Practice, and The IEEE Transactions on Engineering Management.* Her current writing focuses on innovation of environmentally sensitive products and processes. This work has been presented at International Greening of Industry Network Conferences since 1998. Ms Heller holds a PhD in Management from the Wharton School of the University of Pennsylvania and a PhD in Organizational Development from Temple University.

Robert C. Hornal, MBA, is a graduate of Business Administration from Simon Fraser University in Burnaby, Canada. His research and consulting interests are in corporate environmental strategy, stakeholder relations and human resource development.

Bruce T. Lamont earned his PhD degree from the University of North Carolina-Chapel Hill. He is currently a full Professor at Florida State University. His general research interests deal with the effective management of strategic change as well as natural environment and social responsibility issues confronting corporate managers.

Jeanne Mroczko is the Director of Pollution Prevention and Permit Co-ordination, New Jersey Department of Environmental Protection (DEP). She acts as a liaison between the department's permitting programs and the business and industrial communities and provides comprehensive guidance and management of complex, multi-media projects. Ms Mroczko has helped to implement numerous permit processing improvements at the DEP, and is currently overseeing the development and implementation of the 'Silver and Gold Track for Environmental Excellence,' a program that provides regula-tory and operational flexibility for companies that have demonstrated above-average environmental performance. Previously, she served as DEP's Director of Public Participation, where she worked to improve public information about and access to the department's decision-making processes. Ms Mroczko is an expert in the field of Alternative Dispute Resolution, and conducts training in mediation, negotiation and conflict resolution.

Joyce S. Osland is Professor of International Business at San Jose State University. Her current research and consulting focus includes expatriates, cultural sense-making, global leadership, Latin American management and globalization. Her research appears in journals such as *Academy of Management Review*, *Academy of Management Executive*, *Journal of Management Inquiry* and *HR Management*. Dr Osland is the author of *The Adventure of Working Abroad* (Jossey-Bass, 1995) as well as *Organizational Behavior: An Experiential Approach* (Prentice Hall, 2001) and *The Organizational Behavior Reader* (Prentice Hall, 2001). She was named an Ascendant Scholar for her research by the Western Academy of Management and received the University of Portland's Outstanding Scholar Award and MBA Teaching Award. Dr Osland does organization development and cross-cultural management consulting with business and non-profit organizations in various countries. Prior to becoming an academic, she spent a decade working in Latin America and West Africa in the field of international development.

Gordon P. Rands is an Associate Professor of Management at Western Illinois University, specializing in business and the natural environment, corporate social responsibility and business ethics, and how organizational culture and change affect organizations' ethical, social and environmental performance. He serves as coordinator of the university's environmental studies minor. He has degrees from the University of Michigan (Natural Resources), Brigham Young University (Organizational Behavior) and the University of Minnesota (Business Administration). He has previously taught at Minnesota and Penn State. Dr Rands is one of the co-founders of the Organizations and Natural Environment (ONE) Interest Group of the Academy of Management, and served as its chairperson in 2001–2.

Sanjay Sharma's doctoral dissertation won the Best Dissertation Award from the Academy of Management, examining the reconciliation of corporate environmental strategies with competitiveness in the North American oil and gas industry. He has received several research awards including the Jossey Bass/New Lexington Press Award for the Best Academy of Management Paper on organizations and the natural environment (1997) and the ANBAR Citation of Excellence (1999) for his research. He has received research grants from the Social Sciences and Humanities Research Council of Canada (SSHRC) to examine sustainability strategies in the Canadian forestry industry and has served on the Council's Research Funding Adjudication Committee. His research has been published in the *Academy of Management Review*, *Academy of Management Journal*, *Strategic Management Journal*, *Journal of Applied Behavioral Science*, *Business Strategy and the Environment*, *Journal of Asian Business*, *Journal of Strategic Marketing*, and *Revue Francaise de Gestion*, among others. Dr Sharma was awarded a Fulbright Scholar for 2001–2002 during which he conducted research on corporate sustainability at the Center for Sustainable Enterprise at the University of North Carolina, Chapel Hill. Dr Sharma's biography is listed in *Who's Who in Canadian Business*. Before pursuing an academic career, Dr Sharma had 16 years of senior management experience with multinational corporations on three continents. He was the Director of the EMBA Program at Saint Mary's University, Canada and is currently at Wilfrid Laurier University, Canada. Sanjay Sharma is the current Chair of the Organization and the Natural Environment Interest Group at the Academy of Management, and was the Program Chair for the ONE Interest Group in 2001 and the PDW Chair in 2000 for Academy of Management Annual Meetings.

Donald J. Shemwell is an Assistant Professor of Marketing at East Tennessee State University. He earned all his degrees from a Bachelor in Economics to a PhD in Marketing at The Florida State University. His research has been published in among others the *Journal of Services Marketing*, *Journal of Marketing Communications*, *Journal of Marketing Theory and Practice*, *International Journal of Service Industry Management*, *Journal of Health Care Marketing*, *Journal of Nonprofit and Public Sector*

Marketing, Health Care Marketing Quarterly, Journal of Retail Banking Services, International Journal of Bank Marketing, Journal of Financial Services Marketing, Journal of Customer Service in Marketing and Management, International Journal of Management, Journal of Marketing for Higher Education and Managing Service Quality. He has made dozens of presentations at scholarly meetings and has served as a reviewer for over a dozen scholarly journals. His research has been supported by grants from the Sustainable Communities Network, AFG Enterprises, Appalachian Sustainable Development and the Kellogg Foundation.

W. Richard Sherman, JD, LLM, CPA, is an Associate Professor of Accounting at Saint Joseph's University in Philadelphia. Recipient of several teaching awards including the Lindback Foundation Award for Distinguished Teaching, he has presented papers at national and international conferences and his publications have appeared in academic and professional journals such as the *Academy of Accounting and Financial Studies Journal, Accounting Historians Journal, Accounting Educators' Journal, Business Insights, Critical Perspectives in Accounting*, the *CPA Journal*, the *Journal of Accounting Education*, the *Journal of Financial Planning* and the *Tax Adviser.*

Mark Starik is an Associate Professor of Strategic Management and Public Policy in the George Washington University School of Business and Public Management and directs the GW SMPP Environmental and Social Sustainability Initiative. In addition to teaching courses in Strategic Management and Business and Public Policy, he offers courses in Strategic Environmental Management, Environmental Policy, and Sustainability Values and Strategies. Mark's research interests include strategic stakeholder and environmental management, with particular attention to energy issues. Mark's service activities have included initiating and coordinating the GW Environmental Values and Strategies University Seminar Series, co-founding the Academy of Management Organizations and the Natural Environment Interest Group, and participating actively in the World Resources Institute's Business Environment Learning and Leadership Program. Mark received his doctorate in Strategic Management from the University of Georgia in 1991, his masters in Natural Resources Policy and Administration from the University of Wisconsin in 1978, and his bachelors in Economics from the University of Wisconsin in 1976.

Edward Stead is a Professor of Management at East Tennessee State University. He earned his BS and MBA from Auburn University and his PhD in Management from Louisiana State University in Baton Rouge. Before coming to ETSU in 1982, he held faculty positions at Western Illinois University, the University of Alabama in Birmingham and Louisiana State University. He has written extensively for over 20 years in the field of organizations and the natural environment. His book, co-authored with Jean Garner Stead, *Management for a Small Planet: Strategic Decision Making and the Environment* (Sage Publications, Thousand Oaks, CA, 1992 and 1996), has been used at dozens of universities in the US, Europe and Asia, and it has been widely cited in the field. Ed has served as Program Chair, Chair-Elect and Chair of the Organizations and the Natural Environment Interest Group (ONE) of the Academy of Management. He has also been an active member of the Academy's Social Issues in Management Division (SIM), and he serves on the editorial review board of Business Strategy and the Environment. For the past five years Ed has participated in a number of community sustainability projects in the Southern Appalachian region of the US. He has been the team leader of East Tennessee State University's Center for Community Sustainability, and he currently serves on the Board of Directors of Appalachian Sustainable Development. He is a member of the Northeast Tennessee Development District's Ozone Action Partnership, and he is currently serving as a community sustainability consultant for the Clinch River Chapter of the Nature Conservancy.

Jean Garner Stead is a Professor of Management at East Tennessee State University. She earned her BS and MA from Auburn University, her MBA from Western Illinois University, and her PhD in Business Administration from Louisiana State University in Baton Rouge. Prior to her appointment at ETSU Jean served on the faculty of Western Illinois University. Jean has written extensively for over two decades in the field of organizations and the natural environment. Her book, co-authored with Edward Stead, *Management for a Small Planet: Strategic Decision Making and the Environment* (Sage Publications, Thousand Oaks, CA, 1992 and 1996), received a Choice Outstanding Academic Book Award in 1992. In addition to her research, Jean has held several positions in both the Organizations and the Natural Environment Interest Group and the Social Issues in Management Division of the Academy of Management. For the past five years Jean has been involved in several community sustainability projects in the Southern Appalachian region of the US. She served as a team member in East Tennessee State University's Center for Community Sustainability, and she currently serves on the Board of Directors of Appalachian Sustainable Development. She is also a member of the Northeast Tennessee Development District's Ozone Action Partnership, and she serves on the Eco-loan Committee for the Clinch River Chapter of the Nature Conservancy.

David S. Steingard, PhD, is an Assistant Professor of Management at Saint Joseph's University. His current research and teaching interests include corporate spirituality and transformation, new paradigm and stakeholder management, consciousness-based organizations, the social and environmental responsibilities of business, alternative research methodologies, and the integration of science and spirituality in business and academe. His publication and conference presentations focus on the fields of organizational studies and management education. He has held positions in organizational development and human resources as Director of Human Resources, Internal Consultant for Culture Development and Training Specialist.

Ilan Vertinsky is the Vinod Sood Professor of International Business Studies and Professor of Business Economics and Strategy and Operation Logistics at the University of British Columbia. He is also the Director of the Centre for International Business Studies and the Forest Economics and Policy Analysis Research Unit of the University. He received his PhD in Business from the University of California at Berkeley. He held faculty appointment at Northwestern University and was a visiting professor in several universities including the Hebrew University and the Chinese University of Hong Kong. He also served as a senior fellow of the Science Center in Berlin. He has published more than 200 papers, book chapters, monographs and books. His publications appeared in journals such as the *Administrative Science Quarterly*, *Organizational Behaviour and Human Decision Processes*, *Management Science*, *Operations Research*, the *Journal of International Economics* and the *Journal of Economic Studies*. He has received the UBC Killam Research Prize (1995) and the Faculty Professional Research Excellence Award (2000). He serves on the editorial boards of several international and national journals. His current research interests are focused on strategic management in cutthroat competition and on strategic alliances.

Kristi Yuthas is an Assistant Professor of Accounting at Portland State University. She studies management control and corporate reporting systems, and seeks to demonstrate the limitations of instrumentalist perspectives and envision systems with social and economic benefit. Dr Yuthas has been recognized as one of the leading scholars in the field of accounting information systems. Her papers have appeared in a wide range of journals, including *Journal of Business Ethics*, *Journal of Information Systems*, *Critical Perspectives on Accounting and Information and Management*. Dr Yuthas has consulted in the areas of systems development and process reengineering and was a Boeing Faculty Fellow.

1. Research in corporate sustainability: what really matters?

Sanjay Sharma

'I also have a flower.'
'We do not record flowers,' said the geographer.
'Why is that? The flower is the most beautiful thing on my planet!'
'We do not record them,' said the geographer, 'because they are ephemeral.'
'What does that mean – "ephemeral"?'
'It means, "which is in danger of speedy disappearance."'
'Is my flower in danger of speedy disappearance?'
'Certainly it is.'
(*The Little Prince* by Antoine de Saint-Exupéry, 1945)

Just as natural scientists are concerned about species extinction and the health of Earth's 'ephemeral' ecosystems, organizations and the natural environment (ONE) researchers are concerned also about the possible extinction and survival of organizations that depend on healthy ecosystems and societies. The title of this volume, *Research in Corporate Sustainability: The Evolving Theory and Practice of Organizations in the Natural Environment*, reflects the research streams that approximately represent the future and extant focus of theoretical and empirical inquiry in ONE.[1] The past, albeit a short span, of scholarship in organizations and the natural environment has been mainly focused on theoretical and empirical advances in explaining how organizations interact with the natural environment at various levels of analysis. As these relationships become clearer, researchers have begun to take on the challenge of adding the social dimension and developing a deeper theoretical and empirical understanding of sustainable organizational forms, their antecedents and impacts on ecosystems and social welfare.

The challenge for ONE scholars is to go beyond studying pollution control and prevention or environmental restoration and preservation, and explain how organizations can learn to operate within the carrying capacity of ecosystems (Starik and Rands, 1995) and accrue natural capital for future generations (Hawken et al., 2001). Corporate sustainability additionally requires the incorporation of principles of inter-generational and intra-generational equity across species, societies and marginalized and disadvantaged groups of people (Gladwin et al., 1995). Sustainable organizations will build natural capital, enhance human and societal welfare, and contribute to appropriate economic and technological development (Schumacher, 1973 [1974]). These organizational forms will stretch the boundaries of scholarship for ONE researchers and challenge the creative imagination of corporate leaders.

Why is it important for business scholars to theoretically visualize and empirically measure organizational forms, structures, strategies and outcomes as firms travel on the path to sustainability? Some do not subscribe to arguments that environmental damage, species extinction and increasing global social inequities threaten the long-term survival of our organizations and even, perhaps, the human race. However, it is difficult to deny the desirability of economic and technological development that builds natural capital rather than depletes it, that enhances human welfare and builds healthier societies rather than deepens social divisions that lead to conflicts and acts of terrorism. Sustainable organizations not only have the potential for reversing the ecological and social damage caused by their operations but also for improving the world that we live in.

Before discussing the contribution that the chapters in this volume make to various research streams in organizations and the natural environment, it is useful to take stock of extant research and the gaps in this research that are addressed by the studies in this book. In order to develop the following section on extant research streams and directions for the future, Mark Starik and I polled a convenience sample of fellow scholars in ONE. While the names of these scholars are acknowledged,[2] their extremely valuable contributions have not been attributed individually in each case in this chapter due to space limitations and also because there was a great deal of agreement among the scholars and several common suggestions and ideas were offered.

The next section begins by discussing the streams of extant research on organization in the natural environment and the gaps that need to be addressed by future research. The focus of this chapter is on developing an organizing framework for past and extant ONE research, and future directions are discussed to the extent that they flow directly from the discussions in this section. The concluding chapter in this volume, on the other hand, focuses on suggesting research directions for future scholars. The chapter then discusses the limited extant theoretical contributions on corporate sustainability and the challenges of theoretically visualizing and empirically studying organizational change toward sustainability.

RESEARCH ON ORGANIZATIONS IN THE NATURAL ENVIRONMENT

The first half of this section focuses on the academic disciplines and theories that have influenced research in ONE and the value-added by extant ONE research to business and management literature. The potential areas of future theoretical development in organizations and the natural environment are then discussed. The second half of this section describes the topics and research contexts that have been effectively explored by ONE scholars and the areas that need further development.

A Gathering of Theoretical Streams

Organizations rely on the natural environment for their basic resources such as raw materials, clean air, clean water, land for operating facilities, predictable weather patterns and aesthetic working environments. At the same time, organizations also depend on the natural environment for the assimilation of wastes and emissions that they create (Egri, 1997; Shrivastava, 1995). Organizations are comprised of people who depend on a healthy environment for basic needs of food, security, comfort and quality of life.

> All men have stars...but they are not the same things for different people. For some, who are travelers, the stars are guides. For others they are little more than little lights in the sky. For others, who are scholars, they are problems. For my businessman they are wealth. But all these stars are silent. (*The Little Prince* by Antoine de Saint-Exupéry, 1945)

What distinctive contribution has ONE research made to the traditional business and management literature? Should ONE strive to become a separate academic discipline with its own theories or does the value of ONE research lie in addressing and explaining a unique and important problem context that has been neglected or ignored by other management fields? Much like the field of strategic management (Meyer, 1991), ONE research represents a gathering of diverse theoretical streams. ONE research spans functional areas and crosses levels of analysis by focusing on a problem domain rather than restricting itself to the bounds of a discipline or a theory. The field of strategic management adds value by bringing together insights from diverse disciplines such as economics, psychology and sociology, and diverse theories such as transaction-cost economics and population ecology, to address important issues of organizational competitiveness, performance and growth (Meyer, 1991). Similarly, ONE scholars provide a unique perspective on long-term survival, growth and competitiveness of organizations embedded in global ecosystems and societies.

According to the scholars polled for this volume, the main theoretical streams that have contributed to ONE research have been drawn from sociology (institutional theory, issues management, systems theory, network theory), economics (decision-making theory, natural resource valuation and management, the resource-based view of the firm, industrial organization economics, transaction-cost economics), psychology (environmental values and negotiation theory), anthropology (environmental culture and symbolism within organizations, nation-states, and cross-cultural comparisons), political science (collective action, public policy including theories of regulation), ethics (the role of the organization *vis-à-vis* its community and ecology), and mathematics (complexity theory).

The scholars polled by us saw the following business theories and disciplines as having contributed to ONE research: marketing (environmental advertising, packaging and purchasing behavior), accounting (natural resource-based accounting and auditing), organization theory (reconceptualizing organization theory to include the natural environment), organization behavior (leadership, organizational champions, organizational learning), strategic management (stakeholder theory, competitive strategy, resource-based view), operations management (greening the supply/value chain, environmental standards adoption, industrial ecology), and management information systems.

Similar to the field of strategic management, ONE research integrates theoretical perspectives from non-business and business disciplines in attempting to answer research questions about a complex problem domain. ONE is a research arena wherein diverse disciplines, theories and analytical methods vie to explain organizations in the natural environment. It should be noted that the traditional fields of research in business have rarely generated their own foundational theories or research paradigms. Human resources management and organization behavior mainly use theories from psychology and social psychology; accounting and finance mainly use theories from economics; and marketing research is based largely on theories from economics, psychology and social psychology. Therefore, it is a matter of debate whether it is more important for ONE scholars to generate their own theories, or to build cross-disciplinary and integrative research perspectives that have the potential to generate new perspectives on extant management and organizational theories.

ONE research can be considered more pluralistic than strategic management because it has increasingly drawn in scholars from strategic management, marketing, entrepreneurship, operations management, human resources management, organization behavior, accounting, finance, information systems, public policy, economics, psychology, sociology, political science, philosophy, geography and the natural sciences. Hence, ONE research may have the potential to break down barriers between academic enclaves and turfs, enriching the potential for generating cross-disciplinary knowledge. This integration of theoretical streams is accompanied by potential pitfalls. Meyer (1991: 829) points out that 'such cross-theoretical research requires a deep understanding of each theory in its original disciplinary context and the ability to interpret and apply theories to research problems' in the context of organizations in the natural environment. Therefore, the challenge lies in engaging other disciplines by utilizing the research from these disciplines well and undertaking rigorous research to yield theoretical and empirical insights that the other disciplines find interesting and useful.

In keeping with ONE's focus on a unique problem domain, empirical studies have been dominated by inductive and descriptive research intended to explain how organizations are changing (or not changing) in recognition of their interface with the natural environment. At the same time, the theoretical focus has mainly been on conceptualizations of corporate sustainability (for example, the 1995 *Academy of Management Review* Special Topic Forum on Ecologically Sustainable Organizations).[3] Should research on organizations in the natural environment continue to be driven by descriptions of organizational practice or should scholars increasingly develop prescriptive and normative models that will ultimately drive practice?

Future Theoretical Paths

The scholars polled by us agreed that none of the theoretical perspectives on organizations in the natural environment described above have been explored in great depth. ONE scholars should continue to explore these theoretical streams while increasingly collaborating across disciplines in order to integrate diverse theoretical perspectives and methods of inquiry. Potentially rich insights can be gained by engaging and linking management theories to technical fields such as production and engineering, the natural sciences, and economics and politics.

Some areas of further theoretical development in context of organizations in the natural environment as suggested by our colleagues are pointed out below. When a theoretical stream was suggested by just one or two colleagues as opposed to a general consensus among scholars, attributions have been made.

Hoffman suggested environmental sociology as a sub-discipline or theoretical stream embedded within the home discipline of sociology. This includes the processes by which environmental problems and solutions are culturally and institutionally framed; the political economy of the environment and environmental politics; the formation and evolution of environmental attitudes, values and behaviors; the formation, growth and restructuring of the environmental movement; the implications of environmental concerns for technological development and perceptions of technological risk; the role of corporations as institutional and policy entrepreneurs in guiding the evolution of broader environmental values, norms and beliefs.

Bazerman suggested a focus on environmental decision theory, including non-traditional utility functions, negotiations, collective behavior and social dilemmas. Several respondents felt that theories of planned behavior and charismatic leadership should be explored in greater depth as drivers of corporate environmental strategy. Many urged the need for more work utilizing theories in economics, such as transaction-cost economics and the integration of ecological economics to develop theories about environmentally sustainable international trade mechanisms including tradable pollution permits and taxes.

Another area of research that has been given less attention by extant ONE research relates to lesser-developed countries and development issues. These include the unique processes of organizational change and problems of firms in lesser-developed countries, as well as understanding and resolving the complexity of multi-level global interconnectedness of organizational and environmental issues with multiple governance issues.

Ed Stead and Jean Stead urged for more scholarly research on environmental ethics utilizing theories that draw upon the environmental ethics literature (for example, Carson, 1962; Leopold, 1949; Naess, 1995; Schumacher, 1973). The Steads also suggested that researchers make theoretical linkages to spiritual dimensions of environmental management. In general, scholars urged more research from the perspective of environmental entrepreneurship, marketing, finance and accounting, as well as the impact of the digital economy on organizational change toward greater environmental responsibility (Shrivastava).

Scholars also urged a balance between methods of inquiry used. They urged a space for both: positivist approaches using case studies, surveys and experiments, and critical approaches encompassing postmodernism and symmetrical anthropology approaches.

Extant Empirical Research Contexts and Topics

There was a high degree of agreement among ONE scholars polled by us about the empirical research contexts that have been effectively explored in extant research. These contexts may be indicative of the most critical and visible problems and issues for organizations in the natural environment. Alternatively, these may be indicative of the research contexts that are easier to address with our existing measures and methods of inquiry. Perhaps the high degree of agreement by ONE about extant research contexts may also be indicative of the saturation of empirical inquiry into certain research contexts and a signal of opportunities to move on to other important areas of inquiry. Considering that the field of ONE has focused on applying extant theories to a problem domain rather than generating new theories, I classified extant ONE research based on the main research questions explored within this domain from different levels of analysis.

Types of environmental strategies

An early stream of literature on organizations in the natural environment focused on typologies and classifications of environmental strategies and/or green organizations (Hunt and Auster, 1990; Post and Altman, 1992). In empirical research these increasingly sophisticated environmental strategy classifications gradually collapsed into 'proactive vs. reactive' (Sharma and Vredenburg, 1998) or 'pollution prevention vs. pollution control' (Hart and Ahuja, 1996; Russo and Fouts, 1997) or 'compliance vs. voluntary/beyond-compliance' (Sharma, 2000). The ONE scholars polled by us did not urge the further development of increasingly sophisticated typologies of environmental strategy. Rather, our respondents felt that we needed greater understanding of corporate environmental behavior and how environmental strategies evolve from reactive (pollution control) to proactive (pollution prevention) to clean technologies, design for the environment and product stewardship.

Why do organizations go 'green' or undertake environmental practices/strategies?

This question has been examined at several levels of analysis. At the institutional or external level, research has examined the influence of institutional forces (Hoffman, 1997, 1999), regulations (Majumdar and Marcus, 1999; Rugman and Verbeke, 2000), and stakeholders (Henriques and Sadorsky, 1999; Turcotte and Pasquero, 2001). At the industry level, research has examined this question from a collective action perspective (King and Lenox, 2000). At an inter-organizational level, researchers have looked at the greening of the value-chain (Green et al., 2000) and private–public partnerships between NGOs and businesses (Hartman and Stafford, 1997; Rondinelli and London, 2001).

From an organizational level of analysis, studies have examined competitive drivers (Aragón-Correa, 1998; Christmann, 2000; Dean and Brown, 1995; Hart, 1995; Nehrt, 1996, 1998; Russo and Fouts, 1997; Sharma and Vredenburg, 1998), the influence of organizational context and design (Sharma, 2000; Sharma et al., 1999; Ramus and Steger, 2000), and organizational learning (Marcus and Nichols, 1999). At the individual or managerial level of analysis, studies have examined the role of leadership values (Egri and Herman, 2000), environmental champions (Andersson and Bateman, 2000), managerial attitudes (Cordano and Frieze, 2000), managerial interpretations of environmental issues as threats or opportunities (Sharma, 2000; Sharma et al., 1999), and managerial risk propensity (Sharma and Nguan, 1999). Our respondents agreed that this is a fruitful context for continuing future research.

Does it pay to be green?

If ONE scholars were to agree on a dominant research paradigm, it is likely to be the quest for an answer to the question: Does it pay to be green? Increasing empirical evidence has challenged the traditional perspectives that voluntary environmental practices, not mandated by regulations, involve investments requiring careful cost–benefit analysis (Walley and Whitehead, 1994). For example, Klassen and McLaughlin (1996) found a positive relationship between firms' environmental awards and their stock prices. Judge and Douglas (1998) linked proactive environmental practices to above-average financial performance. This link was partially explained by investments in emissions reductions that led to cost savings as a result of reduced material and energy use. However, such savings reached a plateau after the 'low hanging fruit' of excessive waste was harvested (Hart and Ahuja, 1996). Porter (1991) and Porter and van der Linde (1995) argued that firms whose practices went beyond the requirements of environmental regulations reaped lasting cost and differentiation benefits and, indeed, Nehrt (1996, 1998) found the maintainability of competitive advantage for first-movers into clean technologies.

However, the paybacks from voluntary environmental practices are often intangible, difficult to quantify and slow to emerge. Hence, the resource-based (Barney 1991; Wernerfelt, 1984) view of the firm offered greater explanatory power. Hart (1995) argued that proactive environmental strategies could lead to valuable organizational capabilities. Environmental strategies of pollution prevention or proactiveness (Russo and Fouts, 1997; Sharma and Vredenburg, 1998) were shown to be associated with the above-average returns for firms (Russo and Fouts, 1997) and the development of competitively valuable organizational capabilities (Sharma and Vredenburg, 1998). Christmann (2000) found that complementary capabilities of process innovation and implementation were required within firms for leveraging environmental practices in order to achieve cost reductions. Aragón-Correa and Sharma (2002) argued that a proactive environmental strategy would lead to competitive advantage only under certain contingent conditions in the business environment.

Hence, the research question: Does it pay to be green?, has attracted increasingly sophisticated theoretical integration of strategic management and economic perspectives as well as increasingly sophisticated measures and analytical methods. The ONE scholars polled by us urged continuing research into greater understanding of the factors at various levels of analysis that influence the adoption and evolution of organizational environmental strategies and practices, as well as increasingly sophisticated research to examine the link between environmental strategy and competitive advantage.

Future Empirical Research Contexts and Topics

The empirical research contexts suggested as worth pursuing by the ONE scholars polled by us are classified according to different levels of analysis: global, institutional, inter-organizational, organizational and individual. A brief review is presented below and a more detailed discussion follows in the last chapter of this volume.

Global level

At a macro level, global environmental issues such as climate change and ozone depletion involve complex negotiations between multiple players and can be examined from the perspective of the political economy of the environment in an international system involving relationships between firms, NGOs and governments. To the extent that multinational corporations contribute to such global environmental impacts, what role can they play in international environmental governance regimes? Further, cross-cultural and comparative studies of processes of environmental change in developed and developing countries will help us understand the mechanisms via which North–South partnerships can work to mitigate global environmental and social impacts.

Institutional level

While there was a general consensus that research on typologies and classifications of environmental strategy were not important at the current juncture, several scholars urged an examination of how social norms and institutional environments constantly change the evolving definitions of green companies and proactive environmental practices. From a public policy perspective, research is required into the role of government regulation and information disclosure in changing environmental behavior and creating societal awareness about greening. It is also useful to examine the extent to which regulatory regimes such as the Environmental Protection Agency in the US or similar regulatory agencies are responsive to changing societal expectations (Swanson) in comparison to collaborative voluntary sectoral environmental targets in countries such as the Netherlands. What factors facilitate and/or hinder interactions between state, federal and local agencies in responding to environmental crises or major environmental issues (Swanson)?

From a stakeholder perspective, how do individual stakeholder pressures drive corporate environmental practices? For example, what does the media consider news and how much environmental damage is considered newsworthy (Swanson)? Does the media see its role as creating an environmental consciousness or as selling newspapers via sensational stories of environmental accidents and social injustice? To what extent do industry associations, coalitions and informal networks influence environmental practices of individual firms?

Inter-organizational level

Many organizations find it difficult to individually change their processes, technologies and products in order to minimize their ecological footprint. However, certain unavoidable process wastes and by-products may be used as inputs by other organizations or firms in other countries. Therefore research into networks and alliance development among firms, citizens, governments and NGOs is a fruitful area of inquiry. Perspectives from network theory, strategic alliances and industrial ecology literature can contribute to a greater understanding of how sustainability can be achieved collectively, if not individually, by organizations. Studies of such collaborations, especially public–private partnerships, provide a rich context for studying the process of negotiations and search for common meanings as well as examining the actual outcomes as compared to the desired objectives.

Organizational level

The extant empirical work on the organizational drivers and outcomes of environmental strategy needs to incorporate contingency perspectives. How do our current theories and models of corporate environmental performance change under different general business environments, different stages of economic development and in different cultural settings?

Do certain organizational forms and structures facilitate proactive environmental strategy evolution more than others? Are publicly traded companies more proactive than private firms? What about state-owned or government organizations such as the armed forces? How do different types of corporate governance structures influence environmental performance, for example comparisons of single-unit firms versus diversified firms, and multi-nationals versus conglomerates?

More work is required to understand how elements of organizational structure and design affect environmental performance. Conversely, what effect does the adoption of environmental practices and standards such as ISO 14001 have on organizational structure and design, that is, does environmental certification lead to changes in organizational forms and structures?

In terms of the link between environmental performance and competitiveness, the natural resource-based view is a fruitful research stream that can be further developed to examine and describe the processes through which organizations develop individual green capabilities. Similarly, contingency perspectives can be adopted to explain not 'Does it pay to be green?' but 'When or how does it pay to be green?' What type of competitive benefits are associated with design for the environment and product stewardship? What competitive benefits does environmental certification create for organizations?

Relatedly, is there a link between 'green' management and 'good' management? If we agree that pollution is an indicator of wastage of materials and poor process or product design, would not a 'green' company be better managed? Does managerial information processing that includes the complexities of environmental and social impacts enhance the quality of organizational decisions and outcomes?

At an empirical level, much work remains to be done in developing metrics for measuring environmental performance. Early research has focused on using the Toxic Release Inventory (TRI) data (Hart and Ahuja, 1996; King and Lenox, 2000), or a few environmental indicators in Kinder Lydenburg Domini (KLD) or Investor Responsibility Research Center (IRRC) databases (Russo and Fouts, 1997), or more comprehensive self-report measures developed for industry-specific studies (Sharma and Vredenburg, 1998; Sharma, 2000). The TRI data are very limited and provide information on chemical emissions rather than overall corporate environmental performance. The self-report measures suffer from lack of objectivity. Some scholars urge the development of tools for managers in order to guide them through the processes of measuring the change and evolution of environmental practices.

Individual level

The role of individuals in organizations in affecting environmental change in organizations has been under-researched. Scholars urge a shift in research focus from changing collective behavior to changing individual behavior – an area into which we have rich theoretical insights from the discipline of psychology. What role do an individual's deeply held values play in managerial environmental decision-making? For example, do deeply held values such as vegetarianism support corporate environmental goals (Swanson)? What deeply held personal values influence an employee to take a stand on whistle-blowing (Swanson)? Has whistle-blowing led to more responsible corporate environmental practices? What role does an organization's executive leadership play in driving environmental change? Is there an interaction effect between values of the organizational leadership and individual values in driving voluntary and proactive environmental practices?

Can we map, and learn from, the decision-making processes that managers adopt in weighing economic, social and environmental factors simultaneously? While there has been some research on the role of managers in driving environmental change, there has been little empirical work on the connection between the rewards, incentives and information that may influence employees' environmental decisions and actions. Finally, are sustainable business practices actually a source of competitive advantage in the employee hiring and employee productivity context?

From the perspective of the individual consumer, marketing researchers need to test and verify the underlying assumptions about whether or not environmental performance of companies matters to consumers. How do consumers weigh the environmental and social attributes of products and services in making purchase decisions? Some basic product attribute studies using conjoint analysis were undertaken in the early 1990s. However, sophisticated empirical experiments can be undertaken using psychometric analysis. At a macro level, does the marketing function have a role in educating the consumer and raising environmental consciousness?

Of course, we also need integrative studies that examine interactions of institutional and organizational variables, as well as organizational and individual variables, in influencing the evolution of organizational 'greenness.'

Management education
Arguing that individual values and attitudes can be shaped in educational programs, some scholars urge a research stream that examines the effective integration of the natural environment into the core curriculum of management subjects. By what methods can ONE educators stimulate student interest in environmental issues and ensure that they become informed and effective environmental decision-makers in corporations?

RESEARCH ON CORPORATE SUSTAINABILITY

The concept of an ecologically sustainable corporation adds complexity to theoretical and empirical research on organizations and the natural environment by adding a third dimension to the economic–natural environment interface: the need to improve social and human welfare while reducing the ecological footprint and ensuring the effective achievement of organizational objectives. Sustainable development is not a new idea. Many cultures over the course of human history have recognized the need for harmony between the environment, society and the economy. Indeed, many aboriginal people and indigenous tribes across the world still adhere to principles of environmental stewardship and harmony between human development and nature. However, recent human history is defined in a major way by the industrial revolution and its systems of mass organization and production that have been constantly at odds with the concept of sustainability. Therefore, the articulation of sustainable principles in context of such global and capital-intensive systems of mass production is new.

There are multiple definitions and interpretations of the concept of sustainable development (for example, see Gladwin et al., 1995; Starik and Rands, 1995). The generally understood modern concept of sustainable development is embodied in *Our Common Future* (also known as the Brundtland Commission Report). This report defines sustainable development as the 'development that meets the needs of the present without compromising the ability of future generations to meet their own needs (WCED, 1989: 43). In simple terms, it implies the improvement of welfare or quality of life equally and fairly for all human beings and also their future generations, while ensuring that the demands made on the natural environment in terms of resources extracted or wastes assimilated are within its carrying capacity. These demands go far beyond the objectives that organizations are currently set up to achieve. Therefore, corporate sustainability research presents unique challenges for ONE scholars. As can be expected, scholars agree that the extant research on corporate sustainability is mainly theoretical, extremely limited and an extremely promising area for future inquiry on a number of topics.

What is a Sustainable Corporation?

Even as scholars in several disciplines debate and discuss the definitions of sustainable development at a global level encompassing all of nature and global human welfare, defining sustainability in a corporate or organizational context presents unique challenges. The challenge of defining corporate sustainability has been undertaken only at a theoretical level (for example,

Gladwin et al., 1995; Jennings and Zandbergen, 1995; Starik and Rands, 1995). It must be noted that besides the *Academy of Management Review*'s Special Topic Form on Ecologically Sustainable Organizations, very little has been written by management scholars on the meaning and operationalization of sustainable organizations.

In the *Academy of Management Review* forum, Gladwin et al. (1995) presented an operationalization of a 'sustaincentric' paradigm, situated between the current technocentric paradigm subscribed to by business and the ecocentric paradigm advocated by deep ecologists. However, even the supposedly practical sustaincentric paradigm (Gladwin et al., 1995) included concepts such as inclusiveness of marginalized societies and future generations that present major operationalization challenges for current organizational forms. Starik and Rands (1995) adopted an open systems concept to show how organizations interface with the natural environment at multiple levels of analysis and offered a research agenda that is still largely untapped by empirical researchers. Jennings and Zandbergen (1995) suggested that the meaning of 'sustainability' is evolving and shaped by social and organizational institutional forces. While the institutional perspective has been adopted by a number of researchers, the focus has been on the evolution of environmental practices rather than sustainable organizations. The theories proposed by the 1995 *Academy of Management Review* research forum still offer ONE scholars a rich vein of untapped research contexts and ideas.

Can we construct unique theories of sustainable corporations or does sustainable development provide a context for gaining new insights into existing theoretical frameworks and perhaps challenging them? It is possible that by integrating the concepts of carrying capacity and the laws of thermodynamics (for example, Throop et al., 1993), as well as measuring and reporting an organization's ecological footprint and the triple bottom line, we will provide clues to sustainable organizational forms. The challenge of improving the welfare of marginalized societies and future generations as well as accruing natural capital for them may have the potential to create new insights into future organizational architectures.

Sustainable Organizational Networks and Communities

In terms of the accepted definitions of sustainability, it is a challenge to conceptualize organizational forms that will be able to prosper and simultaneously improve human welfare and accrue natural capital. For most modern organizations, resource extraction, production, consumption and disposal systems are geographically dispersed. Perhaps, for an organization to operate within the carrying capacity of an ecosystem while improving human welfare, it has to organize its inputs, processes and outputs within a locally identifiable ecosystem rather than as a complex global value chain (Hawken, 1993; Schumacher, 1973 [1974]) Perhaps, sustainability is possible between groups or networks of organizations that operate within definable geographic regions or communities. Practical examples and case studies of industrial ecology (for example, Shrivastava, 1995) have been the first theoretical and empirical forays into this concept.

There are opportunities to conceptualize the composition of such networks, whether as a mix of private firms, or as links between private firms, state agencies and non-governmental organizations. How should such networks be bounded geographically – should they be local, regional or can they even be globally connected and be able to assimilate wastes and ensure social justice? How should such sustainable networks be governed? What role should public policy and regulations play in facilitating such networks? How will the performance of such networks be determined and how will it be measured and monitored? How will the inter-organizational interfaces be managed and how will the designs and structures of individual organizations change to facilitate network objectives? Will such networks emerge as planned entities such as eco-parks or industrial ecology networks or will they be fluid, flexible and constantly evolving?

The concept of local or community self-sufficiency may facilitate the monitoring of the impacts of organizations on the carrying capacity of an eco-system and on the stock of natural and human capital in a bounded geographic region. What will sustainable communities look like? How will they interact with, and exchange resources with, other sustainable communities globally? How will such communities achieve their objectives of smart growth involving better quality of life and the accrual of natural capital?

The Role of Corporations in Global Sustainable Development

Can corporations play a role in the alleviation of global ecological and social problems such as hunger, poverty, human rights, illiteracy and so on? Often, such social problems lead to ecological problems and vice versa. For example, lack of access to renewable energy and integrated rural poverty results in poor societies cutting down trees for fuel, which in turn leads to soil erosion and contamination of water bodies, which in turn restricts agricultural yields and incomes (Chambers, 1984). Ultimately, building localized sustainable communities and networks in developed countries will have minimal positive impacts on the global environmental problems of climate change or the social problems of desperate poverty that can stimulate antisocial behavior and terrorism. Therefore, corporations also have a role in including marginalized societies and ecosystems into sustainable processes.

Practical examples such as the Grameen Bank and Grameen Phone in Bangladesh (Prahalad and Hart, 2002) provide clues to the business models that organizations can adopt to improve the welfare of the poorest people without damaging or depleting natural capital. Non-governmental organizations have been working to manage such social and ecological issues in isolation. Partnerships with private corporations and governments can provide more far-reaching and effective sustainable solutions (Sharma et al., 1994) involving community-based entrepreneurship. Corporations can offer their considerable management expertise to help governments and NGOs manage nutrition, clean water, hygiene and health, via the application of appropriate technologies (Schumacher, 1973) and processes. It is estimated that $30–40 invested per person on primary health in the developing world can yield as much as $186 billion per year in economic benefits via higher productivity and economic innovation (Tyson, 2002). Top-down trickle-down approaches of handing out large sums to developing countries' governments have not been very successful in improving primary health care. Hence, there are opportunities for private corporations to provide management expertise in partnership with NGOs and governments to deliver primary care at the grass-roots level.

Further, digital technologies and virtual business models can be leveraged for sustainable third world development by leapfrogging environmentally damaging and socially unjust and divisive technologies. Corporations may also have a role in fostering more responsible consumption in the developed world. However, before taking on these roles, corporations need to forecast how such strategies will affect their long-term survival and competitiveness.

Sustainable Business Models and Competitive Advantage

Competitive advantage is a powerful driver for organizations that move toward sustainable networks and partnerships. Shrivastava (1995) and Hart (1995, 1997) visualized links between sustainable organizations and their competitiveness. Hart and Milstein (1999) argued that sustainable business models involved Schumpeterian creative destruction and disruptive innovations, and hence the potential for competitive leapfrogging. We need research that tells us whether these hypotheses are true: do sustainable business models contribute to long-term competitiveness?

ABOUT THIS VOLUME

Nine chapters in this volume were selected from the papers accepted for the Organizations and the Natural Environment Interest Group Scholarly Program at the 2001 Academy of Management meetings. The Ellis, Cordano and Lamont chapter was the only one that was drawn from the ONE Program at the 2000 Academy of Management meetings. A brief version of their study was included in the 2000 Academy of Management Best Paper Proceedings. Therefore, each of these papers had already been double-blind reviewed by three reviewers before being selected for the ONE program at the Academy of Management. These papers were selected either for the uniqueness or quality of ideas presented, or the importance of research questions addressed, or the quality of empirical design and analysis, or a combination of these factors. Two papers went through one editorial review by the two co-editors in addition to the changes made in response to the three double-blind reviews for the ONE program at the Academy meetings. Eight papers went through two to four rounds of additional editorial reviews after the authors incorporated comments by the AOM reviewers.

The research studies reported in this volume make important contributions in addressing some of the gaps in research on organizations in the natural environment identified above. Seven studies in this volume tend to be focused mainly on pollution control and prevention issues. While these studies do not explicitly tackle the range of complexities of corporate sustainability, they do provide new insights into external and internal drivers of corporate behavior on the path to sustainability. Three studies venture further into the realm of sustainability: one describes a system of sustainable stakeholder accounting that integrates a firm's environmental and social performance into its financial statements, another examines citizen readiness for community sustainability in a remote mountain community in the United States, and the third examines the impacts of globalization on sustainability.

Due to ONE's recent history, there have been just a few collections of theoretical and empirical research on organizations in the natural environment. Such collections include special volumes and journal issues including the 1995 JAI volume *Research on Corporate Social Performance and Policy: Sustaining the Natural Environment* (Collins and Starik), the 1995 *Academy of Management Review* Special Topic Forum on Ecologically Sustainable Organizations and the 2000 *Academy of Management Journal* Special Research Forum on Organizations in the Natural Environment (Starik et al., 2000). The chapters in this volume draw from research represented in the volumes mentioned above and other ONE related articles published in a wide variety of journals, to enhance our understanding of the organization – natural environment interface and provide useful directions for future research. In doing so, the studies reported also address many of the gaps in extant research identified by ONE scholars discussed above. These studies are classified on the basis of the level of analysis at which the authors approach environmental and sustainability issues.

Global Level of Analysis

Osland, Dhanda and Yuthas's chapter 'Globalization and environmental sustainability: an analysis of the impact of globalization using the Natural Step framework' addresses an important gap identified by the ONE scholars: the lacuna of studies on the impacts of globalization and international trade on ecosystems and the environment. Osland et al. question a central assumption underlying international business research, lending policies of international agencies, government economic policies and international agreements. This assumption is that globalization and international trade have positive effects on sustainable development. Their study uses the four system conditions of the Natural Step framework to examine the extant literature on globalization and sustainability. This framework provides a systemic lens to examine major areas in the globalization debate: key dimensions of environmental sustainability along with inequality, labor conditions and rights, national sovereignty, and cultural and community impact. Their review found that globalization is an uneven process that has had a few positive but many negative effects on the four system conditions. The current models of globalization have involved trade-offs, for example, economic development and jobs at the cost of serious environmental degradation and weakened labor protection. They conclude with a recommendation to include these trade-offs in the globalization debate, in international business research and in computations of the cost of global business.

Community Level of Analysis

Sustainable communities could provide unique operational contexts for individual organizations as well as networks. Stead, Stead and Shemwell's chapter 'Community sustainability comes to the Southern Appalachian region of the USA: the case of Johnson County, Tennessee' reports an action research-based empirical assessment of citizen readiness for a community sustainability process in a remote mountain community in Southern Appalachia in the USA. They found that while government and community leaders supported the process, and that the funding for the process has been acquired from several public and private sources, there was a split among the county's citizens regarding support for the three dimensions critical for the success of the county's community sustainability efforts. These dimensions were: access to the county, demographic diversity and community-wide land-use laws. Thus, one group of citizens wished to improve access to the county, to implement zoning and to encourage new people and organizations to move to the community, while the other group either opposed such measures or was not sure about their value. The authors recommend both an early identification of sources of conflicts between members of a community and a process of consensus building. For example, the current economic problems in the county were partially due to multinational corporations such as Timberland Shoes, Levi Strauss and Sara Lee moving from the county to developing nations. They concluded that hope for community sustainability lay in government and funding agencies (public and private) at regional, state, national and international levels using their resources to forge long-term partnerships between communities and multinational corporations. One suggestion emerging from this study could be that multinational corporations ought to make long-term commitments to communities where they locate and invest substantial corporate resources into sustaining these communities economically, socially and environ-mentally.

Institutional Level of Analysis

Extant research has shown the importance of institutional forces such as environmental regulations in shaping corporate environmental practices (for example, Hoffman, 1997, 1999). Branzei and Vertinsky's chapter 'Eco-sustainability orientation in China and Japan: differences between proactive and reactive firms' is situated within the institutional perspective and also makes a contribution to the lack of cross-cultural empirical ONE research identified by ONE scholars polled by us. This study examined the diffusion of corporate environmental practices in different national contexts – China and Japan. The authors tested propositions regarding the influences of governmental regulations, best practices and stakeholder pressures on eco-sustainability orientation, a firm-level measure of corporate environmental performance, on firms from China and Japan. They found that governmental regulations were more influential in China, while best practices adopted by trade associations were more influential in Japan. Their findings suggested that the effectiveness of institutions depended on each country's degree of socio-economic development. Regulations may be effective initially in order to bring firms up to a minimum level of compliance. As institutional frameworks crystallize, regulations are likely to become more versatile and receive better enforcement, but their effectiveness may diminish. Beyond the minimum level of regulatory compliance, firms may tend to be influenced by best practices that emerge in their organizational fields. They also found that the governments' direct intervention in corporate operations did not foster an improvement of environmental practices. This study confirms Sharma's (2002) findings in the North American context and contributes by examining the influence of interactions between different institutional forces.

Darnall's chapter 'Motivations for participating in a US voluntary environmental initiative: the Multi-State Working Group and EPA's EMS Pilot Program' study makes another useful contribution to the institutional perspective on organizations in the natural environment by integrating the institutional and resource-based perspectives. She argues that an organization's participation in voluntary environmental initiatives (VEI) depends not only on regulatory frameworks but also on its internal environmental capabilities. Her study found that while regulatory pressures encouraged all organizations to behave similarly, their internal environmental capabilities influenced whether or not they participated in VEIs. Darnall's study also addresses another gap identified by ONE scholars: the lack of comparative research on publicly traded, privately owned and government organizations. She found that the continuous innovation and basic environmental management proficiencies embedded in publicly traded facilities' more advanced types of environmental management capabilities motivated VEI participation to a much greater extent as compared to government assistance programs. Privately owned organizations were influenced to a greater extent by external government-sponsored environmental assistance programs to fortify their limited internal environmental capabilities. At the other extreme, government organizations, generally lacking prior environmental pro-ficiencies, participated in VEIs only if their weak internal environmental capabilities were fortified via external assistance from regulators. This study provides a useful foundation for future comparative research on sustainability practices in public, private and government organizations.

Angell and Rands's chapter 'Factors influencing successful and unsuccessful environmental change initiatives' examines organizational environmental change in response to stakeholder pressures and critical environ-mental events. They looked at changes in environmental practices of manufacturing facilities in the US state of Pennsylvania between 1995 and 1998. They found that management's perceptions of stakeholder pressures and critical environmental events drove the level and success of environmental change within manufacturing facilities. They also examined the interaction with organizational context and found that the existence of formal environmental policies, environmental departments and improved waste reduction opportunities increased the number of successful environmental change implementations in surveyed facilities. Alternatively, the threat of punitive events led to a greater number of unsuccessful implementations at the facility level of the firms. Facility managers perceived stakeholder groups to have differential levels of influence over environmental decisions, and to differ in terms of the significance of their impact upon the number of environmental initiatives attempted and the relative success of these initiatives. Similarly, managers perceived critical environmental events as either punitive or regulatory events (threats), waste reduction and external recognition (opportunities) or industry developments (which could be seen as either threats or opportunities). This study is an interesting examination of inter-actions between stakeholder influences and organ-izational factors in driving environmental practices.

Inter-organizational Level of Analysis

Ellis, Cordano and Lamont's chapter 'The altering of a firm's environmental management capability during the acquisition integration process' presents hypotheses for future research about the transfer of environmental capabilities across organizational boundaries during the process of inter-organizational acquisitions. This chapter examines the influence of managerial decisions, during the process of acquisitions, on the environmental performance of facilities operating within the newly combined firm. The authors drew from the literature on the process of acquisitions and environmental strategy to identify five influences on environmental capabilities resulting from managerial activity during the acquisition integration process. They hypothesized that, (1) greater strategic importance accorded to environmental capabilities in the acquisition process facilitates capabilities transfer; (2) early timing of environmental capability consideration in the acquisition process facilitates capabilities transfer; (3) symbiotic integration strategy rather than preservation or absorption integration strategy facilitates capabilities transfer; (4) moderate imple-mentation speed of the acquisition process rather than slow or fast speeds facilitates capability transfer; and (5) the programmability of the acquisition based on prior experience facilitates transfer of environmental capabilities. This chapter takes the first steps toward a research agenda considered extremely important by ONE scholars: how can inter-organizational alliances and networks develop environmental capabilities in order to achieve their sustainability objectives?

Organizational Level of Analysis

Sustainable organizations will adopt an integrated approach to preserve the environment, improve social welfare and enhance economic growth (Starik and Rands, 1995). A number of ONE studies have examined the impact of individual human resource management practices on environmental practices, but none has taken an integrative strategic approach to investigating the incidence and impact of environmental human resource management practices.

Egri and Hornal's chapter 'Strategic environmental human resource management and organizational performance: an exploratory study of the Canadian manufacturing sector' fills this gap by proposing that an effective strategic environmental human resource management (SEHRM) system selects and promotes employees on the basis of their environmental knowledge, skills and leadership abilities; formally identifies environmental job responsibilities; provides education and training that engender environmentally proactive attitudes, skills and behaviors; uses specific and measurable environmental performance criteria and goals in employee performance appraisals; and recognizes and rewards employee environmental contributions and achievements at individual, group and organizational levels. In a study of 37 Canadian manufacturing organizations, they found that a SEHRM approach and environmental proactivity enhanced managerial perceptions of organizational performance. They also found that organi-zational contextual factors such as organization size, environmental organi-zation units and labor unions were related to environmental proactivity and/or perceived organizational benefits of environmental management practices. Their study concluded that the incorporation of environmental objectives and criteria in a wide range of HRM practices affecting a greater variety of employees was perceived to facilitate the achievement of organi-zational performance objectives. These findings not only support the strategic HRM perspective that a high degree of both internal and external fit has a synergistic effect on organizational performance, but also reinforce the link between environmental performance and organizational performance.

Heller and Mroczko's chapter 'Information disclosure in environmental policy and the development of secretly environmentally-friendly products', written primarily as a practitioner-oriented comparative case study of two companies, provides an interesting perspective on why a company may not disclose the positive environmental impacts of its operations to its stakeholders. One company they studied trumpeted the environmental improvements in its product to counter prior criticisms and to target an environmentally-conscious market niche. Another company chose to keep the removal of a toxic ingredient from its product secret in order to hide the fact that it had been previously using the toxic ingredient in a product that was traditionally handed down as a family heirloom. The latter company also wished to hide the fact that it had polluted water bodies for years with its toxic wastes. They concluded that environmental information disclosure depended on the skeletons in the organization's closet or its history, among other factors. They concluded that it is entirely possible that a company's actual environmental performance, in some cases, may be better than that which is publicly disclosed. Therefore, in some cases, a company's 'walk' may actually be greener than its 'talk.' They drew an interesting conclusion that the publicity of positive environmental activity is experienced as rewarding only when it follows after the publicity of a negative environmental impact. Without the visibility of negative environmental impact, the prospect of publicizing positive environmental activity is experienced as a threat that attention will be drawn to negative aspects of the firm's environmental performance. This study presents an interesting hypothesis based on exploratory work and provides a rich ground for in-depth empirical studies about environmental attributes of products and services – an area considered important for future research by the ONE scholars polled by us.

Sherman, Steingard and Fitzgibbons tackle the issue of integrating reporting and information disclosure about social and environmental impacts in conventional accounting systems via sustainable stakeholder accounting. Their chapter titled 'Sustainable stakeholder accounting: beyond complementarity and towards integration in environmental accounting' discusses and describes how environmental performance measures can be integrated directly into financial statements in order to assess a company's financial impact on sustainability. Conventional accounting standards ignore the environmental costs of doing business. Stand-alone corporate environmental reports provide voluntary information about a company's environmental performance. These reports fail to influence the financial performance of a company as reflected in its financial statements. These authors' conception of sustainable stakeholder accounting directly integrates environmental costs, liabilities and sustainable investments into the financial statements. Financial statements prepared under these guidelines provide corporate stakeholders such as investors, managers, customers, communities, environmental groups and suppliers with a more holistic and accurate picture of an organization's impacts, positive or negative, to ecosystems and social welfare. They explain the principles of SSA by applying it to the financial statements of Exxon and Baxter International. Sherman et al. argue that SSA will drive change by providing incentives and competitive advantage for environmental leaders such as Patagonia, Ikea and Interface, who have adopted the Natural Step framework, and impact negatively on the reputation of laggards such as Exxon. They address an important gap in the literature pointed out by ONE scholars by showing how accurate reporting of corporate sustainability impacts can affect a company's future sustainability performance.

Individual Level of Analysis

Cordano and Frieze's chapter 'Enhancing environmental management teaching through applications of toxic release information' presents a study that

addresses two important areas of research identified by ONE scholars: changing individual attitudes and integrating environmental management into
business education. They provided 466 business students with a limited
amount of toxic release data from manufacturing facilities in their neighborhoods. They then examined the impact this information had on student
evaluations of pollution problems, attitudes toward environmental regulation
and limits on property rights, and behavioral intentions for pro-environmental
behavior. The students who viewed information that included descriptions of
potential human health impacts expressed greater envir-onmental concern
when given toxic release information. Influencing students' attitudes is an
important step in changing subsequent managerial attitudes. This technique
could also be used to shape disclosure policies to create concern for pollution
among citizens and create pressures for change.

In summary, Osland et al.'s chapter, one of the first to look at the sustainability impacts of globalization, presents a rich set of research possibilities on
how international trade regimes, nation-states and multinational corporations
can cooperate to reduce the negative environmental and social impacts of
international business. Stead et al. offer us a glimpse of the barriers to
establishing sustainable communities and the extent to which such communities may provide hospitable institutional contexts for business organizations in the future. Branzei and Vertinsky answer the call of ONE scholars for
comparative cross-cultural research on corporate behavior in developing
(China) and developed (Japan) institutional contexts. Their research presents
potential insights into multilateral North–South solutions to sustainability
conundrums. Darnall, as well as Angell and Rands, go beyond just exam-ining
the influence of institutional forces on environmental strategy to looking at the
interactions of these forces with organizational variables such as internal
capabilities, organizational design and managerial interpretations. Their
studies should lead to research designs that investigate interactions between
variables at different levels of analysis to provide us with a more holistic
understanding of organizations in the natural environment.

Ellis et al. propose a theory for operationalization and research by scholars
studying capability transfer during alliances. At an organizational level of
analysis, Egri and Hornal integrate literature on the influence of individual HR
practices on environmental strategy by looking at the influence of an
integrated approach. Heller and Mroczko present a surprising insight into why
some organizations may not 'talk the walk', offering new perspectives on the
role of information disclosure in influencing environmental practices. Sherman
et al. offer a practical management tool that, if implemented, rewards
proactive organizations for beyond compliance performance. Finally, Cordano
and Frieze's findings present opportunities for research on integrating

environmental management into business studies as well as changing managerial and consumer attitudes via controlled information disclosure.

A FINAL NOTE: BRINGING BACK THE STARS

'I know a planet where there is a certain red-faced gentleman. He has never smelled a flower. He has never loved any one. He has never done anything in his life but add up figures. And all day he says over and over, just like you: 'I am busy with matters of great consequence!' (*The Little Prince* by Antoine de Saint-Exupéry, 1945)

If some one loves a flower, of which just one single blossom grows in all the millions of stars, it is enough to make him happy just to look at the stars. He can say to himself: 'Somewhere, my flower is there ...' But if the sheep eats the flower, in one moment all his stars will be darkened ... And you think that is not important! (*The Little Prince* by Antoine de Saint-Exupéry, 1945

The chapters in this volume offer new insights and future research potential for helping scholars, managers and policy-makers understand corporate sustainability better. However, extant ONE research has followed the tradition of most social sciences: incremental progress in slowly unfolding the complexities of a unique problem domain. Do we have the luxury and the time to take a leisurely stroll through incremental science or do we need radical new theories and new research paradigms?

Growing up, I spent hours looking up at the night sky, fascinated, identifying planets, stars and constellations, and contemplating the mysteries of creation. Anyone who has looked at the night sky lately knows that it is impossible to even see the Milky Way in most cities. The unaided eye should be able to see almost 3500 stars and planets in a clear night sky. In most cities, we are lucky if we can see 50 (Cinzano et al., 2001). Light pollution has resulted in almost one-tenth of the world population losing its night vision; it has led to severe habitat loss for species that depend on darkness for survival; and recent medical research has linked excessive night light to the incidence of breast cancer and other human diseases (Cinzano et al., 2001; Mittelstaedt, 2002). In beginning to think about the progress made by research in the arena of corporate sustainability and organizations in the natural environment, I was struck by a tremendous sense of loss and the realization that we have lost a part of nature forever. McKibben (1990) calls it a personal realization of the 'end of nature.' If sustainability involves leaving a legacy for future generations, a brilliant night sky is a legacy that we may not be able to give even with major technological advances over several generations. Unless we travel deep into the countryside, or to remote mountain tops in Hawaii or to the remote deserts of Africa, we will not be able to create the same fascination for the stars in our children that our parents created for us by just walking us to the back yard. The city of Tucson, Arizona has made the Milky Way visible to its residents on good days via managed directed and controlled lighting placement (Mittelstaedt, 2002). This presents us with a ray of hope and a reminder of the few tiny steps we have taken in tackling this incredibly complex problem and at the same time of the great management challenges that lie ahead.

NOTES

1. In a narrow sense, the term ONE could be interpreted as a reference to the membership of the Organizations and the Natural Environment Interest Group at the Academy of Management. However, it is used here to refer to the scholarship generated by all researchers who examine the interface between organizations and the natural environment at various levels of analysis, whether or not they are affiliated with the ONE Interest Group at the Academy of Management.
2. Mark Starik and I owe a debt of gratitude to our colleagues for their valuable suggestions and ideas that contributed a great deal to our ruminations: Pratima Bansal, Max Bazerman, Mark Cohen, Mark Cordano, Alberto Aragón-Correa, Jonathan Doh, Carolyn Egri, Irene Henriques, Andrew Hoffman, John Jermier, David Levy, Mark Milstein, Aseem Prakash, Jorge Rivera, Mike Russo, Mark Sharfman, Paul Shrivastava, Ed Stead, Jean Stead, Diane Swanson, Marie-France Turcotte, Gurneeta Vasudeva, David Wheeler and Monika Winn.
3. Some scholars that we polled disagreed. They felt that extant ONE research has been dominated by predictive and normative studies and we need to shift focus to descriptive studies that empirically explain organizational change and mana-gerial choice.

REFERENCES

Academy of Management Review (1995), 'Special topic forum on ecologically sustainable organizations,' **20**(4): 873–1089.

Andersson, L.M. and T.S. Bateman (2000), 'Individual environmental initiative: championing natural environmental issues in US business organizations,' *Academy of Management Journal*, **43**: 548–70.

Aragón-Correa, J.A. (1998), 'Strategic proactivity and firm approach to the natural environment,' *Academy of Management Journal*, **41**: 556–67.

Aragón-Correa, J.A. and S. Sharma (2002), 'A contingent resource-based view of proactive environmental strategy,' *Academy of Management Review* (forthcoming).

Barney, J.B. (1991), 'Firm resources and sustained competitive advantage,' *Journal of Management*, **17**(1): 99–120.

Carson, R. (1962 [2000]), *Silent Spring*, London: Folio Society.

Chambers, R. (1984), *Rural Development: Putting the Last First*, London: Longman.

Christmann, P. (2000), 'Effects of 'best practices' of environmental management on cost advantage: the role of complementary assets,' *Academy of Management Journal*, **43**: 663–80.

Cinzano, P., F. Falchi and C.D. Elvidge (2001), 'The first World Atlas of the artificial night sky blindness,' *Monthly Notices of Royal Astronomical Society*, **328**: 689–707.

Collins, D. and M. Starik (eds) (1995), *Research in Corporate Social Performance and Policy. Sustaining the Natural Environment: Empirical Studies on the Interface Between Nature and Organizations*, Greenwich, CT: JAI Press.

Cordano, M. and I.H. Frieze (2000), 'Pollution reduction preferences of US environmental managers: applying Ajzen's theory of planned behavior,' *Academy of Management Journal*, **43**: 627–41.

Daly, H.E. (1993), 'The perils of free trade,' *Scientific American*, November: 50–57.

Dean, T.J. and R.L. Brown (1995), 'Pollution regulation as a barrier to new firm entry: initial evidence and implications for future research,' *Academy of Management Journal*, **38**: 288–303.

Egri, C.P. (1997), 'Spiritual connections with the natural environment,' *Organization and Environment*, **10**(4): 407–31.

Egri, C.P. and S. Herman (2000), 'Leadership in the North American environmental sector: values, leadership styles, and contexts of environmental leaders and their organizations,' *Academy of Management Journal*, **43**: 571–604.

Gladwin, T.N., J.J. Kennelly and T.S. Krause (1995), 'Shifting paradigms for sustainable development: implications for management theory and research,' *Academy of Management Review*, **20**: 874–907.

Green, K., B. Morton and S. New (2000), 'Greening organizations,' *Business and Society*, **13**(2): 206–25.

Hart, S.L. (1995), 'A natural-resource-based view of the firm,' *Academy of Management Review*, **20**: 874–907.

Hart, S.L. (1997), 'Beyond greening: strategies for a sustainable world,' *Harvard Business Review*, **75**(1): 66–76.

Hart, S.L. and G. Ahuja (1996), 'Does it pay to be green? An empirical examination of the relationship between emission reduction and firm performance,' *Business Strategy and the Environment*, **5**: 30–7.

Hart, S.L. and M.B. Milstein (1999), 'Global sustainability and the creative destruction of industries,' *Sloan Management Review*, **41**(1): 23–33.

Hartman, C.L. and E.R. Stafford (1997), 'Green alliances: building new business with environmental groups,' *Long Range Planning*, **30**(2): 184–96.

Hawken, P. (1993), *The Ecology of Commerce: A Declaration of Sustainability*, New York: HarperBusiness.

Hawken, P., A. Lovins and H. Lovins (2001), *Natural Capitalism: Creating the Next Industrial Revolution*, Snowmass, CO: Rocky Mountain Institute.

Henriques, I. and P. Sadorsky (1999), 'The relationship between environmental commitment and managerial perceptions of stakeholder importance,' *Academy of Management Journal*, **42**: 87–99.

Hoffman, A.J. (1997), *From Heresy to Dogma: An Institutional History of Corporate Environmentalism*, San Francisco, CA: New Lexington Press.

Hoffman, A.J. (1999), 'Institutional evolution and change: environmentalism and the US chemical industry,' *Academy of Management Journal*, **42**: 351–71.

Hunt, C.B. and E.R. Auster (1990), 'Proactive environmental management: avoiding the toxic trap,' *Sloan Management Review*, **31**(2): 7–18.

Jennings, P.D. and P.A. Zandbergen (1995), 'Ecologically sustainable organizations: an institutional approach,' *Academy of Management Review*, **20**: 1015–52.

Judge, W.Q. and T.J. Douglas (1998), 'Performance implications of incorporating natural environmental issues into the strategic planning process: an empirical assessment,' *Journal of Management Studies*, **35**: 241–62.

King, A. and M.J. Lenox (2000), 'Industry self-regulation without sanctions: the chemical industry's responsible care program,' *Academy of Management Journal*, **43**(4): 698–716.

Klassen, R.D. and C.P. McLaughlin (1996), 'The impact of environmental management on firm performance,' *Management Science*, **42**: 1199–214.

Klassen, R.D. and D.C. Whybark (1999), 'The impact of environmental technologies on manufacturing performance,' *Academy of Management Journal*, **42**: 599–615.

Leopold, A. (1949), *A Sand County Almanac*, New York: Oxford University Press.

Majumdar, S.K. and A.A. Marcus (2001), 'Rules versus discretion: the productivity consequences of flexible regulation', *Academy of Management Journal*, **44**: 170–79.

Marcus, A.A. and M.L. Nichols (1999), 'On the edge: heeding the warnings of unusual events,' *Organization Science*, **10**: 482–99.

McKibben, W. (1990), *The End of Nature*, Toronto: Anchor Books.

Meyer, A.D. (1991), 'What is strategy's distinctive competence?' *Journal of Management*, **17**(4): 821–33.

Mittelstaedt, M. (2002), 'Blinded by the light,' *The Globe and Mail*, 12 January: F1, F6.

Naess, A. (1995), 'Politics and the ecological crisis: an introductory note,' in G. Sessions (ed.), *Deep Ecology for the 21st Century*, Boston, MA: Shambhala.

Nehrt, C. (1996), 'Timing and intensity effects of environmental investments,' *Strategic Management Journal*, **17**: 535–47.

Nehrt, C. (1998), 'Maintainability of first mover advantages when environmental regulations differ between countries,' *Academy of Management Review*, **23**: 77–97.

Porter, M.E. (1991), 'America's green strategy,' *Scientific American*, April: 168.

Porter, M.E. and C. van der Linde (1995), 'Green and competitive,' *Harvard Business Review*, September–October: 120–34, 196.

Post, J.E. and B.W. Altman (1992), 'Models of corporate greening: how corporate social policy and organizational learning inform leading-edge environmental management,' in J.E. Post and L.E. Preston (eds) *Research in Corporate Social Performance and Policy*, Greenwich, CT: JAI Press.

Prahalad, C.K. and S.L. Hart (2002), 'The fortune at the bottom of the pyramid,' *Strategy and Business*, Issue 26: 1–14.

Ramus, C.A. and U. Steger (2000), 'The roles of supervisory support behaviors and environmental policy in employee 'ecoinitiatives' at leading-edge European companies,' *Academy of Management Journal*, **43**: 605–26.

Rondinelli, D.A. and T. London (2001), 'Making corporate and stakeholder environmental partnerships work,' *Environmental Management*, November: 16–22.

Rugman, A.M. and A. Verbeke (2000), 'Six cases of corporate strategic responses to environmental regulation,' *European Management Journal*, **18**: 377–85.

Russo, M.V. and P.A. Fouts (1997), 'A resource-based perspective on corporate environmental performance and profitability,' *Academy of Management Journal*, **40**: 534–59.

Schumacher, E.F. (1973 [1974]), *Small is Beautiful: A Study of Economics as if People Mattered*, London: Sphere.

Sharma, S. (2000), 'Managerial interpretations and organizational context as predictors of corporate choice of environmental strategy,' *Academy of Management Journal*, **43**: 681–97.

Sharma, S. (2002), 'Different strokes: regulatory styles and environmental strategy in the North American oil and gas industry,' *Business Strategy and the Environment*, **11**(1): 344–64.

Sharma, S. and O. Nguan (1999), 'The biotechnology industry and biodiversity conservation strategies: the influence of managerial interpretations and risk propensity,' *Business Strategy and the Environment*, **8** (January–February): 46–61.

Sharma, S, A. Pablo and H. Vredenburg (1999), 'Corporate environmental responsiveness strategies: the role of issue interpretation and organizational context,' *Journal of Applied Behavioral Science*, **35**(1): 87–109.

Sharma, S. and H. Vredenburg (1998), 'Proactive corporate environmental strategy and the development of competitively valuable organizational capabilities,' *Strategic Management Journal*, **19**: 729–53.

Sharma, S., H. Vredenburg and F. Westley (1994), 'Strategic bridging: a role for the multinational corporation in Third World Development,' *Journal of Applied Behavioral Science*, **30**: 458–76.

Shrivastava, P. (1995), 'The role of corporations in achieving ecological sustainability,' *Academy of Management Review*, **20**(4): 936–61.

Starik, M., A.A. Marcus and A.Y. Ilinitch (eds) (2000), 'Special research forum: the management of organizations in the natural environment,' *Academy of Management Journal*, **43**(4): 539–736.

Starik M. and G.P. Rands (1995), 'Weaving an integrated web: multilevel and multisystem perspective of ecologically sustainable organizations, *Academy of Management Review*, **20**: 908–35.

Throop, G.M., M. Starik and G.P. Rands (1993), 'Sustainable strategy in a greening world: integrating the natural environment into strategic management,' in P. Shrivastava, J. Dutton and A. Huff (eds), *Advances in Strategic Management*, **9**, Greenwich, CT: JAI Press.

Turcotte, M.F. and J. Pasquero (2001), 'The paradox of multistakeholder collaborative roundtables,' *Journal of Applied Behavioral Science*, **37**(4): 447–64.

Tyson, L.D. (2002), 'For developing countries, health is wealth,' *BusinessWeek*, 14 January: 20.

Walley, N. and B. Whitehead (1994), 'It's not easy being green,' *Harvard Business Review*, May–June: 46–52.

(WCED) World Commission on Environment and Development (1987), *Our Common Future*, Oxford: Oxford University Press, p. 43.

Wernerfelt, B. (1984), 'A resource-based view of the firm,' *Strategic Management Journal*, **5**: 171–80.

2. Globalization and environmental sustainability: an analysis of the impact of globalization using the Natural Step framework[1]

Joyce S. Osland, Kanwalroop K. Dhanda and Kristi Yuthas

INTRODUCTION

Globalization is becoming an increasingly controversial topic, as shown by recent protests around the world. The purpose of this research is to broaden the boundaries of the debate on globalization and increase our understanding of its impact beyond the economic sphere into the realm of environmental sustainability. We review and summarize the extant empirical literature connecting globalization and sustainability, and use the Natural Step framework to organize this literature.

Our review of the literature, which appears to be the first of its kind, revealed evidence that globalization is an uneven process that has had both positive and negative effects on the system conditions. The Natural Step framework is a useful tool for capturing the benefits and liabilities of globalization because it provides for a systemic perspective that encompasses major areas in the globalization debate: key dimensions of environmental sustainability along with inequality, labor conditions and rights, national sovereignty, and cultural and community impact. Viewing the literature through this frame provides a basis for understanding the tensions embodied in globalization and for exploring the trade-offs faced by policy-makers and managers.

The last decades of the twentieth century were years of increasing globalization, manifested in the rapid growth of world trade, foreign direct investment and cross-border financial flows (Lee, 1996). Some multinational enterprises (MNEs) now have budgets larger than the economies of many countries.

Growth in globalization has been facilitated and driven by rapid improvements in international transportation, technology, telecommunications (Wood, 1995), and the Internet. Global trade policies have also stimulated globalization. Many nation-states have liberalized their trade policies, removing trade barriers and focusing on exports. Globalization has been influenced by international organizations such as the World Bank, the IMF and the WTO, devoted to increasing trade and development.

Many members of the business community, as well as some business scholars, accept globalization as a *fait accompli* whose presence and benefits are unquestioned. Globalization, however, has become a controversial topic, as evidenced by labor protests in Korea and France, student riots in Indonesia and anti-WTO demonstrations in Seattle. Proponents view globalization as an opportunity for economic growth and prosperity while opponents perceive it as a threat to prosperity as well as to political sovereignty and cultural integrity.

In developed countries, a primary concern is the threat to unskilled workers and contracting industries; developing countries worry about political sovereignty and losing control of their economies (Champlin and Olson, 1999). The literature on globalization includes many impassioned ideological arguments, both for and against. Most of these arguments, however, lack empirical support. Furthermore, some of the existing research findings are contradictory. As Champlin and Olson (1999) note, the debate cannot be resolved, not because we lack the definitive econometric analysis, but because the debate is defined or framed in different ways. To some, it is simply an argument about the virtues of free markets and supply and demand. To others, it is a matter of economic fairness, cultural and political institutions and concern for environmental impact. There is plentiful, if sometimes contradictory, research on the financial and economic aspects of globalization; the broader impact of this phenomenon, however, has received much less attention by academics.

The globalization controversy naturally affects the definition of the term itself. Robert Reich refers to globalization as one of those concepts 'that has passed from obscurity to meaninglessness without ever having an intervening period of coherence' (2000: B-1). This meaninglessness can be traced to its usage as an 'all-purpose catchword in public and scholarly debate' (Lechner and Boli, 2000: 1) with different connotations for different parties who support or oppose globalization.

One popular definition of globalization is the absence of borders and barriers to trade between nations (Ohmae, 1995). Dicken (1992) defined globalization as shifts in traditional patterns of international production, investment and trade. The IMF describes globalization as 'the growing economic interdependence of countries worldwide through the increasing volume and variety of cross-border transactions in goods and services and of international capital flows, and also through the more rapid and widespread diffusion of technology' (IMF, in Wolf, 1997). While these definitions convey a sense of dynamic change and boundarylessness, they view the outcomes of globalization too narrowly. In contrast, others define globalization as the interconnections between the overlapping interests of business and society (Brown, 1992; Renesch, 1992). This chapter assumes an even broader definition of globalization that includes the environmental and socio-cultural results of the processes of globalization.

This chapter explores the impact of globalization on the four conditions of sustainability outlined in the Natural Step framework. We seek to contribute to the current literature by (1) expanding the boundaries of the debate to recognize the broad and systemic impacts of globalization on sustainability; and (2) summarizing the arguments supported by empirically-based research about the benefits and liabilities of globalization.

As researchers, our goal has been objectivity and the inclusion of as much substantive evidence as we could gather in what seems to be the first attempt to grapple with a systemic view of an admittedly vast topic. The research is presented in a series of tables that summarize empirical findings about the positive and negative effects of globalization on sustainability. The literature reports more negative than positive effects, perhaps because the majority of researchers interested in sustainability issues, like ourselves, are sensitive to the negative consequences of globalization and pursue research that fits this paradigm.

THE NATURAL STEP FRAMEWORK

The Natural Step is a not-for-profit environmental education organization founded by Dr Karl-Henrik Robèrt. Robèrt, a Swedish pediatric oncologist, was motivated by an anomaly he observed in his work with children suffering from cancer. The parents of these children frequently vowed to do anything they could to save their children, including sacrificing their own lives. Yet, he thought Sweden as a whole was fairly complacent about taking steps to eradicate the environmental causes of cancer. To prevent cancers resulting from pollution, Robèrt began a process of dialogue and consensus building about sustainability with scientists; after numerous iterations, 50 scientists agreed on four basic, non-negotiable system conditions for sustainability (Hinrichs, 1996).

Environmental sustainability is defined as meeting the needs of present generations without compromising the ability of future generations to meet their own needs. The Natural Step program promotes sustainability by encouraging people in organizations to consider the following four system conditions (Hinrichs, 1996) whenever they make decisions.

1. Substances from the earth's crust must not systematically increase in the ecosphere, which means that fossil fuels, metals and other minerals must not be extracted at a faster pace than their slow redeposit and reintegration into the earth's crust. This requires a radically reduced dependence on mined minerals and fossil fuels. Businesses must ask themselves this question: Which materials that are mined from the earth's surface do we use (for example, metals, fuels) and can we use less?

2. Substances produced by society must not systematically increase in the ecosphere. Nature cannot withstand a systematic build-up of substances produced by humans, which means that substances must not be produced at a faster pace than they can be broken down and integrated into the cycles of nature or deposited into the earth's crust. The question for business is: Which unnatural substances does our organization depend on (for example, plastics, chemical compounds) and can we use less?

3. The physical basis for productivity and diversity of nature must not be systematically diminished. Nature cannot withstand a systematic deterioration of its capacity for renewal. In other words, societies cannot harvest or manipulate ecosystems in such a way that productive capacity and biodiversity systematically diminish. This requires that all people critically examine how they harvest renewable resources and adjust consumption and land-use practices to be well within the regenerative capacities of the planet's ecosystems. The question for businesses is: Does our organization depend on activities that encroach on productive parts of nature (for example, overfishing) and can we decrease these activities?

4. For the three previous conditions to be met, there must be fair and efficient use of resources with respect to meeting human needs. Satisfying basic human needs must take precedence over the provision of luxuries, and there should be a just resource distribution. This will result in the social stability and cooperation required to make the changes that will eventually ensure sustainability. The question for businesses is: Is our organization economically dependent on using an unnecessarily large amount of resources in relation to added human value (for example, cutting down forests inhabited by indigenous people whose way of life is thereby threatened) and can we lessen this dependence?

The Natural Step has gained widespread popularity in Swedish society, including Swedish municipalities and multinationals such as Ikea, Electrolux, OK Petroleum and Scandi Hotels. The program has also spread to other countries. In the United States, Interface, the Collins Pine Company and the state of Oregon are among the leading proponents.

THE IMPACT OF GLOBALIZATION ON THE NATURAL STEP CONDITIONS

Key areas of discussion in the globalization debate include global warming, deforestation, ozone depletion, biodiversity, oceans (Lawrence et al., 1996) and pollution. Rhetoric surrounding these issues tends to fall at the extremes. It has often been argued, for example, that the movement of MNEs to countries where environmental laws are absent or not enforced has resulted in greater environmental degradation in these areas. MNEs, however, have also been credited with the development and dispersion of clean technologies, methods and policies.

To date, there are no definitive, system-wide answers to our research question about globalization's impact on the environment. Researchers naturally limit themselves to studying manageable pieces of the enormous interlocking puzzle that comprises our ecosystem and the global economy. Nevertheless, empirical data suggest that globalization has had both positive and negative effects in each aspect of sustainability. As noted earlier, there is generally more research about negative environmental effects than about positive effects. The simple fact that the number of negative articles or arguments is greater, however, does not indicate that the overall effect on the condition is negative. Individual arguments should be considered on their own merits, and their importance will be determined in part by the context within which they are used to evaluate decisions relating to globalization. In the remainder of this chapter, we identify the research findings that link globalization and the individual system conditions of the Natural Step.

System Condition One

The first condition states that substances from the earth's crust must not systematically increase in the ecosphere, stipulating that fossil fuels, metals and other minerals must not be extracted at a faster pace than their slow redeposit and reintegration into the earth's crust. Globalization has had mixed effects on this condition.

On the positive side, globalization facilitates the worldwide dissemination of practices like improved energy efficiency, dematerialization, resource substitution and metal recovery technologies, which are described below.

As a result of technological innovations, pressure from consumer groups and organizations, and regulatory demands, industrialized countries have drastically improved energy efficiency. In association with the export of energy-efficient products and processes, energy use in industrialized countries has decreased substantially over a 30-year period; each unit of output requires only a third of its former energy inputs (Socolow et al., 1994).

Furthermore, the industrial ecology movement has sought to improve environmental responsiveness at the same time as it reduces the global cost of production for corporations. One of its most important emphases has been dematerialization. Multinational corporations have improved production efficiency, eliminated wastes and reduced costs through systematic efforts to reduce overall use of materials and through efforts to enhance the service value of their products while de-emphasizing their physical attributes (Allenby and Richards, 1994).

Similarly, global material sourcing has been accompanied by widespread substitution of more environmentally problematic materials and energy sources for those with reduced environmental impacts. Increased reliance on energy from renewable sources provides an example of this movement (Graedel and Allenby, 1995).

On the negative side, globalization is linked with the exportation of technologies and activities that can have detrimental effects on the ecosphere. For example, globalization of metal recovery technologies have major impacts on the earth's crust. When rudimentary technologies are used, 90 percent of the materials extracted from the ground for conversion into products are discarded. Although less invasive technologies are often available, adoption can be highly capital intensive and unsuitable for adoption in many regions (Socolow et al., 1994).

To illustrate the extent of this effect, Mathis Wackernagel and William Rees (1996) popularized the concept of the 'environmental footprint.' They demonstrated that developed countries require greater per capita material and energy flows, and therefore greater land surface than developing countries. The per capita effect on the earth's crust is greatest in the wealthiest countries that extract resources at a far greater rate than they can be replaced. Globalization of materially affluent lifestyles, promulgated by the media and increased travel, intensifies the demand for extracted materials (Duchin, 1996).

Most of the indigenous industries in the developing world produced simple goods by employing labor-intensive technology. However, lesser-developed countries, lured by the Western concept of development, have switched their production focus to modern goods that require extensive infrastructure and industrial projects.

Importation of modern industrial plants and infrastructure, in turn, require mega-projects in the energy sector. Usually, this energy is provided by large hydroelectric dams and nuclear power stations (Khor, 1996). The dams flood large amounts of land that had previously been forested or used for agriculture, leading to the displacement of numerous people. At times, health concerns surface due to irrigation canals that spread malaria and other water-borne diseases (Khor, 1996). Many of the nuclear power plants located in developing countries do not have the same safety standards found in industrialized countries. If the plant is unsafe, the choice is to either halt operations and incur a loss or to continue operations and run the risk of an accident. If a plant is deemed safe, the issue regarding the disposal of radio-active waste arises (Khor, 1996).

As a result of globalization, more commodities are exported, increasing the exploitation of natural resources. For example, 33 percent of all plywood, 84 percent of coffee, 47 percent of bauxite and alumina, 38 percent of fish, 40 percent of iron ore and 46 percent of crude oil are exported (French, 1993). In Malaysia, timber is a valuable export product that brings in $1.5 billion dollars per year in foreign exchange. The environmental cost, however, is substantial. Whereas 70 to 80 percent of the Malaysian peninsula was forested in 1945, at present most of the forested areas have been cleared resulting in soil erosion, falling water table and an increasing trend of floods and droughts (Goldsmith, 1996).

Tobacco, another export-based crop, depletes soil nutrients at a much higher rate than most other crops (Goodland, 1984). It also requires a large volume of wood to heat tobacco curing barns. It is estimated that 12 000 km^2 of forests per year are logged in order to yield 55 m^3 of cut wood, which in turn is burned for every ton of tobacco cured (Goldsmith and Hildyard, 1990). Other export crops, such as coffee and peanut plantations, also cause significant environmental damage in terms of soil degradation and reduced yields (Borgstrom, 1967; Franke and Chasin, 1981).

In Asia and Latin America, almost half of the world's mangrove forests have been cut down to support the farming and export of prawn. Nearly 120 000 hectares of mangroves have been destroyed in Ecuador, and 100 000 hectares have been destroyed in Thailand (Goldsmith, 1996). Prawn farms also require large amounts of brackish water, a mixture of fresh water and seawater. In the Philippines, this over-extraction of groundwater has led to the creation of shallow wells, the drying up of orchards and ricelands, and the intrusion of salt water from the sea (Wilkes, 1995).

As global appetite for fish increases, more than half of the world's major fishing grounds are in decline, and some have been 'fished out' commercially (Wilkes, 1995). The great cod fisheries in Canada have been closed indefinitely (Goldsmith, 1996). In the north-west Atlantic, total catches have fallen by one-third in the last 20 years, and in Europe, the North Sea mackerel stocks have decreased fiftyfold. Many of the fleets are now moving south as the fish stocks in the north are depleted, thus putting the southern fisheries at risk (French, 1993).

Table 2.1 The impact of globalization on system condition one

Positive effects	Negative effects
Relative efficiency of energy use is improving	Development and increased affluence lead to larger demands for materials and energy
Corporations have achieved systematic dematerialization through manufacturing changes	Export of damaging extraction technologies continues, despite existence of alternatives
Damaging materials and energy sources can be substituted to reduce impact	Increased transportation of raw materials uses non-renewable resources
Export of extracted commodities provide valuable foreign exchange	Heavy environmental costs associated with extraction
Countries make a narrower range of products more efficiently	In Malaysia, nearly all the timber forests have been cut down
	Growth in prawn farms led to the cutting down of half of the mangrove forests, and extraction of groundwater has led to other environmental concerns
	Spread of factories requires more infrastructure using extracted materials
	Increased consumption uses more natural resources
	Increased travel of workers and MNE employees uses fossil fuel
	Increased travel contributes to global warming

Environmentalists claim that globalization also encourages greater consumption as more goods are marketed to more people, creating artificial needs and utilizing more natural resources (Goldsmith, 1997; Mander and Goldsmith, 1996). Increased travel by workers seeking jobs (Brown et al., 1998) and MNE employees requires fossil fuel that contributes to global warming. Globalization also promotes the transportation of raw materials and goods using non-renewable resources. The spread of factories around the world has made more infrastructure necessary, which requires extracted substances from the earth.

The increased income of developed countries is due, in part, to increases in production efficiencies. Globalization is thought to have an implicit goal of encouraging countries to make a narrower range of products more efficiently. Global specialization is difficult to manage and predict, however. According to critics, globalization has resulted in simultaneous surplus and scarcity (Brown et al., 1998), which points to a less than perfect utilization of resources.   Table 2.1 summarizes the impact of globalization on system condition one.

System Condition Two

The second condition of the Natural Step framework concerns substances produced by humans, such as plastics, chemical compounds and waste that does not readily decompose. These substances should not systematically increase in the ecosphere at a faster pace than they can be broken down or deposited into the earth's crust.

On the positive side of the ledger, globalization has been responsible for creating and exporting technologies that utilize fewer natural resources. Carbon combustion used to produce energy has decreased steadily and dramatically in recent decades. This is a result of a combination of factors including technologies that produce higher energy outputs from combustion and the worldwide use of hydropower to replace carbon-based inputs (Socolow et al., 1994). Other environmentally sound devices, procedures and knowledge are also transferable. According to the United Nations Conference on Environment and Development, 1992, many technological innovations have been transferred internationally and to developing countries with the result of reduced impact on the earth's atmosphere.

Advances in global information technology help corporations and organizations to monitor the results of their practices. Information technology enables the creation of highly sophisticated models incorporating thousands of interrelated variables and the maintenance and manipulation of vast data banks. Through such innovations, global environmental metrics can be monitored, trends can be projected and simulations can be analyzed (Graedel and Allenby, 1995).

Globalization is also associated with negative impacts on condition two. At the same time as countries export clean technologies and systems, they export technologies that can have detrimental environmental effects. For example, developing countries have adopted technologies for fossil fuel combustion, which has led to the large-scale emission of gases and particles into the atmosphere (Socolow et al., 1994).

Some multinational corporations have moved operations to the developing world, where environmental regulations tend to be less stringent. For example, in the case of the Bhopal gas tragedy, a corporation adopted safety standards in India that were lower than acceptable levels in its home country (Khor, 1996). Negative environmental effects that would not be permitted in the home countries can be exported as a result of globalization.

Table 2.2 The impact of globalization on system condition two

Positive effects	Negative effects
Transfer of efficient technologies to assist developing countries in increasing production	Developing nations are exposed to toxic or dangerous technologies
Green revolution introduced to increase crop yield through new seed varieties and imported technology	Requires high doses of chemical fertilizers, pesticides, agricultural machinery and irrigation
Carbon combustion has decreased through the use of alternative energy sources	Increasing fossil fuel combustion emits gases and particles into the atmosphere
Environmentally sound production technologies and knowledge can be transferred	Increased affluence is associated with increased generation of wastes and energy-related pollutants
Countries make a narrower range of products more efficiently	Hazardous products are pushed to developing countries in form of pesticides, pharmaceutical drugs, contraceptives
Creation and transfer of more efficient technologies	Degradation due to agribusiness and logging
	Increased environmental degradation from factories in countries without environmental protection laws
	Increased travel contributes to global warming

Some corporations attempt to sell products that are banned in the home country. Examples are pharmaceutical drugs, contraceptives and pesticides banned in Europe, America or Japan but sold to developing countries. The exportation of DDT is the most notable example of this practice.

The generation of energy-related pollutants also increases with general industrial development. Globalization is associated with increases in per capita income. This, in turn, is associated with increases in both atmospheric pollutants and other forms of waste. Affluent countries produce wastes at very high rates relative to developing countries (International Bank for Reconstruction and Development, World Bank, 1992). Table 2.2 presents the impact globalization has had on this condition.

System Condition Three

The third condition stipulates that the physical basis for productivity and diversity of nature should not be systematically diminished, going beyond the ecosystem's capacity for renewal. The positive effects of globalization lie in its potential to protect and improve the regenerative capacity of the earth's ecosystems.

Bioengineering is a highly controversial practice directly related to system condition three that can have positive ecosystem effects. It concerns the patenting of genetically engineered species. The patenting process began with bacteria and has progressed to plants, animals and human genes. It is currently possible to patent animals. Although human beings cannot be patented, their tissues, cells and organs can be. These need not only be genetically engineered components. They can include naturally occurring parts, such as stem cells (Kimbrell, 1996).

The environmental consequences of private control over genetic material are not yet known. However, global management of genetic material can have positive effects; for example, genetic engineering can help preserve and create new species. Endangered species can be preserved through the use of biological techniques, and new species that are better suited for current transportation and usage demands can also be created. 'Golden rice,' genetically engineered to address certain health problems in developing regions, is an example of new species that serve potentially useful roles.

Another important development arises from global coordination of ecosystem management efforts. Global projects exist that preserve species for anthropological and other purposes. The Human Genome Diversity Project seeks to store samples from unique indigenous human communities around the world (Kimbrell, 1996). Additionally, globally coordinated maintenance of seed banks have preserved numerous plant species that might otherwise be endangered.

Globalization, however, has also had negative effects on biodiversity and productivity. The creation of new species through rearrangement of genetic structures and intermixing affects biological systems. Researchers have created thousands of new plants, animals and microbes, and research in this area is proceeding rapidly. Like the introduction of non-native species into a region, introduction of new species can have unpredictable effects on existing ones and can permanently alter biological systems (Kimbrell, 1996).

Commonly accepted and widely used production techniques have also been detrimental to biological systems. In developing countries, traditional fishing employed simple trap nets with mesh large enough to avoid trapping small fish. As a result, breeding grounds were left undisturbed and fish stocks could multiply (Khor, 1996). With the global introduction of modern trawl fishing, there has been an increase in the number of trawlers run for profit with the goal of maximum catch for immediate revenue. This has led to significant overfishing, and the gear used in the trawlers has scraped the bottom of the seabed and disturbed breeding grounds (Khor, 1996). As a result, fish stocks have decreased in many parts of the developing world for traditional and trawl fishermen. Furthermore, fish resources in some rivers have been destroyed by industrial toxic effluents and by the pesticide run-off from farming (Khor, 1996).

Another ecosystem resource that is impacted by globalization is tropical forests. Indigenous peoples living in forests have practiced 'swidden agriculture,' an ecologically sound agricultural system that causes minimal soil erosion in hilly areas. The widespread logging efforts of transnational corporations have led to the chopping down of trees for export or to clear land for cattle grazing areas. This massive deforestation has had impacts such as heavy soil erosion due to removal of tree cover, reduced intake of rainwater in catchment areas, extensive flooding in downstream rural and urban areas, climate change, and loss of land rights for indigenous or tribal peoples (Khor, 1996).

Deforestation of tropical forests and global adoption of technological innovations in agriculture has also resulted in habitat denial and the extinction of species (Rackham, 1986). According to the World Resources Institute, tropical forests are home to almost half of all known plant and animal species on earth, and this is the only home for most of these species. Many more are found in the coastal regions of non-industrialized countries and are affected by corporatization and tourism. The effects of globalization on condition three are summarized in Table 2.3.

Table 2.3 The impact of globalization on system condition three

Positive effects	Negative effects
Genetic engineering can preserve existing species and create new varieties	Corporations can patent genetically engineered species and human tissues, cells and organs
Samples of plant and animal species can be archived	Genetically engineered species can have unpredictable effects on biological systems
Modern trawl fishing maximized catch for maximum immediate revenue	Gross overfishing and modern equipment led to a decrease in fish stocks
Creation and transfer of more efficient technologies	Industrial toxic effluents and pesticide run-offs destroyed riverine fish resources
	Deforestation can cause extinction; half of known species live in tropical forests
	Most of the fishing grounds in northern hemispheres are declining and fishing fleets are moving south
	Cultivation of tobacco is harsh on the soil, and curing of tobacco requires a large amount of wood

System Condition Four

This condition concerns the fair and efficient use of resources to meet basic human needs globally. It is generally agreed by proponents of the Natural Step framework that the first three conditions, which deal with ecological and biological systems, cannot be met without also addressing basic human needs and resource distribution. The complexity of social outcomes, however, makes it difficult to assess the relationship between the distribution of resources and environmental impact as they relate to global trade. Therefore, the discussion of condition four differs from the previous conditions in two ways. First, the positive and negative consequences are intermixed to a greater degree; in other words, the impacts identified for this condition tend to be both positive and negative. For example, in terms of the overall relationship between income and the environment, the 1992 GATT annual report argued that increased incomes resulting from globalization could result in higher rather than lower environmental quality if income gains are spent on environmental protection. 'Environmentalists [by contrast,] argue that increased trade inevitably results in increased consumption and production and, hence lowered environmental quality' (Whalley, 1996: 82). Therefore, increased income has both positive and negative impact on the environment.

The second difference in the discussion of condition four concerns the organization of the findings. Because of the large body of research concerning this condition, we have divided the discussion into four subtopics: inequality; labor conditions and rights; national sovereignty; and cultural and community impact. As with the previous conditions, most of the empirical research addresses negative consequences.

Inequality
The fairness requirement of system condition four relates to inequality and economic well-being. For consumers in many countries, globalization has yielded positive benefits due to increased access to more goods (Evenett, 1999) and reduced prices due to competition with local monopolies. Poor people in certain countries have been able to buy cheaper imported goods rather than shoddy goods produced by local monopolies (Graham and Krugman, 1991). Globalization is responsible for creating more jobs in some developing countries, resulting in heightened wage levels in some areas. Furthermore, in some countries, the food supply has increased due to industrial agriculture (Mander and Goldsmith, 1996).

Despite its productive potential, however, an economic analysis of income levels reveals that globalization has resulted in both winners and losers (Lee, 1996). According to one estimate, 30–40 percent of the world population has benefited from globalization, while the rest has not (Valadskakis, 1998).

Globalization is blamed for increasing the chasm between new groups of haves and have-nots – between the well educated and the poorly educated, between the technologically skilled and the unskilled, and between those living in countries that compete successfully in the global economy and those that do not (Frank and Cook, 1995; Pritchett, 1997; UNDP, 1999). There have been examples of spectacular development, as in South-East Asia, as well as examples of economic marginalization, as in countries in Sub-Saharan Africa. Some developing countries have suffered job losses in local industries that cannot compete with foreign multinationals once liberalization occurs and formerly protected markets are open to everyone (Lee, 1996). There are, however, many factors other than globalization that influence whether nations are poor or wealthy (Landes, 1998).

The gap between the richest and poorest 20 percent of the world population has widened significantly from 1960 when the income ratio of the richest to the poorest was 30:1, to 82:1 in 1995 (UNDP, 1996). The richest fifth of the world's population receives 82.7 percent of the income (UNDP, 1992). A total of 358 people own as much wealth as 2.5 billion people own together – nearly half the world's population (UNDP, 1996). The global income of the poorest fifth of the world dropped from 2.3 percent to 1.4 percent between 1989 and 1998 (Giddens, 2000). In virtually all developed countries, the gaps between skilled and unskilled workers in wages and/or unemployment rates have widened (OECD, 1997; Gottschalk and Smeeding, 1997; Murphy and Topel, 1997).

In the East Asian economies, trade liberalization contributed to reduced wage inequality accompanied by rapid economic growth (Lee, 1996). In Latin America, however, wage inequality increased following liberalization, meaning that skilled workers benefited disproportionately (Berry, 1996; Robbins, 1995; see also UNCTAD, 1997; and Wood, 1997).

Researchers agree that the gap between rich and poor has widened; they disagree, however, about whether globalization has caused the gap. Although US wages rose only 5.5 percent between 1979 and 1993, some economists claim this is not the fault of globalization since international trade and investment have had little impact (Lawrence, 1995; Sachs and Schatz, 1994). Some studies estimate that shifts in product market demand, including the effect of imports, account for less than 10 percent of the increase in wage differential (Slaughter and Swagel,1997). Other economists attribute labor inequalities to technological changes (Lawrence and Slaughter,1993; OECD, 1997) rather than globalization. Another contingent of scholars, however, points to globalization as the cause of inequality (Wood, 1994; Rodrik, 1997; Leamer, 1998). More recent research by Wood (1998) indicates a causal relationship between globalization and the increased demand for skilled rather than unskilled workers in developed countries. Furthermore, Zhao's research (1998) found that foreign direct investments adversely affect union wages and employment.

Nowhere is the inequality between the rich and the poor as great as in the United States. The worth of the average hourly wage is 12 percent lower than it was in 1973 (Longworth, 1999). In the US, the average pay for a CEO is $13.1 million despite weakening returns in the economy (Lavelle, 2001). The after-tax income of the richest 1 percent of US households increased 72 percent from 1977 to 1994 while that of the poorest 20 percent of US households decreased by 16 percent (Scott et al., 1997). As in other countries, some parts of the United States, like Silicon Valley, have benefited more than others.

Some economists and political scientists worry about the threat to political stability since, historically, large and apparently insurmountable gaps between rich and poor have been a factor in revolutions (Marquand, 1996). In the opinion of Anthony Giddens, Director of the London School of Economics, 'Along with ecological risk, expanding inequality is the most serious problem facing world society' (2000: 34). While globalization may not be the only factor involved in growing social inequality, there is evidence that it has produced winners and losers on both the individual and the country level. The increasing gap between the haves and the have-nots raises the question of fairness; intense debates over the fairness of the competitive advantages held by various countries are fought out at WTO meetings and trade negotiations. Table 2.4 summarizes the impact of globalization on inequality.

Table 2.4 The impact of globalization on inequality

Positive effects	Negative effects
Increased access to more goods	
Reduced prices due to competition with local monopolies	
Increased food supply due to industrial agriculture in some countries	Created a greater chasm between haves and have-nots for both individuals and countries
Increased wages for the well-educated	Some downward pressure on wages for the poorly educated
Increased wages for technologically skilled	Some downward pressure on wages for technologically unskilled
Improved economic conditions in countries that successfully compete in global economy	Worsened economic conditions in countries marginalized from the global economy
Rich have become richer	Poor have become poorer
Certain regions of some countries have prospered	Certain regions of some countries have declined

Labor conditions and rights

Job displacement and disparate labor conditions are among the most tangible aspects of globalization; both relate directly to the fairness requirement of condition four. Increasing imports from low-wage countries are perceived by some as a threat to manufacturing jobs in industrialized countries, particularly in labor-intensive sectors (Wood, 1994). Firms in developed nations with high wages move their manufacturing or processing operations to low-cost, lesser-developed countries (LDCs). This, of course, is advantageous for the LDCs and the recipients of new jobs. However, the LDCs compete against one another to attract foreign employers to free trade zones, or export processing zones (EPZs). MNEs are wooed with the lure of tax-free status for a set number of years, facilities and infrastructure, and, in some countries, exemptions from adhering to the national labor code. Five of the 11 nations examined in a US Department of Labor study restricted their citizens' labor rights in EPZs by allowing foreign firms to ignore national labor laws that were enforced elsewhere in the country (Charnovitz, 1992). According to some sources, EPZ workers are often temporary workers who are fired and rehired as needed to avoid having to provide them with benefits or career paths. When zone workers complain about working conditions, they may be fired (Klein, 2000).

The form of ownership and the transitory nature of many overseas factories have resulted in a different form of social contract between employer and employee. The reliance of some MNEs on local subcontractors who run their factories means that workers do not 'belong' to the MNE. This arm's-length relationship facilitates the closure of factories when labor costs rise prohibitively and another country becomes more attractive. In these cases, the social contract between employer and employee is limited to the simplest, most expedient transaction – pay for work, which is a stripped-down version of the social contract that exists in most developed countries.

The exploitative practices most commonly cited in EPZs and outsourced factories are: child labor, hazardous and unhealthy working conditions, absence of collective bargaining, repression of labor unions (Lawrence et. al., 1996) and forced overtime (Klein, 2000). Labor union advocates and others fear that 'exploitative practices in low-wage exporting countries artificially depress labor costs, leading to unfair competitive advantage in world markets and a downward pressure on labor standards in rich countries' (Lawrence et al., 1996: 12). There is evidence that globalization has caused downward pressure on wages (Lawrence, 1995) as well as pensions and benefits (Krishnan, 1996; Sutherland, 1998) and has diminished the power of unions (Levi, 2000). Other economists argue that globalization has had very little negative impact on labor conditions and wages (Krugman, 1994).

The onset of globalization served as a trigger event for positive change in some companies – a wake-up call that people must work more efficiently and more intelligently, which resulted in increased productivity (Evenett, 1999). The labor movement and human rights advocates, however, argue that globalization has had a negative effect on labor standards and threatens hard-won improvements in labor conditions. They warn about the 'race to the bottom,' which assumes that competition will drive labor standards to the lowest common denominator. Interestingly, another aspect of globalization, worldwide telecommunications and the Internet, has contributed to calls for basic labor standards. The increased publicity and communications about poor working conditions in other countries, what is known as the 'CNN effect,' has resulted in greater pressure from human rights groups and labor unions (Lawrence, 1996; Lee, 1997). The threat of Internet-driven international boycotts of goods made by offending MNEs exerts a counter-balancing force for better labor practices in some cases. Companies that engage in exploitative practices are subject to boycotts, negative publicity and loss of both good will and revenue (Dohrs and Garfunkel, 1999). Wide-spread criticism from consumers and protesters induced some MNEs, like NIKE, to demand that their subcontractors provide better working conditions.

Table 2.5 The impact of globalization on labor conditions

Positive effects	Negative effects
Increased employment opportunities in some countries	Job displacement affected individuals as companies moved operations to cheaper labor markets
Increased wages for some workers	Certain industries were forced out of business
Upgraded education system in some countries	Lowered labor standards
Increased opportunity for education and training in some countries	Caused downward pressure for wages*
	Decreased the power of unions
	Decreased labor rights
	Produced a diminished social contract between employer-employee
	Poor health conditions for workers in some countries

Note: * contradictory research findings

Another benefit of globalization for labor is that some workers in LDCs have received more education and training from multinational companies. Furthermore, there is some evidence that increased competition has resulted in upgrading education systems to produce a more highly qualified workforce (Schmidheiny, 1992; Mander and Goldsmith, 1996). As noted in the previous section on inequality, workers have more employment opportunities in some countries and less in others where certain industries and firms (for example, the import sector, small farmers) have been put out of business by global competition (Mander and Goldsmith, 1996). Daly (1996) notes that some people have less choice about how they make their living as a result of globalization. Table 2.5 summarizes the positive and negative impacts of globalization on labor conditions and rights.

National Sovereignty

Historically, governments played a major role in promoting their country's economic development and managing its economy, albeit in a variety of forms. Today, however, some critics argue that government matters less and less in a global economy. Nation-states are just another actor on the global stage, not the directors. Aggressive global production systems and capital markets now occupy the commanding heights of global development, forcing governments on the defensive and pressuring them to deregulate, downsize and privatize many of the social management functions assumed during the past century (Yergin and Stanislaw, 2000). Nation-states, defined by political boundaries, are at a disadvantage when they confront the unique pressures of a boundaryless global economy. Who governs a global economy? 'Information technology – through computers – is creating a "woven world" by promoting communication, coordination, integration, and contact at a pace and scale of change that far outrun the ability of any government to manage. The accelerating connections make national borders increasingly porous – and, in terms of some forms of control, increasingly irrelevant' (Yergin and Stanislaw, 2000: 215). The growing power of globalized financial markets limits the scope of national policy (Lee, 1996). If nations make different rules for their territory, others (firms, workers, citizens and governments) may complain that the playing field is not level. Yielding one's power to international governing bodies like the WTO or the IMF, however, constitutes a grave threat to national sovereignty (Longworth, 1999).

From the governmental viewpoint, globalization has resulted in more economic development and expanded infrastructure for some countries. Certain countries have benefited from the transfer of modern, more effective management techniques to their business sector. Some observers believe that the increased interdependence of trading and investment partners will draw countries closer together and serve as a deterrent against war (Harris and Goodwin, 1995; Tyson, 1999).

Globalization and international competitiveness have influenced public policy in some countries by encouraging them to lower labor standards (Lee, 1997). Furthermore, governments of developed countries with extensive entitlement programs – social security systems, health care programs, unemployment pay or welfare systems – are experiencing greater pressure to decrease such expenditures because they raise the rate of taxation (Longworth, 1999). Nevertheless, Lee (1996) concludes that in spite of increasing globalization, national policies still determine levels of employment and labor standards. He warns, however, that there is a worldwide trend toward smaller government, which is evident in public expenditure reductions, lower taxes, less support for redistributive measures and greater deregulation of markets, including the labor market. Thus, governments are less likely to compensate the losers from globalization at a time when globalization increases the demand for social insurance (Sutherland, 1998). A global economy allows companies (and the wealthiest citizens) to base their tax-paying in countries with the lowest rates, thereby decreasing the taxes local governments receive from formerly 'local' companies. Capital mobility weakens the tax base, which means there is less capacity for social insurance (Sutherland, 1998).

Table 2.6 The impact of globalization on national sovereignty

Positive effects	Negative effects
Increased economic development in some countries	Power of MNEs has increased at the expense of governmental power and sovereignty
Expanded infrastructure in some countries	MNEs externalize some of their costs to countries
Transfer of modern management techniques into business sector	Competition for factories and FDI leads some countries to give MNEs too many concessions
Greater interdependence among trading and investment partners may deter war	Some foreign firms influence local government policy and threaten to leave if their demands are not met
	Companies incorporate in countries with low tax rates, depriving their own country of revenue
	Developed countries are pressured to reduce social benefits to reduce the tax rate

Grunberg (1998) claims that governments have less funds available as a result of globalization. Many EPZs grant tax-free status for the first years, but some MNEs shut down operations and leave as soon as the period is over, because they can take advantage of the same tax-free status elsewhere (Klein, 2000). Furthermore, MNEs sometimes influence local government policy and threaten to leave if their demands are not met. In this way, corporations externalize their costs to others.

As governments struggle (or give up the struggle) with the challenges of regulating global business, a growing number of NGOs are trying to counterbalance the proponents of globalization (Dohrs and Garfunkel, 1999). Many experts agree that governments are not designed or structured to deal with the problems of global business (Giddens, 2000), particularly problems like global warming and environmental degradation, which are inevitable by-products of economic development (Lechner and Boli, 2000). Table 2.6 summarizes the positive and negative impacts of globalization on governmental sovereignty.

Culture and community
Globalization may be a positive force for greater cross-cultural understanding via more cross-cultural exposure and closer cross-border ties. 'A world of complex connectivity (a global market-place, international fashion codes, an international division of labour, a shared eco-system) thus links the myriad small everyday actions of millions with the fates of distant, unknown others and even with the possible fate of the planet' (Tomlinson, 1999: 25). Tomlinson refers to the increased connectivity of the world as a double-edged sword that provides new and wider understanding at the same time it takes away of the securities of one's local world (1999: 30).

Another criticism leveled at globalization is the development of a mono-culture via 'cultural colonialism.' In this view, weakened cultural traditions, along with the importation of foreign media, stores and goods encourage cultural homogenization. Multinational news outlets, like CNN and Rupert Murdoch's News Corporation, provoked the complaint that the flow of information (a term that includes both ideas and attitudes) was dominated by multinational entities based in the most powerful nations (MacBride and Roach, 2000: 286). Chains like Wal-Mart, with lower prices and an extensive, standardized inventory, force uniquely local small stores out of business. Monbiot (1995) claims the use of English as the language of business and in the media drives out and threatens minority languages. As transnational corporations grow and become more powerful, there is a concern that the culture of capitalism (heavily influenced by Western or US culture and commoditization) will develop into a world monoculture. While cultures have always influenced one another, often enriching them in the process, Hamelink, based on personal observation, concludes that cultural synchronization has been occurring at an unprecedented rate and 'never before has one particular cultural pattern been of such global dimensions and so comprehensive' (2000: 312).

There are, however, opposing views to these arguments. Communication experts maintain that the media has been decentralizing with the development of regional centers (for example, Mexico for Spanish television, India for film, Hong Kong for East Asian film and television) and indigenized programming. Thus, they argue that the homogenizing forces of the media, like satellite television, exist in tension with 'heterogenization' (Sinclair et al., 1996). Tomlinson agrees with Hamelink that cultural synchronization is an unprecedented feature of global modernity but argues that, 'Movement between cultural/geographical areas always involves interpretation, translation, mutation, adaptation, and "indigenization" as the receiving culture brings its own cultural resources to bear, in dialectical fashion, upon "cultural imports"' (1999: 84). Other observers point out that globalization may be responsible for the increasing popularity of indigenous movements to maintain ethnic identity (Karliner, 2000). While globalization was not the only cause of the Islamic revolution in Iran, it provided a target for rebellion and also forced the Muslims to 'identify' themselves and determine how they wanted to live in a global society (Lechner and Boli, 2000).

Critics claim that globalization has irrevocably changed the social landscape of communities and constitutes a threat to national culture. For example, transnational agribusiness has replaced family farms in some areas; similarly, cutting down forests inhabited by indigenous people makes it difficult if not impossible for them to maintain their traditional way of life (Keck and Sikkink, 2000; Brown et al., 1998). The spread of newer cultures and technologies may result in the loss of knowledge about traditional practices and arts that may be more compatible with natural systems. EPZs draw people from rural areas, moving them out of reach of their traditional safety nets. It is difficult to pinpoint how much of this movement of people from their traditional communities and ways of life can be attributed directly to globalization versus normal economic and industrial development and a desire to better one's life. Table 2.7 summarizes the positive and negative impacts of globalization on culture and community.

Table 2.7 The impact of globalization on culture and community

Positive effects	Negative effects
Increased cultural exposure and understanding	Exacerbated the desire for mobility, disrupting rural life, and moving people out of reach of their traditional safety nets
Closer cross-border ties	Disintegration of local communities
Encouraged the proliferation of indigenous organizations and movements to preserve ethnic identity	Damaged self-sufficiency of rural life
	Encourages cultural homogenization and a global monoculture

CONCLUSION

The short answer to: 'What is the impact of globalization on environmental sustainability?' is: It's mixed, but there is a growing body of evidence pointing to harmful effects on the environment. Globalization is an uneven process that has resulted in both positive and negative consequences, both winners and losers. A systemic perspective indicates that globalization is neither a panacea nor an unmitigated scourge. It involves serious trade-offs – economic development and jobs at the cost of serious environmental degradation and weakened labor protection, to name only two. The important lesson is to include these trade-offs in the debate, in our research and in the total cost of global business.

Much of the literature on globalization has an ideological bent, which means there is a need for more objective research on its impact and more questioning about the basic assumptions of globalization itself. Using Burrell and Morgan's (1979) taxonomy, we see that the majority of US international business research tends to be both accepting of the *status quo* and objective – falling squarely into the functionalist paradigm with descriptions of the new global economy, its forms and lessons. Given the unprecedented reach of the current form of globalization with its heightened integration, interdependence and powerful consequences, we would argue that functionalist research alone is insufficient. Furthermore, the US acceptance of globalization as the *status quo* may reflect cultural and historical influences. In his Pulitzer Prize-winning book *The Global Squeeze*, journalist Richard Longworth made this conclusion:

The global economy is not an act of God, like a virus or a volcano, but the result of economic actions taken by human beings and thus responsive to human control. There is no need to say, as many American economists and businesspeople do, that the market knows best and must be obeyed. This cultural capitalism is confined mostly to the United States and the other English-speaking nations. Other nations, in Europe and in Asia, see the market as the source of both bountiful benefits and lethal damage, and are determined to temper this force to their own priorities (Longworth, 1999: 4–5).

Given the ever-evolving history of economic development and trade, there is little reason for scholars to assume that globalization as we know it today is the final incarnation. Such an assumption is dangerous if it prevents us from seeing other possibilities as well as the systemic consequences.

This brings us back to the question of how the globalization debate is defined and framed. Once the debate is broadened to include more than economic arguments, it seems obvious that free trade without any regulations or constraints has not been wholly successful (Giddens, 2000). The wealthy nations that advocate free trade are successful in part because they also have laws and institutions that serve as regulators and checks and balances that do not exist in all countries. Leaving workers, governments and the environment to the mercy of an ideology that places unbridled maximization of profit ahead of all else produces mixed results. In Giddens's view, 'Trade always needs a framework of institutions, as do other forms of economic development. Markets cannot be created by purely economic means, and how far a given economy should be exposed to the world market-place must depend upon a range of criteria'(Giddens, 2000: 35). Scholars could help identify these criteria and broaden the scope of their research to include the systemic impact of globalization.

Research on the systemic impact of globalization will never be a simple proposition due to the scope and interdependent nature of the topic. Almost all the empirical research we reviewed focused on small pieces of the puzzle. To do otherwise requires well-funded, multidisciplinary research teams with access to scientific, economic and social science data, sometimes longitudinal in nature. This is arguably the type of research that could be sponsored by international and government agencies.

Case studies of the impact of TNS on individual firms are more manageable and have proved useful in tracking experience with TNS (Bradbury and Clair, 1999). TNS is a relatively new concept that would develop more rapidly if TNS scholars and experts created a research clearing house that collected studies, determined the criteria for valid and rigorous TNS studies and identified the gaps in the literature. For example, two key evaluation questions that drive the more practical side of TNS research are: Does it influence environmental sustainability in a positive direction? and: Utilizing a balanced scorecard that includes financial and other measures of organizational effectiveness and efficiency, do firms benefit from using TNS over the long term?

How do we define corporate accountability in the face of globalization? At present corporate accountability is understood by many as a corporation's non-binding response to the demands of those affected by its activities – its investors, the community in which it is operating – or as a company's voluntary reporting of environmental information (Karliner, 2000). Given the negative results of globalization reported here, it seems obvious that this approach is outdated and overly circumscribed. Business people (as well as politicians, policy-makers and the general public) should be educated about the broader impact of globalization. Social accounting that figures in all the costs of making products, including the cost to the environment and the local community, is a step in the right direction. While there are few quick, easy answers to the problem of an outdated conception of corporate accountability, the Natural Step may be part of the solution.

There are concerns about the limitations of TNS. As a Swedish innovation, it may not work as successfully in countries with different cultural values and history (Bradbury and Clair, 1999). Furthermore, it is too soon to tell whether TNS will have an economic pay-off for all companies that adopt it (Bradbury and Clair, 1999). There are other paths to sustainable business and organizations will need to select the framework most appropriate to their situation and organizational culture.

Nevertheless, the Natural Step framework facilitated a systemic analysis of globalization, which seems to include most of the major controversies in the globalization debate. The fairness issue in system condition four takes the analysis beyond environmental sustainability to include a wide variety of human issues. This leads us to believe that the Natural Step approach could also help MNEs see the broader picture and guide their decision-making on complex issues and trade-offs that characterize a global economy dependent on natural resources.

NOTE

1.   This chapter was funded by CIBER at the University of Washington under a grant from the US Department of Education.

REFERENCES

Allenby, Braden R. and Deanna Richards (1994), *Greening of Industrial Ecosystems*, Washington, DC: National Academy Press.

Berry, Albert (1996), 'The income distribution threat in Latin America,' Paper prepared for the Comparative Economic Association Panel on the 'Distributional impact on market-oriented reforms,' San Francisco: CA.

Borgstrom, Georg (1967), *The Hungry Planet*, New York: Collier.

Bradbury, Hilary and Judith A. Clair (1999), 'Promoting sustainable organizations with Sweden's natural step,' *The Academy of Management Executive*, (4): 63–74.

Brown, Chester R., Michael Renner and Christopher Flavin (1998), *Vital Signs*, New York: W.W. Norton.

Brown, Juanita (1992), 'Corporation as community: a new image for a new era,' in John Renesch (ed.), *New Traditions in Business*, San Francisco, CA: Berrett-Koehler.

Burrell, Gibson and Gareth Morgan (1979), *Sociological Paradigms and Organizational Analysis: Elements of the Sociology of Corporate Life*, London: Heinemann.

Burtless, Gary, Robert Z. Lawrence, Robert E. Litan and Robert J. Shapiro (1998), 'Globaphobia: confronting fears about open trade,' Washington, DC: Brookings Institute.

Champlin, Dell and Paulette Olson (1999), 'The impact of globalization on US labor markets: redefining the debate,' *Journal of Economic Issues*, 33(2): 443–51.

Charnovitz, Steve (1992), 'Environmental and labour standards in trade,' *The World Economy*, 15(8): 343.

Daly, Herman (1996), 'Free trade and globalization vs. environment and community,' *Beyond Growth*, Boston: Beacon Press, pp.145–57.

Dicken, Peter (1992), *Global Shift*, New York: Guilford Press.

Dohrs, Larry and Jon Garfunkel (1999), 'Time to talk about trade and human rights?' *Trade and Human Rights: A Pacific Rim Perspective*, A Source Handbook, Seattle, WA: Global Source Education.

Duchin, Faye (1996), 'Population change, lifestyle, and technology: how much difference can they make?' Population and Development Review, 22(2): 321–30.

Evenett, Simon J. (1999), 'The world trading system: the road ahead,' Finance and Development, 36(4): 22.

Franke, R. and B.H. Chasin (1981), 'Peasants, peanuts, profits and pastoralists,' *Ecologist*, 11(4): 156–68.

Frank and Cook (1995), *The Winner-Takes-All Society*, New York: Free Press.

Freeman, Richard B. (1997), 'Does globalization threaten low-skilled Western workers?' in John Ohilport (ed.), *Working for Full Employment*, New York: Routledge.

French, Hillary (1993), 'Costly tradeoffs reconciling trade and the environment,' Washington, DC: WorldWatch Institute.

Giddens, Anthony (2000), *Runaway World: How Globalization is Reshaping our Lives*, New York: Routledge.

Goldsmith, Edward (1996), 'Global trade and the environment,' in Jerry Mander and Edward Goldsmith (eds), *The Case Against the Global Economy*, San Francisco, CA: Sierra.

Goldsmith, Edward (1997), 'Can the environment survive the global economy?' *The Ecologist*, 27(6): 242–9.

Goldsmith, Edward and Nicholas Hildyard (1990), *The Earth Report No. 2*, London: Mitchell Beazley.

Goodland, Robert (1984), 'Environmental management in tropical agriculture,' Boulder, CO: Westview Press.

Gottshalk, P. and T. Smeeding (1997), 'Cross national comparisons of earnings and income inequality,' *Journal of Economic Literature*, **35**(2): 633–87.

Graedel, Thomas E. and Braden R. Allenby (1995), 'Industrial Ecology,' New York: Prentice-Hall.

Graham, Edward M. and Paul R. Krugman (1991), 'Foreign direct investment in the United States,' 2nd edn, Washington, DC: Institute for International Economics.

Grunberg, Isabelle (1998), 'Double jeopardy: globalization, liberalization and the fiscal squeeze,' *World Development*, **26**(4): 591–605.

Hamelink, Cees (2000), cited in John Tomlinson, 'Cultural Imperialism,' in Frank J. Lechner and John Boli (eds), *The Globalization Reader*, Oxford, UK: Blackwell.

Harris, J.M. and N.R. Goodwin (1995), *A Survey of Ecological Economics*, Washington, DC: Island Press.

Held, David, Anthony McGrew, David Goldblatt and Jonathan Perraton (1999), *Global Transformations: Politics, Economics and Culture*, Cambridge: Polity Press.

Hinrichs, Doug (1996), 'The natural step: an interview with Paul Hawken,' *Ecological Economics Bulletin*, **1**(4): 6–10.

Howes, D. (ed.) (1996), *Cross-cultural Consumption: Global Markets, Local Realities*, London: Routledge.

IMF World Economic Outlook, cited in Martin Wolf (2000), 'Why this hatred of the market?,' *Financial Times*.

Karliner, Joshua (2000), 'Grassroots globalization: reclaiming the Blue Planet,' in Frank J. Lechner and John Boli (eds), *The Globalization Reader*, Oxford: Blackwell.

Keck, Margaret E. and Kathryn Sikkink (2000), 'Environmental advocacy networks,' in Frank J. Lechner and John Boli (eds), *The Globalization Reader*, Oxford: Blackwell, 392–99.

Khor, Martin (1996), 'Global economy and the Third World,' in Jerry Mander and Edward Goldsmith (eds), *The Case Against the Global Economy*, San Francisco, CA: Sierra.

Klein, Naomi (2000), *No Logo*, New York: Picador

Korten, David (1995, 1997), *When Corporations Rule the World*, London: Earthscan.

Krimbell, Andrew (1996), 'Biocolonization: the patenting of life and the global market in body parts,' in Jerry Mander and Edward Goldsmith (eds), *The Case Against the Global Economy*, San Francisco, CA: Sierra.

Krishnan, Raghu (1996), 'December 1995: the first revolt against globalization,' *Monthly Review*, **48**(1): 1–23.

Krugman, Paul (1994), 'Does third world growth hurt first world prosperity?,' *Harvard Business Review*, **72**(4): 113–21.

Landes, David S. (1998), *The Wealth and Poverty of Nations*, New York: W.W. Norton.

Lavelle, Louis (2001), 'Executive Pay,' *Business Week*: 76–80.

Lawrence, Robert A. (1995), 'US wage trends in the 1980s: the role of international factors,' *Federal Reserve Bank of New York Economic Policy Review*, **2**(1): 18–25.

Lawrence, Robert Z., Dani Rodrik and John Whalley (1996), 'Emerging agenda for global trade,' in *Emerging Agenda for Global Trade: High Stakes for Developing Countries*, Washington, DC: Overseas Development Council.

Lawrence, Robert Z. and Matthew Slaughter (1993), 'Trade and US wages in the 1980s: giant sucking sound or small hiccup?,' *Brookings Papers on Economic Activity: Microeconomics*, 2: 161–210.

Leamer, E. (1998), 'In search of Stolper-Samuelson linkages between international trade and lower wages,' in S. Collins (ed.), *Imports, Exports, and the American Worker*, Washington, DC: Brookings Institution Press.

Lechner, Frank J. and John Boli (2000), *The Globalization Reader*, Oxford: Blackwell.

Lee, Eddy (1996), 'Globalization and employment: is anxiety justified?' *International Labour Review*, 135(5): 486–97.

Lee, Eddy (1997), 'Globalization and labour standards: a review of issues,' *International Labour Review*, 136(2): 173–89.

Levi, Margaret (2000), speech on Labor Unions and the WTO, University of Washington, Seattle, Washington.

Longworth, Richard C. (1999), *The Global Squeeze*, Chicago: Contemporary Books.

Mander, Jerry and Edward Goldsmith (eds) (1996), *The Case Against the Global Economy*, San Francisco, CA: Sierra.

Marquand, David (1996), 'The great reckoning,' *Prospect*, London.

Martin, Hans-Peter and Harald Schumann (1997), *The Global Trap: Globalization and the Assault on Democracy and Prosperity*, New York: Zed Books.

Martin, Peter (2000), 'The moral case for globalisation,' in Frank J. Lechner and John Boli (eds), *The Globilization Reader*, Oxford: Blackwell, 12–13.

Monbiot, G. (1995), 'Global villagers speak with forked tongues,' *Guardian*, August 24, 13.

Murphy, K. and R. Topel (1997), 'Unemployment and nonemployment,' *American Economic Review*, 87(2): 295–300.

OECD (1997), 'Trade, earnings and employment: assessing the impact of trade with emerging economies on OECD labour markets,' *OECD Employment Outlook*, 93–128.

Ohmae, Kenichi (1995), *The End of the Nation State*, New York: Free Press.

Parker, Barbara (1998), *Globalization and Business Practice: Managing Across Borders*, London: Sage.

Pritchett, Lant (1997), 'La distribution passee et future du revenue mondial,' (The once and future distribution of world income), *Economie Internationale*, 0(71) (3rd Trimester), 19–42.

Reich, Robert (2000), quoted in Steve Duin, 'Reich displays designer hips and a deft mind,' *The Oregonian*, 3 December B-1.

Renesch, John (ed.) (1992), *New Traditions in Business*, San Francisco, CA: Berett-Koehler.

Robbins, Donald J. (1995), *Trade, Trade Liberalization and Inequality in Latin America and East Asia: Synthesis of Seven Country Studies*, Mimeo, Cambridge, MA: Harvard University.

Rodrik, Dani (1996), 'Labor standards in international trade: do they matter and what do we do about them?' in R.Z. Lawrence, D. Rodrik and J. Whalley (eds), *Emerging Agenda for Global Trade: High Stakes for Developing Countries*, Washington, DC: Overseas Development Council.

Rodrik, Dani (1997), 'Has globalization gone too far?' Washington, DC: Institute for International Economics.

Sachs, Jeffrey and Howard Shatz (1994), 'Trade and jobs in US manufacturing,' Washington, DC: Brookings Papers on Economic Activity, 1, 1–84.

Schmidheiny, Stephan (1992), *Changing Course*, Cambridge, MA: MIT Press.

Scott, Robert E., Thea Lee and John Schmitt (1997), 'Trading away good jobs: an examination of employment and wages in the US 1979–94,' Washington, DC: Economic Policy Institute.

Sinclair, John, Elizabeth Jacka and Stuart Cunningham (1996), *New Patterns in Global Television: Peripheral Vision*, Oxford: Oxford University Press.

Slaughter, Matthew J. and Phillip Swagel (2000), 'Does globalization lower wages and export jobs?' in Frank J. Lechner and John Boli (eds), *The Globilization Reader*, Oxford: Blackwell, 177–80.

Socolow, Robert, Clinton Andrews, Frans Berkhout and Valerie Thomas (1994), *Industrial Ecology and Global Change*, New York: Cambridge University Press.

Sutherland, Peter D. (1998), 'Sharing the Bounty,' *Banker*: 148(873), November 1.

Takashi, Iwase (1997), 'Changing Japanese labor and employment system,' *Journal of Japanese Trade and Industry*, 16(4): 20–24.

Taylor, C. Robert (2000), quoted in Bill Christison, 'The impact of globalization on family farm agriculture,' a speech presented at the RIAD International Forum 5 July 2000 Porto Alegre, Brazil.

Tomlinson, John (1999), *Globalization and Culture*, Chicago: University of Chicago Press.

Tyson, Laura D'Andrea (1999), 'Why the US should welcome China to the WTO,' *Business Week*, 31 May.

UNCTAD (1997), *Trade and Development Report*, Geneva: UNCTAD.

UNCTAD (1999), *North-South Trade, Employment and Inequality: Changing Fortunes in a Skill-Driven World*, Oxford: Clarendon Press.

UNDP (1992), *Human Development Report*, New York: Oxford University Press.

UNDP (1996), *Human Development Report*, New York.

UNDP (1999), *Human Development Report*, New York.

Valadskakis, Kimon (1988), 'The challenge of strategic governance: can globalization be managed?' *Optimim*, 28(2): 26–40.

Wackernagel, Mathis and William Rees (1996), *Our Ecological Footprint*, Gabriola Island, BC: New Society Publishers.

Whalley, John (1996), 'Trade and environment, the WTO, and the developing countries,' in R.Z. Lawrence, D. Rodrik and J. Whalley (eds), *Emerging Agenda for Global Trade: High Stakes*, Washington, DC: Overseas Development Council.

Wilkes, Alex (1995), 'Prawns, profits and protein: aquaculture and food production,' *Ecologist*, 25: 2–3.

Wood, Adrian (1994), *North-South Trade, Employment and Inequality: Changing Fortunes in a Skill-Driven World*, Oxford: Clarendon Press.

Wood, Adrian (1995), 'How trade hurt unskilled workers,' *Journal of Economic Perspectives*, 9(3): 57–81.

Wood, Adrian (1997), 'Openness and wage inequality in developing countries: the Latin American challenge to East Asian conventional wisdom,' *World Bank Economic Review*, 11(1): 33–57.

Wood, Adrian (1998), 'Globalization and the rise in labour market inequalities,' *Economic Journal*, **198**(450): 1463–83.

World Economic Outlook (1997), Washington, DC: International Monetary Fund, May, 45.

Yergin, Daniel and Joseph Stanislaw (2000), 'The commanding heights: the battle between government and the marketplace that is remaking the modern world,' in Frank J. Lechner and John Boli (eds) *The Globalization Reader*, Oxford, UK: Blackwell.

Zhao, Laixun (1998), 'The impact of foreign direct investment on wages and employment,' *Oxford Economic Papers*, **50**(2): 284–302.

3.   Community sustainability comes to the Southern Appalachian region of the USA: the case of Johnson County, Tennessee[1]

W. Edward Stead, Jean Garner Stead and Donald J. Shemwell

INTRODUCTION

Community sustainability involves participative community planning processes that attempt to establish synergy among the community's economy, natural environment and socio-cultural system. This chapter reports the results of an action research-based empirical assessment of citizen readiness for a community sustainability process in a remote mountain community in Southern Appalachia in the USA. Government and community leaders support the process, and funding has been acquired from several public and private sources. However, the results of our assessment indicate a potential split among the county's citizenry regarding support for three dimensions critical for the success of the county's community sustainability efforts – access to the county, diversity and zoning (community-wide land-use laws). The results of this study add credence to the two-worlds hypothesis. They indicate that whereas Southern Appalachia may be in greater need of community sustainability than any other region in the US, it may be the last region in the US to embrace the idea. The results from this study have implications for community sustainability change agents, multinational corporations and funding agencies.

At the heart of current efforts to achieve some semblance of sustainability on the planet are a wide variety of initiatives that can be categorized under the title 'community sustainability.' Communities are complex social networks, ethical support systems and places where people have deep attachments to nature, culture and each other. (Daly and Cobb, 1989; Etzioni, 1993; Mehrhoff, 1999; Shuman, 1998; Stead and Stead, 1996). Community sustainability involves participative community planning processes that attempt to establish synergy among the community's economy, natural environment and socio-cultural system. These processes require that government, business, NGOs and private citizens work together to restore ecosystems, improve land use, provide quality jobs, promote cultural diversity, encourage environmentally sensitive business, preserve cultural and environmental resources, provide affordable housing and improve social services and transportation (Euston, 1997; PCSD, 1999).

We believe that there are few places in the USA as ripe for community sustainability as the remote mountain communities of the Southern Appalachians – a region of the US that extends from Southern Pennsylvania to Northern Alabama and is known for its natural beauty, coal mining, social ills, poverty and cultural and physical isolationism. Many of these communities are in serious need of economic and social development, and all of them are treasure troves of natural beauty and cultural heritage. Currently many Southern Appalachian communities are attempting to institute community sustainability planning processes. However, there may be a major obstacle to the success of these efforts. Hsiung (1997) demonstrates that the people of the Southern Appalachians have historically divided themselves into two worlds, each with a very different view of progress, defined by Hsiung and others as the steady improvement of the economic and social well-being of a given community or society. One group wants to see the region open itself up to development as well as the ideas and people from outside while the other group favors regional isolationism and resists change. Hsiung documents that these groups have clashed over the nature of economic and social development in the region for some 200 years, with the former group referring to the latter group as 'backward.'

In this chapter, we report on an ongoing community sustainability effort in Johnson County, Tennessee, an isolated Southern Appalachian community. Specifically, we will report our empirical findings regarding the readiness of this community to undertake the long-term process of change that will be necessary if it is to achieve community sustainability status. As you will see, our findings indicate that Hsiung's two worlds are alive and well in Johnson County, Tennessee, and that their existence does not bode well for the success of community sustainability efforts in the county or elsewhere in the region for the near future.

It is important for readers to note as they proceed that the data for this study were gathered as part of an action research project in which the paper's authors acted as participants as well as observers at several stages of the process. It is also important to note that the authors did not act as either survey respondents or focus group participants in this case, and the analyses of the survey and focus group data were conducted in objective, scientific ways. Thus, the study reflects certain biases of the authors, such as their belief that sustainability is good and that community sustainability provides a viable vehicle for progress in the future in Southern Appalachia. However, the data and subsequent analyses reported herein were gathered and conducted in ways to minimize the effect of these biases on the results reported in this chapter.

WHAT IS COMMUNITY SUSTAINABILITY?

As mentioned above, community sustainability refers to a pot-pourri of efforts designed to integrate a community's economy, environment and socio-cultural system into a synergistic whole that will allow all three to flourish over the long term. Community sustainability has deep roots in sustainable development efforts in developing countries, but it has arrived in the developed world in recent years. According to the US President's Council on Sustainable Development (PCSD, 1999) federal, state and local governments in the USA allotted $7.5 billion in tax money to community sustainability efforts in 1998. These monies were spent to create environmentally sensitive infrastructures, to improve land use, to revitalize communities, to develop rural enterprises and to improve materials use and resource efficiency (PCSD, 1999). In addition to the money allocated to community sustainability efforts, there were 240 community sustainability ballot initiatives passed by US voters in 1998, and in that same year 32 US governors identified smart land use and smart development as goals for their states (PCSD, 1999).

Principles

The principles of community sustainability are numerous and varied. However, several principles seem common among most authors (Berry, 1999; Covy, 1998; Daly and Cobb, 1989; Euston, 1997; Mehrhoff, 1999; PCSD, 1999; Shuman, 1998; Stead and Stead, 1996; Thomas, 1998; Wheatley and Kellner-Rogers, 1998) (see Table 3.1): One is that community sustainability efforts are by definition participative – requiring a consensus among and between government, business, NGOs and the citizenry throughout the process. A second principle is that community sustainability requires that communities identify the economic, environmental, social and cultural elements that comprise their common wealth. Third, sustainable communities should pursue economic development that stresses the local over the global, allowing them to keep more of the wealth created within their communities (discussed in more depth below). Fourth, sustainable communities should be designed for the young and the old; by doing so, communities are created that are comfortable, safe, accessible and affordable for all. Fifth, sustainable communities should seek to enhance and protect their social, cultural and environmental diversity in order to ensure long-term community buoyancy and vibrancy. Sixth, sustainable communities should seek energy efficiency and independence. Seventh, sustainable communities should give local nature – land, air, water and native species – community membership.

Table 3.1 Principles of community sustainability

- It is a participative process involving government, business, NGOs and the citizenry
- It requires identifying economic, environmental, social and cultural dimensions of the community's common wealth
- It involves pursuing economic development that stresses the local over the global
- It involves designing the community for the young and the old
- It requires enhancing and protecting social, cultural and environmental diversity
- It requires that the community seek energy efficiency and independence
- It requires that local nature – air, water, land and species – be given community membership

---

As is probably clear from a cursory examination of these principles, comprehensive community zoning processes are critical for the successful implementation of community sustainability. Zoning is a term commonly used in the USA to refer to community land-use ordinances. These ordinances generally classify all of the property in the community according to various zones – industrial, commercial, residential, public use and so forth. The designated zone of a particular parcel of land determines how it can be used, how it can be landscaped, how it should be maintained and so forth. As such, zoning is generally considered necessary to protect the natural environment, to create favorable conditions for emergence of sustainable business, to protect the community's cultural artifacts, to create and maintain sustainable neighborhoods, to provide affordable housing, to develop adequate public transportation systems and so forth.

Process

Community sustainability is an ongoing process that requires long-term commitment and actions that support the above principles. Establishing community sustainability requires completing a four-stage process (Berry, 1999; English et al., 1998; Euston, 1997; Kinsley, 1997; Mehrhoff, 1999; Nature Conservancy, 1997) (see Table 3.2). The first stage is community education and consensus building. This stage involves letting community members know what community sustainability is and soliciting their involvement and support in the process. This consensus building requires working with public institutions such as community government and schools, working with the community's environmental, social and cultural NGOs, conducting public forums, publishing newsletters and using other media to increase awareness. The second stage is community analysis, which involves conducting surveys of community members regarding their visions and their perceptions of community assets and challenges, conducting environmental resource inventories, conducting cultural resource inventories, conducting economic resource inventories, identifying social and educational trends and so forth. The third stage of community sustainability is community visioning and planning. Effective visioning and planning require creating a community profile from data gathered during community analysis and conducting visioning workshops with community groups in order to develop long-term community goals as well as short-term objectives and action plans. The fourth stage is the development and institution of community indicators designed to measure the community's progress toward community sustainability. These indicators should be relevant to sustainability, based on reliable and timely information, developed via community participation, understandable to the community at large, link the pillars of community sustainability together over the long term and be fed back regularly to the community so that adjustments and changes can be made. There are dozens of community sustainability indicators that have arisen in North America from successful grass-roots community sustainability efforts in places like Chattanooga, Tennessee, Seattle, Washington, San Francisco, California and Calgary, Alberta. These indicators include such items as income distribution, unemployment, drinking water quality, timber growth-to-removal rates, population diversity, educational attainment and births to single mothers. However, it is important to note that relevant indicators are likely to vary from community to community depending on sound community analysis of resources and needs.

Table 3.2 Community sustainability process

Community education and consensus building
Community analysis:
      survey of community assets and challenges
      environmental resource inventory
      cultural resource inventory
      economic resource inventory
Community visioning and planning
Development of community indicators that:
      link the 3 pillars of sustainability
      are based on reliable and timely information
      are understandable
      are fed back regularly to the community

Going Local

One of the most ominous threats to community sustainability (a threat very relevant to this study) is corporate mobility. Shuman (1998) and Daly and Cobb (1989) discuss the perils for local communities when they put too many of their economic eggs in the baskets of mobile corporations that are free to search the globe for lower-priced resources and labor. Shuman (1998) points to four ways that unchecked and uncontrolled corporate mobility threatens communities: it causes a decline in the quantity and quality of jobs, it imposes huge costs on all levels of government, it contributes to the gradual destruction of local culture and it undermines the capacity of communities to plan for the future. According to Shuman (1998: 9) 'The growing power and will of corporations to move without notice or warning has presented communities with a terrible dilemma: either cut wages and benefits, gut environmental standards and offer tax breaks to attract and retain corporations, or become a ghost town.'

Shuman says that the antidote for these ills is going local. According to Shuman (1998: 6) 'Going local means nurturing locally owned businesses which use local resources sustainably, employ local workers at decent wages, and serve primarily local consumers. It means becoming more self-sufficient and less dependent on [the global market].' This strategy keeps a larger share of the dollars generated by business activity circulating within the community. By keeping a greater portion of the economic multiplier, levels of employment increase in the community, local businesses grow, income levels rise, public welfare improves, cultural heritage is preserved and the natural environment is protected.

THE SOUTHERN APPALACHIANS: A REGION RIPE FOR COMMUNITY SUSTAINABILITY

We believe that there are few stretches of land in the USA that better exemplify both the need and the potential for community sustainability than Southern Appalachia. Located in this region are the temperate rain forests of the Smoky and Blue Ridge Mountains, and the region has been identified as among the most biodiverse in North America. The three pillars of community sustainability – the environment, the socio-cultural system and the economy – rest extremely delicately on the edge of a precipice throughout this region.

Environmentally, the Southern Appalachians provide a plethora of some of the richest geological, faunal and floral wonders in the world. For many years this region was isolated, with much of its natural beauty virtually impervious to outside forces. Today, however, it is being penetrated by a combination of forces that threaten the integrity of the natural environment, including excessive pollution from automobiles and industry, unsustainable forestry and agricultural practices and random economic development.

Socio-culturally, this region is a mixture of rich cultural heritage and socio-economic deprivation. Culturally, we believe that there are few places in the USA that sport a more impressive and more unique heritage. Native Americans hunted bison in the region thousands of years before European settlers discovered the area. The region is the heart of traditional American folklore and the birthplace of traditional American country and bluegrass music. Some of the oldest communities and historical artifacts in the USA reside there. The region has spawned US heroes like Daniel Boone, the Over-the-Mountain Boys, Davey Crockett and Sergeant York. Yet, in the midst of this cultural richness are found some of the US's most serious and acute social ills. High levels of poverty, isolation, illiteracy, teen pregnancy, homelessness, domestic violence and underemployment plague this region like no other in the USA. Parts of the region compare favorably in certain ways to the developing world.

Economically, the region demonstrates a serious split. On the one hand, several of the windy back roads that were once the only access into the area have been replaced by a web of interstate highways that provide easy access to the largest markets in the Eastern US. Communities along these highways such as Chattanooga, Tennessee (one of the nation's most famous sustainable communities), Knoxville, Tennessee, Asheville, North Carolina, Roanoke,

Virginia and Tri-Cities, Tennessee/Virginia have seen rapid economic development. Yet, economic devastation has hit many of the isolated mountain communities in the Southern Appalachia. Much of the economic development in these communities has been built on US federal tobacco allotments. These communities have also attempted to compete on some of the same criteria as developing nations – cheap available labor, tax breaks and promises of minimal government intervention. Whereas these strategies were in many cases effective in the short run, the long-term benefits are now being called into serious question. Tobacco allotments have been cut by 75 percent over the last three years, which has caused serious hardships. Allotments are generally very small (one-half to two acres), and many of the region's most needy citizens rely on them for income. Further, in today's global economy firms that are seeking cheap labor, tax breaks and minimal government intervention are fleeing the borders of the US in favor of developing nations. As a result, many rural mountain communities in Southern Appalachia are slowly losing their economic foundation as the income from tobacco dries up and company after company relocates to the developing world, leaving closed plants, lost jobs and economic troubles in their wake.

THE TWO-WORLDS HYPOTHESIS

Led primarily by concerned citizens and regional NGOs, there have been numerous efforts in recent years to institute community sustainability in the remote mountain communities of the Southern Appalachians. These efforts have been funded by a wide variety of government agencies such as the Tennessee Valley Authority, the Appalachian Regional Commission, the US Environmental Protection Agency, the US Department of Agriculture, the US Forest Service and the US Economic Development Administration, as well as prominent NGOs such as the Nature Conservancy and Appalachian Sustainable Development. These efforts, though nascent, have been as broad as the definition of community sustainability would indicate. They have included the development of community sustainability planning processes, the institution of local value-added micro-enterprise incubators, the implementation of sustainable forestry practices, the development of eco-tourism and the creation of organic produce markets, to name but a few.

As encouraging as efforts like these have been, they have not been without their problems. In several cases community sustainability efforts have begun only to be cut short before they had much of a chance to succeed. For example, in Rogersville, Tennessee, efforts to begin a community sustainability process have been consistently stymied by a lack of cohesion among the various community stakeholders. Also, Unicoi, Tennessee accepted $5000 in US Environmental Protection Agency seed money (via the Sustainable Communities Network) to establish a community sustainability process, but 12 months later newly elected town officials turned down a $50 000 US Environmental Protection Agency Sustainable Development Challenge Grant to complete the process. The officials claimed that accepting the grant would lead to interference by outside intellectuals (educated community citizens not born and raised in the town) and government agencies. A similar occurrence happened in St Paul, Virginia, which won accolades for its community sustainability plan only to have newly elected government officials create roadblocks to implementing the plan.

A basic theme runs through these examples as well as many other thwarted community sustainability efforts in Southern Appalachia – the constant tension between those citizens who support new ideas and want progress for the region and those who do not. This is always an issue in any type of community change process, of course, but according to the research of noted Appalachian historian David Hsiung (1997) the problem is particularly acute in the Southern Appalachians. In his book, *Two Worlds in the Tennessee Mountains* (based on his dissertation at the University of Michigan) he empirically demonstrates that for the past 200 years the citizens of Southern Appalachia have fallen into two camps with regard to their attitudes toward economic and social progress. One group, which lives primarily in the accessible areas of Southern Appalachia, is outwardly oriented and eclectic. According to Hsiung's data its members tend to value education, and they want the region to be as progressive as the rest of the US. Hsiung (1997) documents a long history in the region of members of this group who worked tirelessly to bring rail service and improved roads that would attract business and make the region more accessible. Unfortunately, there is also a very inwardly focused group of citizens in Southern Appalachia that seems to have no use for economic and social progress because it means potential exposure to people and ideas from outside the region. Hsiung's data suggest that they live mostly in the inaccessible areas of the region, they are essentially isolationists, they often devalue (and are suspicious of) education and they do not want progress because it means accepting new ideas, new people and new ways of doing things. They want things to stay they are, and they will work very hard to ensure that they do. Hsiung documents a clear historical rift between these two groups, and he believes that it is the primary reason why the entire region has been so slow to progress over the years.

Hsiung's work applied to the many examples of thwarted community sustainability efforts in Southern Appalachia leads us to a hypothesis regarding the implementation of community sustainability processes in the remote mountain communities of the region. Drawing from the name of his book, we refer to this as the two-worlds hypothesis, and we state it as follows:

> Community sustainability efforts in the remote mountain communities of Southern Appalachia will lag behind the rest of the US because of the traditional historical rift in the region between its more progressive outwardly focused citizens and its less progressive inwardly focused citizens.

COMMUNITY SUSTAINABILITY COMES TO THE TENNESSEE MOUNTAINS

Johnson County, Tennessee is located in the mountains in the extreme north-eastern tip of Tennessee, on the border with North Carolina and Virginia. The county typifies the remote mountain communities of Southern Appalachia. It consists of a network of small towns and pastoral valleys snugly nestled between three mountain ranges – Holston, Iron and Doe. The Doe and Watauga Rivers flow through the county, and the Appalachian Trail traverses its heights. The county consists of three small towns, Mountain City, Shady Valley and Butler, but many of the county's citizens live in remote isolated 'hollers.' ('Hollers' is the traditional Appalachian pronunciation of the word 'hollows.' Hollows are deep geological indentions in mountains, and people are drawn to them as places to live because they are typically small water-rich fertile valleys protected on three sides by mountains.) Access to the county from any direction is limited to windy mountain roads that are often impassable during the winter months. The citizens of the county are primarily white and Christian, and the overall educational attainment among the county's residents is quite low (reports indicate as many as 53 percent of residents over age 25 are functionally illiterate). As with many isolated communities in the US today, the county has a very difficult time retaining its best and brightest citizens. The young people who go beyond high school seldom return to live and work in the county. As is also typical of remote Appalachian communities, there is a small but vocal group of generally wealthy, highly educated, mostly retired newcomers in Johnson County who moved to the community because of its natural beauty and cultural charm. Johnson County is especially attractive to such residents because it is relatively close to the resort communities of Boone and Blowing Rock in North Carolina.

The county's economy was fueled by a very vibrant agricultural industry throughout most of its history, first with beans and more recently with tobacco. It was also successful in attracting companies looking for highly productive unskilled and semi-skilled workers willing to accept low wages for their work, such as Timberland Shoes, Sara Lee Clothing and Levi Strauss. Unfortunately, as Shuman (1998) and Daly and Cobb (1989) predict for US communities that attempt to compete based on low wages, Johnson County has fallen victim to the new global economy. All three of the aforementioned firms (and others as well) have left Johnson County for cheaper labor in developing nations, and tobacco is becoming less and less viable as an agricultural base as tobacco allotments continue to decline in the US. The county's hospital has closed and there is a chronic shortage of available health care. Unemployment has been above 14 percent recently (highest in Tennessee), and about half of the employed residents must drive 45 minutes or longer to jobs outside the county. The biggest boost to the economy in recent years has been the location of a prison in the community. Ironically, when the prison began hiring, it was discovered that there was a shortage of people with the skills necessary for the jobs that were open, so prison officials had to go outside the county to find employees.

Community Sustainability Efforts in Johnson County

It is against this backdrop that community sustainability efforts in Johnson County have taken place. These began in 1995, when two Johnson County High School agriculture instructors developed a plan to revitalize the school's struggling agricultural program, revitalize the county's depressed agricultural industry and keep some of the county's best and brightest young people at home. They shifted the focus of their agriculture program from traditional farming methods to closed-loop hydroponics methods. The instructors raised hundreds of thousands of dollars from the Tennessee Valley Authority and several community businesses to build a geothermally heated aquaculture facility. The program has been operated primarily by the students, and markets have been created for the fish and produce.

Early on these markets were sufficient to cover the program's production and distribution costs. However, as costs rose and prices fell, especially due to competition from Asian fish producers, these programs became a financial burden on the school. Thus, in the fall of 1999, Johnson County High School entered into a Kellogg Foundation-funded partnership with the authors of this chapter, who were associates in the Center for Community Sustainability at East Tennessee State University. The essential purpose of the partnership was to create a viable sustainable marketing plan for the school's fish and produce (see Fuller, 1999, for a thorough discussion of sustainable marketing).

At the same time, broader discussions were taking place about the future of the county. The largest employer, Levi Strauss, had announced that its Johnson County plant was closing, and county officials and citizens were groping with what to do. What emerged from these discussions was an eclectic group composed of the County Executive, the County Commissioners, the county's Kellogg Foundation-sponsored New Century Council, educational leaders, health care professionals, business leaders and several citizen activists. This group worked with East Tennessee State University to procure funding and assistance in establishing a community sustainability process in the county. Funding for the process was procured from an US Economic Development Administration grant and from the Levi Strauss Foundation. East Tennessee State University pledged its support via its Kellogg Community Partnerships program. There is no doubt that the efforts in Johnson County met one key principle of community sustainability: they were very participative, involving a wide coalition from government, business, education, health care and the community at large.

In the spring of 2000, the community sustainability planning process in Johnson County got under way when the above-mentioned group of Johnson County officials, quasi-officials, professionals, business leaders and activist citizens began the long process of creating a plan. Their first order of business was to assess the community's readiness for community sustainability and to identify its strengths and weaknesses regarding its economy, natural environment and socio-cultural system. The participants in the planning process formed themselves into appropriate groups (economic development, culture, environment and so on), and each group took responsibility for gathering data related to its particular area of responsibility.

Assessing Readiness for Community Sustainability in Johnson County

The authors of this study assumed responsibility for gathering most of the data to serve as initial input to the community sustainability planning process in Johnson County. In keeping with the requirements of the community analysis stage of the process, the data gathering efforts were designed to assess citizen readiness to embrace the principles of community sustainability in Johnson County. To do this, three basic questions were embedded into the assessment: What are the precious natural, cultural and economic resources in the county that should be sustained? What issues need to be addressed to sustain these resources? What actions can be taken to achieve community sustainability in Johnson County?

Two data-gathering tools were employed to conduct the assessment: focus groups and a countywide survey. Thirty-two Johnson County residents participated in the focus groups. The planning group (discussed above) selected the focus group participants on the basis of their community influence, interest in the process and/or ability to make things happen in the community. In fact, many of the members of the planning group actually participated in

the focus groups (including all of the members of the environment and culture sub-groups). Thus, this group can be characterized as self-selected and,
for the most part, already committed to the community sustainability process.
Their education and income levels were significantly above the average
county resident, and many of them had relocated into the community from
outside the area. The focus groups employed the nominal grouping technique
(NGT), which involved a three-stage process of incubation (independent
generation of ideas), idea sharing and idea prioritizing. Four questions were
selected for the focus groups: (1) What are the socio-cultural issues in
Johnson County? (2) What are the environmental issues in Johnson County?
(3) What cultural points of interest in Johnson County have the potential for
sustainable economic development? (4) What environmental points of interest
in Johnson County have the potential for sustainable economic development?
There were four facilitators, one for each question. The 32 focus group
participants were formed into four groups of eight, and each group rotated
through all four focus questions.

The community sustainability survey was designed with input from the
Johnson County planning group. The survey consisted of 24 items with seven
possible responses (a seven-point Likert scale) ranging from 'very beneficial'
to 'very harmful.' The items were chosen for their relevance to the principles
of community sustainability and to the needs of the community. In general,
the items were broken into question sets that measured attitudes toward
developmental regulations (zoning, described earlier), economic
development, environmental issues and socio-cultural issues. In addition to
the 24 quantitative items, five qualitative questions were asked: What type of
shopping or services do you have to leave the county for? What is your
favorite place to go in the county to enjoy nature? What one thing do you like
most about the county? What one thing do you like least about the county?
What one thing could the people of the county do to make it a better place to
live? Demographic data on the respondents was also gathered. The survey
was distributed to 1272 county residents (1276 were mailed and 4 were
returned), and 228 responded (18 percent). Eight hundred of the surveys were
mailed to residents who agreed in advance by phone to fill out the survey,
while 476 were sent to randomly selected residents without prior notice. A
MANOVA analysis found no significant differences in survey responses
between these two groups, so the data sets were merged. Demographically, 82
percent of the respondents were over 40 and 66 percent were over 50 while
only 5 percent were 29 years old or younger. The average respondent was a
long-time resident of the county (32 years), and the majority of the
respondents had been to college (34 percent attended, 19 percent completed
baccalaureate degrees, and 10 percent completed graduate degrees). The age
and years of residency in the county of the respondents are reflective of the

current trend in the county of an aging population with a loss of young people. However, the educational level attained by the respondents is skewed well above what would be expected in the general population in the county. Relevant data from the surveys and focus groups are summarized in Table 3.3 and Table 3.4.

Table 3.3 Sustainable community actions suggested by survey respondents

Action	Level of Support (%)
Maintain high-quality drinking water	99
Protect local streams	91
Protect forests	81
Protect natural beauty	96
Preserve the Appalachian culture	92
Prevent toxic wastes	85
Restrict logging	81
Avoid environmentally harmful development	85
Improve literacy rates	96
Provide better jobs	98
Reduce dependence on tobacco farming	80
Create parks and recreation areas	88
Building sidewalks, river walks and trails	78
Building better roads	70
Protecting neighborhoods and property values	86
Encouraging responsible development	70

Regarding the first question related to citizen readiness for community sustainability – What are the precious common resources of the county? – the citizens who were surveyed and those who participated in the focus groups were essentially of one mind. Preserving the natural beauty and resources of the county was seen as paramount in both groups. Survey respondents agreed that high-quality drinking water (99 percent), local streams (91 percent), forests (81 percent) and the county's natural beauty (96 percent) were all important to sustain. Focus group respondents identified 15 specific environmental points of interest that should be preserved and promoted, among them Lake Watauga, the Appalachian Trail, Sink Mountain, the Shady Valley cranberry bogs, Laurel Gorge, the Cherokee National Forest and all of the county's trout streams. Preserving the Appalachian culture of the county was also paramount to both the survey respondents and the focus group parti-

Table 3.4 Sustainable community actions suggested by focus groups

Action

Protect air and water quality
Preserve/promote Lake Watauga
Preserve/promote the Appalachian Trail
Preserve/promote Sink Mountain
Preserve/promote the Shady Valley cranberry bogs
Preserve/promote Laurel Gorge
Preserve/promote the Cherokee National Forest
Preserve/promote the community's trout streams
Preserve local history
Preserve/promote mountain heritage
Preserve/promote Native American heritage
Preserve/promote bluegrass and country music
Develop/expand the hydroponics and aquaculture industries
Make education a high priority
Improve the school system
Expand the school curricula
Improve the library
Clean up trash along roadways
Prevent unchecked logging
Prevent harmful development
Develop river walks and hiking/biking trails
Promote eco-tourism
Promote cultural tourism
Preserve/promote wildlife
Promote fall foliage tours
Promote local crafts
Strengthen community organizations
Enact road expansion and improvement
Enact zoning

cipants. Ninety-two percent of the survey respondents supported the need to preserve the county's Appalachian culture. The focus group participants cited the need to maintain the history of the county, the need to preserve and promote its mountain heritage, the need to preserve and promote the county's home-grown music and the need to celebrate the county's Native

American heritage as cultural aspects that should be sustained. Interestingly (but not surprisingly, given the county's current economic situation) except for the economic potential provided by the county's natural beauty and unique cultural heritage, few current economic resources were identified. The focus groups did cite the high school's hydroponics and aquaculture operations as a sustainable economic resource.

Regarding the second question – What environmental, socio-cultural and economic issues need to be addressed? – the responses were as follows. Environmentally, survey respondents saw a need to prevent toxic wastes (85 percent), place restrictions on logging interests (81 percent) and avoid environmentally harmful development (85 percent). Also, 'eliminating trash dumping' was one of the major suggestions given by survey respondents to the qualitative question regarding the one thing that could be done to make the county a better place to live. Trash along the roadways was also seen as a major issue by the focus group participants, as were unchecked logging and environmentally harmful development. The focus groups also identified air quality and water quality as environmental issues in the county. Socio-culturally, the most dominant issue identified by both the survey respondents and the focus group participants was illiteracy and the poor educational system in the county. Ninety-six percent of the survey respondents saw illiteracy as an issue, and the focus groups said that education was too low a priority in the county, that library facilities were weak, that the school curriculum was too limited and that the school system needed to be improved. Economically, 98 percent of the survey respondents agreed that the county needed better jobs available for the citizens, and 80 percent felt that tobacco should be replaced as the county's agricultural mainstay. Interestingly, few economic issues were identified by the focus groups. Only four focus group participants identified the high unemployment rate as an issue, and the need to replace tobacco with more viable agriculture was not mentioned at all. However, we believe that this disparity can be attributed primarily to how the questions were asked in the focus groups rather than what the participants thought.

According to the survey and focus group data there are several actions the community can take to protect the community's precious resources, deal with the community's issues and thus create a sustainable community (question 3). Eighty-eight percent of the survey respondents and virtually all of the focus group participants were in favor of creating parks and recreation areas in the county. Seventy-eight percent of the survey respondents favored building more sidewalks, river walks and trails. The focus group participants were also in virtually unanimous agreement regarding this matter, and they made several suggestions for locations for these pathways. Eco-tourism and cultural tourism were both very popular suggestions in the focus groups as ways to enhance the county's economy while protecting its natural and cultural resources. Suggestions were made to promote the county's mountains, waterways, wildlife and fall foliage to hikers, bikers and other tourists seeking an experience with nature. Similar suggestions were made regarding the promotion of local bluegrass and country music, crafts and cultural artifacts. Also, the survey respondents supported the development and maintenance of volunteer action groups in the community, and the focus groups agreed, suggesting the strengthening of the Newcomers Club, the Arts Council, the Historical Society and the Chamber of Commerce. Interestingly, there was both a lot of support and a lot of opposition to building better roads into the county that would improve access to outside markets. Seventy percent of the survey respondents wanted to build a four-lane road into the county, but 19 percent thought that such an action would be harmful to the county and 11 percent were not sure. The focus groups identified road expansion and improvement as a necessary action but debated its pros and cons rather vigorously.

The Two Worlds Show Themselves

To this point it would seem that there is significant potential for successful community sustainability efforts in Johnson County, Tennessee. The survey and focus group data reported above show that the citizens of the county have a deep appreciation and desire to preserve the natural beauty that surrounds them. This is also true for their unique cultural heritage and artifacts. The data also show support for the creation of a sustainable economic system that serves to preserve and promote the county's natural and cultural resources rather than to destroy them. Suggestions of promoting eco-tourism, cultural tourism, hiking trails, biking trails, river walks, music festivals, arts and crafts festivals and community theatre are music to the ears of community sustainability devotees. If we ended the chapter here, it would be easy to conclude that Johnson County, Tennessee is on track for a successful community sustainability effort.

But there are potentially serious problems. The data indicate that there are three factors that could prove to be major hindrances to the county's community sustainability efforts (see Table 3.5). Interestingly, taken together these three factors indicate that the two-worlds hypothesis is alive and well in Johnson County.

Table 3.5 Survey data supporting the two-worlds hypothesis

Action	Supported by (%)	Opposed to/not sure (%)
Building new roads	70	30
Zoning:		
Protecting neighborhoods and property values	86	14
Encouraging responsible development	95	5
Limiting options of landowners	49	51
Encouraging different types of people to move to the county	52	48

The first of these factors is improved access to the county, which is critical if the county is to reduce its isolation and open itself up to new people and new ideas. As mentioned above, whereas 70 percent of the survey respondents think that improving roads in order to improve access to outside markets and tourists would be beneficial, 30 percent think it would be harmful or are not sure, and the focus groups reflected a similar split. This is the same type of attitude split that Hsiung (1997) discovered when he studied community support for railroads in Southern Appalachia in the nineteenth century.

The second factor indicating a potential two-worlds split among the residents of Johnson County with regard to community sustainability relates to the citizens' attitudes toward zoning. Whereas zoning is considered critical for the successful implementation of community sustainability, zoning is a new idea for Johnson County (as well as for most isolated Southern Appalachian communities). There are currently no meaningful zoning regulations in the county, and the people have a long-held belief (common in Southern Appalachia) that people should be able to do whatever they wish with their property. Although the survey respondents responded rather favorably to soft-peddled zoning questions related to protecting neighborhoods and property values (86 percent of the survey respondents thought this would be beneficial) or encouraging responsible development (95 percent of the survey respondents thought that this would be beneficial), when asked their opinions about 'protecting and enhancing property values even if it means limiting the options of individual land owners' the data changed significantly. Only 49 percent agreed that such actions would be beneficial while 28 percent thought such actions would be harmful and 23 percent were not sure. Interestingly, this same split was not apparent among the focus group respondents, who seemed to support significant changes in the zoning laws of the county. This was probably because the respondents were self-selected for the stated purpose of discussing community progress; thus, by definition, the focus group participants all probably fall into the progressive group.

The third factor indicating a two-worlds split in Johnson County is population diversity. Only 52 percent of the survey respondents thought that 'encouraging different types of people to come to live in Johnson County' would be beneficial, while 48 percent thought that this would be either harmful or were not sure. The issue of diversity was never raised in any meaningful way in the focus groups. One person did mention the need to have more Christian denominations represented in the county, but this comment received little attention, and even if it had, the idea does not represent much of a leap forward for diversity.

In sum, there seems to be a two-worlds split in Johnson County. One group of citizens who wish to improve access to the county, to implement zoning, and to encourage new people to move to the community, and one group of citizens that either opposes such measures or is not sure about their value. It is important to note at this point that the splits among the survey respondents regarding these three issues may have been even more pronounced had they better reflected the general population in the county with regard to education and literacy. Remember that all of the survey respondents were literate and that the majority of the survey respondents had been to college. Hsiung's data (1997) demonstrated that the more educated members of a community tend to fall into the outwardly focused progress-oriented group, whereas the less-educated members of the community tend to fall into the inwardly focused isolationist group. Had the illiterate and lower-educated citizens of Johnson County been better represented in the survey, the split may lean even more heavily toward attitudes of isolationism and resistance to change.

CONCLUSIONS

In drawing conclusions, we recognize that the data in this study are action research-based and from a single case study of one community's ongoing efforts to implement community sustainability, and this limits our ability to generalize. However, we do believe that it is safe for us to generalize our results from the Johnson County, Tennessee case to the other remote mountain communities in Southern Appalachia that share the same natural beauty, rich culture and serious economic and social ills. Similar tales could be told about Hancock County, Tennessee; Hawkins County, Tennessee; Granger County, Tennessee; Dickenson County, Virginia; Lee County, Virginia; Wise County, Virginia; and Letcher County, Kentucky, to name but a few.

It is unlikely that any other region of the USA has more need for and potential for community sustainability than the remote mountain communities of Southern Appalachia. All of the ingredients are there: a need for sustainable economic development that provides viable career options for local residents and encourages local financial resources to remain in the community; myriad social ills, including poor education, poverty, homelessness, drug and alcohol abuse and domestic violence that could be improved with the development of viable sustainable communities in the region; a rich natural environment that is as unique, diverse, beautiful and fragile as any in the world; a cultural heritage that has spawned some of the US's most important stories, heroes, music, art and crafts.

The US government has been supportive of community sustainability efforts in the region. Money, advice and direct assistance for the planning, implementation and maintenance of community sustainability efforts in the remote communities of Southern Appalachia has been available from the Appalachian Regional Commission, the US Environmental Protection Agency, the US National Forest Service and the US Department of Agriculture. Support from state and local governments for community sustainability efforts in the region has been less consistent but encouraging. Local government support in the Johnson County case was and continues to be very high, with a lot of involvement by county officials. Our experiences indicate, however, that the degree of local government support for community sustainability in the remote communities of Southern Appalachia may depend on which 'world' (Hsiung, 1997) dominates the local government (as the earlier cited examples of Rogersville, Tennessee; Unicoi, Tennessee; and St Paul, Virginia demonstrate).

There also seems to be support for community sustainability among key NGOs and citizen activists in Southern Appalachia. In Johnson County the New Century Council, the Chamber of Commerce, the Newcomers Club and other community groups have been very active in the community sustainability process, and a group of private citizens are working with the Nature Conservancy to restore and protect the Shady Valley cranberry bogs. In other parts of the region NGOs such as Appalachian Sustainable Development, the Nature Conservancy, Clinch-Powell Resource Conservation and Development Council, the Jubilee Project and others have made strides to bring community sustainability to Southern Appalachia.

Lack of support among the general citizenry of Southern Appalachia represents a potentially serious stumbling block to the successful long-term implementation of community sustainability efforts in the region. Even in an effort like the one in Johnson County with funding, government support and broad participation by a wide variety of stakeholders, overcoming the region's two-worlds history and culture will be difficult. The data from Johnson

County indicate that the two worlds still exist, and this does not bode well for community sustainability there or in the other remote mountain communities in Southern Appalachia. As long as a significant percentage of the population remains committed to isolating themselves from new ideas and other people, communities in Southern Appalachia will struggle to implement community sustainability efforts. The region will likely lag behind the rest of the nation in its pursuit of community sustainability just as it did in its pursuit of railroads in the nineteenth century (Hsiung, 1997). And this leads us to our basic conclusion, which is embedded with irony. There are few regions in the United States in more need of community sustainability than Southern Appalachia, but it may very well be the last place in that nation where the idea is embraced.

IMPLICATIONS

The methods and data reported in this study were designed and gathered in the early stages of the community sustainability process – community education and consensus building, and community analysis. These are critical stages for many reasons, of course, one being that they set the psychological stage for the all-important community visioning processes to follow. The apparent two-worlds split among the people of Johnson County provides a significant psychological barrier to achieving the consensus necessary for a truly shared vision in the community, and this in turn puts the entire community sustainability process in jeopardy (as we stated in our conclusions above). This observation holds an important message for community sustainability change agents. We highly recommend from our experience that change agents put consensus building at the top of their agendas throughout the process. We suggest testing for consensus early and often throughout the community sustainability process, and we suggest trying to identify potential sources of conflict – like the two-worlds split we found in Johnson County – as soon as possible. At a minimum, keeping continuous track of consensus can give change agents a more realistic perspective on the potential for a successful community sustainability intervention in the community. In some cases it may even help change agents to predict potential conflicts so that they may find ways to head them off and keep the community sustainability process alive and moving forward.

As we reported above, the current economic problems in Johnson County, Tennessee have been exacerbated by the migration of multinational corporations such as Timberland Shoes, Levi Strauss and Sara Lee from the county to developing nations. According to Shuman (1998) this is a common problem throughout the developed world. One of the hopes for a sustainable world is that multinational corporations across the globe will commit themselves to the triple bottom line – strategic processes designed to achieve economic, social and ecological synergy in all of a firm's operations. If Shuman's point is valid, and our data certainly point in that direction, then commitment to the triple bottom line will require that multinational corporations commit themselves to the concept and principles of going local. This means making long-term commitments to communities where they locate, and investing as many corporate resources as possible into sustaining these communities economically, socially and environmentally.

This same message holds true for public and private regional, state, national and international funding agencies interested in supporting and promoting community sustainability. We highly recommend that these agencies use their resources to forge long-term partnerships between communities and multinational corporations based on the local principles and practices discussed above. We believe that such an approach would help to ensure that economic progress in the communities funded and supported by these agencies is sustainable over the long term because it is founded on sound principles of economic, social and ecological synergy.

LIMITATIONS

As stated earlier, it is important to remember that the data in this study are the result of an action research intervention. Action research interventions are organizational change processes that employ sound scientific data-gathering and analysis to guide and encourage change. Thus, action research is not pure objective research methodology. The primary role of the researcher in action research is that of change agent, not scientific observer. As such, action research interventions include an overlying value system that represents the values of the clients and the change agents (for a complete discussion of action research, see French and Bell, 1999). There is no doubt that we, the authors, entered the Johnson County, Tennessee intervention with the express purpose of bringing community sustainability to the community because we believed that it was the right thing for them to do and because we wanted to help them do it, and we fully admit that this can cause potential bias on our part. We also admit that our values probably significantly influenced our use of two value-loaded terms in the chapter – 'sustainability' and 'progress.' Specifically, there is a core value reflected throughout this chapter that sustainability is good. Three instrumental values are also clearly reflected in this chapter: community sustainability is a good and admirable goal for communities to seek; progress is a good and admirable goal for communities to seek; and community sustainability represents progress.

While these values certainly influenced our interpretation of the terms 'sustainability' and 'progress,' we have confidence that they did not significantly influence our survey design, focus group design or interpretations of the data. Thus, we strongly believe that the data reported herein accurately portray the climate for community sustainability in Johnson County, Tennessee. Specifically, the two-worlds split highlighted in this study was in no way preconceived by the authors. Rather, it appeared out of the data.

NOTE

1. This research was partially funded by grants from the W.K. Kellogg Foundation and the Economic Development Administration.

REFERENCES

Berry, W. (1999), 'Community in 17 sensible steps,' *Community and Society*, hhtp://www.unte.com/lens/cs/11cswberry.html.
Covy, S. (1998), 'The ideal community,' in F. Hesselbein, M. Goldsmith, R. Beckhard and R. Schubert (eds), *The Community of the Future*, San Francisco: Jossey-Bass Publishers.
Daly, H. and J. Cobb (1989), *For the Common Good*, Boston, MA: Beacon Press.
English, M., J. Peretz and M. Manderschied (1998), *Smart Growth for Tennessee Towns and Counties: A Process Guide*, Knoxville, TN: Energy, Environment and Resources Center, University of Tennessee.
Euston, A. (1997), *Local Community Sustainability Strategies*, Washington, DC: Office of Community Planning and Development, US Department of Housing and Urban Development.
Etzioni, A. (1993), *The Spirit of Community*, New York: Crown Publishers.
French, W. and C. Bell (1999), *Organization Development*, 6th edition, Upper Saddle River, NJ: Prentice-Hall.
Fuller, A. (1999), *Sustainable Marketing,* Thousand Oaks, CA: Sage Publications.
Hsiung, D. (1997), *Two Worlds in the Tennessee Mountains*, Lexington, KY: University of Kentucky Press.
Kinsley, M. (1997), *Economic Renewal Guide: A Collaborative Process for Sustainable Community Development*, Snowmass, CO: Rocky Mountain Institute.
Mehrhoff, W. (1999), *Community Design: A Team Approach to Dynamic Community Systems*, Thousand Oaks, CA: Sage Publications.
Nature Conservancy (1997), *Pathways to Building a Local Initiative for Compatible Economic Development*.
President's Council on Sustainable Development (PCSD) (1999), *Towards a Sustainable America*, Washington, DC: PCSD Publications.
Shuman, M. (1998), *Going Local: Creating Self-Reliant Communities in a Global Age*, New York: Free Press.
Stead, W. and J. Stead, (1996) *Management for a Small Planet*, Thousand Oaks, CA: Sage Publications.

Thomas, R. Jr. (1998), 'Diversity in Community,' in F. Hesselbein, M. Goldsmith, R. Beckhard and R. Schubert (eds), *The Community of the Future*, San Francisco, CA: Jossey-Bass Publishers.

Wheatley M.J. and M. Kellner-Rogers (1998), 'The paradox and promise of community,' in F. Hesselbein, M. Goldsmith, R. Beckhard and R. Schubert (eds), *The Community of the Future*, San Francisco, CA: Jossey-Bass Publishers, pp. 9–18.

4. Eco-sustainability orientation in China and Japan: differences between proactive and reactive firms

Oana Branzei and Ilan Vertinsky

INTRODUCTION

This chapter examines the diffusion of corporate environmental practices in different national contexts. Using an institutional theory framework, we articulate propositions regarding the influences of governmental regulations, 'best practices,' and stakeholder pressures on eco-sustainability orientation, a firm-level measure of corporate environmental performance. We test these propositions on two random samples of firms from China (Shanghai) and Japan. The chapter contrasts the importance of different institutional influences for Chinese and Japanese firms, and analyzes their impact on proactive and reactive firms within each national context. We find that Chinese firms, especially the proactive ones, are mainly responsive to 'best practices' endorsed by regulatory agencies. Japanese firms, especially the reactive ones, are more sensitive to the influences of their trade associations. In both countries, firms' eco-sustainability orientation was positively influenced by the societal views regarding the role governments should play in environmental protection, and by the perceived effectiveness of governmental regulations. However, we find that governments' direct intervention in firms' operations did not foster an increase in their eco-sustainability orientation.

> We have in the more recent past been forced to face up to a sharp increase in economic interdependence among nations. We are now forced to accustom ourselves to an accelerating ecological interdependence among nations. Ecology and economy are becoming ever more interwoven – locally, regionally, nationally, and globally – into a seamless net of causes and effects. (WCED, 11987: 5, quoted by Pezzoli, 1997: 552).

Environmental crises, such as climate change and loss of biodiversity, are cross-national in scope. Firms from different countries often depend on resources from a common ecosystem. The increasing levels of economic concern, as well as ecological and economic interdependence can facilitate the transfer of environmental technologies and production processes across national boundaries (Adler, 1983; Dunlap and Mertig, 1994; Ronen, 1986; Christmann and Taylor, 2001).

Corporate actions are constrained by specific geographical and demographic conditions and by the expectations arising from the national cultures in which the firms are embedded (Child, 1981; Trice and Beyer, 1993: 333). Countries have different degrees of economic development and specific biophysical environments (Egri and Pinfield, 1996: 476), and may espouse different paradigms regarding the relationships among their economic, social and natural environments (Jennings and Zandbergen, 1995). National culture influences these relationships by shaping the environmental values held collectively and individually in a society (Gooch, 1995), as well as the social expectations regarding corporate environmental actions. The impact of national and cultural differences upon firms' environmental approaches has been insufficiently addressed by existing studies (Starik and Marcus, 2000).

This chapter adopts an institutional perspective and examines the impact of firms' national context on their environmental responses. We investigate which institutions help diffuse new environmental guidelines and practices among firms in China and Japan. Within each national context, the study compares the impact of national governmental regulation (Walley and Whitehead, 1994) and of social, self-imposed norms (King and Lenox, 2000; Ostrom, 1990; Tolbert and Zucker, 1983) on the environmental responses of firms. We discuss several sources of social influence – the 'best practices' promoted by environmental agencies, trade associations and competing organizations, and the pressures exerted by the media and local communities (Henriques and Sadorsky, 1999; Hoffman, 1999; Scott, 1995). Oliver (1991: 160) suggested that organizational responses vary depending on 'who is exerting institutional pressures on the organization'. Firms are more likely to respond to institutional pressures when they depend on the source of influence for resources or for legitimacy (DiMaggio and Powell, 1983) and when the demands of different sources are convergent (Oliver, 1990). Firms' strategic orientations shape their responses to these institutional influences: some firms are more open to change and have more resources available than others (Fox-Wolfgramm et al., 1998). There is only limited research on the precipitating and enabling institutional influences on different groups of firms (that is, early movers versus late movers, Greenwood and Hinings, 1996; or between 'cleaner' and 'dirtier' firms, King and Lenox, 2000; Lyon and Maxwell, 2001; Russo and Fouts, 1997). To fill this gap, we examine which institutional influences are more important for firms with low and high levels of environmental performance.

The study is organized as follows. The next section compares the environmental paradigms espoused in North America, China and Japan, and introduces a firm-level concept of environmental performance, eco-sustainability orientation. The third section discusses the influences of specific institutions on the eco-sustainability orientation of Chinese and Japanese firms. We suggest that these institutions may have a differential impact on firms with a weak eco-sustainability orientation (reactive firms) than on firms with a strong eco-sustainability orientation (proactive firms). The fourth section describes the institutional contexts of China and Japan in the late 1990s, our samples and the measures used. The fifth section presents the results and is followed by a discussion which contrasts the findings of the current study with prior research in the North American context and explores their theoretical and practical implications. It also identifies the limitations of the study, and suggests avenues for future research.

THE CONCEPT OF ECO-SUSTAINABILITY ORIENTATION IN DIFFERENT CULTURES

Three sets of environmental paradigms, summarized in Table 4.1, have influenced the relationships between nature, economy, and society in Western and Eastern nations (Daly and Cobb, 1994; Egri and Pinfield, 1996: 461; Gladwin et al., 1995; Kalland and Asquith, 1997; Miyamoto, 1967; Sakamaki, 1967; Yukawa, 1967; Zhang, 1989). (1) the dominant social paradigm, equivalent to Hsun Tzu in China, and Lao Tzu in Japan, stresses human mastery over nature; (2) reform environmentalism, similar to Yi Zhuang in China, and Wa and Fukko Shinto in Japan, emphasizes harmony between man and nature; and (3) radical environmentalism, represented by Chuang Tzu, Confucianism, and Taoism in China, and by the traditional Shinto in Japan, highlights human submission to, and awe of natural forces. Husserl (1970) and Dy (1989) suggest that similar relationships between nature and society exist in most countries, and that these relationships have evolved over time from a state of total dependence upon nature to a state of submission of nature to mankind.

Most societies impose a wide range of economic, legal and ethical constraints on corporate activities (Carroll, 1979). In both Eastern and Western nations, many firms seek to balance the utilization and the conservation of the natural environment (Table 4.1), and implement environmentally responsible

Table 4.1 Views of the natural environment in Eastern and Western cultures

Context	Narrow economic self-interest	Firms' social responsiveness	Conservation of natural ecosystem
Western nations	**Dominant social paradigm** Anthropocentric values. Unlimited progress based on exploitation of natural resources (Daly and Cobb, 1994; Egri and Pinfield, 1996).	**Reform environmentalism** Ecological sustainability (Starik and Rands, 1995). Corporate activities seek to balance economic returns and environmental risks. Firms comply or exceed governmental policies and regulations for environmental protection, develop principles of responsibility and implement environmental actions.	**Radical environmentalism** Bio-centric values. Forgoing economic advancement for natural harmony.
China	**Hsun Tzu** 'Dominating, transforming, and harnessing nature' to improve the quality of human life. Instrumentality, present needs, and human control, and pays scarce attention to natural equilibrium (Zhang, 1989).	**Yi Zhuan** 'the harmony of heaven (nature) and man'; 'ecological balance.' Man adjusts to nature and assists in its change. 'Acknowledges the objectivity of natural changes and their laws, on the one hand, and affirms the initiative of the subject, on the other' (Zhang, 1989: 11).	**Chuang Tzu, Confucianism and Taoism** 'Let nature run its own course and follow it.' Nature is inviolable and beyond man's control. Laments man-centeredness and the artificial interventions of humans in natural ecosystems. Advocates man's return to a perfect, original state of nature.
Japan	**Lao Tzu** Nature considered insensate (never popular in Japan).	**'Wa,' the spirit of harmony** 'the ideal of attaining a complete union of man and nature, and accordingly, of resolving any kind of alienation between them' (Yukawa, 1967: 59). **Fukko-Shinto (Return to Antiquity Shinto)** Proper principles of human conduct are shaped through careful observation of nature, and communication with nature.	**Traditional Shinto** 'Man's awe for Nature' (Miyamoto, 1967: 4). 'Man was treated as an integral part of the whole, closely associated with and identified with the elements and forces of the world about him' (Sakamaki, 1967: 24).
'Universal' attitudes	**Means to human ends** Man 'attempts to master, to grasp its inner workings so as to control and utilize it for man's ends'. Nature becomes 'tamed and harnessed for the goals of human civilization' (Dy, 1989: 220–21).	**Objective support for human activities** Nature offers a physical support for human activities and becomes a means to increase human freedom.	**Mythico-religious submission to nature** Nature represents an ambiguous, inescapable force that sustains and pervades man's life. Humans fear and obey nature's mysterious force.

actions to different extents (Dechant and Altman, 1994; Henriques and Sadorsky, 1999; Hunt and Auster, 1990; Roome, 1992; Wartick and Cochran, 1985). Some firms adopt only pollution reduction measures in order to meet governmental policies and regulations (that is, reactive firms, Hunt and Auster, 1990). Other firms seek competitive advantages based on environmentally friendly technologies and practices. Those firms that devote persistent efforts and resources to addressing environmental issues eventually internalize environmental values and develop ecologically sustainable strategies and practices (Hart, 1995; Shrivastava, 1995; Starik and Marcus, 2000; Stead and Stead, 2000). These firms are considered environmentally proactive (Ackerman, 1975; Nasi et al., 1997; Preston and Post, 1975). Firms' environmental actions, and their environmental performance, are comparable across countries (Karagozoglu, 2001).

The variety of corporate responses to environmental issues can be described using a firm-level concept, eco-sustainability orientation. This concept includes principles of organizational responsibility, processes of environmental responsiveness and internal strategies and actions (Klassen, 2001; Wartick and Cochran, 1985; Wood, 1991).[1] At the firm level, eco-sustainability orientation is higher when: (1) environmental issues become legitimate corporate concerns (Bansal and Roth, 2000; Winn, 1995); (2) firms dedicate adequate resources to implement environmental actions (Post and Altman, 1992; Sharma, 2000); and (3) organizational members, at all levels, feel personally responsible for their firms' environmental actions (Egri and Herman, 2000).

INSTITUTIONAL INFLUENCES ON ECO-SUSTAINABILITY ORIENTATION

In this section, we investigate how firms' eco-sustainability orientation 'is shaped, mediated, and channeled by the institutional environment' (Hoffman, 1999: 351) in different national contexts. Institutional theory examines how societal and organizational fields influence the diffusion of rules and practices among firms (DiMaggio and Powell, 1991; Hoffman, 1997; Jennings and Zandbergen, 1995; Meyer and Scott, 1983; Scott, 1995). Corporate actions are chosen from a narrowly defined set of options, which are shaped or legitimated by the institutions in firms' societal and organizational fields (Scott, 1991).

Societal Fields

Societal fields are largely shaped by: (1) nation states, (2) social movements, and (3) industry-level innovations (Giddens, 1984; Jennings and Zandbergen, 1995). In industrialized countries, the state exerts pervasive influence on all aspects of economic life (Jennings and Zandbergen, 1995). For example, the state sets the type and the level of environmental regulations. Social movements, which include environmental non-governmental organizations (ENGOs), are instrumental in introducing environmental issues into public debate, and shape both public opinion and government policy. Through direct social actions (strikes, demonstrations and so on) social movements can change industry practices. Industry-level innovations, such as new product and process technologies, influence the public demand for environmentally friendly goods, and increase the governmental requirements regarding the standards of environmental performance for new and existing firms.

In their pursuit of economic goals, firms tend to respect the legal environmental requirements set by their governments (Carroll, 1979; Henriques and Sadorsky, 1999; Sexton et al., 1999). Regulations influence firm-level responses (Walley and Whitehead, 1994). They encourage corporations to initiate environmental actions sooner than self-interest alone would dictate, and try to ensure that the costs of undoing negative environmental impacts are borne by those who generated the damage (Marcus, 1984). Environmental regulation attempts to establish controls for the material and energy impacts of each society upon its biophysical environment (Cohen, 1987; Sanchez, 1997). The governmental sector uses a combination of command and control mechanisms (for example, legislation and sanctions, Sanchez, 1997; Scott, 1994) and market-based mechanisms (Meyer and Scott, 1983; Sanchez, 1997; Sharma, 2000). Effective command and control mechanisms specify clear regulations, with strict enforcement, which trigger firms' compliance. Market-based mechanisms are flexible arrangements through which governments can stimulate firm-level environmental innovations beyond regulatory requirements by providing incentives (Cairncross, 1993; Sanchez, 1997).

Firms' reactions to governmental regulation may vary depending on the society's views about the role firms ought to assume in protecting the environment, the general effectiveness of governmental regulations regarding environmental protection and the degree to which governmental regulations have a direct impact on firms' operations.

Environmental proactivism is driven by a combination of the 'stick' of governmental regulation and the 'carrot' of improved market performance, which could result from a cleaner corporate image (Lawrence and Morell, 1995: 102). 'Significant government intervention, including carrots and sticks, may be necessary to stimulate change in industrial sectors bogged down with inertia and attitudinal problems' (Ashford, 1993: 296). In nations with statist views, governments shoulder the responsibility for environmental protection and rely on command and control mechanisms to trigger firms' compliance with environmental policies. However, excessive emphasis on regulatory compliance, conventional end-of-pipe technologies, and discharge standards, are often costly and effort-intensive for firms and may block firm-level environmental initiatives (Ashford, 1993; Sanchez, 1997). Liberal nations delegate broader social responsibilities to firms, expect a higher degree of firm-level initiative and advocate market-based mechanisms, which stimulate firm-level environmental initiatives (Post, 1994; Williams et al., 1993). In Canada, for example, firm-level voluntary actions are expected to work more quickly and more effectively than the traditional regulatory approach, and to be more cost-effective for both the government and industry (Ibbotson and Phyper, 1996: 39). Emphasis on improved market performance helps decision-makers frame environmental investments as 'opportunities' to 'gain' a cleaner environment (Feyerherm, 1995: 251; Sharma, 2000). As a result, they may be more likely to engage in risk-seeking environmental investments (Kahneman and Tversky, 1979) aimed at reducing their firms' ecological footprint (proactive behavior), than in risk-averse investment to minimize economic losses (reactive behaviors).

Firms generally increase their environmental performance when governmental regulations demand a higher level of performance and are effectively enforced (Sanchez, 1997; Nehrt, 1998). Reactive firms may adopt environmental responses because they think that other firms will also comply with governments' regulations, and thus the required initial investments will not damage their competitive position. Governments' apparent leadership in environmental protection can also reinforce proactive corporate behaviors. When proactive firms perceive governmental actions as credible and effective means to alleviate their negative environmental impact, they will be more strongly motivated to adapt their voluntary initiatives in response to governmental regulations (Sanchez, 1997).

These firms accept greater environmental responsibility because they recognize that pollution and waste may signal inefficient practices, or because they expect stronger demands from their stakeholders in the near future (Williams et al., 1993). These firms will be more inclined to respond to those governmental environmental policies and regulations when these are viewed as effective means of protecting the ecosystem.

Finally, firms are more likely to comply with governmental regulations that include clear, specific requirements and apply directly to firms' operations. 'The degree to which the requirements of a regulation are strictly enforced may influence the willingness of an industrial sector to innovate' (Ashford, 1993: 283). Interviews with state and federal personnel suggest that 'stringent and certain regulatory demands (such as emission, effluent, or exposure standards, or product bans or phase-outs) [are effective in achieving] pollution prevention' (Ashford, 1993: 296). We anticipate that:

H1: Firms' eco-sustainability orientation will be positively related to:
(1) the liberal views regarding governments' role in environmental protection held by firms;
(2) their perceptions of the general effectiveness of the environmental regulatory system;
(3) the degree of direct impact of governments' environmental regulations on firms' operations.

Within each nation, firms generally comply with regulatory requirements that affect their operations directly, and are strictly enforced, resulting in sanctions in case of non-compliance (Aragón-Correa, 1998; Henriques and Sadorsky, 1999). However, the introduction of new policies or regulatory changes are likely to have a stronger impact on reactive firms which have to strive to keep up with regulatory requirements than on proactive firms which generally exceed and anticipate regulatory requirements (Carroll, 1979; Sethi, 1979; Stead and Stead, 2000).

H2: Within the same national context, governmental regulations will have a stronger impact on eco-sustainability orientation for reactive firms and a weaker impact on eco-sustainability orientation for proactive firms.

Organizational Fields

Organizational fields operate within societal fields (DiMaggio and Powell, 1991; Meyer and Scott, 1983). An organizational field includes a set of firms and institutions that are guided by the same purposes, produce similar products and services, or interact on a regular basis. Organizational fields may include 'constituents such as the government, critical exchange partners, sources of funding, professional and trade associations, special interest groups, and the general public' (Hoffman, 1999: 352). Scott (1995: 56) defines an organizational field as 'a community of organizations that partakes of a common meaning system and whose participants interact more frequently and fatefully with one another than with actors outside the field'. In the early development stages of a field, technical performance requirements are more important, while in the later (mature) stages, institutional pressures become more salient (Greenwood and Hinings, 1996; Tolbert and Zucker, 1983). Mature fields have clear organizational templates and articulated mechanisms for transmitting these templates (the state, regulatory agencies, trade associations, and leading firms, Fligstein, 1991; Hinings and Greenwood, 1988; Kikulis, Slack and Hinings, 1995).

We are interested here in the organizational fields that form around environmental issues. Our study investigates the influence of five types of institutions: (1) governmental environmental agencies that establish pollution, production, and/or process standards; (2) trade and industry associations; (3) firms' competitors within the main industry; (4) media; and (5) local communities. Governmental agencies, trade and industry associations, and competing firms exert normative influences on firms' eco-sustainability orientation by setting rules of thumb, standard operating procedures and social or professional standards (King and Lenox, 2000). Firms also mimic their competitors' environmental practices to reduce their costs, improve their products or expand their share of environmentally conscious market segments (Hart, 1995; Stead and Stead, 2000). Governmental agencies, trade associations, competing firms, media and local communities can also exert coercive influences by sanctioning those firms who have failed to adopt the accepted environmental practices or by rewarding those who do (Scott, 1991).

Environmental standards
Environmental standards reflect the 'best practices' in an organizational field. In mature fields, there is a well-developed network of regulatory agencies, and regulatory pressures for compliance with these standards are clear and reinforced (Greenwood and Hinings, 1996). Firms are likely to adopt these standards, due to regulatory pressures (Kikulis et al., 1995) and to gain legitimacy (DiMaggio and Powell, 1991). We propose that the existence of clear standards will be positively associated with higher eco-sustainable orientation at the firm level.

> H3: The more explicit are the 'best practices' in the organizational field, the stronger firms' eco-sustainability orientation.

The degree to which environmental standards are adopted by firms depends on the general acceptability of the ecological sustainability concept within each country (Jennings and Zandbergen, 1995). Jennings and Zandbergen proposed that the greater the association made by a state between sustainability and modernity, the more firms within that state will accept the sustainability concept. This association is stronger in developed countries than in developing countries, where economic and technological factors dominate concepts of modernity. Therefore, compared to firms in developing countries, firms in developed countries would be more likely to adopt environmental standards that help them promote long-term ecological sustainability.

H4: The influence of environmental 'best practices' on firms' eco-sustainability orientation will be stronger in developed than in developing countries.

Within each country, the extent of adoption of environmental standards may also differ between reactive and proactive firms (Greenwood and Hinings, 1996; King and Lenox, 2000; Lyon and Maxwell, 2001; Russo and Fouts, 1997). In the early stages of an organizational field, innovative (proactive) firms establish new standards, but these standards may not be visible, or enforced. As the field matures, and these standards become more transparent, other firms may seek to adopt them. However, firms that focus on preserving their *status quo* (reactive firms) adopt only those standards that are legally reinforced, whereas firms that are open to changes (proactive firms) are more likely to implement these standards (Fox-Wolfgramm et al., 1998).

H5: The influence of 'best practices' on firms' eco-sustainability orientation will be stronger for proactive than for reactive firms within the same national context.

Trade associations

Norms and practices are also promoted through self-regulation (Ostrom, 1990) within professional, industry and trade associations (Kelley, 1991; King and Lenox, 2000). Trade associations exert coercive influences by developing explicit sanctions and rewards and diffuse information on 'best practices' amongst their members (Nash and Ehrenfeld, 1997). Trade associations influenced the performance of both members and non-members. By facilitating the transfer of 'best practices' among firms, self-regulation increases firm-level and collective performance (Kraatz, 1998).

H6: There will be a positive relationship between the influence of trade associations and firms' eco-sustainability orientation.

Trade associations are more effective at coordinating and diffusing environmental technologies and practices in mature fields, where environmental regulations and standards have become established (Klassen and Whybark, 1999). Self-imposed standards are also more effective when they are backed by governmental agencies (King and Lenox, 2000). We propose that the influences of trade associations will be more salient in developed countries, where environmental norms and practices are well established, than in developing countries where there is little consensus among firms regarding the appropriate type and level of their environmental responses.

H7: The influence of trade associations on firms' eco-sustainability orientation will be stronger in developed than in developing countries.

Trade associations rely on coercive, normative and mimetic mechanisms to diffuse 'best practices' amongst their members. Firms with poorer performance face higher social pressures for change (embarrassment and shaming, King and Baerwald, 1998), have a greater need to align their values to those in the field (Gladwin et al., 1995), and are influenced to a greater extent by the 'best practices' in their field (King and Lenox, 2000). Trade associations exert a greater influence on 'dirty' firms (Lyon and Maxwell, 2001).

H8: The influence of trade associations on firms' eco-sustainability orientation will be stronger for reactive than for proactive firms within the same national context.

Competitors

Firms that develop innovative responses establish reputations as leading organizations in their fields (Kondra and Hinings, 1998). These firms may have more resources for additional initiatives (Sharfman et al., 1988; Sharma, 2000) and achieve superior financial performance (Fligstein, 1991). Other firms tend to mimic these legitimate and profitable leading organizations (Zucker, 1988), especially in mature, closely integrated fields (Hinings and Greenwood, 1988).

H9: There is a positive relationship between the competitors' adoption of environmental practices and firms' eco-sustainability orientation.

Media and communities

In addition to self-regulating mechanisms (Ostrom, 1990), institutional templates may also derive from contextual expectations which channel dominating beliefs and ideologies (Pettigrew, 1987) and affect all the firms in an organizational field (Greenwood and Hinings, 1996). Media and local community pressures can mobilize regulators, governmental agencies and self-regulating bodies against those firms that lag behind their peers in environmental protection (King and Baerwald, 1998; Lawrence and Morell, 1995). Their efforts concentrate on visible firms – larger firms (Deephouse, 1996; Henriques and Sadorsky, 1999), with visible negative environmental impact (Getz, 1995). Proactive firms, which are less likely to cause environmental damage, generally attract less public scrutiny and fewer complaints from stakeholders.

H10(1): There is a negative relationship between media pressures for firms' responsible environmental practices and firms' eco-sustainability orientation.

H10(2): There is a negative relationship between community pressures for improved environmental practices and firms' eco-sustainability orientation.

METHOD

Research Context

We tested the influences of societal and organizational fields on firms' eco-sustainability orientation in two important and very large Asian countries, China and Japan. These countries have cultures which are similar in some dimensions (for example, a high level of collectivism and power distance), but distinct political regimes and different types of environmental regulations.

China

Rapid economic growth and benign neglect of the environment has resulted in a significant degradation of the environment in China (He, 1991). In the late 1970s, the Chinese government recognized the need to internalize pollution costs into firms' decision-making, introducing the 'Pay for pollution' principle in 1979 and requiring environmental impact assessments for new plants. During the 1980s, China's regulatory structure expanded, but the dual role of the government as both regulator and owner of Chinese firms impeded the effective implementation of environmental protection policies. Economic reforms during this decade resulted in a rapid growth of small township enterprises which showed little concern for environmental quality and could not be monitored effectively by governmental agencies (Zhang et al., 1999). Continued deterioration of environmental conditions led the central government to declare, in 1996, environmental protection as an essential requirement for the nation's survival and for China's economic development. However, government commitment did not result in large investments in firms' environmental protection programs. The schedule of fines for pollution, and the public funds available for environmental protection and enforcement, did not provide strong incentives for firms to change their environmental practices (Yu, 1991).

The National Environmental Protection Commission (NEPC), established in 1983, continues to oversee all corporate environmental actions and coordinates the Environmental Protection Committees and Environmental Protection Bureaus within each ministry. Large firms are directly affiliated with specific ministries, which provide technical and financial support for firms' environmental activities. In parallel, party representatives promote the environmental regulations at different levels (individuals, departments and so on) inside Chinese firms (Zhang, 1997). Chinese media promotes the explicit environmental policies of the government (party), but does not serve as an independent watchdog for implementation (Zhang et al., 1999). Only firms' actions that result in extremely negative or highly visible environmental emergencies – such as bubbling soapsuds in the drinking water of Shanghai – trigger media coverage and reactions from local communities (Zhang et al., 1999).

Japan
In the 1950s and 1960s, concerns of growth and economic development dominated the government agenda and firm-level decisions in Japan. The resulting increase in pollution levels caused irreversible damage to Japan's environment. Serious health problems (for example, Minamata disease and prevalence of severe asthma) mobilized public opinion to demand government action. However, the environmental legislation of the late 1960s proved ineffective. In the 1970s, a series of amendments to the Basic Law of Pollution Control (1967) and the Air Pollution Law (1968) improved the efficacy of Japan's regulatory system. Through technological development, Japanese firms were successful in turning the energy and environmental challenges they faced in the 1960s and 1970s into opportunities for profits, both domestically and in their markets abroad.

During the last three decades, firm-level environmental awareness and responsibility has been encouraged by the concerted effort of governmental agencies, which promoted new environmental regulations and supported their implementation. Regulatory measures have also been supported by economic incentives. For example, Japanese firms are entitled to receive 'necessary and appropriate financial assistance' from governmental agencies, such as low-interest loans for pollution control and energy efficiency investments, and special depreciation rates for pollution abatement equipment (Basic Law on the Environment, 1993). Also, MITI trains, qualifies and appoints environmental specialists to the environmental departments of large, or highly polluting, private firms.

The implementation of governmental regulations has often been based 'on building a consensus between members of the regulated community and [the governmental] authorities' (OECD, 1994: 103). Trade associations informally enforce, translate and supplement governmentally set standards. Endorsement by Keidanren, the Japan Federation of Economic Organizations, creates higher expectations for firm-level adoption of environmental regulations.

Trade associations also adopt and promote their own action plans. For example, the 'responsible care program' initiated by the Japan Chemical Industry Association has been embraced by 96 percent of its members (OECD 1994: 104).

Governmental efforts, amplified by supportive media coverage, have increased the mobilization of public communities, but have not led to the emergence of powerful environmental NGOs. Voluntary initiatives of firms (their discretionary environmental actions beyond legal requirements) are open to public scrutiny. To protect or enhance their legitimacy, some Japanese firms also negotiate separate voluntary agreements with local communities (9 percent of the voluntary agreements negotiated in 1991–92, OECD, 1994).

Samples

Two random samples of manufacturing firms were drawn from China (Shanghai) and Japan in 1997.[2] In China, we selected 300 firms from the 'List of Large and Medium Shanghai Enterprises,' compiled by the Shanghai Municipal Government in 1994. We administered one questionnaire per firm, soliciting the response from senior or middle managers directly in charge of their firms' environmental activities. Completed surveys were endorsed with the official company seal. In China, 30 research assistants, all senior students in management sciences, delivered and collected back the questionnaires from the selected firms to ensure the reliability of the distribution. Two hundred and twenty four completed questionnaires were obtained in China, for a response rate of 74.6 percent. In Japan, we randomly selected 600 Japanese manufacturing firms from the First Section of the Tokyo Stock Exchange, and mailed the questionnaires to the highest executive in charge of the firms' environmental activities from each company (either a senior or middle-level environmental manager or a senior operations or strategy executive). Completed questionnaires were returned by mail, in pre-addressed envelopes. Responses from 193 Japanese firms were received, for a response rate of 32 percent.

Survey Instrument

We used the same survey instrument in China and Japan. The questionnaire items were formulated in English by a joint team of Canadian, Japanese and Chinese researchers, and then translated into Chinese and Japanese, following the back-translation method (Brislin, 1983). The survey instrument included three sections. The first part assessed the criterion variable, eco-sustainability orientation. The second part recorded predictor variables, societal and organizational field influences. The third and final part included the control variables.

Criterion: eco-sustainability orientation

To assess firms' eco-sustainability orientation, we developed 29 questions (Branzei et al., 2001) regarding firms' environmental plans and policy commitments, internal environmental practices and environmental attitudes and responsibilities of individual organizational members. Factor analyses indicated three orthogonal dimensions of firms' eco-sustainability orientation – embeddedness, capacity and responsibility.[3] Embeddedness represented the extent to which environmental issues were addressed by firms' goals, plans, strategy and practices, were supported by internal organizational norms, and were role-modeled by the top management (Waddock and Graves, 1997). Capacity reflected the resources, such as funds, expert knowledge and discretionary slack (Sharfman et al., 1988; Sharma, 2000), which were allocated to environmental actions. Responsibility summarized the environmental commitments of individual organizational members (Winn, 1995). These findings suggest that eco-sustainability orientation has three different facets: policy commitment to environmental issues, capacity for environmental actions and individual responsibility of organizational members. Firms can increase their eco-sustainability orientation by increasing any of these facets. For example, firms may develop environmental policies or foster individual responsibility even if they do not have adequate resources and skills for taking environmental actions. Also, firms may develop environmentally friendly goals, missions or corporate cultures, without committing adequate resources and without nurturing individual responsibility for their implementation. However, reactive firms would tend to have low scores on all three dimensions, and proactive firms would have high scores on all dimensions. Therefore, we derived a non-compensatory aggregate measure of eco-sustainability for each firm, by multiplying their embeddedness, capacity and responsibility scores, and then extracting the cubic root of the resulting product.

Figures 4.1 and 4.2 show the frequency distributions of the eco-sustainability orientation measure for Chinese and Japanese firms. Within each country, firms with low eco-sustainability orientation (lower quartile) were considered reactive, and firms with high eco-sustainability orientation (the upper quartile) were considered proactive (Hunt and Auster, 1990). For reactive firms, the upper cut-off scores were 3.23 for China and 3.24 for Japan. For proactive firms, the lower cut-off scores were 3.82 for China and 3.90 for Japan.

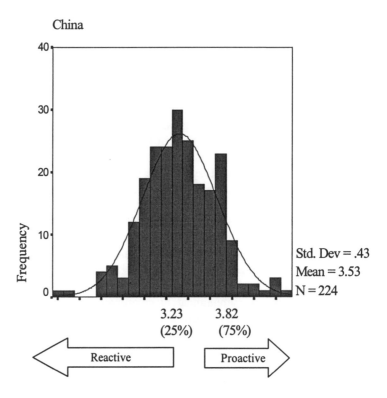

Figure 4.1 Proactive versus reactive firms in China

Predictors: societal and organizational field influences
We developed three questions regarding governments' regulatory influences on firms' eco-sustainability orientation (Sanchez, 1997) and five questions regarding the impact of organizational field institutions on firms' eco-sustainability orientation (Hoffman, 1999; Scott, 1995). These questions are shown in Table 4.2 (items 5–7 for societal field influences and items 8–12 for organizational field influences). Each question was measured on a Likert-type five-point scale, with verbal anchors from 1, 'strongly disagree' to 5, 'strongly agree.'

Controls and sample comparability
Firms operating in more polluting industries face higher regulatory pressures and higher compliance costs (Hunt and Auster, 1990). Larger firms often have more financial resources and better internal abilities (knowledge and expertise) for implementing environmental protection activities. Also, larger

firms are more visible, and more susceptible to social scrutiny and influence (Getz, 1995; Henriques and Sadorsky, 1999). They are also held to higher standards (Deephouse, 1996).

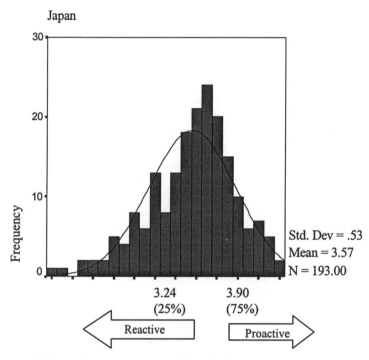

Figure 4.2 Proactive versus reactive firms in Japan

For each firm, we recorded their industry and size (Table 4.2). This data was verified and approved by each company in China and matched with publicly available corporate records for the Japanese firms. We grouped firms' total annual sales in three categories that reflected the proportion of medium-sized, large and very large companies in each country. Since, in general, manufacturing firms were significantly larger in Japan than in China, we adjusted the cut-off points based on country-specific sales averages (Table 4.2). For each sector, and for each size category, the eco-sustainability orientation of Chinese and Japanese firms did not differ significantly.

Leaders' demographic variables have also been shown to influence firms' strategic orientation (Chaganti and Sambharya, 1987). For each respondent, we recorded their age and level of environmental training (Table 4.2). In our sample, the majority of the Japanese respondents were over 50 (71.5 percent), while the majority of the Chinese respondents were younger than 50 (71.9

percent). About a quarter (23.8 percent) of the Japanese respondents and about half of the Chinese respondents reported higher levels of environmental training compared to their peers in similar firms. We found no significant influences between Chinese and Japanese scores on eco-sustainability orientation when respondents fell within the same age-group or category of environmental training.

Data Analysis

Statistical controls for common method variance

Since the study relied on self-reported data, we took several steps to alleviate the concerns that common method biases might have inflated the reported relationships (Podsakoff and Organ, 1986). First, we assessed the criterion variable with an aggregated, non-compensatory measure, derived by factor analyzing 29 different items.[4] Only a third of the zero-order correlations between this criterion and the control and predictor variables were significant for each country. All significant correlations showed moderate effects (for example less than 0.345, Table 4.2). This pattern of correlations suggests that respondents neither followed a consistent line in their answers, nor gave indiscriminately high reports on all variables.

We also used Harman's one-factor test (Podsakoff and Organ, 1986). Common method variance represents a serious concern if a single factor emerges from an unrotated factor analysis, or if one general factor accounts for the majority of the covariance of the independent and dependent variables. Using all 13 variables we obtained five different factors for the Chinese sample, which explained 58 percent of the total variance. The first factor accounted for 16 percent of this variance. In the Japanese sample, four different factors explained 51 percent of the variance. The first factor accounted for 18.7 percent of this variance. These results suggest that common method variance did not have a substantial effect on the findings.

Table 4.2 also reports the partial correlations of eco-sustainability orientation with the control and predictor variables (controlling for Harman's first factor scores, cf. Podsakoff and Organ, 1986). In the Chinese sample, three of the four significant zero-order correlations remained significant, in the same direction, and of similar magnitude after accounting for the effects of this general factor. This suggests that Chinese responses were not significantly affected by common method biases. In Japan, there was less agreement between the zero-order and the partial correlations (Table 4.2). However, the differences may simply indicate a stronger functional relationship between the predictor and criterion variables in the Japanese sample (Podsakoff and Todor, 1985).

Tests of hypotheses

We used hierarchical regression models to estimate the impact of the control variables, and societal and organizational field influences on firms' eco-sustainability orientation. Table 4.3 reports the results for three hierarchical models: (1) for all firms; (2) for proactive firms; and (3) for reactive firms. These models were estimated separately for China and Japan. We also tested six matching structural equation models, using AMOS 4.0. To obtain a conservative test of our hypotheses, we fixed the measurement error terms for all indicators at zero – assuming that all predictors were accurately and independently measured. These models fit the data well and confirmed the results of the hierarchical regression models (all main effects were in the same direction and of similar magnitude).

To test the hypothesized differences between the Chinese and Japanese samples, and between the reactive and proactive firms within each country, we compared these models with nested models in which we constrained the hypothesized effects to be equal between the two groups (Hayduk, 1987). Significant chi-square differences between the unconstrained and the constrained models suggest significant differences between the groups. Non-significant differences indicate that similar relationships were present in both groups

RESULTS

Table 4.3 summarizes the results of the hierarchical regression models for corporate sustainability. In the first step of each model, we controlled for firm and respondent characteristics. Societal field influences were entered in the second step. Organizational field influences were entered last.

Control Variables: Respondent and Firm Characteristics

Respondent and firm characteristics explained significant variance in firms' eco-sustainability orientation in Japan (15.9 percent, $\rho < 0.001$) but not in China (3.5 percent, $\rho = 0.102$). In Japan, respondents' age (Beta = 0.192, $\rho < 0.05$) and firms' size (Beta = 0.320, $\rho < 0.05$) had a positive and significant influence on eco-sustainability orientation. In China, firms' size had a small positive influence on eco-sustainability orientation (Beta = 0.125, $\rho < 0.10$). Control variables did not have a significant effect on eco-sustainability orientation for proactive and reactive firms in China, and proactive firms in Japan. For Japanese reactive firms, only respondents' age had a positive influence on eco-sustainability orientation (Beta = 0.479, $\rho < 0.05$, 26.4 percent variance explained, $\rho = 0.009$). These findings suggest that size and

Table 4.2 Zero order and partial correlations between criterion and predictor variables

		Eco-sustainability Orientation								
		China				Japan				
Variables	Questions (5-point Likert-type scales, unless specified)	Mean	SD	Zero order	Partial	Mean	SD	Zero order	Partial
1. Age	(1) 20–39, (2) 40–49, and (3) over 50.	1.897	0.811	0.051	0.025	2.632	0.633	**0.229**	0.056
2. Environmental training	(1) < = the national average, (2) > the national average.	1.522	0.501	0.127	-0.005	1.238	0.427	0.091	**-0.155**
3. Sector	(1) low, (2) medium, and (3) high pollution.	2.156	0.732	0.037	-0.042	2.176	0.604	0.117	**-0.172**
4. Firm size (annual sales)	Chinese RMB: (1) less than 30 million, (2) between 30 and 100 million, and (3) over 100 million. Japanese Yen: (1) less than 100 billion, (2) between 100 and 300 billion, and (3) over 300 billion.	2.152	0.817	**0.146**	**0.140**	1.777	0.727	**0.345**	0.060
5. Liberal views of government	'It is the role of government not the enterprise to protect the environment' *(reverse coded)*.	4.161	0.894	**0.143**	0.061	4.423	0.621	**0.171**	**0.132**
6. General effectiveness	'Government regulations are effective in protecting the environment.'	3.601	0.962	0.127	-0.017	3.869	0.841	0.132	0.027
7. Degree of direct impact	'My organization is subject to a lot of governmental regulation regarding environmental matters.'	3.687	0.952	-0.023	**-0.213**	3.358	1.188	**0.170**	**-0.150**

8.	Standards	'Governmental agencies have established pollution, production, and process standards, and we have to make sure that we do not breach these standards.'	4.212	0.673	**0.314**	**0.205**	4.534	0.621
9.	Trade associations	'My organization's trade and industry associations have influenced our environmental practices.'	3.512	0.825	-0.033	**-0.173**	2.557	1.065
10.	Competitors	'My organization's environmental practices have been influenced by what other organizations from our industry have done.'	3.612	0.769	0.053	-0.102	3.423	0.832
11.	Media	'Newspapers and TV have created a lot of concern about environmental issues and this has put pressure on our company to improve our environmental performance.'	3.258	1.112	**-0.195**	**-0.371**	3.319	0.956
12.	Community	'A pollution incident could ruin our corporate image and market, so we must pay full attention to such issues before they become a concern of the public/local communities.'	4.180	0.748	0.105	-0.083	3.912	1.154

0.230	**-0.024**
0.218	**-0.158**
0.166	**-0.215**
0.117	**-0.350**
-0.094	**-0.200**

Note: Correlations significant at $\rho < .05$ appear in bold.

experience facilitate the general implementation of environmental initiatives, may be more salient for firms from developed countries, and have little impact on the reactive and the proactive firms (that is at low and at high levels of eco-sustainability orientation).

Societal Field Influences

After controlling for firm and respondent differences, the societal field had a small but significant influence on firms' eco-sustainability orientation in China (3.9 percent variance explained, $\rho = 0.032$) and Japan (3.7 percent variance explained, $\rho = 0.040$).

Hypothesis 1 proposed that firms' eco-sustainability orientation is higher when (1) the society holds more liberal views regarding the role of their government in environmental protection; (2) governmental regulations are considered effective in reaching their goals; and (3) governments place clear and direct environmental demands on firms. H1(1) was supported in both China (Beta = 0.141, $\rho < 0.05$) and Japan (Beta = 0.126, $\rho < 0.10$). H1(2) was supported in China (Beta = 0.124, $\rho < 0.10$), but rejected in Japan (Beta = 0.109, ns). These findings suggest that the perceived effectiveness of regulations may have a stronger influence on firms' eco-sustainability orientation in newly developed fields, where regulations are emergent. Interestingly, the degree of direct impact on firms' operations did not influence firms' eco-sustainability orientation either in China (Beta = -0.065, ns) or in Japan (Beta = 0.103, ns). H1(3) was rejected for both countries. These findings may be due to conflicting impacts of direct regulatory approaches on firms with different levels of environmental performance (Cairncross, 1993; Sanchez, 1997). Direct regulations may have a positive effect on reactive firms, but a negative effect on proactive firms. H2 examines this contrast.

H2 proposed that, within the same national context, governmental regulations would have a stronger positive impact on eco-sustainability orientation for reactive firms and a weaker impact on eco-sustainability orientation for proactive firms. Indeed, in China, the regulations directly related to firms' operations had a stronger positive influence on eco-sustainability orientation for reactive firms (Beta = 0.265, $\rho < 0.05$) than for proactive firms (Beta = -0.004. ns). The nested model comparison further supported H2 in China: setting an equality constraint between Chinese proactive and reactive firms resulted in a significant worsening of fit ($\Delta\chi^2 = 3.5$, $\rho < 0.10$) over the unconstrained model ($\chi^2 = 26.1$, df = 34, $\rho = 0.833$, GFI = 0.966, RMSEA = 0). However, in Japan, H2 was not supported: governmental regulations did not have a significant influence on eco-sustainability orientation for reactive or for proactive firms.

Table 4.3 Results of hierarchical regression analyses

	All firms		Proactive firms		Reactive firms	
	China	Japan	China	Japan	China	Japan
Step 1: Respondent and firm characteristics						
Age	0.047	0.192**	-0.015	0.134	0.113	0.479*
Environmental training	0.098	0.010	0.137	-0.014	-0.183	-0.180
Sector	0.038	0.077	-0.002	0.053	0.161	0.056
Firm size (Sales)	0.125*	0.320**	0.270*	0.249	-0.057	0.165
R^2	0.035	0.159	0.117	0.090	0.073	0.264
Adjusted R^2	0.017	0.145	0.047	0.005	0.000	0.195
R^2 change	0.035	0.159	0.117	0.090	0.073	0.264
F change	1.958	11.872	1.686	1.059	1.004	3.853
ρ	0.102	$\rho < 0.001$	0.168	0.388	0.414	0.009
df	219	189	51	43	51	43
Step 2: Societal field influences (Government's environmental regulations)						
Liberal views	0.141**	0.126*	0.199	0.311**	0.015	0.094
General effectiveness	0.124	0.109	-0.104	0.192	-0.060	0.050
Degree of direct impact	-0.065	0.103	-0.004	0.064	0.265*	-0.022
R^2	-0.073	0.201	0.163	0.244	0.132	0.278
Adjusted R^2	0.043	0.171	0.041	0.111	0.006	0.152
R^2 change	0.039	0.037	0.046	0.154	0.059	0.014
F change	2.999	2.825	0.886	2.717	1.096	0.262
ρ	0.032	0.040	0.455	0.057	0.360	0.852
df	216	180	48	40	48	40
Step 3: Organizational field influences						
Standards	0.275**	0.101	0.267*	0.118	0.210	0.090
Trade associations	0.000	0.147**	0.017	-0.071	-0.030	0.506**
Competitors	0.038	0.113	-0.202	-0.127	-0.040	-0.321*
Media	-0.189**	-0.051	-0.010	-0.137	-0.195	-0.240
Community	0.005	-0.081	0.151	0.138	-0.136	-0.246*
R^2	0.190	0.252	0.290	0.319	0.188	0.494
Adjusted R^2	0.144	0.202	0.092	0.085	--	0.320
R^2 change	0.117	0.051	0.127	0.075	0.056	0.216
F change	6.116	2.435	1.538	3.152	0.593	2.980
ρ	p<0.001	0.036	0.198	0.579	0.705	0.024
df	211	180	43	35	43	35

Note: Entries are standardized coefficients (Betas). Levels of significance: $\rho < 0.10$*, $\rho < 0.05$**

In this study, societal field influences on eco-sustainability were similar for Chinese and for Japanese firms, with only one exception: Chinese reactive firms were more likely to respond to governmental regulations. This finding suggests that regulations may have a greater impact on reactive firms operating in new regulatory frameworks, yet, as regulations diffuse amongst firms and become more fine-tuned, they tend to elicit similar levels of compliance from both reactive and proactive firms.

Organizational Field Influences

Organizational field institutions explained significant variance in firms' eco-sustainability orientation in China (11.7 percent, $\rho < 0.001$) and Japan (5.1 percent, $\rho = 0.036$), after controlling for firm and respondent characteristics and for the impact of governmental regulations.

Environmental standards

H3 proposed that eco-sustainability orientation would be stronger when explicit standards of 'best practice' are identified in the firm's organizational field. H3 was supported in China (Beta = 0.275, $\rho < 0.05$), but was not supported in Japan (Beta = 0.101, ns).

H4 proposed that the influence of 'good practice' standards on firms' eco-sustainability orientation would be stronger in developed countries (Japan) than in developing countries (China). Contrary to this hypothesis, in our sample, the effect of environmental standards was almost three times as strong in China as in Japan.[5] We found no support for H4.

H5 proposed that, within the same national context, 'good practice' standards would have a stronger influence on eco-sustainability orientation for proactive than for reactive firms. In our Chinese and Japanese samples, the influence of environmental standards on eco-sustainability orientation was slightly stronger for proactive firms than for reactive firms (Betas in China 0.267, $\rho < 0.10$, and 0.210, ns; Betas in Japan, 0.118, ns and 0.090, ns). However, the nested model comparison did not support H5. The influence of environmental practices on eco-sustainability orientation was not significantly different between proactive and reactive firms (in the Chinese sample, $\Delta\chi^2 = 0$, ns, $\chi^2 = 26.1$, df = 34, $\rho = 0.833$, GFI = 0.966, RMSEA = 0, and in the Japanese sample, $\Delta\chi^2 = 0$, ns, $\chi^2 = 29.7$, df = 34, $\rho = 0.677$, GFI = 0.957, RMSEA = 0).

Trade associations

H6 proposed that there would be a positive relationship between trade associations' influences and firms' eco-sustainability orientation. H8 was supported in Japan (Beta = 0.147, p < 0.005), but not in China (Beta = 0.000, ns).

H7 proposed that the positive influence of trade associations on firms' eco-sustainability orientation would be stronger in developed countries (Japan) than in developing countries (China). In our sample, trade associations have a significant positive influence on the eco-sustainability orientation of Japanese firms and no effect on Chinese firms. However, the nested model comparison suggests that the hypothesized influence was not significantly different between Chinese and Japanese firms ($\Delta\chi^2$ = 2.24, ns, over the unconstrained model, χ^2 = 26.1, df = 34, p = 0.833, GFI = 0.991, RMSEA = 0). We found marginal evidence, but no statistical support for H7.

H8 proposed that, within the same national context, the influence of trade associations on firms' eco-sustainability orientation will be stronger for reactive than for proactive firms. In China, trade associations did not have a significant influence on eco-sustainability orientation for reactive firms (Beta = -0.030, ns) or for proactive firms (Beta = 0.017, ns). The nested model comparison also suggested that the influence of trade associations was not significantly different for proactive and for reactive firms in China ($\Delta\chi^2$ = 0, ns, χ^2 = 26.1, df = 34, p = 0.833, GFI = 0.966, RMSEA = 0). In Japan, trade associations had a strong positive influence on the eco-sustainability orientation of reactive firms (Beta = 0.506, p < 0.05), and did not have a significant influence on the eco-sustainability orientation of proactive firms (Beta = -0.071, ns). The nested model comparison confirmed that these effects were significantly different ($\Delta\chi^2$ = 10.2, p < 0.05, χ^2 = 29.7, df = 34, p = 0.263, GFI = 0.944, RMSEA = 0). Thus, H8 was supported in Japan.

Competitors

H9 proposed that competitors' adoption of environmental practices would have a positive influence on firms' eco-sustainability orientation. H9 was not supported for the Chinese firms (Beta = 0.038, ns) or the Japanese firms (Beta = 0.113, ns) included in our sample. This finding suggests that mimicking competitors' environmental practices did not improve firms' own eco-sustainability orientation.

Media and communities

H10(1) proposed that media pressures would be higher for firms with lower levels of eco-sustainability orientation. H10(1) was supported in China (Beta = -0.189, p < 0.10), suggesting that the Chinese media tends to pay attention mainly to firms with low levels of environmental concern or performance. H10(1) was not supported for Japanese firms (Beta = -0.051, ns), suggesting that media pressures are felt more evenly across all firms, irrespective of their eco-sustainability orientation.

H10(2) proposed that the pressures for improved environmental practices of local communities would be more likely to be felt by firms with lower levels of eco-sustainability orientation. In this study, H10(2) was supported neither in China (Beta = 0.005, ns) nor in Japan (Beta = -0.051, ns).

DISCUSSION

The results of our study highlight both similarities and differences in the paths of Japan and China towards eco-sustainability. We focused on the eco-sustainability orientation of firms in these countries and the role institutions play to promote it. We found surprising similarities in the average level and distribution of eco-sustainability orientations in the two countries but showed that different institutions have differential impacts in each country. In particular, the results suggest that the role of informal institutions increases with the degree of political and economic development of the country. The spread of liberal concepts of government gives impetus to the rise of commitment and voluntary actions by firms to protect the environment. At the micro level, the results suggest that institutions have differential impacts depending on whether the firms are reactive or proactive. The specific nature of these differences, however, depends on the national context.

In both China and Japan, the degree to which governmental regulations have a direct impact on firms' operations has not improved firms' eco-sustainability orientation. This suggests that, when more discretion is granted (Carroll, 1979), firms focus more on voluntary measures to increase their readiness for unexpected environmental contingencies. However, when government imposes stringent regulations, firms focus their energy on compliance and may become less internally committed to implement environmental protection initiatives (Sanchez, 1997). Indeed, in our study, the degree of direct regulatory impact appeared beneficial only for Chinese reactive firms, with few resources for adopting voluntary environmental initiatives. The perceived effectiveness of governmental regulations was more apparent in Chinese than in Japanese firms. In Japan, regulations have been in place for a longer time, and firms have come to accept their effectiveness. Greater efforts for marketing newly introduced regulations can elicit stronger compliance from firms, especially in emergent institutional fields (Greenwood and Hinings, 1996; Oliver, 1991). Liberal views, which place greater responsibility on firms for protecting the environment, helped improve firms' eco-sustainability in China and Japan, showing that societal expectations can be an important driver for firm-level environmental actions. This effect was notably strong for Japanese proactive firms, suggesting that, at high levels of environmental performance, firms are motivated most by societal expectations and least by direct regulations.

In developed institutional fields, firms with low levels of environmental performance tend to pay more attention to informal norms and values. Informal and self-imposed venues (trade and industry associations, competitors, media and communities) were important for reactive firms in Japan, but had no significant influence on reactive firms in China. As fields mature, reactive firms tend to be driven into compliance more by accepted norms and values than by regulations. To maximize the impact of their interventions, over time, policy-makers need to shift from a coercive model to one that encourages voluntary actions.

In both China and Japan, media and communities target those firms with lower eco-sustainability orientation (Henriques and Sadorsky, 1999). However, these influences depended on the maturity of firms' institutional fields. Media and community pressures had no influence on Chinese reactive firms, but they had a strong influence on Japanese reactive firms. Our results also show that proactive firms were more likely to increase their eco-sustainability orientation in response to pressures from local communities (Henriques and Sadorsky, 1999), suggesting that vibrant media attention and empowered communities may provide effective monitoring of firm-level environmental actions when regulations have become taken for granted.

Managerial Implications

The similarities found in the levels and distribution of eco-sustainability orientation between Chinese and Japanese firms may suggest the applicability of the international model of organization for multinationals' environmental management. In this model, the headquarter's culture is assumed to apply universally and the same management approach is considered best for all countries (Adler, 1983). The differences found in this study however suggest that a multi-domestic approach is more appropriate, allowing managers in each country to respond in different ways to environmental challenges. The focus of the managers working in China must be, at least at present, on the environmental regulatory system. They must dedicate resources to build relationships (*Guanxi*) with regulators to facilitate information flows and negotiate constraints. In Japan, environmental regulations are regarded as a minimum requirement for legitimacy. The relationships of a firm with its organizational field are paramount, as the field is the primary source of information about environmental standards and 'best practices.'

Limitations and Future Research

The study has a number of limitations. First, our arguments regarding the roles played by different institutions in fostering eco-sustainability orientation are restricted to the Chinese and Japanese context. These institutional influences depend on the socio-economic, political and cultural environments of each nation (Jennings and Zandbergen, 1995; Starik and Marcus, 2000; Starik and Rands, 1995). To establish an empirical link between degree of economic development and the average level of firms' eco-sustainability orientation, future studies need to compare the impact of various institutional influences on firms' eco-sustainability orientation across multiple countries, with various degrees of economic development. This study underscores the fact that national political regimes may influence the type and perceived effectiveness of environmental regulations. However, more nuanced comparisons of various regimes may shed additional light on the impact of regulations on firm-level environmental actions. Finally, the relationship between national cultural norms and firms' eco-sustainability orientation merits further investigation. China and Japan share many cultural characteristics. Future studies may attempt to disentangle the impact of cultural norms by studying nations with similar socio-economic development and political regimes, but different cultural norms (for example, European Union states).

Secondly, both the predictors and criterion variables used in this study have been collected with the same instrument. Our design considerations (negative wording of items with high social desirability, aggregate criterion variable) and post-hoc statistical procedures (Harman's one-factor test and partial correlations) suggested that common method variance did not have a significant impact on our findings. However, future studies may obtain the measures for the predictors and criterion variable from different respondents within the same firm.

In this study we relied on the perceptions of key informants, who were knowledgeable about their firms' environmental practices (Ackerman, 1975; Miles, 1987). However, the responses of these key informants were likely colored by their own values and biases (Wally and Baum, 1994; Wood, 1991). Additional studies that contrast the reports of key informants with external measures of the corporate environmental performance are needed. Researchers can compile measures of institutional influences using internal corporate documents (such as minutes for executive meetings) and firms' press releases. Firms' eco-sustainability orientation could also be independently assessed by industry experts (for example, using environmental certification schemes).

The direction of causality implied in our study is based only on theoretical assumptions, since both the predictor and the criterion variables were collected at the same point in time. Longitudinal data from firms with different levels of eco-sustainability orientation, and their perceived institutional influences at different points in time, would be required to establish the direction of causality.

CONCLUSION

This study employs a holistic firm-level concept, eco-sustainability orientation, to assess corporate environmental actions in China and Japan, and tests the influence of different institutions in helping or constraining firms' environmental efforts. We find that governmental regulation and the environmental standards developed by regulatory agencies are more influential in China, and that 'best practices' adopted by trade associations are more influential in Japan. The findings suggest that the effectiveness of institutions may depend on each country's degree of socio-economic development. Regulations are effective initially and bring firms up to a minimum level of compliance. As institutional frameworks crystallize, regulations become more versatile and receive better enforcement, but their effectiveness may diminish. Beyond the minimum level of regulatory compliance, firms tend to be influenced by the 'best practices' that emerge in their organizational fields. The study also suggests that, within nations, institutional influences are not homogenous for firms with different levels of environmental performance. In China, for example, governmental regulations are more important for reactive firms, and environmental standards developed by regulatory agencies are more important for proactive firms. In Japan, 'best practices' and pressures exerted by local communities are more influential on the eco-sustainability orientation of reactive firms. Japanese proactive firms are driven mainly by societal expectations for a greater role of firms in environmental protection. Regulators and policy-makers can improve firms' environmental responses and stimulate their environmental initiatives by using a set of fine-grained institutional influences specifically targeted towards firms with different levels of eco-sustainability orientation. In particular, policy-makers may wish to distinguish between the levers of influence for reactive and proactive firms. They can develop and emphasize better command and control instruments for the former and more versatile market-based mechanisms for the latter (Sanchez, 1997). Emphasizing 'best practices' may elicit little improvement from reactive firms, and emphasizing regulations can hold back the progress of proactive firms. Overall, the findings suggest that future research needs to pay more attention to the dynamic aspects of eco-sustainability, to understand which institutions can help increase firms' eco-sustainability orientation over time, and to establish the fine-grained impacts of these institutions on firms with different levels of environmental performance

Appendix Elements of firm-level eco-sustainability orientation

---

Embeddedness

---

1. Clear and strong signals have been sent from our top managers that better environmental management is a requirement in our organization, not a choice
2. Environmental concerns have been integrated into the decision-making of my organization's senior management
3. Many top level managers in my organization are personally and actively involved in developing environmental protection policies and monitoring their implementation
4. My organization has detailed written policies concerned with protecting the environment
5. Most people in my organization are very aware of the need to protect the environment and are well informed about our environmental policy
6. My company has a written environmental policy that states goals for improving our environmental performance
7. Environmental protection is an explicit component of my organization's strategic (long-term) plan
8. Ideas on pollution management are shared freely among lower, middle and upper levels within my organization
9. Environmental protection is an integral part of my organization's culture
10. The people in charge of environmental protection in my organization have sufficient authority
11. In my organization we are constantly looking for advances in technology to reduce our pollution levels
12. Environmental managers or those chiefly responsible for environmental management in my organization have adequate authority over capital investment decisions
13. My organization has an environmental officer at the senior management level.
14. My organization has a long-term plan to lower our pollution control costs in order to be more competitive in the market
15. The record of my organization on environmental protection is significantly better than other organizations in our industrial sector
16. The people in charge of environmental protection in my organization have the authority to stop operations if they perceive a significant risk of environmental degradation

---

Capacity

---

1. My organization cannot act on its own to improve environmental performance because we have insufficient resources
2. I have insufficient authority to influence the environmental performance of my organization

3. There is no consensus in my organization about the desirable level for environmental protection
4. My organization cannot act on its own to improve environmental performance because we must remain competitive
5. Economic growth objectives must assume a higher priority in my organization than environmental protection objectives for the time being
6. Complying with regulations and preventing environmental incidents are all that is required from a business enterprise like ours
7. I have insufficient knowledge to influence the environmental performance of my organization

Responsibility

1. Polluters should pay fully for the damage they cause, and be responsible for cleaning up their pollution
2. Those who use natural resources should pay the full cost of using them even though the resources are public
3. An activity should only proceed if the risk to the environment from the activity can be fully evaluated and controlled
4. Those firms which use energy inefficiently are as responsible for environmental damage as those firms which directly pollute their immediate environment
5. I feel it is my personal responsibility to ensure that my organization improves its environmental performance
6. It is the role of each individual, no matter what his or her position, to see to it that the environment is protected

NOTES

1. Our definition of eco-sustainability does not include broader societal and ecological outcomes of eco-sustainable strategies 'designed to shift the firm's markets toward the developing nations of the world [and] provide developing nations with the kind of investments they need to improve education, health-care, civil rights, and economic opportunities' (Stead and Stead, 2000: 326), which depend on macro-economic, social and ecological conditions (Starik and Rands, 1995). The concept used in this study was derived from a literature review of North American studies (Branzei, 2001), and then tested in China and Japan (Branzei et al., 2001).
2. The authors thank Masao Nakamura and Weijiong Zhang for facilitating access to the data sets.
3. These three factors explained 45.38 percent of the total variance in the combined sample (Branzei et al., 2001) and were robust in China and Japan (Van de Vijver and Leung, 1997). The scale reliabilities for embeddedness (16 items), capacity (7 items), and responsibility (6 items) were 0.90, 0.71 and 0.73 for the Chinese sub-sample, and 0.92, 0.76 and 0.53 for the Japanese sub-sample.
4. Please see Branzei et al. (2001) for additional details on how these items were developed and the questions used in the survey instrument.
5. However, nested model comparison suggested that the influence of existing standards of 'good practice' was not significantly different between Chinese and

Japanese firms ($\Delta\chi^2 = 1.5$, ns, over the unconstrained model, $\chi^2 = 26.1$, df = 34, ρ = 0.833, GFI = 0.991, RMSEA = 0).

REFERENCES

Ackerman, R.W. (1975), *The Social Challenge to Business*, Cambridge: Harvard University Press.

Adler, N.J. (1983), 'Organizational development in a multinational environment,' *Journal of Applied Behavioural Science*, 19(3): 249–365.

Aragon-Correa, J.A. (1998), 'Strategic proactivity and firm approach to the natural environment,' *Academy of Management Journal*, 41(5): 556–67.

Ashford, N.A. (1993), 'Understanding technological responses of industrial firms to environmental problems: implications for governmental policy,' in K. Fisher and J. Schot (eds), *Environmental Strategies for Industry: International Perspectives on Research Needs and Policy Implications*, Washington, DC: Island Press.

Bansal, P., and K. Roth (2000), 'Why companies go green: a model of ecological responsiveness,' *Academy of Management Journal*, 43: 717–37.

Basic Law on the Environment (1993). http://www.mekonglawcenter.org/download/-0/china.htm

Branzei, O. (2001), 'Green interpretations across cultures – global dimensions of corporate environmentalism,' *Best Paper Proceedings, International Business Division, Administrative Sciences Association of Canada*: 25–35.

Branzei, O., I. Vertinsky, T. Takahashi and W. Zhang (2001), 'Corporate environmentalism across cultures: a comparative field study of Chinese and Japanese executives,' *International Journal of Cross Cultural Management*, 1(3): 287–312.

Brislin, R.W. (1983), 'Cross-cultural research in psychology,' *Annual Review of Psychology*, 34: 363–400.

Cairncross, F. (1993), *Costing the Earth: The Challenge for Governments, the Opportunities for Business*, Boston: Harvard Business School Press.

Carroll, A.B. (1979), 'A three-dimensional conceptual model of corporate performance,' *Academy of Management Review*, 4(4): 497–505.

Chaganti, R. and R. Sambharya (1987), 'Strategic orientation and characteristics of upper management,' *Strategic Management Journal*, 8(4): 393–401.

Child, J. (1981), 'Culture, contingency, and capitalism in the cross-national study of organizations,' in L.L. Cummings and B.M. Staw (eds), *Research in Organizational Behaviour, 3*, Greenwich, CT: JAI Press.

Christmann, P. and G. Taylor (2001), 'Globalization and the environment: determinants of firm self-regulation in China,' *Journal of International Business Studies*, 32(3): 439–58.

Cohen, I. (1987), 'Regulation and deregulation,' *California Management Review*, 29 (4): 169–83.

Daly, H.E. and J.B. Cobb Jr. (1994), *For the Common Good*, 2nd edn, Boston: Beacon Press.

Dechant, K. and B. Altman (1994), 'Environmental leadership: from compliance to competitive advantage,' *Academy of Management Executive*, 8(3): 7–27.

Deephouse, D.L. (1996), 'Does isomorphism legitimate?,' *Academy of Management Journal*, 39: 1024–39.

DiMaggio, P.J. and W.W. Powell (1991), 'The iron cage revisisted: institutional iso-morphism and collective rationality in organizational fields,' in W.W. Powell and P.J. DiMaggio (eds), *The New Institutionalism in Organizational Analysis*, Chicago: University Press.

Dy, M. (1989), 'On nature and values, ideology and hope,' in Y.J. Tang, Z. Li and G.F. McLean (eds), *Man and Nature: The Chinese Tradition and Future*, Washington, DC: University Press of America, 219–28.

Egri, C. and S. Herman (2000), 'Leadership in the North American environmental sector: values, leadership styles, and contexts of environmental leaders and their organizations,' *Academy of Management Journal*, **43**: 571–604.

Egri, C.P. and L.T. Pinfield (1996), 'Organizations and the biosphere: ecologies and environments,' in S. Clegg, C. Hardy and W. Nord (eds), *Handbook of Organization Studies*, London: Sage.

Feyerherm, A.E. (1995), 'Changing and converging mind-sets of participants during collaborative environmental rule-making: two negotiated regulation case studies,' in J.E. Post, D. Collins and M. Starik (eds), *Research in Corporate Social Performance and Policy*, 1, Greeenwich, CT: JAI Press.

Fligstein, N. (1991), 'The structural transformation of American industry: an institutional account of the causes of diversification in the largest firms, 1919–1979', in W.W. Powell and P.J. DiMaggio (eds), *The New Institutionalism in Organizational Analysis*, Chicago: University of Chicago Press.

Fox-Wolfgramm, S.J., K.B. Boal and J.G. Hunt (1998), 'Organizational adaptation to institutional change: a comparative study of first-order change in prospector and defender banks,' *Administrative Science Quarterly*, **43**: 87–126.

Getz, K.A. (1995) 'Implementing multilateral regulations: a preliminary theory and illustration,' *Business and Public Policy*, **34**(3): 280.

Giddens, A. (1984), *The Constitution of Society*, Berkeley, CA: University of California Press.

Gladwin, T.N., J.J. Kennelly and T.S. Krause (1995), 'Shifting paradigms for sustainable development: implications for management theory and research', *Academy of Management Review*, **20**(4): 874–907.

Gooch, G.D. (1995), 'Environmental beliefs and attitudes in Sweden and the Baltic States,' *Environment and Behaviour*, **27**(4): 513–39.

Greenwood, R. and C.R. Hinings (1996), 'Understanding radical organizational change: bringing together the old and the new institutionalism,' *Academy of Management Review*, **21**(4): 1022–54.

Hart, S.L. (1995), 'A natural-resource-based view of the firm,' *Academy of Management Review*, **20**: 986–1014.

Hayduk, L.A. (1987), *Structural Equation Modeling with LISREL*, Johns Hopkins University Press: Baltimore and London.

He, B. (1991), *China on the Edge: The Crisis of Ecology and Development*, San Francisco, CA: China Books and Periodicals.

Henriques, I. and Sadorsky, P. (1999), 'The relationship between environmental commitment and managerial perceptions of stakeholder importance,' *Academy of Management Journal*, **42**: 87–99.

Hinings, C.R. and R. Greenwood (1988), *The Dynamics of Strategic Change*, Oxford: Basil Blackwell.

Hoffman, A. (1997), *From Heresy to Dogma*, San Francisco, CA: New Lexington Press.

Hoffman, A.J. (1999), 'Institutional evolution and change: environmentalism and the US chemical industry,' *Academy of Management Journal*, **42**(4): 351–71.

Hunt, C.B. and E.R. Auster (1990), 'Proactive environmental management: avoiding the toxic trap,' *Sloan Management Review*, **31**(2): 7–18.

Husserl, E. (1970), *The Crisis of European Sciences and Transcendental Phenomenology*, translated by David Cars, Evanston, IL: Northwestern University Press.

Ibbotson, B. and J.D. Phyper (1996), *Environmental Management in Canada*, Mc-Graw-Hill Ryerson Limited: Toronto.

Jennings, P.D. and P. Zandbergen (1995), 'Ecologically sustainable organizations: an institutional approach,' *Academy of Management Review*, **20**(4): 1015–52.

Kahneman, E. and A. Tversky (1979), 'Prospect Theory,' *Econometrica*, **47**: 263–91.

Kalland, A. and P.J. Asquith (1997), 'Japanese perceptions of nature: ideals and illusions,' in P.J. Asquith and A. Kalland (eds), *Japanese Images of Nature: Cultural Perspectives*, Richmond: Curzon Press.

Karagozoglu, N. (2001), 'Economic development and environmental management: comparing environmental management practices in Turkey and the United States,' *The Mid-Atlantic Journal of Business*, **37**(2–3): 111–22.

Kelley, P.C. (1991), 'Factors that influence the development of trade associations' political behaviors,' in J.E. Post (ed.), *Research in Corporate Social Performance and Policy*, **12**, Greeenwich, CT: JAI Press.

Kikulis, L.M., T. Slack and T.R. Hinings (1995), 'Sector specific patterns of organizational design change,' *Journal of Management Studies*, **32**: 67–100.

King, A. and S. Baerwald (1998), '"Greening" arguments: opportunities for the strategic management of public opinion,' in K. Sexton, A.A. Marcus and K. Easter (eds), *Better Environmental Decisions: Strategies for Governments, Business, and Communities*, Washington, DC: Island Press.

King, A.A. and M.J. Lenox (2000), 'Industry self-regulations with sanctions: the chemical industry's responsible care program,' *Academy of Management Journal*, **43**(4): 8–716.

Klassen, R.D. (2001), 'Plant-level environmental management orientation: the influence of management views and plant characteristics,' *Production and Operations Management*, **10**(3): 257–75.

Klassen, R.D. and D.C. Whybark (1999), 'Environmental management in operations: the selection of environmental technologies,' *Decision Sciences*, **30**(3): 601–31.

Kondra, A.Z. and C.R. Hinings (1998), 'Organizational diversity and change in institutional theory,' *Organization Studies*, **19**(5): 743–67.

Kraatz, M. (1998), 'Learning by association? Interorganizational networks and adaptation to environmental change,' *Academy of Management Journal*, **41**: 621–43.

Lawrence, A.T. and D. Morell (1995), 'Leading-edge environmental management: motivation, opportunity, resources, and processes', in J.E. Post (ed.), *Research in Corporate Social Performance and Policy*, **7**, Greenwich, CT: JAI Press.

Lyon, T.P. and J.W. Maxwell (2001), '"Voluntary" approaches to environmental regulation: a survey,' in M. Franzini and A. Nicita (eds), *Economic Institutions and Environmental Policy*, Brookfield, VT: Ashgate.

Marcus, A.A. (1984), *The Adversary Economy*, Westport, CT: Quorum Books.

Meyer, J.W. and W.R. Scott (1983), *Organizational Environments: Ritual and Rationality*, Beverly Hills, CA: Sage.

Miles, R.A. (1987), *Managing the Corporate Social Environment*, Englewood Cliffs, NJ: Prentice-Hall.

Miyamoto, S. (1967), 'The relation of philosophical theory to practical affairs in Japan,' in C.A. Moore (ed.), *The Japanese Mind: Essentials of Japanese Philosophy and Culture*, University Press of Hawaii, Honolulu, pp. 4–23.

Moore, C.A. (1967), *The Japanese Mind: Essentials of Japanese Philosophy and Culture*, University Press of Hawaii, Honolulu.

Nash, J. and J. Ehrenfeld (1997), 'Codes of environmental management practice: assessing their potential as a tool for change,' in R.W. Socolow (ed.), *Annual Review of Energy and Environment*, 22, Palo Alto, CA: Annual Reviews.

Nasi, J., S. Nasi, N. Phillips and S. Zyglidopoulos (1997), 'The evolution of corporate social responsiveness,' *Business and Society*, 36: 296–321.

Nehrt, C. (1998), 'Maintainability of first mover advantages when environmental regulations differ between countries,' *Academy of Management Review*, 23: 77–98.

OECD (1994), *OECD Environmental Performance Review: Japan*, Paris: OECD.

Oliver, C. (1991), 'Strategic responses to institutional process,' *Academy of Management Review*, 16: 145–79.

Ostrom, E. (1990), *Governing the Commons: The Evolution of Institutions for Collective Action*, New York: Cambridge University Press.

Pezzoli, K. (1997), 'Sustainable development: a transdisciplinary overview of the literature,' *Journal of Environmental Planning and Management*, 40(5): 549–74.

Podsakoff, P.M. and D.W. Organ (1986), 'Self-reports in organizational research: problems and prospects,' *Journal of Management*, 12(4): 531–44.

Podsakoff, P.M. and W.D. Todor (1985), 'Relationships between leader reward and punishment behavior and group processes and productivity,' *Journal of Management*, 11: 55–73.

Post, J.E. (1994), 'Environmental approaches and strategies: regulation, markets, and management education,' in R.B. Kolluru (ed.), *Environmental Strategies Handbook*, New York: McGraw-Hill.

Post, J.E. and B.W. Altman (1992), 'Models of corporate greening: how corporate social policy and organizational learning inform leading-edge environmental management,' *Markets, Politics, and Social Performance. Research in Corporate Social Performance and Policy*, 13: 3–29.

Preston, L.E. and J.E. Post (1975), *Private Management and Public Policy: The Principle of Public Responsibility*, Englewood Cliffs, NJ: Prentice-Hall.

Ronen, S. (1986), *Comparative and Multinational Management*, New York: John Wiley.

Roome, N. (1992), 'Developing Environmental Management Strategies,' *Business Strategy and the Environment*, 1: 11–24.

Russo, M. and Fouts, P. (1997), 'A resource-based perspective on corporate environmental performance and profitability,' *Academy of Management Journal*, 40: 534–51.

Sakamaki, S. (1967), 'Shinto: Japanese ethnocentrism,' in C.A. Moore (ed.), *The Japanese Mind: Essentials of Japanese Philosophy and Culture*, University Press of Hawaii, Honolulu.

Sanchez, C.M. (1997), 'Environmental regulation and firm-level innovation: the moderating effects of organizational and individual-level variables,' *Business and Society*, 36(2): 140–68.

Scott, W.R. (1991), 'Unpacking institutional arguments,' in W. Powell and P. DiMaggio (eds), *The New Institutionalism in Organizational Analysis*, Chicago, IL: University Press.

Scott, W.R. (1994), 'Institutional analysis: variance and process theory approaches', in R.W. Scott, J.W. Meyer and associates (eds), *Institutional Environments and Organizations: Structural Complexity and Individualism*, Thousand Oaks, CA: Sage.

Scott, W.R. (1995), *Institutions and Organizations*, London: Sage.

Sethi, S.P. (1979), 'A conceptual framework for environmental analysis of social issues and evaluation of business response patterns,' *Academy of Management Review*, 4: 63–74.

Sexton, K., A. Marcus, K.W. Easter and T. Burkhardt (1999), *Better Environmental Decisions*, Washington, DC: Island Press.

Sharfman, M.P., G. Wolf, R.B. Chase and D.A. Tansik (1988), 'Antecedents of organizational slack,' *Academy of Management Review*, 13(4): 601–14.

Sharma, S. (2000), 'Managerial interpretations and organizational context as predictors of corporate choice of environmental strategy,' *Academy of Management Journal*, 43: 681–97.

Shrivastava, P. (1995), 'The role of corporations in achieving ecological sustainability,' *Academy of Management Review*, 20: 936–60.

Starik M. and A. Marcus (2000), 'Special research forum on the management of organizations in the natural environment: a field emerging from multiple paths, with many challenges ahead,' *Academy of Management Journal*, 43: 539–47.

Starik, M. and G.P. Rands (1995), 'Weaving an integrated web: multi-level and multi-system perspectives of ecologically sustainable organizations,' *Academy of Management Review*, 20: 908–35.

Stead, J.G. and E. Stead (2000), 'Eco-enterprise strategy: standing of sustainability,' *Journal of Business Ethics*, 24(4): 313–29.

Tolbert. P.S. and L.G. Zucker (1983), 'Institutional sources of change in the formal structures of organizations: the diffusion of civil service reform, 1880–1935,' *Administrative Science Quarterly*, 28: 22–39.

Trice, H.M. and J.M. Beyer (1993), *The Cultures of Work Organizations*, Englewood Cliffs, NJ: Prentice-Hall.

Van de Vijver, F. and K. Leung (1997), *Methods and Data Analysis for Cross-Cultural Research*, Thousand Oaks, CA: Sage Publishing.

Waddock, S.A. and S.B. Graves (1997), 'The corporate social performance – financial performance link,' *Strategic Management Journal*, 18(4): 303–19.

Walley, N. and B. Whitehead (1994), 'It's not easy being green,' *Harvard Business Review*, 72(3): 46–51.

Wally, S. and J.R. Baum (1994), 'Personal and structural determinants of the pace of decision making,' *Academy of Management Journal*, 37: 923–40.

Wartick, S.L. and P.L. Cochran (1985), 'The evolution of the corporate social performance model,' *Academy of Management Review*, 10: 758–69.

Williams, H.E., J. Medhurst and K. Drew (1993), 'Corporate strategies for a sustainable future,' in K. Fisher and J. Schot (eds), *Environmental Strategies for Industry: International Perspectives on Research Needs and Policy Implications*, Washington, DC: Island Press.

Winn, M. (1995), 'Corporate leadership and politics for the natural environment,' in D. Collins and M. Starik (eds), *Sustaining the Natural Environment: Empirical Studies on the Interface between Nature and Organizations*, Greenwich, CT and London: JAI Press.

Wood, D.J. (1991), 'Corporate social performance revisited,' *Academy of Management Review*, 16(4): 691–718.

Yu, Y. (1991), *The Chinese Environmental Management System*, Beijing: Chinese Environmental Science Publications.

Yukama, H. (1967), 'Modern trend of Western civilization and cultural peculiarities in Japan,' in C.A. Moore (ed), *The Japanese Mind: Essentials of Japanese Philosophy and Culture*, University Press of Hawaii, Honolulu, 52–65.

Zhang D., I. Vertinsky, T. Ursacki and P. Nemetz (1999), 'Can China be a clean tiger?, growth strategies and environmental realities,' *Pacific Affairs*, **72**(1): 23–37.

Zhang, D.N. (1989), 'Theories concerning man and nature in classical Chinese philosophy,' in Y.J. Tang, Z. Li and G.F. McLean (eds), *Man and Nature: The Chinese Tradition and Future*, Washington, DC: University Press of America.

Zhang, K. (1997), 'Sustainable development and its practice in China,' *Shanghai Environmental Science,* **16**: 1–5.

Zucker, L.G. (1988), *Institutional Patterns and Organizations: Culture and Environment*, Cambridge, MA: Ballinger.

5. Motivations for participating in a US voluntary environmental initiative: the Multi-State working group and EPA's EMS pilot program

Nicole Darnall[1]

INTRODUCTION

While many different types of organizations in the United States are better managing their environmental activities, a relatively small proportion of them are also choosing to participate in voluntary environmental initiatives. This study addresses why organizations participate in these programs and examines how motivations vary for different types of enterprises. It emphasizes the importance of external and internal factors that influenced three types of facilities' (publicly traded, privately owned and government) decisions to participate in the Multi-State Working Group and the Environmental Protection Agency's EMS Pilot Program. The results show that despite the vast differences among these enterprises, a common theme in their motivation was the importance of regulatory pressures, which supports the idea that these pressures encourage all organizations to behave similarly. The results also support the suggestions posited by the 'natural' resource-based view of the firm and show that continuous innovation and basic environmental management proficiencies are embedded in publicly traded facilities' more advanced types of environmental management capabilities. Privately owned and government facilities, however, are lacking in these prior proficiencies, but appear to be fortifying their internal capacities by seeking external assistance from regulators, thus enabling them to participate in the voluntary environmental initiative.

Over the last 30 years, many US organizations are better managing their environmental activities, although a relatively small proportion of them have chosen to participate in a voluntary environmental initiative (VEI). Little is known about the factors that influence organizations to participate in a VEI and how these motivations differ among various types of enterprises.

Previous studies have considered aspects of these decisions (Arora and Cason, 1996; King and Lenox, 2000; Welch et al., 2000; Khanna and Damon, 1999) and attributes of firms' decisions to employ industry codes of conduct (Nash and Ehrenfeld, 1996; Howard et al., 2000). These studies, however, only consider either large publicly traded organizations or all types of organizations in aggregate (for example, they include publicly traded, privately owned, government or non-profit operations together), without making distinctions among them. Yet different types of organizations are participating in VEIs, and little is known about their similarities and differences. These prior studies, moreover, evaluate only the external factors that motivate organizations' participation decisions. But multiple internal capabilities are likely to play an important role (see for example, Cordano and Frieze, 2000; Rugman and Verbeke, 1998; Sharma, 2000; Russo and Fouts, 1997; Welford, 1992; Egri and Herman, 2000; Sharma and Vredenburg, 1998; Andersson and Bateman, 2000; Klassen, 2000; Hart, 1995, 1997; Christmann, 2000; Florida, 1996). As such, a deeper understanding of organizations' prior internal capabilities seems key in examining the rationales for why different organizations participate in a VEI.

This study addresses these issues by taking an integrative approach, exploring both the external and internal factors that comprise the participation decisions for three types of organizations – publicly traded, privately owned and government enterprises. The first half of this study relates institutional theory to an organization's decision to join a VEI to assess the external factors that encourage participation. This analysis is then coupled with an examination of the resource-based view of the firm (RBV) to consider the internal factors that influence participation. These two theoretical contexts are then applied to discussion of the three types of organizations to hypothesize how various external and internal factors affect their participation decisions differently. The second half of this study explains the research methods used to test the differences between facility-level decisions to participate in a VEI that encourages environmental management system (EMS) adoption. Using data from the National Database on Environmental Management Systems (NDEMS) the results show that basic organizational capabilities are embedded in their decisions, although some types of organizations possess greater levels of these capabilities than others. The study ends with a discussion of the theoretical implications of this research.

EXTERNAL PARTICIPATION DRIVERS

External drivers comprise all factors outside an organization that influence its routines and competencies (Aldrich, 1999) and motivate it to participate in a VEI. While multiple theories have emerged which define the factors that shape firms to appear and behave similarly, DiMaggio and Powell's (1983) framework has gained substantial prominence in organizational studies. The authors suggest three types of external pressures – coercive, mimetic and normative – shape organizational isomorphism.

Coercive pressures are the formal and informal forces exerted on organizations by institutions that they are dependent on. They include regulatory forces, market pressures such as mandates upon suppliers and demands from customers and cultural or societal expectations, while mimicry is the actions taken by organizations to model themselves on other enterprises (DiMaggio and Powell, 1983). Normative pressures are related to professionalism and psycho-emotional factors (Bansal and Roth, 2000), and a result of networks such as industry associations and educational processes. When these networks are formalized they have a greater influence on organizational isomorphism.

Building on this framework, recent studies have considered this neo-institutional paradigm by examining the motivators for organizations' decisions to behave in an environmentally proactive manner. They suggest, for example, that regulatory pressures influence organizations' environmental actions (Henriques and Sadorsky, 1996, 1999; Hart, 1995; Jaffe et al., 1995; Hoffman, 2000; Khanna and Damon, 1999; Porter and van der Linde, 1995; Welch et al., 2000; Arora and Cason, 1996). These pressures come in various forms and include coercive mandates to adopt specific control technology, apply for operating permits, monitor and report on its media-specific environmental discharges, allow regulatory audits of their environmental activities and address any emissions violations, potential violations or legal implications of non-compliance. To the extent that organizations can influence the formation of regulation, managing their environmental impacts may serve as a signal to lawmakers to increase restrictions for industry as a whole (Salop and Scheffman, 1983) or to preempt more stringent environmental regulation (Welch et al., 2000; Lutz et al., 2000). There may be informal regulatory benefits from participating in a VEI, including increased recognition by government officials and improved relations with regulators.

Regulatory pressures are also taking on a new shape as EPA and states expand their basket of VEIs. Increasingly regulators are offering technical assistance grants as incentives for organizations to participate in VEIs and achieve their environmental goals (Davies et al., 1996). The Multi-State

Working Group on Environmental Management Systems (MSWG) and EPA's EMS Pilot Program, EPA's Performance Track Program and EPA's Region I StarTrack Program are just a few examples of VEIs that offer participants technical assistance as incentives for participation in programs that encourage EMS development. While still operating as an institutional pressure, these regulatory incentives are less coercive than is the traditional regulatory regime, and as such may lead to greater variation in organizational responses (Jennings and Zandbergen, 1995).

Prior literature also emphasizes the importance of market pressures on organizations' environmental change (Arora and Cason, 1996; Hoffman, 2000; Bowen, 2000; Khanna and Damon, 1999; Konar and Cohen, 1997). Market pressures refer to the interplay of all potential buyers and sellers involved in the production, sale or purchase of a particular commodity or service. Markets include consumers, customers and competitors who are influencing companies to proactively manage their environment management strategies (Hoffman, 2000). As information has become more readily available about companies' environmental activities, customers and firms have increasingly considered the environment when making their purchasing decisions (Arora and Gangopadhyay, 1995; Marshall and Mayer, 1991). Some firms, for example, may seek only to do business with factor suppliers that have adopted certified EMSs, as doing so helps to ensure that their final product is more environmentally conscious (Bowen., et al. 2001; Darnall et al., 2000; Darnall et al., 2001). By participating in a VEI suppliers may better satisfy these market demands.

Finally, social pressures also influence organizations' environmental actions (Klassen and McLaughlin, 1996; Henriques and Sadorsky, 1996, 1999; Arora and Cason, 1996; Konar and Cohen, 1997; Welch et al., 2000; Garrod and Chadwick, 1996; Hoffman, 2000). These pressures are derived from an organization's external constituents that must be actively managed in order to develop effective and successful operating strategies (Hoffman, 2000). Constituents include environmental groups, citizens groups and the media, and can mobilize public sentiment, alter accepted norms and change the way people think about the environment and the role of the organization in protecting it (Hoffman, 2000). Social drivers have gained increasing attention since the 1980s due to the heightening influence of stakeholders on organizational strategy (see for example, Klassen and McLaughlin, 1996; Henriques and Sadorsky, 1996, 1999; Arora and Cason, 1995; Konar and Cohen, 1997; Welch et al., 2000; Garrod and Chadwick, 1996; Hoffman, 2000; Muoghalu et al., 1990; Hamilton, 1995). Part of this changing focus may be due to highly publicized stories of catastrophic environmental disasters like the nuclear accident at Three Mile Island, the Union Carbide toxic gas leak in Bhopal and the Exxon oil spill, which has personalized the importance of organizations' environmental management activities (Rajan, 2001).

The basic premise of all of these institutional views is that organizational tendencies toward conformity with external influences lead to homogeneity in organizational behavior (Oliver, 1997). The organization is thus cast as a passive participant that responds to external pressures and expectations. This view is criticized, however, by researchers who argue that organizations are dynamic and evolving, and can respond to external pressures in a variety of ways based on the resources and capabilities that they posses (Oliver, 1997; Perrow, 1986). As such, an understanding of an organization's prior internal capabilities may be important factors that affect why different organizations participate in a VEI.

INTERNAL PARTICIPATION DRIVERS

RBV suggests that external factors, while important in shaping organizational strategy, cannot alone lead to valuable resources (Barney, 1986). Instead, an organization's competitive strategies depend significantly on its specific capabilities (Sharma and Vredenburg, 1998) and its ability to put these proficiencies to routine productive use (Grant, 1991; Collis and Montgomery, 1995; Russo and Fouts, 1997). These capabilities include less tangible knowledge-based advantages such as socially complex organizational processes and reputational assets (Barney, 1991; Rumelt, 1984, 1991; Penrose, 1959; Wernerfelt, 1984; Oliver, 1997) and are necessarily path-dependent in that they are a function of unique organizational actions and learning that accrue over a period of time (Barney, 1991; Hart, 1995).

Applied to environmental management, RBV informs why enterprises might also participate in a VEI. Recent literature in this area can be categorized into two frameworks. The first framework consists of studies that focus on 'human capital' as capabilities that foster environmental action. This framework emphasizes the importance of managerial attitudes and views (Cordano and Frieze, 2000; Sharma et al., 1999; Sharma and Nguan, 1999), managerial interpretations (Sharma, 2000), environmental values and leaders (Egri and Herman, 2000) and environmental champions (Andersson and Bateman, 2000). In each case key individuals influence management decisions and explain in part why organizations engage in particular environmental activities.

A second framework focuses on 'higher-order learning processes' as capabilities, which are triggered by environmental responsiveness (Sharma and Vredenburg, 1998; Hart, 1995; Christmann, 2000) and continuous improvement strategies (Hart, 1995; Russo and Fouts, 1997; Florida, 1996;

Rugman and Verbeke, 1998; Sharma and Vredenburg, 1998). This framework focuses on actual management practices and suggests that in order to engage in environmental management practices that rely on higher-ordered learning proficiencies, basic capacities must first be in place (Hart, 1995; Christmann, 2000). For example, to achieve greater levels of internal environmental competency and efficiency (such as product stewardship) an organization must first be proficient in basic environmental capabilities (such as pollution prevention) (Hart, 1995). Organizations that adopt environmental strategies without these basic-level competencies lack the capabilities to support them and are less likely to achieve their organizational goals (Christmann, 2000).

While developing 'foundational' proficiencies are necessary to lead to competitive advantage, they are not sufficient. Competitors will over time replicate effective learning systems (Sharma and Vredenburg, 1998), and for this reason organizational competencies must be continually improved (Sharma and Vredenburg, 1998; Russo and Fouts, 1997; Hart, 1995) in order to generate a stream of innovations and achieve competitive advantage (Sharma and Vredenburg, 1998). Organizations that possess continual improvement processes, moreover, are more competent at transferring general basic capabilities and generating momentum to encourage commitments in environmental management (Klassen, 2000; Hart, 1995), and achieve proactive environmental change (Lawrence and Morell, 1995; Florida, 1996; Andrews et al., 2001).

An organization's environmental management proficiencies – in both RBV frameworks – depend on its ability to allocate resources towards achieving basic competencies (Russo and Fouts, 1997; Aragón-Correa, 1998; Arora and Cason, 1996). Slack resources provide a foundation for environmental management by creating opportunities for organizations to develop their internal capabilities and assist them in moving beyond compliance (Bowen, 2000; Arora and Cason, 1996; McGuire et al., 1988; McGuire et al., 1990; Lawrence and Morell, 1995; Hart and Ahuja, 1996; Waddock and Graves, 1997). More specifically, managers that possess greater levels of discretionary slack (Sharma, 2000) have a greater ability to attempt costly or risky environmental investments (Henriques and Sadorsky, 1996; Ahmed et al., 1998).

These two RBV perspectives – the 'human capital' and the 'higher-order learning process' – are complements in that organizational leaders are likely to champion the basic organizational activities that are embedded in the more sophisticated environmental action, which the second framework describes. Data constraints limit this study to considering only the second structure and its role in organizational decisions to participate in a VEI. Within this framework, continuous improvement capabilities, environmental management resources and access to resources emerge as factors that may affect organizations' participation decisions. While organizations' internal resources and capabilities may be controlled by the enterprise itself, different types of organizational structures may affect the enterprise's ability to access them. Various types of organizations, moreover, are also likely to respond differently to the institutional pressures exerted on them. It is thus important to address how external and internal drivers for VEI participation differ among varying types of organizations.

ORGANIZATIONAL DIFFERENCES AND HYPOTHESES FOR VEI PARTICIPATION

The population of organizations that are choosing to participate in VEIs varies along many dimensions including size, structure, resources and other factors. However one key distinction that can be made among the population of enterprises is in the goals that they aspire towards, especially among for-profit organizations – both publicly traded and privately owned – and government organizations. This difference accounts for many broader distinctions that can be hypothesized about the external and internal drivers that motivate organizations to participate in a VEI.

For-Profit Organizations

Neo-classical economics suggests that both publicly traded and privately owned organizations operate with the goal to increase profits. Ownership in the publicly traded organization is widely dispersed among many shareholders, who themselves do not make the daily decisions about prices, output, employment and other factors. Instead, managers supervise routine operations. Such an arrangement creates a 'separation' in organizational goals, as shareholders wish to maximize their shareholder revenues and managers wish to ensure their job security by maximizing sales (Browning and Browning, 1992). This separation, however, does not diminish the publicly traded organization's ability to increase profits, as managers enjoy some degree of discretion inasmuch as they are able to achieve a minimum-profit constraint (Baumol, 1976; Alchian and Demsetz, 1972).

Privately owned firms, in contrast, are owned by one or a handful of individuals who operate the business. For these companies, the owner(s) is often engaged directly in decisions concerning which inputs to use, who to hire or fire and what price to charge for their product. This structure creates a tighter 'coupling' between the organization's ownership and profit-focused goals.

As resources enter either type of for-profit firm, they are allocated towards achieving operational efficiency (Browning and Browning, 1992). If allocated efficiently, the company has a greater opportunity to grow and generate slack resources. There are differences, however, in firms' abilities to achieve this end, which largely rest on their structural variations. Publicly traded organizations are generally larger than private businesses and are more likely to have a parent company with multiple facilities and divisions. Because of their larger scale of operations, publicly traded firms are also more likely to have a greater market share and access to resources for environmentally innovative behavior (Greening and Gray, 1994; Russo and Fouts, 1997; Bowen, 2000).

In contrast, the vast majority of privately owned organizations are small and medium-sized enterprises. Because of their smaller presence in the market place, private companies are less likely to have the same level of market share and access to resources than are publicly traded firms. The combination of all these factors suggests that private companies will have more modest internal capabilities that support environmental action than do publicly traded firms.

H1: Publicly traded organizations have stronger internal environmental capabilities than do privately owned organizations prior to participating in a VEI.

An organization's modest internal resources may be moderated, however, by external regulatory drivers. These drivers include government assistance programs in pollution prevention, management system training, environmental monitoring and continual improvement, or government grants to hire consultants. Access to these programs may facilitate privately owned organizations' decisions to participate in a VEI, because they are less likely to have the higher-order learning processes and capacities to manage their environmental activities.

H2: Privately owned organizations are more influenced by the availability of environmental technical assistance programs than are publicly traded organizations when deciding to participate in a VEI.

Because of their profit-focused goals, market pressures are expected to influence both types of for-profit organizations similarly. There is one exception, however. With their greater market share, publicly traded companies are more likely to have operational units in foreign countries and do business with international customers. For this reason, they are also more likely to be influenced by the demands of international customers.

H3: Publicly traded and privately owned organizations are influenced similarly by all market drivers (except international customers' pressure) when deciding to participate in a VEI.

Finally, as noted earlier, larger-scaled organizations generally have greater access to resources. Publicly traded organizations are generally larger than privately owned companies and more likely to have parent companies that can support their facility-level environmental management activities.

H4: Publicly traded organizations have greater access to resources prior to participating in a VEI than do privately owned enterprises.

Government Organizations

The generalized view of the government organization is that it exists for the purpose of increasing public welfare. It thus operates differently from the for-profit firm. In making its operational decisions, the government enterprise not only considers the benefits to the organization of its action or inaction, but also the benefits to society. Because of its societal interest, the government organization is more likely than is the for-profit firm to invest in activities that attempt to improve social well-being (Stokey and Zeckhauser, 1978).

Government's ability to improve public welfare, however, is often confounded by the diverging goals between and among its owners, political appointees and managers. Government's ownership is widely dispersed among taxpayers, voters and interest groups who influence the legislative process, but do not manage the resulting public programs. Instead, political appointees oversee program implementation while career officials manage the details (Levine and Kleeman, 1992; Ingraham and Rosenbloom, 1990). Both political appointees and career officials have an incentive to ensure their job security, and do so by increasing their political capital and cultivating relationships with influential political actors, rather than pursuing exclusively the goal of increasing social well-being (Wilson, 1989; Kettl, 1993; Blais and Dion, 1991; Levine and Kleeman, 1992; Ingraham and Rosenbloom, 1990). This structure creates a similar (although more extreme) 'separation' in the goals of government enterprises than is seen in the publicly traded firm and tends to produce goals that are complex and varied, and which often conflict with public welfare ideals (Kettl, 1993). It also creates a tendency for government officials to focus on inputs rather than outcomes (Behn, 1981), which further separates the goals of political appointees and career officials from the goals of voters, taxpayers and interest groups.

This scenario is further complicated because of government's not-for-profit structure, lengthy documentation procedures and fewer performance criteria (Kettl, 1993). These factors make it difficult for government entities to remove career officials who do not confine their self-interests. Once created and institutionalized, moreover, government operations are difficult to disassemble and the threat of their demise is small, which allows self-interested managers to persist and flourish (Wilson, 1989; Blais and Dion, 1991). Fiscal rules, moreover, restrict more efficient government enterprises from keeping their surplus revenues (Wilson, 1989). Such a structure encourages organizational inefficiencies that are less tolerated by the for-profit firm and hampers government's ability to achieve its social and legislative goals (Kettl, 1993).[2]

Government's capacity to garner resources also differs from the for-profit organization. The resources available to governmental organizations are derived from the taxpayer and the legislative process, and while the number of taxpayers is vast the resources available to these entities has become progressively more constrained. Since the early 1990s, US voters have become less and less willing to accept additional tax burdens and government's fiscal budgets have become increasingly reduced (Gordon and Milakovich, 1998).

The combination of government's less-efficient resource allocation and reduced access to resources hampers its ability to develop assets, capabilities and less tangible knowledge-based advantages that facilitate VEI participation. Void of a competitive advantage environment, moreover, government organizations have fewer reasons to invest (Kettl, 1993) in developing these capabilities.

H5: Compared to publicly traded and privately owned organizations, government entities have weaker internal environmental capabilities prior to participating in a VEI.

While RBV might suggest that investments in developing internal proficiencies will lead to greater organizational efficiencies, because government managers are motivated to maximize their political capital, this efficiency argument is undermined. For these reasons, the pressure exerted on government organizations to participate in a VEI is more likely to be derived from external factors such as regulatory and social pressures. This is expected to be true for all external drivers except market drivers, as government organizations are less affected by market because of their not-for-profit status.

H6: Government organizations are more likely to be influenced by external pressures (other than market pressures) than internal pressures when deciding to participate in a VEI.

H7: Market pressures exert less influence on government organizations' decisions to participate in a VEI than they do for profit-oriented organizations.

Similar to privately owned companies, government organizations' more modest internal resources may be moderated by external factors including government assistance programs such as those described earlier.

H8: Government enterprises, like privately owned organizations, are more likely to be influenced by the availability of environmental technical assistance programs than are publicly traded organizations when deciding to participate in a VEI.

Finally, traditional regulatory pressures are expected to have similar influence on all three types of organizations (Henriques and Sadorsky, 1996). Regardless of an organization's goals, it must address its regulatory compliance or risk additional regulatory scrutiny and the threat of being shut down. For these reasons, all organizations are expected to seek regulatory relief if possible. By better managing their regulatory pressures, moreover, all organizations have the potential to change their relationships with regulators by moving from a highly coercive regulatory regime to a more cooperative one, which is expected to be attractive for all three types of enterprises.

H9: All three types of organizations – publicly traded, privately owned and government – are influenced similarly by traditional regulatory pressures when deciding to participate in a VEI.

METHODOLOGY

To evaluate these hypotheses, an organization's decision to participate in a VEI was applied to facilities' decisions to participate in the EMS Pilot Program. This program was initiated with support from the Multi-State Working Group for EMSs (MSWG), whose members[3] in concert with EPA initiated ten state-level pilot programs to encourage and facilitate EMS adoption in approximately 60 US-based facilities. The pilot program was designed to determine the potential EMSs have for environmental performance and future regulation. States recruited many different types of enterprises to participate and as a condition for their participation facilities were required to contribute EMS adoption data to a publicly accessible database called the National Database on EMSs (NDEMS).[4] In return, EPA and MSWG states offered technical assistance, small grants for EMS design training, consultant support and data collection assistance, in addition to public recognition. Regulatory compliance was a requirement for program participation, as was a pledge by pilot facilities to implement an EMS.[5]

NDEMS contains data for all pilot program participants. The data were collected from environmental managers in each pilot facility using a standardized set of protocols that were reviewed by multiple researchers, government officials and facility managers prior to pilot testing and final utilization. NDEMS contains information on facilities' baseline operations during the three years prior to adopting an EMS, in addition to data on the processes by which they designed and implemented their EMSs. In the future, the database will also contain post-EMS performance data that may be used to determine the overall impact of EMS adoption on participants' environmental performance.

Facility data included in this analysis were for all pilot program participants that had contributed baseline and EMS design data between 1998 and July 2001.[6] The sample consists of 46 facilities (21 publicly traded, 17 privately owned and 8 government facilities) that had provided complete information for the measures of interest.

Measures

External drivers

Regulatory drivers were measured by six variables. The first five variables represent traditional regulatory pressures and focus on regulatory compliance. They are measured by whether the organization had incurred at least one environmental compliance violation, non-compliance and/or potential non-compliance during the three years prior to participating in the VEI.[7] These variables were coded as dichotomous responses, 1 if yes and 0 otherwise. In addition, pilot managers reported using a three-point ordinal scale (high, medium, low)[8] to express whether they participated in the pilot program because they believed that it would improve their compliance with environmental regulations. Finally, two incentive-based regulatory drivers were also included. Using the same three-point ordinal scale (high, medium, low) pilot facility managers reported (1) whether they participated in the pilot program in hopes that doing so would lead to regulatory benefits in the future, and (2) whether government assistance programs (that included technical assistance, small grants for EMS design training and consultant support and periodic meetings in which facility managers could share their participation experiences) made participation in the pilot program attractive.

Market drivers were measured by eight variables, all of which were based on facility managers' perceptions. Pilot managers reported on a three-point ordinal scale (high, medium, low) whether they participated in the pilot program because they believed that EMS adoption (1) was being pressured by domestic customers, (2) was being pressured by international customers, (3) may be a valuable marketing tool, (4) may provide a competitive advantage, (5) was increasingly being supported by environmental management professionals, (6) was being pressured by shareholders, (7) might reduce their costs, (8) might increase their revenues. While including information about facilities' factor supplier pressures would also be a relevant to include, NDEMS does not contain these data.

Social drivers were the last category of external drivers considered and were measured by the number of public inquiries each facility received about its environmental activities during the three years prior to participating in the pilot program. Responses were coded in three ordered categories: less than ten inquiries per year, between 11 and 50 inquiries per year and greater than 50 inquiries per year. In addition, pilot managers reported on an ordinal scale (high, medium, low) whether they participated in the pilot program because they believe that (1) outside interested parties were pressuring them to do so, and (2) it may be a valuable public relations tool.

Internal capabilities
To measure an organization's continuous improvement capability facilities were asked whether they had implemented either total quality management principles (TQM) prior to EMS implementation or ISO 9000 quality management systems (QMS). The latter measure is a more advanced form of a continuous improvement capability that is certified by independent auditors, while TQM is a more basic form. These variables were coded 1 if yes and 0 otherwise.

Facilities' environmental management proficiency was measured by whether they had engaged in any pollution prevention activities prior to adopting an EMS. In addition, a second more advanced form of pollution prevention capability was also included – whether or not facilities had adopted a formal pollution prevention plan (Henriques and Sadorsky, 1996) prior to participating in the VEI. Both variables were coded 1 if yes and 0 otherwise.

Finally, facilities' slack resources were measured by three variables. The first variable, facility size (employees), was coded in three ordered categories: less than 100 employees, between 101 and 299 employees, and 300 or more employees. While a more precise measure of organizational slack would have incorporated specific information about discretionary slack (Sharma, 2000) or separated the effects of slack from societal visibility (Bowen, 2000), such data were unfortunately not available. The two parent organization measures were also included to measure slack resources because implementation of environmental initiatives in multi-plant organizations depends on the incentives and the resources available to facilities (Bowen, 2000). It was first determined whether the facilities had parent organizations, and if so whether the parent organization provided EMS adoption assistance (financial support, technical assistance or support from sister facilities). Both measures were coded as dichotomous variables, 1 if yes and 0 otherwise.

Responses were grouped by the external and internal drivers described above for each of the three types of facilities. Because two types of responses were elicited – ordinal and discrete – the data were evaluated independently rather than by employing an index. In addition to evaluating the statistical results of the three-point ordinal responses, these data were also assessed by combining high and medium responses and comparing them to low responses. This additional comparison was performed because external and internal pressures that have a moderate or high influence are more likely to prompt organizational action than are factors with low influences.

Data comparisons were performed using Fisher's exact test for contingency tables. This non-parametric approach was employed because the NDEMS sample was necessarily small and as such typical parametric approaches lead to poor approximations and model misspecification (Hess and Orphanides, 1995; Stokes et al., 1995). Used extensively in biostatistics and the social sciences, Fisher's exact test was used to determine the strength of the association between each participation driver and the three different facility types.

In adjusting for sample size, Fisher's exact test estimates highly conservative ρ-values. For this reason, in addition to conventional levels ($\rho <$ 0.05) more liberal levels of significance ($\rho < 0.10$) are also reported (Grusky, 1959; Rice, 1988; Kahn and Goldenberg, 1991; Hirota et al., 1999; Beirle and Konisky, 2000). Two-tailed statistical tests were performed on all comparisons.

Facility descriptions
The descriptive statistics show that publicly traded and privately owned enterprises were largely manufacturing operations (SIC codes 2000–3999), as seen in Table 5.1, although there were a few non-manufacturing facilities that had chosen to adopt an EMS.[9] Of the government facilities, five were local governments. The others consisted of two national-level government facilities and a university.

Table 5.1 Numbers of sample organizations by industry type

Facility type	**Industrial type**		
Publicly Traded Facilities (21)	17 = manufacturing	3 = electric services	1 = wholesale furniture
Privately Owned Facilities (17)	16 = manufacturing	1 = lab research	—
Government Facilities (8)	5 = local government	2 = national government	1 = university

Prior to participating in the pilot program almost all of the publicly traded companies were marketing their products (95 percent) and producing their goods internationally (86 percent), as seen in Table 5.2. This contrasts with the privately owned companies, which were more subdued in the international arena. Sixty-five percent of the privately owned companies were marketing their products internationally and 35 percent were involved in international production prior to participating in the pilot program. As might be expected, the government facilities were much less involved in the international arena.

Table 5.2 Numbers of sample organizations involved in international production and international marketing[a]

Facility Type	**International Production**	**International Marketing of Products**
Publicly Traded Facilities (21)	86% (18)	95% (20)
Privately Owned Facilities (17)	35% (6)	65% (11)
Government Facilities (8)	0% (0)	25% (2)
Facility Total (46)	52% (24)	72% (33)

Note: [a] Some facilities were engaged in both international production and foreign marketing of their products, while others were involved in one but not the other. A few facilities were not involved in either international activity.

Finally, all three types of facilities were certifying their EMSs to ISO 14001 while participating in the pilot program, although certification occurred at different rates. Seventy-six percent of the publicly traded facilities were certified or were in the process of seeking ISO 14001 registration and 71 percent of privately owned facilities were doing the same, as shown in Table 5.3. In contrast, 38 percent of the government facilities were registered or were seeking registration. Other differences were related to the influence of facilities' parent organizations. Compared to single-facility operations (40 percent), nearly twice (72 percent) as many pilot facilities that belong to a larger organization have certified their EMS to ISO 14001. Parent organizations, as noted earlier, are hypothesized to be an important influence on facilities' access to resources, and are a topic for discussion in the following sections.

Table 5.3 Sample organizations' relationship with ISO 14001

Facility type	Facility with parent organization			Single facility		Total ISO certified[b] facilities
	Total	*ISO 14001*	*Parent Requires or Encourages EMS[a]*	*Total*	*ISO 14001*	
Publicly traded (21)	95% (20)	75% (15)	90% (18)	5% (1)	100% (1)	76% (16)
Privately owned (17)	65% (11)	82% (9)	64% (7)	35% (6)	50% (3)	71% (12)
Government (8)	62% (5)	40% (2)	20% (1)	38% (3)	33% (1)	38% (3)
Facility Total *(46)*	*78% (36)*	*72% (26)*	*72% (26)*	*22% (10)*	*40% (4)*	*67% (31)*

Notes:
a EMS may or may not be ISO 14001 certified.
b Denotes those facilities that were certified to ISO 14001 or were seeking third-party certification to ISO 14001. Facilities that declared 'self-certification' or did not utilize third party registration were excluded from these counts.

External Drivers

The empirical results of the factors that affect facilities' rationales for EMS adoption are illustrated in Table 5.4. The table describes the influences of the external and internal pressures on participation decisions for the three types of pilot facilities.

Regulatory drivers
Of the external drivers, all three types of facilities reported that traditional regulatory pressures had the greatest influence on their decisions to adopt an EMS. Between 29 percent and 62 percent of each type of facility had experienced a violation, non-compliance or potential non-compliance in the three years prior to participating in the pilot program. Most of the facilities,

Table 5.4 Statistical analysis results

Drivers	Publicly traded (n = 21) (in %)			Private (n = 17) (in %)			Government (n = 8) (in %)		
	H	M^a	L	H	M^a	L	H	M^a	L
EXTERNAL DRIVERS:									
Regulatory drivers									
1. Number of violations	37	–	63	44	–	56	29	–	71
2. Number of non-compliances	44	–	56	29	–	71	62	–	37
3. Number of potential non-compliances	39	–	61	38	–	62	62	–	38
4. Improve compliance	48	28	24	53	29	18	75	25	0
5. Potential regulatory benefits	33	28	38	23	41	35	75	0	25
6. Environmental technical assistance	0	9	91	35	12	53	25	63	12
Market drivers									
1. US customer pressures	19	19	62	12	12	76	0	0	100
2. International customer pressures	14	19	67	12	0	88	0	0	100
3. Potential marketing tool	35	35	30	18	24	59	0	0	100
4. Increase competitive advantage	33	52	14	29	41	29	0	25	75
5. Environmental professionals support EMSs	5	35	60	12	18	71	0	25	75
6. Shareholders/owner pressures	14	14	71	12	6	82	0	0	100
7. Potential cost reduction	43	33	23	41	47	12	38	25	38
8. Potential revenue increases	16	47	37	13	25	63	0	0	100
Social drivers									
1. Number of stakeholder requests	10	9	71	6	12	82	12	38	50
2. Stakeholder pressures	0	5	95	0	0	100	0	0	100
3. Improve public relations	19	29	52	24	47	29	38	35	37
Continual improvement capability									
1. Total Quality Management Principles	48	–	52	29	–	71	12	–	88
2. ISO 9000	71	–	29	71	–	29	0	–	100

Drivers	Facility type								
	Publicly traded *(n = 21)* *(in %)*			*Private* *(n = 17)* *(in %)*			*Government* *(n = 8)* *(in %)*		
	H	M[a]	L	H	M[a]	L	H	M[a]	L
Environment management capability									
1. Pollution prevention activities	91	–	9	94	–	6	62		38
2. Pollution prevention plan	57		43	53	–	47	25	–	75
Resources									
1. Number of employees	71	19	10	47	24	29	50	0	50
2. Parent organization exists	100	–	0	65	–	35	62	–	38
3. Parent organization offers EMS technical support	90	–	10	66	–	34	60	–	40

*Note:*Sums of percentages that do not total 100 percent are due to rounding.
[a] '–' represents a dichotomous variable.

moreover, adopted an EMS to improve their compliance with environmental regulations, as between 75 and 100 percent of them reported that the possibility of compliance improvement had either a high or a moderate influence on their EMS adoption decisions.

Consistent with Hypothesis 9, traditional regulatory drivers affected all three facilities' decisions similarly, and there is no statistically significant difference between them (see Table 5. 5). There are two exceptions, however, which relate to non-traditional regulatory factors. Despite the high pressure that facilities perceive by environmental requirements, the influence of potential regulatory benefits motivated government facilities' EMS adoption decisions more than they did for publicly traded and privately owned facilities ($p < 0.04$). It is unclear why these differences exist, but they may be due to the slightly higher number of regulatory non-compliances and potential non-compliance that government facilities experienced prior to participation (72 percent). While regulatory benefits have yet to be realized, pilot facilities had anticipated that they would come in the form of expedited and consolidated permitting. Some facilities also hoped that regulators would waive some state and federal regulations if they achieved environmental results that are superior to those otherwise required by law.

Table 5.5 Statistical differences of individual drivers

Drivers	Statistical differences (p value <, two-tail test) between:	
	Govt. and for-profit facilities	Publicly traded and private facilities
EXTERNAL DRIVERS:		
Regulatory drivers		
Regulatory benefits	0.04	—
Environmental technical assistance	0.01	0.01
Market drivers		
Marketing tool	0.01	—
Competitive advantage	0.01	—
Increase revenues	0.03	—
INTERNAL DRIVERS:		
Continual improvement Capability		
ISO 9000	0.01	—
Parent organization existence	—	0.03
Parent organization offers EMS technical support	0.05	0.04

Perhaps the most important finding related to regulatory drivers is the role that government assistance programs played in influencing privately owned and government facilities' participation decisions. These programs influenced 47 percent of private organizations and 88 percent of government pilots. In contrast, only 9 percent of publicly traded facilities were motivated by receiving aid ($p < 0.01$). These differences support Hypotheses 2 and 8 and suggest that privately owned and government facilities were more influenced than were publicly traded facilities by the availability of environmental technical assistance programs.

Market drivers

In general, market pressures had only a moderate influence on all facility-level decisions and there are no statistically significant differences between publicly traded and privately owned facilities. These findings partially confirm Hypothesis 3, which suggests that while all market drivers influence both types of organizations similarly, they differ in the level of pressure endured by international customers' pressure. Despite the fact that publicly traded facilities operate more in the international domain ($\rho < 0.05$) than do the other facility groups, publicly traded facilities did not experience greater pressures from international customers than did privately owned organizations.

Market drivers are less relevant, however, to government facilities, and confirm Hypothesis 7. These differences are statistically significant ($\rho < 0.01$) across two dimensions – that implementing an EMS in the VEI was expected to be a useful marketing tool and that it might help them gain a competitive advantage. For publicly traded and privately owned facilities, these two pressures had a greater influence on their participation decisions. The other market drivers lack statistical significance because publicly traded and privately owned facilities also reported them to have a low influence on their EMS adoption decisions.

Additionally, publicly traded and privately owned facilities see in EMSs the possibility of increasing their revenues (63 percent and 38 percent respectively) and reduce costs (76 percent and 89 percent report them as high or medium influences), which suggest that these facility managers are considering an EMS as a tool to increase organizational efficiency. In contrast, government facilities only considered half of the efficiency argument. That is, they reported that while reducing costs was an important factor in their EMS adoption decisions, the possibility of increasing revenue was not. Part of this difference may be ascribed to the fact that for-profit organizations derive their revenues from sales, while government organizations are funded through the political process, which generally appropriates funding based on political and legislative factors rather than efficiency arguments.

Social drivers
Social drivers are the least influential of the external drivers for all three types of facilities. Low relevance of stakeholder pressures in addition to low numbers of stakeholder requests yielded no differences among the three facility groups. It is worth noting, however, that when designing the VEI, regulators had hoped that the pilot program facilities might be influenced to adopt an EMS if they were offered benefits in the form of enhanced publicity (that is press releases and announcements, media events, pollution prevention awards and highly advertised annual conferences). It appears that increased public relations opportunities did moderately influence all pilot participants' EMS adoption decisions.

Internal Drivers

When considering the differences among for-profit facilities, statistical variation in their internal drivers was more prevalent. For government facilities, moreover, while the overall influence of internal drivers was an important factor, regulatory drivers appear more important to their decision to participate in the pilot program, as was anticipated by Hypothesis 6.

Continuous improvement capability

In evaluating facilities' continuous improvement capabilities, prior to EMS adoption many (71 percent) of publicly traded and privately owned facilities had ISO 9000 capabilities in place. Because of this pre-existing capability, EMS implementation likely demanded fewer internal resources and was more easily integrated into the facilities' management practices (Sarkis and Kitazawa, 2000). This is in stark contrast to government facilities ($p < 0.01$), of which none had in place a certified QMS prior to EMS adoption.

The resource-based view of the firm advises that because TQM practices are a more basic form of the principles embodied in ISO 9000, facilities should thus adopt TQM practices prior to ISO 9000. Customer requirements for ISO 9000, however, have no doubt disrupted this natural progression. For those facilities that were not pressured by such influences, simply following the TQM principles may have been sufficient to satisfy their continual improvement needs. Because of ISO 9000's relatively high prevalence in publicly traded and privately owned facilities, an additional investigation was done to determine its relevance to facility decisions to participate in the pilot program. Environmental managers in five (three publicly traded and two privately owned) facilities were interviewed. They reported that their pre-existing ISO 9000 QMS offered a foundation upon which to integrate their EMS. These facility managers all confirmed that in making their decision to participate in the pilot program, they believed that by utilizing their QMS, they could reduce the transaction costs of participation, because they were higher up the learning curve in documenting their internal operations. All five facilities, moreover, integrated their EMS into their QMS, so as to formalize their environmental goals as a component of their quality-focused production (see Darnall et al., 2001, for a greater discussion).

Environmental management capability

With respect to facilities' prior environmental management capability, most of the publicly traded and privately owned facilities had engaged in pollution prevention activities prior to EMS adoption (91 and 94 percent, respectively) while only 62 percent of government facilities had done so ($p < 0.05$). Despite these differences when considering whether facilities had adopted a formal pollution prevention plan prior to adopting an EMS there is no statistical difference between the three types of facilities. While engaging in pollution prevention activities demonstrates a basic level of environmental management capability, a formal pollution prevention plan requires additional levels of organizational commitment, capabilities and transaction costs. As such, few of all the pilot facilities had these capabilities in place prior to EMS adoption.

Slack resources

In comparing facility sizes, 71 percent of publicly traded facilities had over 300 employees and 10 percent had less than 100 employees. Privately owned and government facilities were more diverse, however, in that between 47 and 50 percent of them, respectively, had 300 or more employees. These differences are statistically significant ($p < 0.10$). Facilities also differed in whether or not they had parent companies in that all of the publicly traded enterprises belong to larger organizations, while 65 percent of privately owned ($p < 0.03$) and 62 percent of the government facilities had parent organizations. Finally, of those organizations that had parent companies, publicly traded facilities were more likely than privately owned facilities to receive financial and technical support from them ($p < 0.04$) and government facilities were less likely than for-profit organizations to receive this support ($p < 0.05$). These findings support Hypothesis 4 that publicly traded facilities have greater access to resources prior to participating in the pilot program than do privately owned and government enterprises.

Collectively, the internal driver results offer insight on publicly traded facilities' internal capabilities, as these enterprises had greater overall access to resources and proficiencies that support EMS adoption. They also confirm Hypotheses 1 and 5, which proposed that publicly traded facilities have greater internal capabilities that support VEI participation than do privately owned facilities and government facilities. Government facilities, moreover, had the lowest internal capabilities to support their VEI participation.

In summary, the empirical results offer support for the nine hypotheses, as described in Table 5.6.

DISCUSSION AND IMPLICATIONS

This study begins to understand the occurrence of VEI participation by exploring why facilities participated in the MSWG/EPA's EMS pilot program. It extends previous research by evaluating how motivations vary for different types of organizations, emphasizing that both external and internal organizational-level factors comprise participation decisions.

Table 5.6 Summary of findings

Hypotheses	Evidence offered
H1: Publicly traded facilities have stronger internal environmental capabilities than do privately owned facilities prior to participating in a VEI	Some
H2: Privately owned organizations are more influenced by the availability of environmental technical assistance programs than are publicly traded organizations when deciding to participate in a VEI	Yes
H3: Publicly traded and privately owned facilities are influenced similarly by all market drivers (except international customers' pressure) when deciding to participate in a VEI	Yes
H4: Publicly traded facilities have greater access to resources prior to participating in a VEI than do privately owned and government enterprises	Yes
H5: Compared to publicly traded and privately owned facilities, government entities have weaker internal environmental capabilities prior to participating in a VEI	Some
H6: Government facilities are more likely to be influenced by external pressures (other than market pressures) than internal pressures when deciding to participate in a VEI	Yes
H7: Market pressures exert less influence on government facilities' decisions to participate in a VEI than they do for profit-oriented facilities	Yes
H8: Government enterprises, like privately owned organizations, are more likely to be influenced by the availability of environmental technical assistance programs than are publicly traded organizations when deciding to participate in a VEI	Yes
H9: All three types of facilities – publicly traded, privately owned, and government – are influenced similarly by traditional regulatory pressures when deciding to participate in a VEI	Some

The results of this analysis, while somewhat limited due to sample size constraints, underscore the importance of the US environmental regulatory system as a motivator for VEI participation for all facility types. They also support Henriques and Sadorsky's (1996) suggestion that the presence of the regulatory system itself fosters facilities' decisions to consider environmental management goals as part of their profit generating goals.

The regulatory system, however, while traditionally coercive has recently begun to incorporate incentives for good behavior through the use of VEIs (Davies et al., 1996). This change has created a more cooperative institutional arrangement for organizations (Jennings and Zandbergen, 1995) that choose to participate in voluntary programs. It also has resulted in greater variation in the influence that different regulatory incentives have on facility-level decisions to participate in a VEI. More specifically, publicly traded facilities were influenced less by regulatory incentives, while privately owned facilities were influenced moderately and government facilities were influenced greatly by them.

This variation is also likely due to an interaction between external drivers and facilities' internal capabilities. Publicly traded facilities, for example, had stronger internal capabilities that fortified their EMS adoption decisions, making external resources such as government assistance less relevant to them. As such, a greater understanding of organizations' prior internal capabilities appears to be an important factor in examining the rationales for why the different organizations participate in a VEI.

In examining these interactions, a relevant issue that this study brings to the fore is the embeddedness of organizations' internal capabilities and their relationship with external resources. Consistent with previous research, this study shows that continuous innovation (Hart, 1995; Sharma and Vredenburg, 1998) and basic environmental management capabilities (Hart, 1995; Christmann, 2000) are embedded in facilities' decisions to employ advanced forms of environmental management such as EMS development in a VEI. Interestingly, while some of the facilities in this study were lacking in these prior capabilities they relied on external assistance from regulators to fortify their internal capacities, thus enabling them to participate in the pilot program.

As cooperative arrangements between regulators and organizations expand, additional research is needed that explores the interaction between external and internal pressures on environmental change. While several researchers have recognized the importance for such integration of institutional and RBV (Rugman and Verbeke, 1998; Henderson and Mitchell, 1997; Christmann, 2000; Oliver, 1997), the field is ripe for additional explanation and empirical examination. In exploring these issues further, we may better understand the relationship that emerging regulatory arrangements have for organizations' internal capabilities, and whether they may create competitive advantage for the enterprises that utilize them. As future research emerges, it will also be interesting to know how the experiences of US organizations differ from other types of enterprises in different countries.

Finally, in considering future research on EMSs, two topics merit future exploration. First, while EMS adoption occurs at the facility level, many facilities' decisions about their environmental management strategies are made at the corporate level. Evidence of this corporate-level influence is seen in the descriptive statistics above – 75 percent of the publicly traded facilities adopted their EMSs because of corporate mandate and 15 percent more did so because they were encouraged by their parent company. Thus, a key question for future research on EMSs is what factors influence parent organizations to mandate or encourage EMS adoption in their facilities and how they might differ from facility-level adoption decisions.

Second, the results of this study apply to facilities that participated in the MSWG/EPA's EMS pilot program. Future research should study how these facilities and their parent organizations differ from facilities that do not adopt an EMS and whether they differ from facilities that adopt an EMS outside a voluntary environmental program. It is likely that the pilot facilities, because of the program's environmental compliance requirements for participation, had compliance records that were better than average. In order to achieve these better-than-average compliance records, these facilities and their parent organizations were likely to have greater internal capacities than did non-participating enterprises, which suggests that the availability of external resources may be even more relevant for participation by the broader organizational landscape.

There is still much that can be learned about the voluntary environmental management activities that lead to an organization's decision to participate in a VEI. The information presented here provides a framework for exploring these decisions by integrating both the external and internal factors that influence organizational decisions (see Figure 5.1), and offers preliminary evidence about how these factors vary for different types of enterprises.

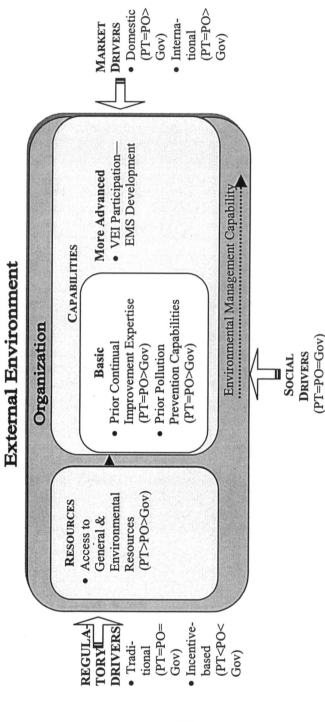

Figure 5.1 Interaction among external pressures, organizations' basic capabilities and their higher-level environmental management capabilities[a]

Notes: [a]'PT' = Publicly traded facility, 'PO' = Privately Owned facility, 'Gov' = Government-owned facility

NOTES

1. The author acknowledges the helpful comments and suggestions from Sanjay Sharma, Mark Starik, three anonymous AOM reviewers, Richard N.L. Andrews, Mark Milstein and Deborah Rigling Gallagher. She is particularly grateful to Daniel Edwards, Jr. for his skillful data assistance and thoughtful observations. The US Environmental Protection Agency sponsored a portion of this research and the pilot facilities and state EMS pilot-project managers provided in-kind support, for which the author is indebted. All conclusions and any errors are solely the responsibility of the author, and do not represent the position of EPA or state regulatory agencies.

2. Some researchers have identified similarities among quasi-government institutions and publicly traded organizations. Similarities are evident, for example, between public utilities and for-profit utility providers as well as between the US Postal Service and its for-profit competitors. The characterization offered here, however, emphasizes the differences between traditional government and for-profit firms, and while there are no doubt exceptions to the traditional view, the differences between the goals and revenue sources for government and for-profit firms create inherently different incentive structures for them. The literature on these arguments is voluminous. See, for example, Blais and Dion (1991); Niskanen (1971); Tullock (1965); Borcherding (1977); Miller and Moe (1983); Kettl (1993); Wilson (1989).

3. The Multi-State Working Group on Environmental Management Systems (MSWG) was initiated in 1997 by government officials in ten states, EPA, NGOs, universities and industry associations with the collective goal to determine whether EMSs increase the environmental performance of organizations that adopt them. Today nearly all US states participate in the MSWG, which by November 2001 had over 200 participants. The National Database on Environmental Management Systems, however, contains data from pilot facilities in the original ten MSWG states, as they are the only states participating in the EMS Pilot Program.

4. States solicited NGOs, government facilities, privately owned firms and facilities, as well as operational units of publicly traded companies, to participate in the pilot program.

5. One pilot facility was removed from the program when it was unable to adhere to the program's minimum compliance requirements.

6. Fifteen facilities were excluded from this study because they had not provided completed baseline and EMS design data by July 2001.

7. A violation is defined as any environmental non-compliance that resulted in a formal enforcement action against the facility. Similarly, a non-compliance is any non-conformity in fulfilling environmental regulatory requirements that resulted in no enforcement action.

8. Actual NDEMS data employ a four-point scale ordinal scale (high, medium, low and not applicable). Because of the lack of strong distinction between low and not applicable pressures, these responses were collapsed into a single category.

9. The sample size constraints unfortunately restricted an extensive examination of the types of industries that these facilities comprise.

REFERENCES

Ahmed, N.U., R.V. Montagno and R.J. Firenze (1998), 'Organisational performance and environmental consciousness: an empirical study,' *Management Decision*, **36**(2): 57–63.

Alchian, A. and H. Demsetz (1972), 'Production, information costs, and economic organization,' *American Economic Review*, **62**(5): 777–95.

Aldrich, Howard E. (1999), *Organizations Evolving*, London: Sage Publications.

Andersson, L.M. and T.S. Bateman (2000), 'Individual environmental initiative: championing natural environmental issues in US business organizations, *Academy of Management Journal*, **43**(4): 548–70.

Andrews, Richard N.L, Nicole Darnall, Deborah Rigling Gallagher, Suellen Terrill Keiner, Eric Feldman, Mathew Mitchell, Deborah Amaral and Jessica Jacoby (2001), 'Environmental management systems: history, theory, and implementation research,' Cary Coglianese and Jennifer Nash (eds), *Regulation from the Inside: Can Environmental Management Systems Achieve Policy Goals?* Resources for the Future: Washington, DC.

Aragón-Correa, J.A. (1998), 'Strategic proactivity and firm approach to the natural environment,' *Academy of Management Journal*, **41**(5): 556–68.

Arora, S. and T. Cason (1996), 'Why do firms volunteer to exceed environmental regulations? Understanding participation in EPA's 33/50 program,' *Land Economics*, **72**(4): 413–32.

Arora, S. and S. Gangopadhyay (1995), 'Toward a theoretical model of voluntary overcompliance,' *Journal of Economic Behavior and Organization*, **28**(3): 289–309.

Bansal, P. and K. Roth (2000), 'Why companies go green: a model of ecological responsiveness,' *Academy of Management Journal*, **43**(4): 717–36.

Barney, J. (1986), 'Strategic factor markets: expectations, luck, and business strategy,' *Management Science*, **32**(10): 1231–41.

Barney, J. (1991), 'Firm resources and sustained competitive advantage,' *Journal of Management*, **17**(1): 99–120.

Baumol, William J. (1976), *Business Behavior, Value and Growth*, rev. edn, New York: Harcourt, Brace and World.

Behn, R. (1981), 'Policy analysis and policy politics,' *Policy Analysis*, **7**(2): 199–226.

Beirle, T.C. and D.M. Konisky (2000), 'Values, conflict, and trust in participatory environmental planning,' *Journal of Public Policy Analysis and Management*, **19**(4): 587–602.

Blais, Andre and Stephane Dion (eds) (1991), *The Budget-Maximizing Bureaucrat: Appraisals and Evidence*, Pittsburgh, PA: University of Pittsburgh Press.

Borcherding, Thomas (ed.) (1977), *Budgets and Bureaucrats: The Origins of Government Growth*, Durham, NC: Duke University Press.

Bowen, F.E. (2000), 'Does size matter? A meta-analysis of the relationship between organisation size and environmental responsiveness,' paper presented at the International Association for Business and Society Annual Meeting, Vermont.

Bowen, F.E., P.D. Cousins, R.C. Lamming and A.C. Faruk (2001), 'The role of supply management capabilities in green supply,' *Production and Operations Management*, **10**(2), 174–89.

Browning, Edgar K. and Jacquelene M. Browning (1992), *Microeconomic Theory and Applications*, 4th edn, New York: HarperCollins.

Christmann, P. (2000), 'Effects of 'best practices' of environmental management on cost competitiveness: the role of complementary assets,' *Academy of Management Journal*, **43**(4): 663–880.

Collis, D.J. and C.A. Montgomery (1995), 'Competing on resources: strategy in the 1990s,' *Harvard Business Review*, **73**(4): 118–28.

Cordano, M. and I.H. Frieze (2000), 'Pollution reduction preferences of US environmental managers: applying Ajzen's theory of planned behavior,' *Academy of Management Journal*, **43**(4): 627–41.

Darnall, Nicole, Deborah R. Gallagher and Richard N.L. Andrews (2001), 'ISO 14001: greening management systems,' in Joseph Sarkis (ed.), *Greening Manufacturing and Operations: From Design to Delivery and Back*, Sheffield: Greenleaf Publishing.

Darnall, N., D.R. Gallagher, R.N.L. Andrews and D. Amaral (2000), 'Environmental management systems: opportunities for improved environmental and business strategy,' *Environmental Quality Management*, **9**(3): 1–9.

Davies, Terry, Janice Mazurek, Nicole Darnall and Kieran McCarthy (1996), *Industry Incentives for Environmental Improvement: Evaluation of US Federal Initiatives*, Washington, DC: Resources for the Future, Center for Risk Management.

DiMaggio, P. and W. Powell (1983), 'The iron cage revisited: institutional isomorphism and collective rationality in organizational fields,' *American Sociological Review*, **48**(2): 147–60.

Egri, C.R. and S. Herman (2000), 'Leadership in the North American environmental sector: values, leadership styles, and contexts of environmental leaders and their organizations,' *Academy of Management Journal*, **43**(4): 561–604.

Florida, R. (1996), 'Lean and green: the move to environmentally conscious manufacturing,' *California Management Review*, **39**(1): 80–105.

Garrod, B. and P. Chadwick (1996), 'Environmental management and business strategy: towards a new strategic paradigm,' *Futures*, **28**(1): 37–50.

Gordon, George J. and Michael E. Milakovich (1998), *Public Administration in America*, Boston, MA: Bedford/St Martin's.

Grant, R.M. (1991), 'The resource-based theory of competitive advantage,' *California Management Review*, **33**(3): 114–35.

Greening, D.W. and B. Gray (1994), 'Testing a model of organizational response to social and political issues,' *Academy of Management Journal*, **37**(3): 467–98.

Grusky, O. (1959), 'Organizational goals and the behavior of informal leaders,' *American Journal of Sociology*, **65**(1): 59–67.

Hamilton, J.T. (1995), 'Pollution as news: media and stock market reactions to the toxics release inventory data,' *Journal of Environmental Economics and Management*, **28**(1): 98–113.

Hart, S. (1995), 'A natural-resource-based view of the firm,' *Academy of Management Review*, **20**(4): 986–1014.

Hart, S. and G. Ahuja (1996), 'Does it pay to be green? An empirical examination of the relationship between emission reduction and firm performance,' *Business Strategy and the Environment*, **5**(1): 30–7.

Henderson, R. and W. Mitchell (1997), 'The interactions of organizational and competitive influences on strategy and performance,' *Strategic Management Journal*, **18**(7): 5–14.

Henriques, I. and P. Sadorsky (1996), 'The determinants of an environmentally responsive firm: an empirical approach,' *Journal of Environmental Economics and Management*, **30**(3): 381-95.

Henriques, I. and P. Sadorksy (1999), 'The relationship between environmental commitment and managerial perceptions of stakeholder importance,' *Academy of Management Journal*, **42**(1): 89–99.

Hess, G. and A. Orphanides (1995), 'War politics: an economic, rational-voter framework,' *American Economic Review*, **85**(4): 828–46.

Hirota, S., T. Saijo, Y. Hamaguchi and T. Kawagoe (1999), 'Does the free-rider problem occur in corporate takeovers? Evidence from laboratory markets,' Paper presented at New Developments in Experimental Economics Conference, Osaka, Japan.

Hoffman, Andrew (2000), *Competitive Environmental Strategy: A Guide to the Changing Business Landscape*, Washington, DC: Island Press.

Howard, J., J. Nash and J. Ehrenfeld (2000), 'Standard or smokescreen? Implementation of a voluntary environmental code,' *California Management Review*, **42**(2): 63–82.

Ingraham, P.W. and D.H. Rosenbloom (1990), 'Political foundations of the American federal service: rebuilding a crumbling base,' *Public Administration Review*, **50**(2): 210–9.

Jaffe, A., S. Peterson, P. Portney and R. Stavins (1995), 'Environmental regulation and the competitiveness of US manufacturing: what does the evidence tell us?,' *Journal of Economic Literature*, **33**(1): 132–63.

Jennings, P.D. and P.A. Zandbergen (1995), 'Ecologically sustainable organizations: an institutional approach,' *Academy of Management Review*, **20**(4): 1015–52.

Kahn, K. and E. Goldenberg (1991), 'Women candidates in the news: an examination of gender differences in US Senate campaign coverage,' *Public Opinion Quarterly*, **55**(2): 180–99.

Kettl, Donald (1993), *Sharing Power: Public Governance and Private Markets*, Washington, DC: Brookings Institution Press.

Khanna, M. and L.A. Damon (1999), 'EPA's voluntary 33/50 program: impact on toxic releases and economic performance of firms,' *Journal of Environmental Economics and Management*, **37**(1): 1–25.

King, A. and M. Lenox (2000), 'Industry self-regulation without sanctions: the chemical industry's responsible care program,' *Academy of Management Journal*, **43**(4): 698–716.

Klassen, R.D. (2000), 'Exploring the linkage between investment in manufacturing and environmental technologies,' *International Journal of Operations and Production Management*, **20**(2): 127–47.

Klassen, R.D. and C.P. McLaughlin (1996), 'The impact of environmental management on firm performance,' *Management Science*, **42**(8): 1199–214.

Konar, S. and M. Cohen (1997), 'Information as regulation: the effect of community right to know laws on toxic emissions,' *Journal of Environmental Economics and Management*, **32**(1), 109-24.

Lawrence, A.T. and D. Morell (1995), 'Leading edge environmental management: motivation, opportunity, resources and processes,' *Research in Corporate Social Performance and Policy*, Supplement 1: 99–126.

Levine, Charles H. and Rosalyn S. Kleeman (1992), 'The quiet crisis for civil service,' in Patricia W. Ingraham and Donald Kettl (eds), *Agenda for Excellence: Public Service in America*, Chatham, NJ: Chatham House.

Lutz, S., P.L. Thomas and J.W. Maxwell (2000), 'Quality leadership when regulatory standards are forthcoming,' *Journal of Industrial Economics*, **48**(3): 331–48.

Marshall, M.E. and D.W. Mayer (1991), 'Environmental training: it's good business,' *Business Horizons*, March/April: 54–7.

McGuire, J.B., T. Schneeweis and B. Branch (1990), 'Perceptions of firm quality: a cause or result of firm performance,' *Journal of Management*, **16**(1): 167–80.

McGuire, J.B., A. Sundren and T. Schneeweis (1988), 'Corporate social responsibility and firm financial performance,' *Academy of Management Journal*, **31**(4): 854–72.

Miller, G.J. and T.M. Moe (1983), 'Bureaucrats, legislators, and the size of government,' *American Political Science Review*, **77**: 297–322.

Muoghalu, M., H.D. Robinson and J.L. Glascock (1990), 'Hazardous waste lawsuits, stockholder returns, and deterrence,' *Southern Economic Journal*, **57**(2): 357–70.

Nash, J. and J. Ehrenfeld (1996), 'Code green,' *Environment*, **38**(1): 16–45.

Niskanen, William A. (1971), *Bureaucracy and Representative Government*, Chicago: Aldine, Atherton.

Oliver, C. (1997), 'Sustainable competitive advantage: combining institutional and resource-based views,' *Strategic Management Journal*, **18**(9): 679–713.

Penrose, Edith (1959), *The Theory of the Growth of the Firm*, 3rd edn, Basil Blackwell: Oxford.

Perrow, Charles (1986), *Complex Organizations: A Critical Essay*, 3rd edn, New York: Random House.

Porter, M. and C. van der Linde (1995), 'Green and competitive: ending the stalemate,' *Harvard Business Review*, September/October: 120–37.

Rajan, R. (2001), 'What disasters tell us about environmental violence: the case of Bhopal,' in Michael Watts and Nancy Peluso (eds), *Violent Environments*, Ithaca, NY: Cornell University Press.

Rice, W.R. (1988), 'A new probability model for determining exact p-values for 2X2 contingency tables when comparing binomial proportions,' *Biometrics*, **44**(1): 1–22.

Rugman, A. and A. Verbeke (1998), 'Corporate strategies and environmental regulations: an organizing framework,' *Strategic Management Journal*, **19**(4): 363–75.

Rumelt, Richard P. (1984), 'Towards a strategic theory of the firm,' in Robert B. Lamb (ed.), *Competitive Strategic Management*, Englewood Cliffs, NJ: Prentice-Hall.

Rumelt, R.P. (1991), 'How much does industry matter?,' *Strategic Management Journal*, **12**(3): 167–85.

Russo, M. and P. Fouts (1997), 'A resource-based perspective on corporate environmental performance and profitability,' *Academy of Management Journal*, **40**(3): 534–59.

Salop, S.C. and D.T. Scheffman (1983), 'Raising rivals' costs,' *American Economic Association Papers and Proceedings*, **73**(2): 267–71.

Sarkis, J. and S. Kitazawa (2000), 'The relationship between ISO 14001 and continuous source reduction programs,' *International Journal of Operations and Production Management*, **20**(2): 225–48.

Sharma, S. (2000), 'Managerial interpretations and organizational context as predictors of corporate choice of environmental strategy,' *Academy of Management Journal*, **43**(4): 681–97.

Sharma, S. and O. Nguan (1999), 'The biotechnology industry and strategies of biodiversity conservation: the influence of managerial interpretations and risk propensity,' *Business Strategy and the Environment*, **8**(1): 46–61.

Sharma, S., A. Pablo and H. Vredenburg (1999), 'Corporate environmental responsiveness strategies: the role of issue interpretation and organizational context,' *Journal of Applied Behavioral Science*, **35**(1): 87–109.

Sharma, S. and H. Vredenburg (1998), 'Proactive corporate environmental strategy and the development of competitively valuable organizational capabilities,' *Strategic Management Journal*, **19**(8): 729–53.

Stokes, Maura E., Charles S. Davis and Gary G. Koch (1995), *Categorical Data Analysis: Using the SAS System*, Cary, NC: SAS Institute.

Stokey, Edith and Richard Zeckhauser (1978), *A Primer for Policy Analysis*, New York: W.W. Norton and Co.

Tullock, Gordon (1965), *The Politics of Bureaucracy*, Washington, DC: Public Affairs Press.

Waddock, S. and S. Graves (1997), 'The corporate social performance – financial performance link,' *Strategic Management Journal*, **18**(4): 303–19.

Welch, E., A. Mazur and S. Bretschneider (2000), 'Voluntary behavior by electric utilities: levels of adoption and contribution of the climate change program to the reduction of carbon dioxide,' *Journal of Public Policy Analysis and Management*, **19**(3): 407–25.

Welford, R. (1992), 'Linking quality and the environment: a strategy for the implementation of environmental management systems,' *Business Strategy and the Environment*, **1**(1): 25–34.

Wernerfelt, B. (1984), 'A resource-based view of the firm,' *Strategic Management Journal*, **5**(2): 171–80.

Wilson, James Q. (1989), *Bureaucracy: What Government Agencies Do and Why They Do It*, New York: Basic Books.

6. Factors influencing successful and unsuccessful environmental change initiatives

Linda C. Angell and Gordon P. Rands

INTRODUCTION

This chapter empirically explores the relationship between the strategic formulation and implementation of environmental change in Pennsylvania's manufacturing facilities between 1995 and 1998. Findings develop richer models of dominant stakeholder pressures and critical environmental events, and generally confirm the conceptual framework suggesting that management's perceptions of stakeholder pressures and critical environmental events drive the level and success of environmental change within manufacturing facilities. Aspects of the facility's organizational context influence this relationship. Formal environmental policies, environmental departments and improved waste reduction opportunities increase the number of successful environmental change implementations in surveyed facilities. Alternatively, the threat of punitive events leads to a greater number of unsuccessful implementations at the facility level of the firm.

Manufacturing facilities face ever-increasing pressures to address their environmental impact. But how do these pressures influence environmental activities within these organizations? This chapter empirically studies the process of environmental improvement within a broad cross-section of Pennsylvania's manufacturing facilities. In doing so, this study seeks to determine how management perceptions of external environmental pressures drive environmental change in manufacturing. Specifically, the research question focuses on the extent to which dominant stakeholder pressures and the development of critical environmental events support and facilitate the successful implementation of environmental change initiatives.

In the next section of this chapter, we review the literature and develop a conceptual framework in which the environmental change process is diagrammed and the expected interaction among the main components of environmental change is stated and explained. After the conceptual development, we present the methodologies employed in this research study, including descriptions of the sample data and the data analysis. The subsequent sections explain and discuss the empirical results. Finally, in the last section, we summarize the limitations, key contributions and future directions for this research.

CONCEPTUAL DEVELOPMENT

The literature on corporate-level environmental management, stakeholders and organizational change provides an overall context for the study of the environmental change at the facility level (Figure 6.1), and suggests that external pressures relating to the natural environment drive the strategic formulation and implementation of environmental initiatives in manufacturing facilities. However the facility's organizational context serves as a filter that both shapes management's interpretation of external pressures and adds some form of internal pressure, and therefore influences the process of environmental improvement. Figure 6.1 shows the general research constructs along with the operationalized variables.

External Pressures, Organizational Context and Strategic Formulation

External pressures
External environmental pressures facing manufacturing facilities stem from government actions, dominant stakeholders and critical environmental events (Ramus and Steger, 2000; Mitchell et al., 1997). From a facility-level perspective, corporate-level environmental management directives (sometimes resulting from previous environmental audits or overarching strategic programs) add to these external pressures. Regulations are the most frequently cited external drivers for environmental action, often impacting firms at the local, state, national and international levels (Andersson and Bateman, 2000; Bansal and Roth, 2000; Hart, 1997; Hass, 1996; Jaffe et al., 1995; Jose, 1995; Lawrence and Morell, 1995; Porter and van der Linde, 1995; Rugman and Verbeke, 1998).

Environmental stakeholders can place enormous pressures on firms (Henriques and Sadorsky, 1999). Freeman defines stakeholders as 'any group or individual who can affect or is affected by the achievement of the organization's objectives' (1994: 46). Clarkson (1995) and others qualify this very broad, bi-directional view of stakeholders, arguing that stakeholders can be divided into primary versus secondary groups based upon the extent to which the firm depends upon the participation of the stakeholder group for survival.

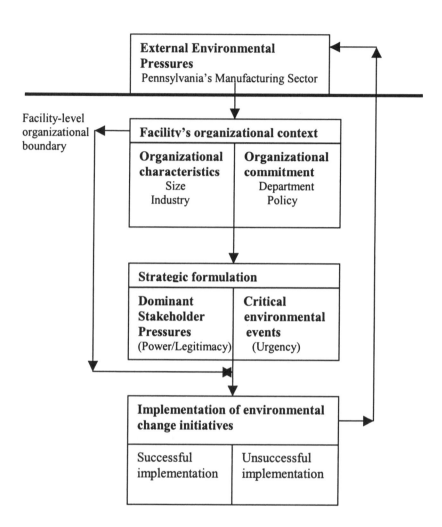

Figure 6.1 Conceptual framework with operational variables

Certainly, manufacturing facility managers face significant pressures from primary stakeholder groups such as shareholders, employees, customers, suppliers, governments and communities. Both industrial customers and end consumers often demand product stewardship – the 'cradle-to-grave' management of products throughout their entire life cycle (Hanna and Newman, 1995). Industrial customers, in particular, can influence their suppliers by requesting product and process information as new environmental regulations are introduced. Suppliers sometimes encourage environmental change by developing an infrastructure for the return, reuse and/or recycling of containers and pallets (Angell, 1996). Local communities often require nearby industrial facilities to commit to the continual improvement of their environmental impact (Jose, 1995).

Secondary stakeholder groups can also have a significant impact upon manufacturing operations. Environmental advocacy groups may induce corporate environmental change by using both cooperative and confrontational tactics (Clair et al., 1995; Girard and Perras, 1994; Stead and Stead, 1995). Other external stakeholders influencing environmental change in firms can include the news media (Lawrence and Morell, 1995), insurance industry (Eckel-Kächele, 1995), competitors (Meffert and Kirchgeorg, 1994), and voluntary industry standards such as the chemical industry's Responsible Care program (Hass, 1996; Hoffman, 1999; King and Lenox, 2000).

Mitchell et al. (1997) develop the stakeholder concept even further by arguing that stakeholders should be classified in terms of their power, legitimacy and urgency as perceived by management. They define 'dominant stakeholders' as those maintaining both power and legitimacy (for example, board of directors, creditors, community leaders, employees, customers) and suggest that these same stakeholders become 'definitive' stakeholders when facing an urgent development. They go on to state that managers perceive 'a clear and immediate mandate to attend to and give priority to [a definitive] stakeholder's claim' (Mitchell et al., 1997: 878). Thus, Mitchell et al., (1997) clearly indicate that the combination of both dominant stakeholder pressures and developing critical events can combine to generate a compeling show of power, legitimacy and urgency to drive management action.

Actual critical environmental events that can promote environmental action include: environmental accidents or spills (Hanna and Newman, 1995; Jose, 1995; Lawrence and Morell, 1995), resource depletion and raw material scarcity (Jose, 1995; Swinth and Vinton, 1992), the existence of environmental hazards (Lawrence and Morell, 1995), and corporate-level directives for environmental management programs (King and Lenox, 2000; Klassen and Whybark, 1999).

Organizational context

The facility's organizational context creates a filter through which external environmental pressures are experienced, acknowledged and considered by management within a manufacturing facility. The nature of this filter is influenced by such factors as organizational characteristics (such as size and industry) and for the purposes of environmental change, the structure of a facility's environmental management program.

Corporate-level research suggests that organizational characteristics which may influence decisions about environmental change include: size (Aragón-Correa, 1998; Henriques and Sadorsky, 1995; Russo and Fouts, 1997; Sharma, 2000), resource availability (Lawrence and Morell, 1995), industry regulatory burden (Brown and Fryxell, 1995), level of vertical integration (Brown and Fryxell, 1995), propensity to innovate (Cordano, 1993), learning capacity (Jose, 1995; Winn, 1996), corporate culture (Wehrmeyer and Parker, 1996) and relationships with environmental groups (Clair et al., 1995). The current study focuses on those characteristics most applicable and relevant to the facility level of an organization, specifically facility size and industry.

Organizational commitment toward environmental management programs, as indicated by the existence of an environmental department and/or policy statement (Dillon and Fischer, 1992; Henriques and Sadorsky, 1995; Hunt and Auster, 1990; Ramus and Steger, 2000), also affects the likelihood of environmental change. Corporate-level research suggests that an organization which regularly engages in environmental audits, environmental reporting, environmental accounting and/or life cycle analysis is more likely to maintain a proactive environmental change program (Hanna and Newman, 1995; Lawrence and Morell, 1995; Moors et al., 1995; Swinth and Vinton, 1992). The current study focuses on the extent to which facility-level indicators of organizational commitment influences environmental change within manufacturing facilities.

Strategic formulation

The unique organizational context within any particular facility influences the extent to which management views external environmental stakeholder pressures and/or critical environmental events as threats or opportunities. Facility management's perception of these pressures as either threats or opportunities can influence the process by which they strategically formulate an approach toward environmental change (Andersson and Bateman, 2000; Jackson and Dutton, 1988; Mitchell et al., 1997; Sharma, 2000; Tushman and Romanelli, 1985).

Previous research suggests that initially reactive responses to stakeholder and event pressures can evolve over time into proactive responses to perceived opportunity (Angell, 1996; Halme, 1996). The organizational context described above could influence management to view various dominant stakeholders and critical environmental events as providing opportunities to: voluntarily reduce the environmental impact of operations by adopting innovative technologies (Russo and Fouts, 1997; Sharma, 2000) and collaboratively interact with stakeholders (Sharma and Vredenberg, 1998); increase economic returns and competitive position (Cordano, 1993; Girard and Perras, 1994; Hart, 1995; Jose, 1995; Stead and Stead, 1995); enhance legitimacy and image (Cordano, 1993; Lawrence and Morell, 1995); recruit a more socially concerned employee base (Eckel-Kächele, 1995); and gain new facilities, products and processes (Lawrence and Morell, 1995). Ramus and Steger (2000) argue that clear organizational commitment to environmental issues (as demonstrated by the existence of a formal environmental policy) leads to an increased willingness to attempt environmental initiatives.

Alternatively, the facility's organizational context could influence management to perceive dominant stakeholders and critical environmental events as posing a threat of increased material costs (Byrne and Deeb, 1993; Gouldson, 1994), increased investment requirements (Byrne and Deeb, 1993; Girard and Perras, 1994), and unstable markets (Gouldson, 1994). Interpretations of environmental stakeholder pressures as a threat could result in managers developing compliance oriented strategies emphasizing pollution control (Sharma, 2000), which do not bring about significant environmental performance improvement. An organization may find that its established performance measurement and compensation system does not reward environmental change activity, and therefore acts as a disincentive (Gabel and Sinclair-Desgagne, 1994). General resistance to threats and/or change is often a barrier to new programs (Shrivastava, 1995).

In either case, external and corporate-level environmental pressures serve to create a motivation for environmental change, and researchers find that strong motivation is essential for a firm to become proactive in their approach to environmental management (Lawrence and Morell, 1995). The occurrence of environmental change significantly increases in firms faced with broader and more varied external pressures (Winn, 1996). However, the very nature of the current business market place works against environmental change because environmental considerations are not included in pricing, but are external to any transaction (Shrivastava, 1995).   An organization may find that technological transformations are threatened by cultural, economic, institutional and knowledge barriers. Often the technology required for environmental change remains undeveloped (Moors et al., 1995).

Strategic Formulation and Change Implementation

Implementation of environmental change initiatives

Environmental changes may take place at any point along the value chain or within the organizational hierarchy. Some of the most proactive environmental changes take place with the development and installation of overarching programs for environmental management such as operating standards (Sarkis, 1995), total quality environmental management (Dambach and Allenby, 1995; Starik, 1995), environmental accounting (Magretta, 1997), risk management (Eckel-Kächele, 1995), technology assessment (Shrivastava, 1995), environmental audits (Murphy et al., 1996), life cycle analysis (Young, 1997), environmental information systems (Black, 1997; Magretta, 1997), cradle-to-grave programs (Hart, 1997; Young, 1997) and design for the environment (Young, 1997; Starik, 1995; Stead and Stead, 1995).

However, much environmental change is tactical, falling under the jurisdiction of operations management. For example, external environmental pressures can influence decisions about site location (Bowman, 1995; Taylor and Welford, 1993), suppliers and procurement (Bowman, 1995; Byrne and Deeb, 1993; Girard and Perras, 1984; Hass, 1996; Murphy et al., 1996; Sarkis, 1995; Stead and Stead, 1995) and human resources (Starik, 1995). A number of environmental change activities take place in the marketing arena, as well. For example, advertising and public relations can pursue eco-labeling options (Stead and Stead, 1995) and promote sustainable consumption practices (Shrivastava, 1995). Also, redesigned logistical systems can reduce environmental impact (Murphy et al., 1996; Sarkis, 1995).

Successful versus unsuccessful implementation

In addition to the nature of the environmental strategies formulated and the number and types of environmental changes attempted, attention also focuses on processes used to implement environmental changes. Some of the factors which appear to be relevant to the successful implementation of environmental change are the tactics used by those championing environmental issues (Andersson and Bateman, 2000), the values of environmentally innovative employees and leaders (Egri and Herman, 2000; Hostager et al., 1998), the organizational support provided to environmental innovators (Hostager et al., 1998; Keogh and Polonsky, 1998) and the signals of organizational and supervisory encouragement to such employees (Ramus and Steger, 2000). In general, the literature suggests that stronger pressures from stakeholder groups holding power, legitimacy and – with the development of critical environmental events – urgency, should lead to a higher number of successfully implemented environmental changes within affected organizations.

Christmann (2000) suggests that not all companies that implement environmental changes derive the full benefits of them; whether this reflects incomplete or mediocre implementation, or adequate implementation but failure to capture expected benefits is not clear. Non-environmental capabilities and resources, such as the abilities to innovate and to implement process modifications in general, may serve as complementary assets and affect the abilities of a firm to gain competitive advantages from its environmental activities (Christmann, 2000). Certainly, we can infer from the literature that the lack of convincing pressure from stakeholders holding significant power, legitimacy and urgency would doom the successful implementation of environmental change initiatives within manufacturing facilities.

Hypotheses
The current study predicts that the extent to which individual facilities will attempt the implementation of environmental change initiatives, and the success of these initiatives, depends upon both the facility's organizational context and management's perceptions of the drivers that they face. The conceptual framework developed in the preceding discussion suggests the following exploratory hypotheses:

Hypothesis 1: Facility management's perceptions of dominant stakeholder pressures drive environmental change in manufacturing facilities.

H1(1): As pressures from dominant stakeholder groups are perceived to increase, the number of environmental change initiatives attempted will also increase.

H1(2): As pressures from dominant stakeholder groups are perceived to increase, the number of successful environmental change implementations will also increase.

H1(3): As pressures from dominant stakeholder groups are perceived to increase, the number of unsuccessful environmental change implementations will decline.

Hypothesis 2: Facility management's perceptions of the development of critical environmental events drive environmental change in manufacturing facilities.

H2(1): As critical environmental events are perceived to develop, the number of environmental change initiatives attempted will also increase.

H2(2): As critical environmental events are perceived to develop, the number of successful environmental change implementations will also increase.

H2(3): As critical environmental events are perceived to develop, the number of unsuccessful environmental change implementations will decline.

Hypothesis 3: Aspects of the facility's organizational context will modify the relationship between the strategic formulation and implementation of environmental change in manufacturing facilities.

H3(1): The organizational context will significantly influence the extent to which perceived stakeholder and critical event pressures affect the number of environmental change initiatives attempted within a facility.

H3(2): The organizational context will significantly influence the extent to which perceived stakeholder and critical event pressures affect the number of successful environmental change implementations.

H3(3): The organizational context will significantly influence the extent to which perceived stakeholder and critical event pressures affect the number of unsuccessful environmental change implementations.

This study tests these hypotheses empirically using a sample of manufacturing facilities operating throughout the state of Pennsylvania in the eastern USA.

RESEARCH METHODS

Sample and Survey Instrument

This study tested the relationship between the strategic formulation and implementation of environmental change initiatives using an eight-page survey questionnaire administered to operations and environmental managers in Pennsylvania's manufacturing facilities in mid-1998. Preliminary interviews with four diverse manufacturers located in central Pennsylvania in the fall of 1997 assisted in the formulation of appropriate mail survey questions. The mailed questionnaire survey contained five main sections, gathering information about demographics, environmental improvement activities, determinants of successful environmental initiatives, performance outcomes and the general environmental management approach within the organization. Data analyzed for the purpose of this study primarily involves seven-point Likert scale and forced-choice types of questions.

The target population for the survey was selected from the Pennsylvania Manufacturers Register (Manufacturing News, 1997), and included 1521 manufacturing facilities employing 100 or more people within the eight largest industries in Pennsylvania. This research was limited to the manufacturing sector in only one state in an attempt to control the various aspects of the external environment acting upon the study participants (that is, regulations, consumers, action groups, environmental degradation). Pennsylvania's industrial base has historically encompassed the traditional, more environmentally sensitive manufacturing sectors (Porter and van der Linde, 1995; Schell, 1997), and thus faces a relatively stringent regulatory context.

A total of 532 facilities responded out of 1521 surveyed, for an effective response rate of 35 percent. Responding facilities had an average of 340 full-time equivalent (FTE) employees (ranging from 100 to 3200 FTE), and represented the targeted industries as follows: foodstuff (15.5 percent), apparel (2.3 percent), printing and publishing (7.7 percent), rubber and plastics (11.9 percent), primary metals (14.5 percent), fabricated metals (23.4 percent), machinery and computer equipment (12.6 percent) and electronics (12.1 percent). An analysis for non-response bias indicated that non-responding companies did not significantly differ from respondents in terms of FTEs or industry representation.

In an attempt to minimize the potential for bias from a single informant, surveys were specifically addressed to both operations and environmental managers within each facility.   Unfortunately, however, in the overwhelming majority of cases, responses were received from only one of the two managers, with a breakdown as follows: 40.6 percent operations managers, 32 percent environmental managers and 27.4 percent 'other' (such as human resource and general managers). Analysis of variance in responses from each group indicated that the responses of these respondent groups did not significantly differ with regard to dominant stakeholder pressures, the implementation of environmental change initiatives and the success level of these change initiatives. However, environmental managers generally perceived a higher level of pressures from certain categories of critical environmental events (that is, regulatory requirements, waste reduction opportunities and external recognition). This study relies upon a single well-informed middle-management respondent from each facility, which is consistent with prior empirical research in environmental and operations management (Karagozoglu and Lindell, 2000; Klassen and Angell, 1998; Miller and Roth, 1994; Vickery et al., 1993). However, findings may be somewhat affected by the respondents' categorically different responses to some critical environmental events. Future research should explore the impact of these differences on the findings reported in this study.

Construct Measurement

Strategic formulation

The primary predictor constructs of interest, dominant stakeholder pressures and critical environmental events, were assessed using self-reported perceptual scales (Klassen and Angell, 1998; Miller and Roth, 1994; Vickery et al., 1993). Thus, a facility manager reported their perception of a compelling level (or potential level) of threat or opportunity from a dominant stakeholder, or from a recent critical environmental event necessitating action at the facility level of the organization. In general, factor analysis delineated the key scales relating to stakeholder and events drivers, then the average of the items loading strongly upon each factor was used in subsequent analysis.

A total of 17 items (Table 6.1) were drawn from the environmental management literature (Barry et al., 1993; Byrne and Deeb, 1993; Cordano, 1993; Eckel-Kächele, 1995; Girard and Perras, 1994; Gouldson, 1994; Hanna and Newman, 1995; Hass, 1996; Lawrence and Morell, 1995; Meffert and Kirchgeorg, 1994; Porter and van der Linde, 1995; Post and Altman, 1992; Starik, 1995; Stead and Stead, 1995) to measure the frequency of influence of various dominant stakeholders upon the respondent's environmental activities. Factor analysis (principle components) of these 17 items identified four significant factors (that is, eigenvalues > 1) that further expand upon the concept of 'dominant stakeholders' identified in the literature: public stakeholders (that is, federal and state regulators, community groups and environmental advocates); industry stakeholders (that is, consumers, suppliers, industrial customers and competitors); financial stakeholders (that is, lenders and investment analysts); and top management stakeholders (that is, board of directors and corporate management). These four factors retained 59.3 percent of the variation in the original items. Using a varimax rotation (the results did not change with an oblique rotation), four items loaded significantly on the first and second factors, while two items loaded significantly on each of the third and fourth factors. The resulting four 'stakeholder' scales, calculated by averaging the items loading heavily on each factor, reflect satisfactory Cronbach alpha coefficient values (Hair et al., 1995) as follows: public stakeholders (0.76), industry stakeholders (0.77), financial stakeholders (0.81) and top management stakeholders (0.62).

Table 6.1 List of survey items

Environmental Stakeholders:
Indicate the frequency with which you are influenced in your environmental decisions and activities by the environmental concerns of each of these groups:
Board of directors
Competitors
Consumers
Corporate management
Employees
Environmental advocates
Federal regulators
Industrial customers
Industry associations
Insurance companies
Investment analysts
Lenders
Media
Community groups
Shareholders
State regulators
Suppliers

Environmental Events:
During the last three years, our facility has undergone change because of the following factors:
The potential for reduced energy costs
Environmental innovations made by another industry player
Supplier's environmental requests or activities
Growing markets for waste by-products
Environmental award and recognition programs
The potential for improved yield (reduced scrap)
Environmental permitting requirements/procedures
Proposed new environmental legislation/regulations
The potential for reduced environmental regulatory oversight
Increasing opportunities to reuse materials and/or components
A customer's request for environmental information and/or improvements
Waste disposal and treatment costs
The threat of publicity over environmental violations
Opportunities for favorable media attention due to environmental activities
The changing cost and availability of raw materials and their substitutes

Environmental Events:
Our organization's environmental audits
Environmental audit conducted by a government agency
Recent publicized environmental accidents in the industry
Personnel changes in the environmental management area of the firm
The threat of civil or criminal penalties
Conditions of a regulatory/civil settlement
Adverse publicity from legal emissions/activities
Implementation of ISO 14000 or other environmental management systems
The development of our company's environmental philosophy/ethic

Environmental Change Initiatives
The following is a list of activities that may have occurred at your facility in response to environmental concerns. Indicate (1) the extent to which implementation of this activity has been attempted at your facility and (2) how successful you believe the implementation has been in the past three years:
Taking back used product from customers
Outsourcing component production
Changing end-of-pipe pollution controls
Redesigning production processes
Recycling waste materials internally
Conserving energy
Purchasing recycled materials
Selling additional waste materials
Redesigning existing products
Redesigning packaging
Changing facility location/layout
Conducting environmental audits
Conducting life cycle analyses
Modifying human resource management practices
Changing production schedules
Modifying quality management practices
Changing suppliers/vendors
Initiating supplier partnerships

Table 6.2 Descriptive statistics and correlation matrix

Variables	10	11	12	13	14	15	16	17	18	19	20	21	22
1 Successful initiatives													
2 Unsuccessful initiatives.													
3 Total initiatives													
4 Size (employees)													
5 Environmental department													
6 Environmental policy													
7 Foodstuff industry													
8 Apparel industry													
9 Printing & publication													
10 Rubber & plastic													
11 Primary metals	-0.15*												
12 Fabricated metals	-0.20*	-0.23*											
13 Machinery & computers	-0.14*	-0.16*	-0.21*										
14 Electronics	-0.14*	-0.15*	-0.20*	-0.14*									
15 Public stakeholders	-0.09*	0.13*	-0.10*	-0.03	0.09								
16 Industry stakeholders	-0.08	0.03	-0.08	0.03	0.05	0.46*							
17 Financial stakeholders	-0.04	0.09	-0.01	-0.04	0.03	0.38*	0.46*						
18 Top management	-0.07	0.10*	-0.06	0.05	-0.01	0.34	0.38*	0.34*					
19 Punitive events	-0.08	0.12*	-0.07	0.00	0.03	0.35*	0.27*	0.25*	0.21*				
20 Regulatory events	-0.14*	0.09*	-0.02	-0.02	0.05	0.39*	0.31*	0.18*	0.20*	0.53*			
21 Waste reduction opportunities	0.07	0.01	-0.19*	-0.04	-0.03	0.23*	0.26*	0.17*	0.19*	0.39*	0.37*		
22 External recognition	-0.08	0.03	-0.02	-0.05	0.09*	0.27*	0.34*	0.28*	0.22*	0.56*	0.45*	0.45*	
23 Industry development	-0.04	0.00	-0.01	-0.01	0.05	0.26*	0.44*	0.31*	0.21*	0.45*	0.44*	0.46*	0.48*

Note: *p < 0.05

It is very interesting to consider the five items dropped from further analysis because they did not clearly load primarily along any of the four significant stakeholder groups. The measure of pressures from 'employees', considered a key stakeholder group in the literature, loaded relatively evenly across the public, industry and management stakeholder factors. The measure of pressures from 'industry associations' loaded evenly across the stakeholder and industry factors. The measure of pressures from 'insurance companies' loaded fairly evenly across the public, industry and financial stakeholder groups. The 'media' pressures measure loaded evenly across the public and financial groups and shareholders loaded evenly across the financial and stakeholder groups. And finally, the 'shareholders' pressure measure represents another traditionally dominant stakeholder group loading relatively evenly across both the financial and management stakeholder groups.

Thus, while employees, industry associations, insurance companies, the media and shareholders are all likely to influence the extent and success of environmental change initiatives within this sample of manufacturing organizations, their loyalties are divided among several different stakeholder groups and therefore their impact on these initiatives may be diluted accordingly. For the purposes of this study, we focused on clearly defined stakeholder groups, although future research should further investigate the role of these five stakeholder categories upon environmental initiatives.

A total of 24 items (Table 6.1) were drawn from the literature (Byrne and Deeb, 1993; Girard and Perras, 1994; Gouldson, 1994; Hanna and Newman, 1995; Hart, 1995; Hass, 1996; Jose, 1995; Klein and Miller, 1993; Lawrence and Morell, 1995; Porter and van der Linde, 1995; Post and Altman, 1992; Schell, 1997; Starik, 1995; Stead and Stead, 1995) to measure the extent to which the development of critical environmental events had resulted in change within responding facilities over the preceding three years. Factor analysis (principle components) of these 24 items revealed five significant factors (that is, eigenvalues > 1), including punitive events, regulatory events, waste reduction opportunities, external recognition and industry events. Altogether, these five 'events' factors accounted for 57.2 percent of the total variation in the original items; six items were dropped from further analysis due to their unclear loadings on any of the key factors. The resulting five 'events driver' scales, calculated by averaging the items loading heavily on each factor, reflected satisfactory Cronbach alpha coefficient values (Hair et al., 1995) as follows: punitive events (0.85), regulatory events (0.80), waste reduction opportunities (0.70), external recognition (0.64) and industry events (0.73).

The five factors representing environmental 'event drivers' indicated considerable face validity. Six items loaded heavily upon the 'punitive events' factor including: adverse publicity from legal emissions or activities, the conditions of a regulatory or civil settlement, recent publicized environmental accidents in the industry, threats of publicity over violations, governmental audits and threats of civil or criminal penalties. The 'regulatory events' factor contained three items including: permitting requirements or procedures, proposed new legislation or regulations and the potential for reducing regulatory oversight. The factor for 'waste reduction opportunities' contained three items: growing markets for waste by-products, increasing opportunities to reuse materials or components and the potential for improved yield (that is, reduced scrap). Three items loaded on the 'external recognition' factor, including: award or recognition programs, implementation of ISO 14000 or another such environmental management system and opportunities for favorable media attention relating to environmental activities. Finally, the three-item 'industry developments' factor involved: a supplier's requests or activities, innovations made by another industry player and a customer's request for information or improvements.

Implementation of environmental change initiatives
The implementation of environmental change initiatives was assessed via three dependent variables: the total number of environmental change initiatives attempted, the number of successful implementations and the number of unsuccessful implementations. The survey listed a total of eighteen environmental initiatives drawn from the literature (Table 6.1) (Barry et al., 1993; Bowman, 1995; Byrne and Deeb, 1993; Gouldson, 1994; Hart, 1997; Klassen and Whybark, 1996; Lund, 1993; Shrivastava, 1995; Starik, 1995; Stead and Stead, 1995). Respondents indicated whether their facility had attempted the implementation of each of these initiatives during the past three years (1 = attempted and 0 = not attempted) and whether they perceived the implementation of these initiatives to have been successful (using a Likert-type scale with 1 = very unsuccessful and 7 = very successful).

Subsequent analysis attempted to predict the number of environmental change initiatives, the number of successful implementations and the number of unsuccessful implementations based upon the extent of stakeholder pressure and critical events development. The total number of environmental change initiatives is calculated simply as the sum of those indicated as attempted over the 18 items for each facility. The number of successful implementations was calculated by taking the sum of those initiatives indicated as attempted and successfully implemented (that is, rated a 5, 6 or 7 on the Likert-type scale). Conversely, the number of unsuccessful implementations was calculated by taking the sum of those initiatives indicated as attempted and unsuccessfully implemented (that is, rated a 1, 2 or 3 on the Likert-type scale).

Organizational context

Organizational characteristics and commitment are aspects of the facility's organizational context that may moderate the impact of dominant stakeholder pressures upon the implementation of environmental change initiatives. As such, the subsequent analysis controls for facility size, industry, the existence of a formal environmental department and the existence of a formal environmental policy.

Due to a skewed distribution, facility size is measured by the natural logarithmic transformation of the number of full-time equivalent (FTE) employees (Karagozoglu and Lindell, 2000; Klassen and Angell, 1998; Klassen and Whybark, 1999; Wiersema and Bantel, 1992). Murphy et al. (1995) found that larger facilities tend to be more environmentally active than smaller plants, possibly because of their greater self-awareness (Fombrun and Shanley, 1990) and consideration of stakeholders (Pfeffer, 1982). On the other hand, Tushman and Romanelli (1985) found that increased size can lead to increased resistance to change pressures, perhaps due to the attendant increase in organizational complexity (Quinn and Cameron, 1983).

Porter and van der Linde (1995) suggest that various industry sectors may respond differently to environmental action drivers. For example, Karagozoglu and Lindell (2000) argue that firms in 'traditional' manufacturing sectors may face relatively more complex and consuming environmental pressures than firms operating in newer, 'high-tech' industries, and therefore may have more experience in effectively dealing with these pressures. In order to explore the impact of industry membership on the relationship between action drivers and environmental change initiatives, this study developed a series of dummy variables using foodstuffs (SIC = 20) as the reference industry. As a result, seven dummy variables (1 = membership; 0 = non-membership) represent industry in the subsequent analysis: apparel, printing and publishing, rubber and plastic, primary metals, fabricated metals, machinery and computers and electronics (Karagozoglu and Lindell, 2000).

Research suggests that the existence of a formal environmental department and a formal environmental policy statement indicates organizational encouragement and support for environmental initiatives (Dillon and Fischer, 1992; Ramus and Steger, 2000). Previously, Henriques and Sadorsky (1995) found that heavy pressure from various stakeholder groups increased the likelihood of an organization's developing a formal environmental plan. This study, therefore, explores the impact of formal environmental departments and policies upon the relationship between the strategic formulation and implementation of environmental change initiatives. As such, the survey asked respondents to indicate the existence of a separate department for environmental issues within the facility (1 = yes; 0 = no), as well as the existence of a formal written environmental policy (1 = yes; 0 = no).

RESULTS

Table 6.2 presents the means, standard deviations, sample sizes and correlations among the variables. Not surprisingly, this matrix indicates high and significant correlations between the total initiatives undertaken and those that are considered successfully (0.70) and unsuccessfully (0.41) implemented. Generally, the frequency of successful implementations appears to be positively, significantly and moderately correlated with larger facilities, higher organizational commitment (that is, the existence of an environmental policy and department), pressure from industry stakeholders in particular and the full range of critical environmental events. Meanwhile, the frequency of unsuccessful implementations appears to be positively, significantly and mildly correlated with the primary metals industry, pressures from all of the various stakeholder groups and punitive environmental events in particular. The total number of initiatives attempted correlates significantly and positively with measures of facility organizational commitment and all of the various stakeholders and critical events, but negatively relates to firms in the rubber and plastics industry. Also, in line with our arguments in the literature review, Table 6.2 indicates that the various stakeholder groups and critical events categories are moderately, significantly and positively correlated with one another.

The research question focuses on the extent to which environmental stakeholders and critical events support and facilitate the implementation of environmental change initiatives. The following three sections further explore the impact of management drivers to action upon: (1) the total number of initiatives attempted, (2) the number of successfully implemented initiatives and (3) the number of unsuccessfully implemented initiatives.

Total Number of Initiatives Attempted

We test Hypotheses 1(1) and 2(1) by regressing the total number of initiatives attempted upon the control variables and the strategic formulation measures (Table 6.3), using separate regression equations for five models: (1) control variables only, (2) control and stakeholder variables, (3) control and events variables, (4) the full model, and (5) the adjusted full model containing only significant variables (Wiersema and Bantel, 1992).

In model 1, regressing the total number of initiatives attempted on the control variables (facility size, environmental department, environmental policy and industry) indicates that the existence of an environmental policy is highly significant and positively related to the total number of initiatives attempted. In addition, these results indicate that facilities operating in the rubber and plastic (SIC = 30) and machinery and computer (SIC = 35) indus-

Table 6.3 Regression analysis for total initiatives attempted[a]

Variables	Model 1 Control Variables	Model 2 Stakeholder variables	Model 3 Event Variables	Model 4 Full model	Model 5 Adjusted full model
Control variables					
Size (employees) [b]	-0.05	-0.03	-0.09*	-0.06	
Environmental department	0.07	0.05	0.07	0.05	
Environmental Policy	0.23***	0.21***	0.14***	0.16***	0.14***
Apparel	-0.05	-0.05	-0.01	-0.02	
Printing & publishing	-0.01	-0.01	0.00	0.00	
Rubber & plastic	-0.13**	-0.12**	-0.12**	-0.13**	-0.10**
Primary metals	-0.03	-0.04	-0.02	-0.02	
Fabricated metals	-0.07	-0.11	-0.01	-0.05	
Machinery & computers	-0.09*	-0.13**	-0.03	-0.08	
Electronics	-0.03	-0.05	-0.02	-0.02	
Potential drivers of change					
Public stakeholders		0.00		-0.06	
Industry stakeholders		0.18***		0.14**	0.17***
Financial stakeholders		0.03		0.00	
Top management stakeholders		0.07		0.04	
Punitive events			0.09	0.13**	0.12**
Regulatory events			0.04	0.01	
Waste reduction Opportunities			0.20***	0.19***	0.22***
External recognition			0.09	0.05	
Industry developments			0.04	-0.01	
Summary statistics					
R^2	0.07	0.14	0.18	0.20	0.19
Adjusted R^2	0.05	0.11	0.15	0.16	0.18
F statistic	3.72***	4.60***	6.44***	4.86***	20.79***
n	500	422	460	397	447

Notes:

[a]Values shown are the standardized regression coefficients
[b]Because of a skewed distribution, a natural logarithmic transformation was used for analysis

* $\rho <= 0.10$
** $\rho <= 0.05$
*** $\rho <= 0.01$

tries tend to attempt fewer environmental change initiatives than those facilities operating in the reference group (that is, the foodstuff industry, SIC = 20). However, model 1, although highly significant ($\rho < = 0.01$), only accounts for a small percentage of the variation in total number of initiatives attempted (adjusted $R^2 = 0.05$).

Regressing total initiatives attempted on the control and stakeholder variables in model 2 partially supports our hypothesis (H1(1)) that stakeholder pressures will lead to a higher number of environmental initiatives attempted. The significant control variables from model 1 remain significant, but also, pressure from industry stakeholders significantly and positively relates to the total number of initiatives attempted. The addition of the stakeholder pressure variables increases the explanatory power of the model (adjusted $R^2 = 0.11$).

Model 3, which considers the impact of both control and events variables, indicates that the development of waste reduction opportunities (as one category of critical events) strongly and positively relates to the total number of initiatives attempted. The effect of the control variables changes somewhat in the move from model 2 to model 3, in that the machinery and computer industry variable becomes insignificant while the size variable becomes marginally negatively significant. Overall, model 3 increases in explanatory power over models 1 and 2 (adjusted $R^2 = 0.15$).

Model 4, the full model including the control, stakeholder and events variables, provides some support for the hypotheses (H1(1), H2(1)) that stakeholder pressures and critical events together lead to an increase in the total number of environmental change initiatives attempted within a manufacturing facility. This model indicates that industry stakeholder pressures, punitive events and waste reduction opportunities all lead to a higher number of change initiatives. Furthermore, model 4 clarifies the role of the control variables (providing support for H3(1)), indicating that the existence of an environmental policy strongly supports attempted environmental initiatives, and that the rubber and plastics industry clearly engages in fewer change initiatives than the foodstuff industry. The full model explains 20 percent of the variance in the dependent measure (adjusted $R^2 = 0.16$). Model 5 is the adjusted full model including only the significant variables (adjusted $R^2 = 0.18$). The signs of the coefficients and the statistical significance levels are consistent across the models for all but three variables (machinery and computers industry, facility size and punitive events.

Table 6.4 Regression analysis for successful implementations[a]

Variables	Model 1 Control variables	Model 2 Stakeholder variables	Model 3 Event variables	Model 4 Full model	Model 5 Adjusted full model
Control variables					
Size (employees) [b]	0.00	0.03	-0.04	-0.02	
Environmental department	0.10**	0.11**	0.10**	0.11**	0.10**
Environmental policy	0.28***	0.27***	0.22***	0.25***	0.23***
Apparel	-0.07	-0.09*	-0.05	-0.06	
Printing & publishing	-0.05	-0.06	-0.07	-0.09	
Rubber & plastic	-0.13**	-0.13**	-0.13**	-0.15**	-0.12***
Primary metals	-0.14**	-0.14**	-0.12**	-0.12*	-0.09**
Fabricated metals	-0.11*	-0.16**	-0.07	-0.13*	-0.03
Machinery & computers	-0.12**	-0.15**	-0.05	-0.10*	-0.05
Electronics	-0.04	-0.06	-0.04	-0.06	
Potential drivers of change					
Public stakeholders		-0.07		-0.09	
Industry stakeholders		0.13**		0.08	
Financial stakeholders		-0.04		-0.06	
Top management stakeholders		0.02		-0.03	
Punitive events			-0.08	-0.05	
Regulatory events			0.06	0.04	
Waste reduction opportunities			0.18***	0.19***	0.23***
External recognition			0.05	0.05	
Industry developments			0.10*	0.09	
Summary statistics					
R^2	0.11	0.14	0.18	0.18	0.16
Adjusted R^2	0.10	0.11	0.15	0.14	0.15
F statistic	6.25***	4.55***	6.32***	4.45***	13.36***
n	500	422	460	397	496

Notes:

[a] Values shown are the standardized regression coefficients
[b] Because of a skewed distribution, a natural logarithmic transformation was used for analysis

* $\rho <= 0.10$

** $\rho <= 0.05$

*** $\rho <= 0.01$

Number of Successful Implementations

We use a similar progression of regression models to test Hypotheses 1(2), 2(2) and 3(2) (Table 6.4). Model 1 enters only the control variables. Results indicate that the existence of a facility-level environmental department and policy, both signs of organizational commitment to environmental programs, strongly influence the number of successful implementations in sampled manufacturing facilities. In addition, several industries (that is, rubber and plastic, primary metals, fabricated metals and machinery and computers) show a significant, negative impact upon the number of successful implementations when compared to the foodstuff industry. This preliminary model, although highly significant, only explains 11 percent of the total variation in the dependent variable (adjusted $R^2 = 0.10$).

Model 2, which evaluates the impact of stakeholder variables, suggests that increased pressure from supply chain stakeholders will lead to an increase in successful environmental change implementations. This model shows increased explanatory power over model 1, explaining 14 percent of total variation in successful implementations (adjusted $R^2 = 0.11$). However, model 3 clearly is the best predictive model for success, explaining 18 percent of variation (adjusted $R^2 = 0.15$). This model enters only the critical event variables to the control variables, and indicates that the development of waste reduction opportunities, and possibly critical events relating to industry players, drives an increase in successful change implementation. Models 4 and 5 further refine and clarify this finding, suggesting that some critical environmental events – namely the development of opportunities for waste reduction – strongly increases the likelihood of successful environmental change implementations. These findings generally do not support Hypothesis 1(2), but do provide some support for Hypothesis 2(2). H3(2) is also well supported, indicating the existence of some industry effects, and suggesting that organizational commitment increases the number of successful environmental change initiatives.

Number of Unsuccessful Implementations

Finally, results of regression analyses for Hypotheses 1(3), 2(3) and 3(3) are relatively weak, although highly significant (Table 6.5). Model 1 is only marginally significant, indicating only weak relationships between facility size and the primary metals industry and unsuccessful implementations. Focusing only on stakeholder variables, model 2 indicates marginal positive

Table 6.5 Regression analysis for unsuccessful implementations[a]

Variables	Model 1 Control variables	Model 2 Stakeholder variables	Model 3 Event variables	Model 4 Full model	Model 5 Adjusted full model
Control variables					
Size (employees) [b]	-0.08 *	-0.09 *	-0.09 *	-0.09	
Environmental department	0.01	-0.01	0.03	-0.01	
Environmental policy	-0.03	-0.05	-0.08	-0.07	
Apparel	0.07	0.10 *	0.10 **	0.12 **	0.08 *
Printing & publishing	0.06	0.09	0.10 *	0.14 **	0.08 *
Rubber & plastic	-0.08	-0.06	-0.06	-0.04	
Primary metals	0.10 *	0.08	0.09	0.09	
Fabricated metals	0.00	0.01	0.03	0.06	
Machinery & computers	-0.03	-0.03	-0.03	-0.01	
Electronics	-0.05	-0.05	-0.03	-0.01	
Potential drivers of change					
Public stakeholders		0.11 *		0.04	
Industry stakeholders		0.04		0.08	
Financial stakeholders		0.10 *		0.10 *	0.13 ***
Top management stakeholders		0.01		0.02	
Punitive events			0.19 ***	0.21 ***	0.19 ***
Regulatory events			0.03	0.03	
Waste reduction opportunities			0.07	0.05	
External recognition			0.00	-0.03	
Industry developments			-0.12 **	-0.17 ***	-0.14 ***
Summary statistics					
R^2	0.04	0.08	0.08	0.12	0.06
Adjusted R^2	0.02	0.05	0.05	0.08	0.05
F statistic	1.80 *	2.57 ***	2.55 ***	2.79 ***	5.75 ***
n	500	422	460	397	461

Notes

[a]Values shown are the standardized regression coefficients.
[b]Because of a skewed distribution, a natural logarithmic transformation was used for analysis

* $\rho <= 0.10$
** $\rho <= 0.05$
*** $\rho <= 0.01$

relationships between pressures from public and financial stakeholder groups and the number of unsuccessful environmental change initiatives in sample firms ($p < 0.01$). Model 3 has the same predictive power as model 2; both explain only eight percent of the variation in the number of unsuccessful implementations variable (adjusted $R^2 = 0.05$). This model suggests that increased punitive actions lead to more unsuccessful implementations while more industry-related events lead to fewer unsuccessful implementations. In addition, the apparel and printing and publishing industries both tend to have more unsuccessful implementations than the foodstuff industry, and larger firms may possibly experience fewer unsuccessful implementations.

The full regression model 4 appears to have the best predictive power of all the models, explaining only 12 percent of total variation in the dependent variable. This model suggests that unsuccessful environmental change implementations are more strongly driven by certain critical environmental events (that is, more punitive events and fewer industry-related events), as well as by certain industry effects (that is, apparel and printing and publishing industries are less successful than the foodstuff industry). H1(3) is clearly not supported by these findings; in fact, quite the opposite indications exist that increased pressure from financial stakeholders results in more unsuccessful environmental change initiatives. The results for H2(3) are mixed. While H2(3) is generally upheld for industry-related developments, the relationship is quite the opposite from that predicted when punitive critical events develop. H3(3) is only mildly supported; Table 6.5 indicates the existence of some marginal industry effects, but otherwise does not indicate that the organizational context significantly influences the relationship between stakeholder pressures, critical environmental events and the number of unsuccessful environmental initiatives within a manufacturing facility.

DISCUSSION

We initially proposed that management's perceptions of stakeholder pressure and the development of critical environmental events, coupled with the facility's organizational context, would support the implementation of successful environmental change initiatives in Pennsylvania's manufacturing facilities. Empirical analysis indicates, however, that the concepts of dominant stakeholder pressure and critical environmental events are more complex than originally conceptualized. The implementation and success level of environmental change initiatives depend upon the types of stakeholder pressures and critical event developments that facility managers face. Dominant stakeholders break down into several different groupings, including public, industry, finance and top management stakeholders. Facility managers perceive these stakeholder groupings to have categorically different levels of influence over environmental decisions, and to differ in terms of the significance of their impact upon the number of initiatives attempted and the relative success of these initiatives. Similarly, critical environmental events break down into categories such as punitive events (threats), regulatory events (threats), waste reduction opportunities, external recognition (opportunities) and industry developments (which can be seen as either threats or opportunities). Once again, findings indicate that the pattern of management response to these event groupings is similar within each category, and that these categories differ in terms of their impact on the number and success of environmental initiatives in manufacturing facilities.

We initially expected that facility organizational characteristics (that is, facility size and industry) and commitment (reflected by the existence of a formal environmental department and policy) would significantly influence the extent to which stakeholder pressures and critical event developments would affect change implementation in manufacturing facilities. The results did indicate the existence of some significant industry effects when comparing traditional manufacturing sectors against the more heavily regulated foodstuff industry. Generally, the foodstuff industry appears to be more likely to engage in successful environmental change (and less likely to engage in unsuccessful change) than the other industries surveyed. Surprisingly, however, our findings indicate across the board that facility size plays a very minor role (if any) in environmental change. This contradicts earlier findings in the environmental management literature (Aragón-Correa, 1998; Henriques and Sadorsky, 1995; Russo and Fouts, 1997; Sharma, 2000). Based on the results shown in Tables 6.2, 6.3 and 6.5, we suggest that the influence of various stakeholders and events which are correlated with the facility size variable, are better indicators of environmental change for the purposes of future research. Meanwhile, results clearly show that the existence of a formal environmental department and policy are both good indicators of the potential success of an environmental change initiative. In particular, a formal environmental policy seems important for encouraging increased attempts toward environmental change in manufacturing.

Hypothesis 1 argues that dominant stakeholders support environmental change, and the success of these change initiatives, in the sampled firms. However, findings indicate that only the industry stakeholder group (consumers, suppliers, industrial customers and competitors) motivates managers to attempt environmental change. Because managers may view these types of pressures as opportunities to strengthen their facility's relationship with strategic supply chain partners, they may be more likely to attempt voluntary initiatives than they would when facing pressures that they view as threats (Sharma, 2000). Table 6.4 (models 4 and 5) suggests that none of the stakeholder groups impact the likelihood of successful implementation of change initiatives, while Table 6.5 indicates that pressure from financial stakeholders (that is,, lenders and investment analysts) in particular can lead to more unsuccessful implementations. Pressures from financial stakeholders may be interpreted by managers as quite threatening to their organization. Dutton and Jackson (1987) suggest that managers respond to perceived threats by reducing the level of organizational participation and involvement in change programs. This response may undermine opportunities for successful implementation of the change initiative. To further clarify this finding, future research should investigate the types of environment-related pressures that financial stakeholders place upon manufacturing managers.

Hypothesis 2 suggests that the development of critical environmental events would also support environmental change, and the success of these change initiatives, in the sampled firms. However, findings show that neither regulatory events (that is,, permitting requirements, proposed legislation, potential to reduce regulatory oversight) nor external recognition (that is,, award programs, ISO14000, favorable media attention) influence the number or successful implementation of environmental initiatives in the sample facilities. This finding, along with the lack of significance of the 'public stakeholders' variable from H1, clearly contradicts earlier research, which suggested that regulations were the key drivers of environmental change levels (Andersson and Bateman, 2000; Bansal and Roth, 2000; Hart, 1997; Hass, 1996; Jaffe et al., 1995; Jose, 1995; Lawrence and Morell, 1995; Porter and van der Linde, 1995; Rugman and Verbeke, 1998). Instead, findings indicate that the development of punitive events and waste reduction opportunities both increased the number of total initiatives attempted in manufacturing facilities. Those initiatives deemed successfully implemented were driven by the development of waste reduction opportunities, while those deemed unsuccessfully implemented were driven by the development of punitive events. Meanwhile, although not necessarily increasing the number of successful innovations, industry developments (that is, supplier's and/or customer's requests, innovations made by other industry players) reduce the number of unsuccessful implementations in sampled manufacturing facilities. As suggested earlier, it appears that threatening critical events stand in the way of successful implementation, while critical events deemed as providing opportunity generally help with implementation (Dutton and Jackson, 1987).

More generally, the correlation analysis shown in Table 6.2 indicates that the successful implementation of environmental change relates primarily to the development of critical events, which Mitchell et al. (1987) suggest lends a sense of urgency to dominant stakeholder demands. Alternatively, this table suggests that unsuccessful implementations relate more to broad stakeholder pressures. According to Mitchell et al., this finding makes sense since stakeholder pressures with power and legitimacy, but without urgency, do not command dedicated and whole-hearted management attention. Meanwhile, the total number of initiatives attempted within an organization highly correlates to organizational commitment and both stakeholder pressures (that is, power, legitimacy) and critical event developments (that is, urgency). Thus, our conceptual model generally holds true, although future research will need to explore other relevant variables to help improve the predictive qualities of our preliminary models.

While this exploratory study was meant to provide only a preliminary analysis of the conceptual model, we must acknowledge some significant limitations. First, the target research population was limited to Pennsylvania manufacturing facilities in order to control for the complexity of external environmental pressures facing the surveyed organizations. Nor did we control for statewide variability in regulations and environmental conditions. Future research should attempt to confirm these findings at the local, national and/or even the international levels and possibly expand the scope of inquiry to the service sector. Other industry sectors should also be included in future analyses. Second, this study does not look at the environmental and business performance implications of environmental activity within the sampled organizations. Nor does it attempt to compare actual environmental pressures with management's perceptions of these pressures and the role of organizational context in this relationship. Third, the statistical models in this study do not explain more than 20 percent of the variation in environmental change initiatives reported by responding manufacturing facilities. Future research may examine the role of other dimensions of strategic formulation in determining environmental change. Fourth, we must acknowledge that not all stakeholders have been considered in this study (for example, nature may be included as a stakeholder in future research), and only relatively generic stakeholders were examined. Finally, this study relied on only one well-informed manager-level respondent in each surveyed facility. Future research should explore the differences in perceptions of external environmental pressures based on the respondent's job classification. In addition, future research should attempt a broader response base, perhaps longitudinally, in order to capture the various perspectives and the evolution of environmental change within these facilities.

In conclusion, this study explores the relationship between the strategic formulation and implementation of environmental change in Pennsylvania's manufacturing facilities. Findings suggest richer models of dominant stakeholder pressures and critical environmental events at the facility level of the firm, and generally confirm the conceptual framework outlined in Figure 6.1. Thus, the facility's organizational context modifies the relationship between management's perceptions of stakeholder pressures and critical environmental events, and environmental change within manufacturing facilities. A combination of some aspects of stakeholder and event pressures combine to increase the total number of environmental change initiatives attempted. Formal environmental policies, environmental departments and improved waste reduction opportunities increase the number of successful environmental change implementations in surveyed facilities. Alternatively, the threat of punitive events leads to a greater number of unsuccessful implementations within a firm.

ACKNOWLEDGEMENT

Many thanks to Sanjay Sharma and Mark Starik and to the anonymous reviewers of earlier versions of this study, for all of their helpful and constructive comments. Thanks also to Zsuzsanna Lonti, Qin Gao, Robert Klassen and Colin Campbell-Hunt for all of their insights and ideas during some very enlightening and helpful conversations.

REFERENCES

Andersson, L.M. and T.S. Bateman (2000), 'Individual environmental initiative: championing natural environmental issues in US business organizations,' *Academy of Management Journal*, **43**(4): 548–70.

Angell, L.C. (1996), 'Consumer products manufacturing and the German Packaging Ordinance,' unpublished dissertation, Boston University Graduate School of Management.

Aragón-Correa, J.A. (1998), 'Strategic proactivity and firm approach to the natural environment,' *Academy of Management Journal*, **41**(5): 556–67.

Bansal, P. and K. Roth (2000), 'Why companies go green: a model of ecological responsiveness,' *Academy of Management Journal*, **43**(4): 717–36.

Barry, J., G. Girard and C. Perras (1993), 'Logistics planning shifts into reverse,' *Journal of European Business*, **5**(1): 34–8.

Black, H. (1997), '"Green" manufacturing: one part at a time,' *Environmental Science and Technology*, **31**(2): 90–91A.

Bowman, R.J. (1995), 'Green logistics,' *Distribution*, **94**(6): 48–51.

Brown, R.L. and G.E. Fryxell (1995), 'Changes in toxic air releases and financial correlates: an empirical study of environmental strategies for the petroleum industry,' paper presented at the annual meeting of the Academy of Management, Vancouver.

Byrne, P.M. and A. Deeb (1993), 'Logistics must meet the "green" challenge,' *Transportation and Distribution*, **34**(2): 33–7.

Christmann, P. (2000), 'Effects of 'best practices' of environmental management on cost advantage: the role of complementary assets,' *Academy of Management Journal*, **43**(4): 663–80.

Clair, J.A., J. Milliman and I.I. Mitroff (1995), 'Clash or cooperation? Understanding environmental organizations and their relationship to business,' in D. Collins and

M. Starik (eds), *Research in Corporate Social Performance and Policy – Sustaining the Natural Environment: Empirical Studies on the Interface Between Nature and Organizations*, Greenwich, CT: JAI Press.

Clarkson, M.B.E. (1995), 'A stakeholder framework for analyzing and evaluating corporate social performance,' *Academy of Management Review*, **20**(1): 92–117.

Cordano, M. (1993), 'Making the natural connection: justifying investment in environmental innovation,' paper presented at the Annual Meetings of the International Association for Business and Society, San Diego, CA.

Dambach, B.F. and B.R. Allenby (1995), 'Implementing design for environment at AT&T: organizational and cultural changes,' paper presented at the Fourth International Conference of the Greening of Industry Network, Toronto.

Dillon, P.S. and K. Fischer (1992), *Environmental Management in Corporations: Methods and Motivations*, Medford, MA: Tufts University Center for Environmental Management.

Dutton, J. and R. Duncan (1987), 'The creation of momentum for change through the process of strategic issue diagnosis,' *Strategic Management Journal*, **8**(3): 279–96.

Dutton, J. and S.E. Jackson (1987), 'Categorizing strategic issues: links to organizational action,' *Academy of Management Review*, **12**(1): 76–90.

Eckel-Kächele, D. (1995), 'Environmental management systems and the European Union's eco-audit ordinance: an industry perspective,' paper presented at the annual meeting of the Academy of Management, Vancouver.

Egri, C.R. and S. Herman (2000), 'Leadership in the North American environmental sector: values, leadership styles, and contexts of environmental leaders and their organizations,' *Academy of Management Journal*, **43**(4): 571–604.

Fombrun, C. and M. Shanley (1990), 'What's in a name? Reputation building and corporate strategy,' *Academy of Management Journal*, **33**(2): 233–58.

Freeman, R.E. (1994), 'The politics of stakeholder theory: some future directions,' *Business Ethics Quarterly*, **4**(4): 409–21.

Gabel, H.L. and B. Sinclair-Desgagne (1994), 'From market failure to organisational failure,' *Business Strategy and the Environment*, **3**(2): 50–8.

Girard, G. and C. Perras (1994), 'Green supply chain management: from Europe to the US,' paper presented at the spring meeting of ORSA/TIMS, Boston.

Gouldson, A. (1994), 'Fine tuning the dinosaur? Environmental product innovation and strategic threat in the automotive industry: a case study of the Volkswagen Audi group,' *Business Strategy and the Environment*, **2**(3): 12–21.

Hair, J.F. Jr, R.E. Anderson, R.L. Tatham and W.C. Black (1995), *Multivariate Data Analysis*, 4th edn, Upper Saddle River, NJ: Prentice-Hall.

Halme, M. (1996), 'Shifting environmental management paradigms in two Finnish paper facilities: a broader view of institutional theory,' *Business Strategy and the Environment*, **4**: 94–105.

Hanna, M.D. and W.R. Newman (1995), 'Operations and environment: an expanded focus for TQM,' *International Journal of Quality and Reliability Management*, **12**(5): 38–53.

Hart, S.L. (1995), 'A natural-resource-based view of the firm,' *Academy of Management Review*, **20**(4): 986–1014.

Hart, S.L. (1997), 'Beyond greening: strategies for a sustainable world,' *Harvard Business Review*, **75**(1): 66–76.

Hass, J.L. (1996), '"Greening" the supply chain: a case study and the development of a conceptual model,' in J.P. Ulhoi and H. Madsen (eds), 'Industry and the environment: practical applications of environmental management approaches in business,' Aarhus School of Business, Denmark.

Henriques, I. and P. Sadorsky (1995), 'The determinants of firms that formulate environmental plans', in D. Collins and M. Starik (eds), *Research in Corporate Social Performance and Policy – Sustaining the Natural Environment: Empirical Studies on the Interface Between Nature and Organizations*, Greenwich, CT: JAI Press.

Henriques, I. and P. Sadorsky (1999), 'The relationship between environmental commitment and managerial perceptions of stakeholder importance,' *Academy of Management Journal*, **42**(1): 87–99.

Hoffman, A. (1999), 'Institutional evolution and change: environmentalism and the US chemical industry,' *Academy of Management Journal*, **42**(4): 351–71.

Hostager, T.J., T.C. Neil, R.L. Decker and R.D. Lorentz (1998), 'Seeing environmental opportunities: effects of entrepreneurial ability, efficacy, motivation, and desirability,' *Journal of Organizational Change Management*, **11**(1): 11–25.

Hunt, C.B. and E.R. Auster (1990), 'Proactive environmental management: avoiding the toxic trap,' *Sloan Management Review*, **31**(2): 7–19.

Jackson, S.E. and J.E. Dutton (1988), 'Discerning threats and opportunities,' *Administrative Science Quarterly*, **33**: 370–87.

Jaffe, A.B., S.R. Peterson, P.R. Portney and R.N. Stavins (1995), 'Environmental regulation and the competitiveness of US manufacturing: what does the evidence tell us?,' *Journal of Economic Literature*, **33**(1): 132–63.

Jose, P.D. (1995), 'Greening through strategic adaptation: a process study of selected firms from the Indian industry,' paper presented at the annual Greening of Industry conference, Toronto, Canada.

Karagozoglu, N. and M. Lindell (2000), 'Environmental management: testing the win-win model,' *Journal of Environmental Planning and Management*, **43**(6): 817–29.

Keogh, P.D. and M.J. Polonsky (1998), 'Environmental commitment: a basis for environmental entrepreneurship?,' *Journal of Organizational Change Management*, **11**(1): 38–49.

King, A.A. and M.J. Lenox (2000), 'Industry self-regulation without sanctions: the chemical industry's responsible care program,' *Academy of Management Journal*, **43**(4): 698–716.

Klassen, R.D. and L.C. Angell (1998), 'An international comparison of environmental management in operations: the impact of manufacturing flexibility in the US and Germany,' *Journal of Operations Management*, **16**(3): 177–94.

Klassen, R.D. and D.C. Whybark (1999), 'The impact of environmental technologies on manufacturing performance,' *Academy of Management Journal*, **42**(6): 599–615.

Klein, J.A. and J.G. Miller (1993), 'Balancing the debate,' in J.A. Klein and J.G. Miller (eds), *The American Edge: Leveraging Manufacturing's Hidden Assets*, New York: McGraw-Hill.

Lawrence, A.T. and D. Morell (1995), 'Leading edge environmental management: motivation, opportunity, resources, and processes,' in D. Collins and M. Starik (eds), *Research in Corporate Social Performance and Policy – Sustaining the Natural Environment: Empirical Studies on the Interface Between Nature and Organizations*, Greenwich, CT: JAI Press.

Lund, R.T. (1993), 'Remanufacturing,' in J.A. Klein and J.G. Miller (eds), *The American Edge: Leveraging Manufacturing's Hidden Assets*, New York: McGraw-Hill.

Magretta, J. (1997), 'Growth through global sustainability: an interview with Monsanto's CEO, Robert B. Shapiro,' *Harvard Business Review*, January/February: 79–88.

Meffert, H. and M. Kirchgeorg (1994), 'Market-oriented environmental management: challenges and opportunities for green marketing,' working paper #43, Institute for Marketing, Westfälischen Wilhems-Universität, Münster, Germany.

Miller, J.G. and A.V. Roth (1994), 'A taxonomy of manufacturing strategies,' *Management Science*, **40**(3): 285–304.

Mitchell, R.K., B.R. Agle and D.J. Wood (1997), 'Toward a theory of stakeholder identification and salience: defining the principle of who and what really counts,' *Academy of Management Review*, **22**(4): 853–86.

Moors, E.H.M., D.F. Mulder and P.J. Vergragt (1995), 'Transformation strategies towards more sustainable industrial production systems: a case study of the zinc production industry,' paper presented at the fourth international conference of the Greening of Industry Network, Toronto.

Murphy, P.R., R.F. Poist and C.D. Braunschweig (1995), 'Role and relevance of logistics to corporate environmentalism: an empirical assessment,' *International Journal of Physical Distribution and Logistics*, **25**(2): 5–19.

Murphy, P.R., R.F. Poist and C.D. Braunschweig (1996), 'Green logistics: comparative views of environmental progressives, moderates, and conservatives,' *Journal of Business Logistics*, **17**(1): 191–212.

Pennsylvania Manufacturers Register (1997), Evanston, IL: Manufacturers' News, Inc.

Pfeffer, J. (1982), *Organization and Organization Theory*, Boston, MA: Pitman.

Porter, M.E. and C. van der Linde (1995), 'Green and competitive: ending the stalemate,' *Harvard Business Review*, **73**(5b): 120–37.

Post, J.E. and B.W. Altman (1992), 'Models of corporate greening: How corporate social policy and organizational learning inform leading-edge environmental management', in J.E. Post and S.A. Waddock (eds), *Markets, Politics, and Social Performance: Research in Corporate Social Performance and Policy*, 13, Greenwich, CT: JAI Press.

Quinn, R.E. and K. Cameron (1983), 'Organizational life cycles and shifting criteria of effectiveness: some preliminary evidence,' *Management Science*, **29**(1): 33–50.

Ramus, C.A. and U. Steger (2000), 'The roles of supervisory support behaviors and environmental policy in employee "ecoinitiatives" at leading-edge European companies,' *Academy of Management Journal*, **43**(4): 605–26.

Rugman, A.M. and A. Verbeke (1998), 'Corporate strategy and international environmental policy,' *Journal of International Business Studies*, **29**(4): 819–34.

Russo, M.V. and P.A. Fouts (1997), 'A resource-based perspective on corporate environmental performance and profitability,' *Academy of Management Journal*, **40**(3): 534–60.

Sarkis, J. (1995), 'Supply chain management and environmentally conscious design and manufacturing,' *International Journal of Environmentally Conscious Design and Manufacturing*, **4**(2): 43–52.

Schell, D. (1997), 'The greening of Wilton Armetale: Pennsylvania's first environmentally friendly foundry offers model,' *International Environmental Systems Update*, **4**(3): 12–13.

Sharma, S. (2000), 'Managerial interpretations and organizational context as predictors of corporate choice of environmental strategy,' *Academy of Management Journal*, **43**(4): 681–97.

Sharma, S. and H. Vredenberg (1998), 'Proactive corporate environmental strategy and the development of competitively valuable organizational capabilities,' *Strategic Management Journal*, **19**: 729–53.

Shrivastava, P. (1995), 'The role of corporations in achieving ecological sustainability,' *Academy of Management Review*, **20**(4): 936–60.

Starik, M. (1995), 'Research on organizations and the natural environment: some paths we have traveled, the 'field' ahead,' in D. Collins and M. Starik (eds), *Research in Corporate Social Performance and Policy – Sustaining the Natural Environment: Empirical Studies on the Interface Between Nature and Organizations*, Greenwich, CT: JAI Press.

Stead, W.E. and J.G. Stead (1995), 'An empirical investigation of sustainability strategy implementation in industrial organizations,' in D. Collins and M. Starik (eds), *Research in Corporate Social Performance and Policy – Sustaining the Natural Environment: Empirical Studies on the Interface Between Nature and Organizations*, Greenwich, CT: JAI Press.

Swinth, R.L. and K.L. Vinton (1992), 'Strategies for environmental performance in small organizations: an international comparison,' *International Association of Business and Society Conference Papers*, Leuven, Belgium.

Taylor, G. and R. Welford (1993), 'An integrated systems approach to environmental management: a case study of IBM UK,' *Business Strategy and the Environment*, **2**(3): 1–11.

Tushman, M. and E. Romanelli (1985), 'Organizational evolution: a metamorphosis model of convergence and reorientation,' in L.L. Cummings and B.M. Staw (eds), *Research in Organizational Behavior*, **7**, Greenwich, CT: JAI Press.

Vickery, S.K., C. Droge and R.E. Markland (1993), 'Production competence and business strategy: do they affect business performance?,' *Decision Sciences*, **24**(2): 435–55.

Wehrmeyer, W. and K.T. Parker (1996), 'Identification and relevance of environmental corporate cultures as part of a coherent environmental policy,' in W. Wehrmeyer (ed.), *Greening People*, Sheffield: Greenleaf.

Wiersema, M.F. and K.A. Bantel (1992), 'Top management team demography and corporate strategic change,' *Academy of Management Journal*, **35**(1): 91–121.

Winn, M.I. (1996), 'A resource-based model of strategic factors affecting responses to mandated change: corporate responses to the German packaging law,' unpublished dissertation, University of California, Irvine.

Young, W. (1997), 'Greenhorn engineering: how to avoid environmental quicksand and other mistakes,' *American Ceramic Society Bulletin*, **76**(3): 57–63.

7. The altering of a firm's environmental management capability during the acquisition integration process

Kimberly M. Ellis, Mark Cordano and Bruce T. Lamont[1]

INTRODUCTION

Managers make several decisions during the acquisition process that influence the environmental performance of facilities operating within a newly combined firm. We used the literature on the process perspective of acquisitions and recent research on environmental strategy to identify five influences on environmental capabilities resulting from managerial activity during the acquisition integration process. These influences are the strategic importance of environmental capabilities, the timing of environmental capability evaluation, the integration strategy selected, the implementation speed and the programmability of the acquisition. We discuss applications of our propositions for managers and organizations as well as environmental management research.

The literature on organizations and the natural environment has grown dramatically during the 1990s (Starik and Marcus, 2000). Within this literature, researchers have often examined the development of environmental capabilities and how these capabilities are transferred across organizational boundaries and systems. For example, an ongoing stream of research has examined the external forces that have influenced, or pressured, firms to adopt environmental management systems and practices (Florida and Davidson, 2001; Henriques and Sadorsky, 1995; Stead and Stead, 1995). Researchers have also examined how practices and programs move across firms within an industry (Cebon, 1993) or are championed to the many facilities within large firms (Andersson and Bateman, 2000; Ramus and Steger, 2000; Winn, 1995). One set of boundaries yet to be considered by environmental management researchers involves those existing between firms engaged in acquisitions. Acquisitions create the need to penetrate boundaries that exist in each of the previous firms in order to effectively share as well as transfer environmental management capabilities and other critical resources between the two firms (Haspeslagh and Jemison, 1991). Researchers and managers need to understand how decisions made following acquisitions affect firm-level environmental capabilities and performance, given the increasing frequency of acquisition activity by large firms operating in industries that have significant impacts on environmental quality. We used the literature on the process perspective of acquisitions to consider how managerial decisions could affect the environmental capability for the newly combined firm. In doing so, we identified five variables pertaining to the integration stage of acquisitions that are likely to influence changes in the environmental capabilities of the combined firm.

An examination of the acquisition decision-making process is necessary due to the frequency of this type of business combination in industries that have significant environmental impacts. Table 7.1 provides a summary of the total number of acquisition transactions and the dollar value of these transactions in the United States from 1995 to 2000. It is important to note that there have been a large number of these transactions in the chemical, metal products, oil and gas, paper and pulp, and utilities industries. Therefore, Table 7.1 also summarizes the activity in these environmentally sensitive industries that have been traditionally cited by the Council on Economic Priorities (CEP) as 'dirty' industries due to their high levels of pollution. Among these transactions are well-known deals involving companies such as Crompton and Knowles/Uniroyal, Hercules/ BetzDearborn, Exxon/Mobil, BP Amoco/Atlantic Richfield, International Paper/Union Camp, Jefferson Smurfit/Stone Container, Duke Power/PanEnergy, and Consolidated Edison/Northeast Utilities. It is especially important to understand how a firm's environmental management capability changes during the acquisition integration process in these high polluting industries. The relationships we outline in this chapter establish a basis for researchers to investigate the impact of managerial decisions on environmental capabilities of the combined firm following acquisitions.

Increasingly, senior management has recognized the strategic value of environmental management capabilities within the context of mergers and acquisitions. For example, recently the CEO of Plum Creek Timber Company, the company resulting from the merger of Plum Creek and the Timber Company, identified the combined firm's expertise in forest, land and environmental management among the critical capabilities necessary to achieve synergies following their merger (PR Newswire, 15 August 2001).

Table 7.1 Acquisition activity

	Overall activity[a]		Activity in eco-sensitive industries[b]	
	Dollar value (billions)	Number of transactions	Dollar value (billions)	Number of transactions
1995	374.2	2543	42.3	327
1996	468.4	2973	86.5	422
1997	706.9	3843	90.1	475
1998	1187.8	3859	169.9	491
1999	1076.3	3121	200.4	415
2000	1098.6	2683	213.1	387

Notes: All data obtained from the SDC Mergers and Acquisitions database
[a] Includes only those acquisitions in which both the acquiring and target firm are headquartered in the US and the acquiring firm owns 100 percent interest after the transaction.
[b] Eco-sensitive industry sectors include chemicals and allied products; electric, gas and water distribution; electronic and electrical equipment; metal and metal products; mining; oil and gas; petroleum refining; paper and allied products; and rubber and plastic products

This recognition can be found in service-oriented firms too. Arthur D. Little, a leading international technology and consulting firm, acquired the Mountain View Technology division of ARCADIS Geraghty & Miller in order to enhance the combined firm's unique ability to provide their clients with 'state-of-the-art environment and technology knowledge to effect improved decisions for business and the environment' (PR Newswire, 27 January 2000).

We focused on the acquisition integration process for two reasons. The first reason involves the established industry practices for commercial real estate transactions in the United States. The potential liabilities resulting from acquiring contaminated real estate significantly expose firms within some industries, such as heavy manufacturing, and their lenders to financial risks associated with non-compliance with environmental related laws. To reduce the risk to all parties in these types of transactions, the American Society for Testing and Materials (ASTM) has formalized the due diligence process for assessing past and current environmental management activities involving commercial real estate transactions (see ASTM guidelines for the transaction screen process and environmental site assessment for commercial real estate). Consequently, some aspects of managerial decision-making throughout the courtship stage of an acquisition are rather standardized.

However, the success of the integration stage depends entirely on the actions, and often, experience of the environmental, health and safety managers. Our second reason comes from the corporate strategy literature pertaining to the process perspective of acquisitions. Recent analyses of post acquisition performance point to the management of the integration process as the factor most critical to realizing intended benefits of the deal (Booz Allen & Hamilton, 2001; KPMG, 1999). Organization and natural environment researchers have yet to examine the unique ecological issues raised by acquisitions and how the management of the integration process can influence changes in the combined firm's environmental capability and performance following an acquisition.

We combined the recent findings within the literature on the process perspective of acquisitions with the research on environmental strategy and capability. The environmental strategy and capability literature highlights the role of knowledge-based resources as a base for ecologically proactive behavior ultimately leading to higher firm performance (Christmann, 2000; Hart, 1995; Russo and Fouts, 1997; Sharma and Vredenburg, 1998). The acquisition literature we examined identifies factors that are likely to promote or negate the effective transfer of knowledge resources between firms during and after an acquisition (Haspeslagh and Jemison, 1991; Jemison and Sitkin, 1986; Marks and Mirvis, 1998; Ranft, 1997). Using these two literatures, we identified five potential influences on the environmental management capabilities of a newly combined firm. These determinants include the strategic importance of environmental capabilities, the timing of environmental capability evaluation, the integration strategy selected, the implementation speed and the programmability of the acquisition. Based on the environmental literature, we defined environmental management capability as the collection of resources, technologies and competencies that a firm possesses to respond to issues of environmental importance. Following the acquisition literature, we view the acquisition process as three chronological stages necessary to facilitate the combination of two previously separate firms into a wholly functioning single entity. These are the courtship, integration and completion stages, with special emphasis placed on the second stage.

DEVELOPMENT OF PROPOSITIONS

Environmental Capabilities and Strategies

Companies engage in mergers and acquisition for a variety of reasons. Among the most common motives are the following: (1) to reduce risk and/or tax liabilities, (2) to increase market share and/or power, (3) to achieve economies of scale and/or scope, (4) to enter new geographic and/or product markets, and (5) to enhance skills and knowledge through the sharing, combining or transferring of resources (Trautwein, 1990; Walter and Barney, 1990). The last motive serves as the focus of this chapter and several recent acquisition studies. According to Haspeslagh and Jemison (1991) value-creating acquisitions are characterized by the transfer of strategically important capabilities that improve the acquiring firm's competitive position. In addition, Ranft (1997) outlined the importance of transferring as well as preserving knowledge during the integration stage of acquisitions in the high-tech industry, in order to create long-term value. More recently, Capron (1999) provided additional support that the transfer of strategically important resources, knowledge and capabilities improves both the market coverage and innovation capability of the combined firm. Collectively, these studies suggest that when firms successfully transfer and redeploy resources and capabilities, considered critical to their ability to improve competitive advantage, they create long-term value following the acquisition.

One such strategic capability, especially for firms operating in eco-sensitive industries, is the firm's environmental management capability. The resource-based view of the firm (Barney, 1991; Wernerfelt, 1984) serves as a theoretical lens through which the relationship between a firm's resources and know-how relative to the natural environment and its ability to gain advantages in the market place can be examined. Building on this theoretical perspective, several researchers have developed typologies of environmental management strategies that explain how environmental management competence can be an important component of a firm's strategic repertoire yielding competitive advantages and superior financial performance (Hart, 1995, 1997; Shrivastava, 1995). These initial typologies were built primarily on anecdotal evidence. However, some recent studies have examined whether first-mover advantages associated with adopting proactive environmental strategies result in competitive advantages. Focusing on different industries and varying measures of competitive advantage, Nehrt (1996) found that paper pulp manufacturers making early environmental investments experienced higher levels of profit growth. Christmann (1997) reported that firms in the chemicals industry experienced significant cost and differentiation advantages resulting from the early implementation of environmental strategies with high levels of 'green' competencies. Using a sample of firms from the Canadian oil and gas industry, Sharma and Vredenburg (1998) also demonstrated that proactive environmental strategies can result in unique organizational capabilities that generate various competitive benefits.

Collectively, recent research from the strategic management perspective suggests that environmental management skills, technologies, capabilities and know-how represent important tangible and intangible firm-specific assets (Christmann, 1997, 2000; King and Lenox, 2000; Klassen and McLaughlin, 1996; Nehrt, 1996; Sharma, 2000; Sharma and Vredenburg, 1998). Drawing on the resource-based view of the firm (Barney, 1991; Wernerfelt, 1984), these studies provide evidence explaining how environmental management competence, to the extent that it is valuable, rare, non-substitutable, inimitable and exploited, can be a strategic tool for realizing various types of competitive advantages that eventually lead to superior financial perform- ance. Additionally, emerging evidence supports the fact that proactive environmental strategies further the advancement of not only knowledge- based environmental management competencies that are valuable and rare, but also facilitate the development of other unique organizational capabilities that are often casually ambiguous, difficult to imitate and path-dependent, thus providing sustainable competitive advantages (Sharma and Vredenburg, 1998). As a result, there is a critical need for managers not only to consider the firm's environmental management capability to be of strategic importance, but also to address issues relative to the firm's environmental performance early on in decision-making processes.

Strategic Importance Attached to the Acquired Firm's Environmental Management Capability by the Acquiring Firm

The growing stream of research in environmental management using the resource-based view of the firm highlights the strategic importance of a firm's environmental management capability (Hart, 1995, 1997; Christmann, 2000). Recent evidence suggests that environmental management capabilities and know-how can serve as the basis for cost and revenue advantages that can lead to sustainable competitive advantages and superior financial perform- ance (Christmann, 2000; Sharma and Vredenburg, 1998). Similarly, researchers examining how the ability of firms to share and transfer resources and capabilities affects post-acquisition performance levels have also utilized concepts from the resource-based view of the firm (Capron, 1999; Haspeslagh and Jemison, 1991; Ranft, 1997). Collectively, these studies provide evidence that firms are able to successfully transfer and leverage strategic resources and capabilities that facilitate their ability to create long-term value.

Building on studies in both the acquisitions and environmental management literature, the strategic importance that the acquiring firm attaches to the environmental capabilities and know-how of the acquired firm is likely to influence the extent of changes in environmental management competence within the acquiring firm (Hart, 1995; Haspeslagh and Jemison,

1991). If the acquired firm's environmental capabilities and know-how are considered strategic assets, then these resources will be preserved and transferred in order to improve competitive advantages and create long-term value in the acquiring firm. On the other hand, if environmental capabilities are not viewed as being a potential source of competitive advantage, then few attempts will be made to transfer such skills and capabilities to the acquiring firm. What's more, the environmental capabilities of the acquired firm are likely to be neglected by the acquiring firm, permitting them to atrophy. Consistent with the ideas in this research, we propose that:

> Proposition 1: The more strategic importance attached to an acquired firm's environmental capabilities by the acquiring firm, the greater is the likelihood of enhancing the environmental management capability of the combined firm.

Timing of Consideration by the Acquiring Firm

As stated earlier, acquisitions often provide firms with the opportunity to obtain assets and resources that can improve competitive advantage and ultimately long-term performance. In such acquisitions, these strategic resources, capabilities and knowledge must be identified at the onset of the acquisition decision-making process because of the critical role their transfer plays in the success of the transaction (Mirvis and Marks, 1992). In addition, because managerial attention is often diverted from normal business operations during the combination process, identifying critical resources and know-how at the beginning of the integration stage is likely to place more emphasis on such core competencies, thereby facilitating their effective transfer and enhancement. For example, North States Power and New Century Energies indicated their commitment to continuing and enhancing environmental initiatives at the very beginning of their merger integration efforts (PR Newswire, 17 August 2000). In addition, Environmental Resources Management (ERM) reported that two chemical companies sought their services, before the deal closed, in developing a comprehensive plan to integrate their individual environmental management systems in such a way that maximized the combined firm's competence (Liebs, 1999).

Timing is also important within the context of implementing environmental management practices. For example, Christmann (1997) reports that early timing along with high existing levels of environmental actions generates cost and differentiation advantages, thereby increasing the overall competitiveness of firms in the chemical industry. Moreover, Nehrt (1996) utilizes the concept of first-mover advantages in finding a positive relationship between the early timing of environmental investments and profit growth that ultimately enhances firm competitiveness. In addition, Nehrt (1996), building on the work of Dierickx and Cool (1989), suggests that the late consideration and implementation of environmental actions can lead to disruptions in internal production processes due to time compression diseconomies.

The earlier the acquiring firm assesses the acquired firm's environmental practices and strategies during the integration process, the greater the likelihood that the combined firm's environmental management competence will be enhanced. However, if the assessment of the acquired firm's environmental management resources and capabilities occurs toward the end of the integration stage, it is possible that late attempts to transfer such capabilities could have detrimental effects, thus resulting in deterioration of the combined firm's environmental management competence. Based on this research regarding the timing of consideration, we propose:

Proposition 2: The earlier that environmental capabilities are considered by the acquiring firm, the greater is the likelihood of enhancing the environmental management capability of the combined firm.

Process Perspective of Acquisitions

Mergers and acquisitions remain one of the most popular strategic choices for obtaining capabilities and knowledge despite recent reports that one-half to two-thirds of these deals fail to realize the intended benefits (Booz Allen & Hamilton, 2001; KPMG, 1999). Research based primarily on three issues of fit, strategic fit (Lubatkin, 1987; Singh and Montgomery, 1987), cultural fit (Chatterjee et al., 1992; Weber, 1996) and organizational fit (Datta, 1991; Datta et al., 1991), has produced equivocal results about post-acquisition performance levels. Thus, in an effort to better understand factors that influence whether these transactions are value-creating or value-destroying, scholars have highlighted the need to explore the entire acquisition decision-making process (Haspeslagh and Jemison, 1991; Jemison and Sitkin, 1986; Marks and Mirvis, 1998).

The seminal works of Kitching (1967), Jemison and Sitkin (1986) and Shrivastava (1986) provide the basis for the process perspective of mergers and acquisitions. Building on these works and evidence from extensive case studies, several researchers have classified the acquisition process into three stages labeled, in chronological order, courtship, integration and completion (Haspeslagh and Jemison, 1991; Marks and Mirvis, 1998; Mirvis and Marks, 1992). The courtship stage typically involves the identification and evaluation of potential partners along with the negotiation and due diligence review. The integration stage generally consists of those managerial activities necessary to combine the operations of the two firms. This typically includes transition management teams responsible for the assessment of organizational issues such as the structure of the combined firm, top management composition and responsibilities, culture compatibility and human relation practices. Finally, the completion stage usually entails a review of performance indicators of the combined firm to determine if intended benefits were realized following the conclusion of the integration efforts.

Research examining acquisitions using this three-stage classification points to the management of the integration stage as key to achieving post-acquisition success (Booz Allen & Hamilton, 2001; KPMG, 1999). It is during this stage that critical decisions are made that affect the combined firm's ability to share strategic resources, to transfer dynamic capabilities and to establish the foundation for other activities necessary to reap the intended benefits from the acquisition. There are several activities that are managed during the integration stage that are likely to have substantial impacts on management's ability to combine the operations of the two previous firms. Management decisions, if done well, can minimize potential disruptions and uncertainties thereby increasing the potential to realize synergistic benefits and other performance improvements. Among these are the integration approach chosen (Haspeslagh and Jemison, 1991; Mirvis and Marks, 1992), the speed of carrying out implementation plans (Jemison and Sitkin, 1986; Ranft, 1997) and the programmability of integration efforts that results from prior acquisition experience (Amburgey and Miner, 1992; Eisenhardt and Brown, 1998; Haleblian and Finkelstein, 1999).

Integration Approaches

The approach used to combine the firms' operations into a functioning whole has a major impact on the level of disruption and extent of change in both firms during an acquisition (Buono and Bowditch, 1989). Likewise, the choice of integration approach influences the ability to share, combine and transfer resources and capabilities between the two firms (Haspeslagh and Jemison, 1991; Mirvis and Marks, 1992). Haspeslagh and Jemison (1991) identify three basic approaches to acquisition integration labeled preservation, absorption and symbiotic. These approaches differ along two primary dimensions, the autonomy needed in the acquired firm and the degree of strategic interdependence of the two firms. The preservation approach allows the acquired firm to continue to operate as it did before the acquisition. This often occurs when there are low levels of strategic interdependence between the firms. This high level of autonomy given to the acquired company results in few changes in the existing resources of both firms. On the other hand, the absorption approach, characterized by high strategic interdependence between the firms, but low levels of autonomy for the acquired firm, often involves the acquired firm having to conform to the practices of, and completely assimilate into the culture of, the acquiring firm. As a result, this integration approach is likely to create the highest levels of resistance to change and disruptions during the integration stage. This often inhibits efforts to transfer resources and capabilities between the firms. Finally, the symbiotic approach necessitates high autonomy of the acquired firm and high interdependence between the two firms. This integration approach, which involves initial preservation and gradual permeability of organizational boundaries, focuses on identifying the strengths of each firm and then creating a combined firm comprised of an integration of the 'best' capabilities and practices. Moreover, this integration approach is expected to facilitate the identification and transfer of strategic resources and know-how between the firms. Applying these findings to a firm's environmental management activities, we propose:

Proposition 3: The more symbiotic the integration approach, the greater the likelihood of enhancing the environmental management capability of the combined firm.

Implementation Speed

Implementation speed, or pacing, is a critical factor affecting the ability to share and transfer capabilities since organizational transitions such as acquisitions often require major changes in a firm's management practices as well as decision-making processes (Jemison and Sitkin, 1986). While there is some belief that short implementation periods are necessary to rapidly achieve synergies and institute changes in the acquired firm, other research suggests that escalating momentum can cause acquiring managers to reach quick, premature conclusions that lead to disruptive changes, thus lowering the chances of successfully transferring strategic resources and capabilities (Jemison and Sitkin, 1986; Shrivastava, 1986). More recent research suggests that excessively long integration periods can prolong the 'post-merger drift' period that is characterized by high employee uncertainty and the diversion of management attention from regular business operations toward integrating the firms (Buono and Bowditch, 1989; Mirvis and Marks, 1992). The declines in individual productivity and organizational performance during this period can have detrimental effects on the sharing and transferring of capabilities between firms. Comparing these two extreme views of implementation speed, Schweiger et al. (1993) argued that the integration process should move in a purposeful fashion as firms learn more about each other while being careful not to make changes too quickly nor prolong them unnecessarily, especially as it relates to large mergers and acquisitions.

This recent research suggests that there should be a period of time immediately after a deal closes where no efforts are made to consolidate operations or transfer strategic resources. This waiting period at the beginning of the integration process allows the firms to gain a mutual understanding of each other's operations and capabilities. This wait facilitates acquisition decision-making as well as the preservation and eventual transfer of knowledge-based resources between the firms (Haspeslagh and Jemison, 1991; Ranft, 1997). Based on the reasoning in this research, we propose a non-linear relationship between acquisition implementation speed and changes in environmental management capabilities.

> Proposition 4: Moderate implementation speed will have a greater likeli-
> hood of enhancing the environmental management capability of the com-
> bined firm than slow or quick implementation speeds.

Programmability by the Acquiring Firm

The extent to which acquiring firms have prior experience with acquisitions of the same type also influences the ability to successfully transfer strategic capabilities and resources. Building on theories of organizational routine and managerial cognition, Amburgey and Miner (1992) find evidence that prior experience with a particular type of merger significantly enhanced the probability of engaging in the same type of merger again. The authors further contend that such repetitive momentum could lead to positive performance results as experience accumulates. In a related study, Haleblian and Finkelstein (1999) incorporated concepts from behavioral learning theory to further examine the ability of managers to use prior experience in determining how the organization should proceed during an acquisition. Their findings indicated that managers involved in acquisitions within the same industry are able to apply prior experience and make decisions more likely to enhance post-acquisition performance. In a similar analysis, using the 180-day transition process utilized by Banc One as an example, Eisenhardt and Brown (1998) found that programmability resulting from prior experience led to the establishment of standard, clearly understood transition processes that improved acquisition decision-making, facilitated interface management and enhanced the transfer of best practices between the firms. These outcomes of programmability are all critical to the successful sharing of strategic capabilities between firms during the integration stage. These studies suggest that prior experience with similar acquisitions facilitates the acquiring firm's ability to make the decisions critical to successfully integrating the operations and capabilities of the two firms. Based on this research, we propose that:

Proposition 5: The greater the programmability by the acquiring firm with similar types of acquisitions, the greater the likelihood of enhancing the environmental management capability of the combined firm.

Our primary objective for this analysis is to take an initial step in identifying factors likely to influence whether the environmental management capability of the combined firm is enhanced during the acquisition decision-making process, focusing on the integration stage. In doing so, we have offered some propositions based on the literature in the areas of environmental management strategies and the acquisition integration process. Figure 7.1 summarizes the proposed relationships outlined above.

Implications for Research and Practice

The propositions we outlined can be measured and tested with a variety of methodologies. Some of the constructs in the propositions have been measured in previous research such as timing of consideration, implementation speed and integration approach. The remaining independent variables, strategic importance and programmability, along with the dependent variable, environmental capability, might present new challenges for empirical analyses. An adequate testing of the propositions will require primary data. However, the benefits of such data appear to justify the effort, given the growing prevalence of large acquisitions in highly polluting industries.

Future research examining the degree to which a firm's environmental management competence is altered during the acquisition decision-making process could benefit from the inclusion of potential moderating variables. An important variable would be the environmental management strategy adopted by the combined firm (Hart, 1995; King and Lenox, 2000) and the relative mix of resources, technologies and competencies that make up the firm's environmental management capabilities. For example, if a firm's environmental management capabilities are derived primarily from competencies that are deeply embedded in the routines and processes of the acquired firm then the task of transferring these capabilities to the acquiring firm is much more complex, thus making it likely that the combined firm's capability will remain virtually unaltered (Haspeslagh and Jemison, 1991; Ranft, 1997). Moreover, differences between top managers of the two previous firms, in terms of behavioral preferences, pertaining to environmental management (Cordano and Frieze, 2000) and interpretations of environmental issues (Sharma, 2000)

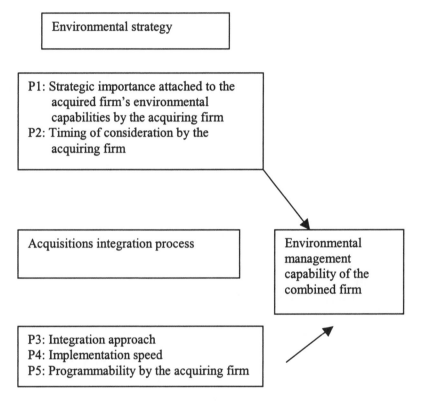

Figure 7.1 Factors influencing changes in environmental management capability during the acquisition, integration stage.

could also moderate the relationships we have proposed. From an organizational level, the degree of fit between the two firms with regard to corporate culture for environmental leadership and compensation systems that reward environmental goals (Sharma and Vredenburg, 1998) may affect the combined firm's environmental management capability following an acquisition. If both firms possess norms and values that encourage environmental leadership, then it is likely that the combined firm's environmental management capability will be enhanced during the acquisition process.

The propositions outlined in this chapter have significant practical implications as well as research applications given the level of acquisition activity in industries where environmental management capability plays a critical role in developing sustainable competitive advantages. Our analysis establishes a groundwork for integrating and applying the growing body of work focused on both environmental management strategy and the acquisition integration process. Findings based on this research should assist managers to make effective decisions during acquisitions. Our hope is to increase the ability of managers to make decisions that lead to the enhancement of environmental management capabilities in highly polluting industries. The due diligence process not only highlights potential liabilities that can kill or alter a deal but also generates information that can help plan the success of the integration of the environmental management systems across the combined organizations. Managers operating in eco-sensitive industries may benefit from identifying environmental management capability as a key objective that should be addressed during the initial stages of the acquisition integration stage. This responsibility, which goes beyond just conducting a due diligence review of potential environmental related liabilities, could be assigned to an integration team and/or the corporate environmental management staff of the combined firm. Finally, from a public policy perspective, our analysis highlights the need for environmental groups, and other external stakeholders, to voice concern during any permit review processes to ensure that issues pertaining to the combined firm's environmental management practices are addressed.

Mergers and acquisitions have long been examined in terms of how they affect two primary stakeholder groups: stockholders (Lubatkin, 1987) and employees (Buono and Bowditch, 1988; Schweiger and DeNisi, 1991). More recent studies have also explored the effect of these business combinations on customers (Baer, 1996; Werden, 1996) and suppliers (Anderson, 2001; Nolan, 1999). Researchers have ignored how acquisitions influence a firm's environmental strategy and performance. Acquisitions are important because a firm's environmental management capability can be changed dramatically following an integration of two firms. It is vital that these critical knowledge-based resources and capabilities are effectively integrated to capitalize on the best environmental capabilities between the two previously separate firms. With the increasing popularity of acquisitions and escalating importance of sustaining our natural environment, our analysis offers researchers and managers some initial guidelines to examine and manage the challenging and stressful decisions during acquisitions so as to enhance the success and environmental performance of large firms in industries that produce significant negative impacts on the natural environment.

NOTE

1. An earlier version of this chapter was presented at 2000 Academy of Management Annual Meeting through the Organizations and Natural Environment (ONE) Interest Group and included in the Conference Best Papers Proceedings.

REFERENCES

American Society for Testing and Materials (2000), *ASTM Standards on environmental site assessments for commercial real estate*. West Conshohoken, PA: ASTM.

Amburgey, T.L. and A.S. Miner (1992), 'Strategic momentum: the effects of repetitive, positional and contextual momentum on merger activity,' *Strategic Management Journal*, **13**: 335–48.

Anderson, H. (2001), 'Can you buy a business relationship? On the importance of customer and supplier relationships in acquisitions,' *Industrial Marketing Management*, **30**: 575–86.

Andersson, L.M. and T.S. Bateman (2000), 'Individual environment initiative: championing natural environmental issues in US business organizations,' *Academy of Management Journal*, **43**(4): 548–70.

Barney, J.B. (1991), 'Firm resources and sustained competitive advantage (the resource-based model of the firm: origins, implications and prospects),' *Journal of Management*, **17**: 99–120.

Baer, W.J. (1996), 'Surf's up: antitrust enforcement and consumer interests in a merger wave,' *Journal of Consumer Affairs*, **30**: 292–321.

Booz Allen & Hamilton (2001), *Merger Integration – Delivering on the Promise*, July., McLean, VA.

Buono, A.F. and J.L. Bowditch (1989), *The Human Side of Acquisitions*, San Francisco, CA: Jossey-Bass.

Capron, L. (1999), 'The long-term performance of horizontal acquisitions,' *Strategic Management Journal*, **20**: 987–1018.

Cebon, P.B. (1993), 'The myth of best practices: the context dependence of two high-performing waste reduction programs,' in J. Schot and K. Fischer (eds), *Environmental strategies for industry: International perspectives on research needs and policy implications*, Washington, DC: Island Press.

Chatterjee, S., M. Lubatkin, D. Schweiger and Y. Weber (1992), 'Cultural differences and shareholder value in related mergers: linking equity and human capital,' *Strategic Management Journal*, **13**: 319–34.

Christmann, P. (1997), 'Environmental strategies of multinational companies: determinants and effects on competitive advantage,' Unpublished doctoral dissertation, University of California at Los Angeles.

Christmann, P. (2000), 'The effects of "best practices" of environmental management on cost advantage: the role of complementary assets,' *Academy of Management Journal*, **43**: 663–80.

Cordano, M. and I.H. Frieze (2000), 'Pollution reduction preferences of US environmental managers: applying Ajzen's theory of planned behavior,' *Academy of Management Journal*, **43**: 627–41.

Datta, D.K. (1991), 'Organizational fit and acquisition performance: effects of post-acquisition integration,' *Strategic Management Journal*, **12**: 281–97.

Datta, D.K., J.H. Grant and N. Rapagopolan (1991), 'Management incompatibility and postacquisition autonomy: effects on acquisition performance,' in P. Shrivastava (ed.), *Advances in Strategic Management*, 7.

Dierickx, I. and K. Cool (1989), 'Asset stock accumulation and sustainability of competitive advantage,' *Management Science*, **35**: 1504–12.

Eisenhardt, K.M. and S.L. Brown (1998), 'Time pacing: competing in markets that won't stand still,' *Harvard Business Review*, **76**(1): 59–69.

Florida, R. and D. Davison (2001), 'Gaining from green management: environmental management systems inside and outside the factory,' *California Management Review*, **43**(3): 64–84.

Haleblian, J. and S. Finkelstein (1999), 'The influence of organizational acquisition experience on acquisition performance: a behavioral learning perspective,' *Administrative Science Quarterly*, **44**: 29–56.

Hart, S.L. (1995), 'A natural-resource-based view of the firm,' *Academy of Management Review*, **20**: 996–1014.

Hart, S.L. (1997), 'Beyond greening: strategies for a sustainable world,' *Harvard Business Review*, **75**(1): 66–76.

Haspeslagh, P.C. and D.B. Jemison (1991), *Managing Acquisitions: Creating Value Through Corporate Renewal*, New York: Free Press.

Henriques and Sadorsky (1995),'The determinants of firms that formulate environmental plans,' in D. Collins and M. Starik (eds), *Research in Corporate Social Performance and Policy*, Greenwich, CT: JAI Press.

Jemison, D.B. and S.B. Sitkin (1986), 'Corporate acquisitions: a process perspective,' *Academy of Management Review*, **11**: 145–63.

King, A. and M. Lenox (2000), 'Does it really pay to be green? Accounting for strategy selection in the relationship between environmental and financial performance,' presented at the Academy of Management, Annual Meetings, Toronto, Canada.

Kitching, J. (1967), 'Why do mergers miscarry?,' *Harvard Business Review*, **45**(6): 84–101.

Klassen, R.D. and C.P. McLaughlin (1996), 'The impact of environmental management on firm performance,' *Management Science*, **42**: 1199–214.

KPMG (1999), 'Unlocking shareholder value: the keys to success,' *Mergers and acquisitions: A global research report*, November.

Leibs, A. (1999), 'Environmental resources plants M&A,' *Mergers and Acquisitions Report*, 17 May.

Lubatkin, M. (1987), 'Merger strategies and stockholder value,' *Strategic Management Journal*, **8**: 39–53.

Marks, M.L. and P.H. Mirvis (1998), *Joining Forces: Making One Plus One Equal Three in Mergers, Acquisitions, and Alliances*, San Francisco: Jossey-Bass.

Mirvis, P.H. and M.L. Marks (1992), *Managing the Merger: Making it Work*, Paramus, NJ: Prentice-Hall.

Nehrt, C. (1996), 'Timing and intensity effects of environmental investments,' *Strategic Management Journal*, **17**: 535–47.

Nolan, A. (1999), 'Mergers?: Quick silver,' *Supply Management*, **4**: 22–6.

PR Newswire (2000), 'Arthur D. Little acquires Mountain View Technology division of ARCADIS/Geraghty & Miller; Combined businesses provide comprehensive technical expertise for energy and transportation industries,' 27 January, Cambridge, MA.

PR Newswire (2000), 'Xcel Energy, Inc. born as merger receives final approval from SEC; Stock trading to begin Aug. 21,' 17 August, Minneapolis, MN and Denver, CO.

PR Newswire (2001), 'Shareholders of Georgia-Pacific and Plum Creek approve timberlands merger,' 15 August, Atlanta, GA.

Ranft, A. (1997), 'Preserving and transferring knowledge-based resources during post-acquisition implementation,' Unpublished doctoral dissertation, University of North Carolina at Chapel Hill.

Ramus, C.A. and U. Steger (2000), 'The roles of supervisory support behaviors and environmental policy in employee "Ecoinitiatives" at leading-edge European companies,' *Academy of Management Journal*, **43**(4): 605–26.

Russo, M.V. and Fouts, P.A. (1997), 'A resource-based perspective on corporate environmental performance and profitability,' *Academy of Management Journal*, **40**: 534–59.

Schweiger D.M., E.N. Csiszar and N.K. Napier (1993), 'Implementing international acquisitions,' *Human Resource Planning*, **16**: 53–70.

Schweiger, D.M. and A.S. DeNisi (1991), 'Communication with employees following a merger: a longitudinal field experiment,' *Academy of Management Journal*, **34**: 110–35.

Sharma, S. (2000), 'Managerial interpretations and organizational context as predictors of corporate choice of environmental strategy,' *Academy of Management Journal*, **43**: 681–97.

Sharma, S. and H. Vredenburg (1998), 'Proactive corporate environmental strategy and the development of competitively valuable organizational capabilities,' *Strategic Management Journal*, **19**: 729–53.

Shrivastava, P. (1986), 'Postmerger integration,' *Journal of Business Strategy*, **7**: 65–76.

Shrivastava, P. (1995), 'Environmental technologies and competitive advantage,' *Strategic Management Journal*, **16**(Summer): 183–200.

Singh, H. and C. Montgomery (1987), 'Corporate acquisition strategies and economic performance,' *Strategic Management Journal*, **8**: 377–86.

Starik, M. and A.A. Marcus (2000), 'Introduction to the special research forum on the management of organizations in the natural environment: a field emerging from multiple paths, with many challenges ahead,' *Academy of Management Journal*, **43**(4): 539–47.

Stead, W.E. and J.G. Stead (1995), 'An empirical investigation of sustainability strategy implementation in industrial organizations,' in D. Collins and M. Starik (eds), *Research in Corporate Social Performance and Policy*, Greenwich, CT: JAI Press.

Trautwein, F. (1990), 'Merger motives and merger prescriptions,' *Strategic Management Journal*, **11**: 283–95.

Walter, G.A. and J.A. Barney (1990), 'Management objectives in acquisitions,' *Strategic Management Journal*, **11**: 79–86.

Weber, Y. (1996), 'Corporate cultural fit and performance in acquisitions,' *Human Relations*, **49**: 1181–202.

Werden, G.J. (1996), 'A robust test for consumer welfare enhancing mergers among sellers of differentiated products,' *Journal of Industrial Economics*, **44**: 409–13.

Wernerfelt, B. (1984), 'A resource-based view of the firm,' *Strategic Management Journal*, **5**: 171–80.

Winn, M.I. (1995), 'Corporate leadership and policies for the natural environment,' in D. Collins and M. Starik (eds), *Research in Corporate Social Performance and Policy*, Greenwich, CT: JAI Press.

8. Strategic environmental human resources management and organizational performance: an exploratory study of the Canadian manufacturing sector

Carolyn P. Egri and Robert C. Hornal

INTRODUCTION

This study of 37 Canadian manufacturing organizations found that a strategic environmental human resource management systems approach (inclusion of environmental objectives and criteria in HRM practices) and environmental proactivity enhances perceptions of organizational performance. The influence of organizational contextual factors (organization size, labor unions) and organizational differentiation (specialized environmental units) on environmental proactivity and organizational benefits of environmental management practices was also investigated. Implications of these findings for future environmental management research and practice are developed.

Regulatory demands, stakeholder forces, consumers, shareholders, cost factors and competitive requirements are among the many forces driving proactive environmental management systems that integrate environmental principles, values and objectives into corporate strategies, cultures and operations (Aragón-Correa, 1998; Berry and Rondinelli, 1998; Frankel, 1998; Gibson, 2000; Hart, 1995; Henriques and Sadorsky, 1999; Hoffman, 2001). To perform on this increasingly important strategic dimension, proactive firms are going beyond simple compliance with regulatory demands to optimize material and energy resource use and reduce their ecological impact (Aragón-Correa, 1998; Russo and Fouts, 1997; Sharma, 2000).

An open systems approach is useful to understand how proactive environmental management contributes to both ecological sustainability and organizational prosperity. Starik and Rands's (1995) multi-system framework identifies the need for ecologically sustainable relationships within and between individual, organizational, political-economic, social-cultural and ecological levels. Thus, ecologically sustainable organizations (ESOs) integrate environmental sustainability objectives in corporate policy statements and business strategies, technological systems (for example, product and process life-cycle analysis and environmental performance improvement programs), administrative systems (environmental audits, environmental cost accounting, evaluation of suppliers' environmental practices and environmental reporting to external stakeholders) and human resource systems (identified positions responsible for environmental issues, and employee environmental awareness and skills training) (Berry and Rondinelli, 1998; Dechant and Altman, 1994; Hart, 1995; Klassen and Whybark, 1999; Lawrence and Morell, 1995; Montabon et al., 2000; Post and Altman, 1992; Russo and Fouts, 1997; Shrivastava, 1995a, 1996; Starik and Rands, 1995). In total, proactive environmental management systems are inclusive and actively engender high employee, supplier and customer involvement and commitment to continuous environmental improvement.

Previous research has found that these environmental management best practices enhance an organization's competitive advantage in numerous ways. Environmental proactivity has been found to reduce production costs (Aragón-Correa, 1998; Christmann, 2000; Hart and Ahuja, 1996; Klassen and Whybark, 1999; Russo and Fouts, 1997; Sharma and Vredenburg, 1998; Willig, 1994; Zhang et al., 1997), regulatory compliance costs (Berry and Rondinelli, 1998; Klassen, 1993; Montabon et al., 2000; Sharma and Vredenburg, 1998) and capital and insurance costs (Anderson, 1999; Gluck et al., 2000; Schmidheiny and Zorraquin, 1996). Other organizational benefits include enhanced market opportunities (Menon et al., 1999; Montabon et al., 2000; Polonsky and Mintu-Wimsatt, 1995), improved shareholder and investor relations (Brill et al., 2000; White, 1995) and higher employee morale and motivation to perform pro-environmental behaviors (Bansal and Roth, 2000; Berry and Rondinelli, 1998; Dechant and Altman, 1994; Ramus and Steger, 2000; Shrivastava, 1996).

In this study, we were particularly interested in Starik and Rands's (1995) propositions concerning organizations' ecological relationships with individuals. Specifically, Starik and Rands (1995: 920) proposed that 'ESOs will include ecological sustainability considerations and criteria in job design, recruitment and selection and training and development systems' and that ESOs have reward systems that promote sustainability-oriented innovation. Our review of the literature revealed that incorporating environmental objectives and criteria in human resource management (HRM) practices is often viewed as critical means to environmental management program success in achieving corporate environmental goals and objectives (Callenbach et al., 1993; Dechant and Altman, 1994; Milliman and Clair, 1996; Russo and

Fouts, 1997; Wehrmeyer, 1996). While a number of environmental HRM best practices have been identified, we found that current knowledge is primarily based on case study and anecdotal evidence. We also found a general lack of empirical research that had taken a strategic human resource management system perspective (Bamberger and Meshoulam, 2000; Lundy and Cowling, 1996) to investigate the potential synergistic benefits of incorporating environmental considerations into all HRM practices such as employee recruitment and selection, job objectives, training and development, performance appraisal, compensation and rewards. In addition, there have been very few empirical studies (Ramus and Steger, 2000; Wehrmeyer, 1996) that examined the relationship between the adoption of a variety of environmental human resource management (EHRM) practices and their impact on organizational performance. One purpose of our study was to address this gap in the literature about the role and contribution of HRM practices in environmental management systems. Specifically, we were interested in the extent to which organizations had incorporated environmental considerations into various HRM practices and had developed strategic environmental human resource management (SEHRM) systems. We were also interested in investigating whether (and if so, how) EHRM practices contributed to organizational performance. In addition, we were interested in learning whether organizational contextual factors (organization size and the presence of labor unions) and the creation of specialized units and roles (an environmental issues unit or department and green teams or task forces) were related to EHRM practice implementation and their impact on organizational outcomes.

For this study, we surveyed a cross-section of Canadian manufacturing organizations to learn about their environmental management systems and HRM practices. We focused on the manufacturing sector given the ecological impacts of product and process manufacturing operations in respect to material and energy resource consumption, pollutant emissions, waste disposal, recycling and product delivery systems (Hart, 1995; Sarkis, 1995; Shrivastava, 1995b; Zhang et al., 1997).

The remainder of this chapter is structured as follows. First, we review the literature and develop hypotheses concerning EHRM practices. We then present the research methods used in this study, followed by the results of our analyses. And finally, we discuss the major findings of this study and their implications for environmental and human resource management theories and practice, as well as identify the limitations of this study and directions for future research.

LITERATURE REVIEW AND HYPOTHESES

The importance of human resource management for successful environmental management system implementation has often been identified (Callenbach et al., 1993; Dechant and Altman, 1994; Milliman and Clair, 1996; Shrivastava, 1996; Starik and Rands, 1995; Wehrmeyer, 1996). The strategic human resource management (SHRM) perspective proposes that systems of HRM practices that are internally consistent (have high internal fit) and are congruent with the firm's overall business strategy (have high external fit) have greater influence on organizational performance than fragmented HRM systems or individual practices (Bamberger and Meshoulam, 2000; Lundy and Cowling, 1996; Youndt et al., 1996). Research has found that the synergistic benefits of an integrative SHRM system are realized when the complete spectrum of HRM practices are aligned not only with each other but also with the goals and objectives of the organization (Arthur, 1994; Delaney and Huselid, 1996; Huselid, 1995).

The SHRM perspective suggests that an effective SEHRM system would incorporate an organization's environmental strategy and objectives into all human resource practices (recruitment and selection, job objectives, training and development, performance appraisal, compensation and rewards). However, as Wehrmeyer (1996) concluded in his review of current HRM practices and environmental management, there is considerable need for modifications to employee recruitment and selection procedures, training programs and reward and recognition programs to take environmental considerations into account. Our review of the research literature revealed that current knowledge about EHRM policies and practices and environmental management success is primarily based on case study evidence (Dechant and Altman, 1994; Lawrence and Morell, 1995; Milliman and Clair, 1996; Shrivastava, 1996). In the majority of empirical studies on environmental management, only a few EHRM practices have been included as a subsidiary focus of investigation. One empirical study that approached a SEHRM system perspective was conducted by Ramus and Steger (2000) who investigated influences on employee environmental initiative. In the remainder of this section, we provide a summary of what is currently known about EHRM practices that would constitute a SEHRM system.

Recruitment and Selection

In a SEHRM system, employee recruitment and selection criteria would include environmental knowledge and skills as well as environmental leadership abilities (Wehrmeyer, 1996). Identifying and attracting candidates who are environmentally concerned would also be a priority. For environmentally proactive organizations this would be an easier task given that organizations' environmental reputation and performance have been found to be important factors in the recruitment and retention of employees (Charter, 1992; Taillieu and Mooren, 1990).

Job Design

In environmentally proactive organizations, responsibility for environmental activities are explicitly identified and written into job descriptions (Starik and Rands, 1995). Employee environmental initiatives have been found to be positively related to managers' sharing of responsibility for achieving corporate environmental objectives (Ramus and Steger, 2000).

Training and Development

One critical facet of EHRM systems is environmental issues training and development to enhance the environmental awareness and competencies of all employees for improved environmental performance (Dechant and Altman, 1994; Milliman and Clair, 1996; Starik and Rands, 1995; Wehrmeyer, 1996). Extensive environmental awareness training raises the salience of environmental issues and the legitimacy of environmentally proactive attitudes and behaviors (Bansal and Roth, 2000; Sharma, 2000) including employee environmental initiatives (Ramus and Steger, 2000).

Employee Performance Appraisal

In an EHRM system, the scope of performance appraisals is extended to include an evaluation of employees' attainment of environmental goals and objectives (Dechant and Altman, 1994). To be effective, environmental performance criteria and goals need to be specific, clear and measurable (Ramus and Steger, 2000), directly linked to the organization's environmental objectives and integrated with other employee performance objectives (Flannery et al., 1996). A systems approach prescribes that employee performance is evaluated on both objective and subjective, specific and holistic, as well as short-term and long-term criteria (Sharma, 2000). However, the practice of environmentally-oriented performance appraisals appears to be underdeveloped with individual performance evaluations not often being included in environmental management systems (Montabon et al., 2000). Although the management of environmental goals and responsibilities has been found to be positively related to employee environmental initiatives (Ramus and Steger, 2000), the inclusion of environmental performance criteria in employee evaluation systems was found to be unrelated to environmental strategy (Sharma, 2000).

Rewards and Compensation

Effective organizational reward systems establish appropriate and specific behavior-reward linkages and provide meaningful, achievable and timely rewards (Agarwal, 1998; Wilson, 1995). An effective environmental reward program would have a diversity of monetary and non-monetary incentives to reflect the high variability in employee motivations and types of contribution (individual, group and organizational). It would also be integrated and consistent with other facets of an organization's reward system (Callenbach et al., 1993; Dechant and Altman, 1994; Flannery et al., 1996).

In contrast to other EHRM practices, there has been considerably more empirical research on the incidence and impact of environmental rewards. Milliman and Clair (1996) reported that organizations use both monetary and recognition rewards to motivate environmental performance and that these incentives are used primarily for managers rather than lower-level employees. Lawrence and Morell (1995) found that environmentally leading-edge chemical companies were more likely to have awards and cash prizes as well as verbal praise to reward managers' environmental accomplishments and that these led to more resource conservation efforts. Ramus and Steger (2000) found that managers' use of rewards and recognition (formal, monetary and informal) was positively related to employee environmental initiatives.

Recent surveys have found that environmental performance was a component of senior management compensation in 38 percent to 60 percent of organizations (Frankel, 1998). However, these surveys did not provide information regarding the forms of compensation for environmental performance nor the incidence for lower-level managers and non-managerial employees. Although skill- or competency-based and variable pay systems have been found to yield positive performance outcomes (Agarwal, 1998; Murray and Gerhart, 1998; Wilson, 1995), there is a lack of empirical research on the use of these compensation systems for motivating environmental performance.

Three critical success factors of environmental recognition reward systems are visibility, diversity and integration (Milliman and Clair, 1996). A wide variety of non-monetary employee recognition rewards for environmental performance have been identified, such as award presentations at highly visible company meetings; team, site or company celebrations; publishing employee achievements in corporate media; giving tokens of appreciation; and providing environmental developmental and decision-making opportunities (for example, training, teams, taskforces, projects) (Callenbach et al., 1993; Milliman and Clair, 1996; Schonberger, 1994).

Summary
As shown in this literature review, there is a lack of empirical research that has taken an integrative strategic approach to investigating the incidence and impact of EHRM practices. In this study, we propose that an effective strategic environmental human resource management (SEHRM) system selects and promotes employees on the basis of their environmental knowledge, skills and leadership abilities; formally identifies environmental job responsibilities; provides education and training that engender environmentally proactive attitudes, skills and behaviors; uses specific and measurable environmental performance criteria and goals in employee performance appraisals; and recognizes and rewards employee environmental contributions and achievements on individual, group and organizational levels (Callenbach et al., 1993; Dechant and Altman, 1994; Flannery et al., 1996; Milliman and Clair, 1996; Ramus and Steger, 2000; Starik and Rands, 1995; Wehrmeyer, 1996).

The SHRM perspective suggests that the adoption of environmental considerations in all facets of a HRM system (high internal consistency) would facilitate the achievement of corporate environmental performance objectives (Bamberger and Meshoulam, 2000; Delaney and Huselid, 1996; Lundy and Cowling, 1996). In addition, a systems perspective suggests that the implementation of EHRM practices throughout an organization (for example, affecting all types of employees) would engender a common focus and commitment to enhancing corporate environmental performance (Russo and Fouts, 1997; Klassen and Whybark, 1999; Montabon et al., 2000; Post and Altman, 1992; Starik and Rands, 1995; Shrivastava, 1995a). Thus, one critical aspect of SEHRM systems is the degree of diffusion of EHRM practices within an organization's human resource system.

Hypothesis 1: Diffusion of EHRM practices will be positively related to the perceived organizational benefits of environmental management practices.

The influence of organizational context

Organization size
Resource dependency theory suggests that larger organizations would have more resources to initiate new environmental programs and may be more motivated to initiate such strategies due to their greater public visibility. Due to greater economies of scale, larger organizations are more likely to have

centralized HRM departments with more developed HRM practices such as formal training and education programs (Saari et al., 1988). The early adoption of administrative innovations in HRM has also been found to be positively related to organization size (Johns, 1993). The majority of studies have found organization size to be positively related to the adoption of proactive environmental management strategies (Montabon et al., 2000; Russo and Fouts, 1997; Sharma, 2000), therefore our hypotheses regarding organization size, environmental proactivity and EHRM diffusion are as follows:

> Hypothesis 2(1): Organization size will be positively related to environmental proactivity.
> Hypothesis 2(2): Organization size will be positively related to the diffusion of EHRM practices.

Environmental organization units

Several authors have advocated the establishment of specialized environmental organization units to provide environmental research support and advice to other parts of the organization (Berry and Rondinelli, 1998; Klassen and Whybark, 1999; Shrivastava, 1996). However, Starik and Rands (1995) were cautious about the benefits of specialized organizational units and roles for environmental responsibility and viewed such organizational differentiation as impeding the diffusion of environmental responsibility, expertise and action throughout an organization. To date, there has been relatively little empirical research on specialized environmental units and previous research has yielded contradictory findings (Henriques and Sadorsky, 1995; Lawrence and Morell, 1995). Even so, environmental organization units should be more prevalent in proactive organizations with extensive environmental management programs that require centralized coordination. Further, the presence of specialized environmental expertise should facilitate the acquisition of knowledge about both environmental technological and administrative innovations and their implementation. Thus, we propose the following hypotheses regarding presence of environmental organization units, environmental proactivity, EHRM diffusion and the organizational benefits of environmental management practices:

> Hypothesis 3(1): The presence of an environmental organization unit will be positively related to environmental proactivity.
> Hypothesis 3(2): The presence of an environmental organization unit will be positively related to the diffusion of EHRM practices.

Hypothesis 3(3): The presence of an environmental organization unit will be positively related to the organizational benefits of environmental management practices.

Labor unions

Historically, improving environmental quality, industrial safety and worker health have been central concerns of labor union movements (Gottlieb, 1993; McElrath, 1988; Yandle, 1985). Although there have been conflicts between labor and environmentalists, especially in natural resource-based industries (Buttel et al., 1992), labor unions have also taken an environmental advocacy role with regulatory agencies and environmental groups (Work and Environment Initiative, 1997). For example, labor unions have collaborated on joint labor–management environmental committees (Cohen-Rosenthal, n.d.) and multi-stakeholder initiatives to develop environmental legislation (Obach, 1999; Schrecker, 1993). Labor unions' support of ecological sustainability objectives suggests that organizations with unionized work-forces would have additional institutional support for their environmental management programs. While collective agreements may affect the scope and type of HRM practices and reward systems, the presence of a labor union should be associated with environmental proactivity and EHRM diffusion as well as be beneficial for environmental initiatives:

Hypothesis 4(1): The presence of a labor union will be positively related to environmental proactivity.
Hypothesis 4(2): The presence of a labor union will be positively related to the diffusion of EHRM practices.
Hypothesis 4(3): The presence of a labor union will be positively related to the organizational benefits of environmental management practices.

In summary, we expect that the diffusion of EHRM practices will be positively related to the perceived organizational benefits of environmental management practices. In addition, we expect that organizations that are larger and those that have environmental organization units and labor unions will be more environmentally proactive and have greater diffusion of EHRM practices. Further, we expect that the presence of environmental units and labor unions will have a positive impact on the perceived organizational benefits of environmental management programs. The empirical model that is tested in this study is presented in Figure 8.1.

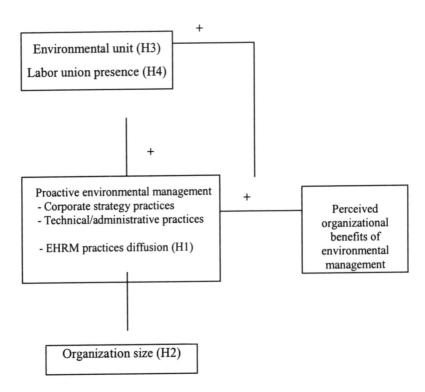

Figure 8.1 Empirical model of perceived organizational performance benefits of environmental management

RESEARCH METHODS

Sample

The sampling frame for this study was all medium-sized and large (over 250 employees) Ontario manufacturing companies listed in the Canadian Business Information database (Canadian Business Information, 1999). The province of Ontario was chosen as a target area because it has the largest and most diverse set of manufacturing firms in Canada. Small companies (less than 250 employees) were excluded from the sampling frame given observations that small companies typically lacked the resources to adopt environmental management policies and practices that go beyond regulatory compliance (Frankel, 1998; Sharma and Vredenburg, 1998).

Each company in the sampling frame was contacted by telephone to obtain the names of potential respondents who would be knowledgeable about HRM and/or environmental management practices. Of the 264 companies listed in the CBI database, 26 were eliminated because of inaccurate mailing addresses or duplicate companies in the database. A total of 238 organizations were mailed the seven-page questionnaire with an accompanying cover letter and a self-addressed, stamped return envelope. Four weeks after the initial mail-out, A postcard reminder was mailed out. A total of 41 questionnaires were received for a 17 percent response rate. Although lower than desired, this response rate is comparable to that obtained in other academic studies that involved mailed survey questionnaires to organizational representatives (Baruch, 1999; Montabon et al., 2000). Three questionnaires were excluded from the study because the respondent had indicated that their organization had fewer than 250 employees. One more questionnaire was unusable because the firm was no longer manufacturing in Canada. As a result, there were 37 manufacturing organizations in the final sample for this study.

Organizations

A wide cross-section of 11 manufacturing industries were represented in the final sample: chemical and allied products (5 percent), electronic and other electrical equipment (5 percent), fabricated metal products (11 percent), food and kindred products (11 percent), industrial and commercial machinery (3 percent), paper and allied products (11 percent), primary metals (14 percent), printing, publishing and allied industries (11 percent), textile mill products (3 percent), transportation (16 percent) and 'other' (11 percent). The seven remaining Standard Industrial Classification (SIC) industry groups that did not respond to the survey were: apparel and other finished products; lumber and wood products except furniture; furniture and fixtures; measuring and analyzing instruments; stone, clay, glass and concrete products; and tobacco products. However, it should be noted that the manufacturing industries that are represented in the sample constituted 91 percent of the total number of organizations that were sent questionnaires. As such, this study's sample could be regarded as representative of organizations in the Ontario manufacturing sector.

In regards to organization size, 32 percent of responding companies had over 1000 employees, 41 percent had 500–999 employees and 27 percent had 250–499 employees. The majority of organizations (70 percent) had unionized workforces and 48 percent of these organizations reported that at least half of their employees were labor union members. The large majority (84 percent) of these manufacturing organizations had a department or unit specifically designated to handle environmental issues.

Respondents
The majority (73 percent) of respondents held environmental positions within their organizations, while the remaining 27 percent of respondents held HRM positions. For the total sample, 24 percent of respondents were executives, 33 percent were managers and 43 percent were in professional or technical positions. This was a relatively well-educated group with 65 percent of respondents having university degrees and 27 percent having college diplomas. The most common area of studies was engineering (28 percent), followed by environmental sciences (19 percent), business administration (19 percent), sciences (17 percent) and arts (14 percent). The average age of respondents was 42 years (s.d. = 10.3) and 63 percent of respondents were male.

Data and Measures

Strategic environmental HRM
Respondents were asked about their organization's use of six EHRM practices: (1) recruitment or selection criteria of environmental knowledge, skills or leadership abilities, (2) environmental objectives in job descriptions, (3) environmental awareness training, (4) environmental performance criteria in regular performance appraisals, (5) financial rewards based on the company's environmental performance, and (6) recognition rewards for employee contributions towards improved environmental performance. For each EHRM practice, respondents indicated whether their organization's CEO, senior environmental executive, other senior executives, plant managers, other managers, other salaried employees and wage employees were affected by each practice. An additional question using the same format asked about the use of variable pay in their organizations.

This question format can be viewed as an organizational gap analysis of EHRM practices. An EHRM diffusion matrix can be constructed to show which employee groups are affected by each practice, as well as which practices are more developed (used with more employee groups) within an organization. This response matrix yields three measures of EHRM practice within an organization. 'Employee group EHRM breadth' (the sum of different EHRM practices; minimum = 0, maximum = 6) indicates the degree of internal consistency of EHRM practices for a particular employee group in an organization. 'EHRM practice depth' (total number of affected organizational levels: CEO, executives, managers, salaried employees, wage employees; minimum = 0, maximum = 5) indicates the prevalence of a particular environmental HRM practice within an organization. The 'EHRM diffusion' summary score was the average number of organizational levels affected by the six EHRM practices.

To investigate the use of environment-related rewards, respondents were asked whether their company used any of six types of recognition rewards for environmental contributions and if so, to evaluate the usefulness of those rewards (using a seven-point Likert-type scale). Respondents were also asked whether their organization had skill- or competency-based compensation systems, employee teams to work on environmental issues or projects and, if so, whether these teams received financial rewards linked to environmental performance. An open-ended question asked respondents to describe the nature of union involvement in improving environmental performance.

Respondents also assessed (on a seven-point Likert-type scale) the effectiveness of their organization's overall reward system in motivating individuals to perform environmental tasks; motivating innovation to improve environmental performance; and motivating employee teamwork to work for environmental performance. These three questionnaire items formed a 'reward system effectiveness' scale ($\alpha = 0.94$).

Environmental proactivity
To determine other facets of environmental proactivity, respondents were asked to indicate the degree (using a seven-point Likert-type scale) to which ten environmental management 'best practices' were practiced in their organizations (Aragón-Correa, 1998; Berry and Rondinelli, 1998; Henriques and Sadorsky, 1999; Sharma and Vredenburg, 1998). These best practices included corporate strategy practices (corporate environmental policy statement, environmental quality improvement business strategy), technical or administrative practices (environmental audit program, environmental performance improvement program, environmental cost accounting, environmental life-cycle analyses of new products, evaluating suppliers' environmental practices) and human resource practices (identified positions

responsible for environmental issues, employee environmental awareness, environmental issues training programs). Given that environmental issues training programs were also measured as an EHRM practice, we excluded this item in the summary scale of environmental proactivity (Cronbach $\alpha = 0.90$, nine items).

Perceived organizational benefits of environmental management practices

Respondents were asked to indicate (using a seven-point Likert-type scale) the extent to which their organizations' environmental practices had resulted in: reduced regulatory compliance costs, reduced material costs, reduced process or production costs, lower employee turnover, higher employee morale, lower insurance premiums, and increased marketing opportunities. Scores for these seven items were averaged to form a 'perceived organizational benefits of environmental practices' scale ($\alpha = 0.87$).

Organizational context

Information regarding the following organizational characteristics was requested: organization's type of manufacturing (categories based on SIC codes), organization size (three categories: 250–499 employees, 500–999 employees, 1000 or more employees), existence of a specialized environmental organizational unit (coded: $1 =$ present, $0 =$ absent) and presence of unionized employees (coded: $1 =$ present, $0 =$ absent) and if yes, percentage of workforce that was unionized.

Analyses

A MANOVA was conducted to test whether EHRM diffusion and environmental proactivity were related to the organization contextual factors of organization size (Hypotheses 2(1) and 2(2)), environmental organization units (Hypotheses 3(1) and 3(2)) and labor unions (Hypotheses 4(1) and 4(2)). The dependent variables in the MANOVA were EHRM diffusion and overall environmental proactivity, and the independent variables were organization size, environmental unit presence and labor union presence.

A summary ANOVA was conducted to test hypotheses concerning the perceived organizational benefits of environmental management practices. In this analysis, the dependent variable was the perceived organizational benefits of environmental management practices scale score. The independent variables were environmental proactivity, EHRM diffusion (Hypothesis 1), environmental organization unit presence (Hypothesis 3(3)), labor union presence (Hypothesis 4(3)) organization size, use of environmental project teams or task forces and environmental effectiveness of organizational reward systems. The use of environmental project teams or task forces was included because they are formed to deal with specific environmental issues and tasks. Environmental effectiveness of organizational reward systems was included based on the logic that an effective reward system should motivate employee actions to achieve desired outcomes.

RESULTS

Descriptive Statistics

Table 8.1 presents the means, standard deviations, ranges and correlations for the dependent and independent variables in this study.

EHRM practices

The diffusion of EHRM practices in these manufacturing organizations was relatively low with only an average of 2.05 organizational levels affected by EHRM practices. As shown in Table 8.2, environmental awareness training (μ = 3.25 organization levels) was the most prevalent EHRM practice in these manufacturing organizations. Including environmental objectives in job descriptions (μ = 2.28), environmental performance criteria in performance appraisals (μ = 2.19), recognition rewards for environmental performance (μ = 2.05) and environmental criteria in job recruitment and selection (μ = 1.89) were the next most prevalent EHRM practices. Financial rewards for environmental performance were the least-used EHRM practice (μ = 0.69).[1]

These data also revealed that CEOs of manufacturing organizations were the least affected by EHRM practices (44 percent reported none; μ = 1.17 EHRM practices). EHRM practices were more prevalent for senior environmental executives (μ = 2.58) than for other executives not specifically charged with this responsibility (μ = 1.67). However, only 38 percent of senior environmental executives were recruited or selected at least partially on the basis of their environmental knowledge, skills or leadership abilities and only one-half of environmental executives had environmental objectives in their job descriptions or environmental criteria in their performance appraisals. Senior environmental executives were slightly more likely than other types of executives to receive financial rewards (respectively, 24 percent and 16 percent) and recognition rewards (respectively, 32 percent and 24 percent) for their environmental contributions.

Given the strong linkage between ecological sustainability and manufacturing operations, it was surprising to find that plant managers were affected by fewer EHRM practices (μ = 2.58) than other types of managers (μ = 2.97) in these organizations. Only one-half of the plant manager employee

Table 8.1 Descriptive statistics and correlations [a]

Variables [b]	Mean	s.d.	1	2	3	3a	3b	3c	3d	3e	3f	4	5	6	7
1. Perceived organizational benefits	4.43	1.15	(0.87)												
2. Environmental proactivity	5.04	1.12	0.71***	(0.91)											
3. EHRM diffusion	2.05	0.93	0.52***	0.58****											
3a. Recruitment	1.89	1.24	-0.32†	0.41*											
3b. Job objectives	2.28	1.41	0.27	0.27		0.48***									
3c. Environmental training	3.25	1.54	0.41*	0.54***		0.41*	0.25								
3d. Performance appraisals	2.19	1.92	0.36*	0.39*		0.62***	0.49**	0.18							
3e. Financial rewards	0.69	1.04	0.52***	0.36*		0.21	0.08	0.19	0.29†						
3f. Recognition rewards	2.05	1.60	0.49**	0.35*		0.46**	0.19	0.33*	0.42**	0.25					
4. Reward system effectiveness	3.98	1.23	0.46***	0.60***	0.36*	0.06	0.18	0.44**	0.35*	0.34*	0.17	(0.94)			
5. Environmental organization unit	0.84	0.37	0.26	0.54***	0.33†	0.31†	0.22	0.69***	0.15	0.10	0.19	0.37*			
6. Environmental project teams	0.61	0.49	0.23	0.26	0.32†	0.27	0.30†	0.48**	0.17	0.30†	0.21	0.31†	0.34*		
7. Organization size	2.05	0.78	0.50**	0.31†	0.15	-0.01	-0.04	0.10	0.18	0.48**	0.04	0.14	0.03	0.25	
8. Labor union	0.73	0.45	0.29†	0.26	0.05	-0.12	0.14	0.10	0.08	0.24	-0.24	0.27	0.06	0.01	0.60***

Notes.

[a] Coefficient alphas are reported, where appropriate, in the parentheses on the diagonals. n = 37.

[b] Categorical variables were coded as follow: organization size: 1 = 250 - 499 employees; 2 = 500 - 999 employees; 3 = 1000 employees or more; environmental organization unit, environmental project teams/task forces, labor unions: 1 = present; 0 = absent. Range of values for other variables were: perceived organizational benefits, environmental proactivity and environmental effectiveness of reward system: 1-7; EHRM diffusion: 1-6; EHRM practices: 1-5.

† p < .10 * p < .05 ** p < .01 *** p < .001

group had job objectives or performance appraisals that included environmental criteria. Only 30 percent of plant managers (compared to 46 percent of other types of managers and 55 percent of other salaried employees) were recruited at least partially on the basis of their environmental knowledge and skills. Environmental awareness training was the most prevalent EHRM practice for plant managers (73 percent), other types of managers (78 percent) and salaried employees (76 percent). And finally, wage employees were the second-least affected by EHRM practices (μ = 1.47) with environmental awareness training (54 percent) being the most-used EHRM practice for this employee group.

Environmental reward practices

As regards environmental reward practices, 65 percent of these manufacturing organizations did not provide financial rewards for environmental contributions. Of the 22 organizations (61 percent) that had employee teams (task forces, committees or 'green teams') to work on environmental projects or issues, only three organizations had team-based financial rewards to encourage improved environmental performance. In contrast, the majority of organizations (72 percent) had non-financial recognition rewards for employee environmental contributions, with 25 percent of these organizations having four or more different recognition awards. The most commonly used recognition awards were publication of environmental achievements in corporate media (46 percent) and providing employees with further training opportunities (43 percent). Being asked to participate in environmental projects with external stakeholders or consultants (35 percent), holding company celebrations for environmental achievements (30 percent), corporate award presentations (30 percent) and giving tokens of appreciation (27 percent) were utilized to a slightly lesser extent. In respect to these recognition rewards' motivational potential, company celebrations of environmental achievements were perceived to be the most useful ($\mu = 6.27$, s.d. = 0.79) with other types of recognition rewards being viewed as being very useful (range of means: 5.45 to 5.70).

Reward system environmental effectiveness

Overall, these manufacturing organizations' reward systems were viewed as neither effective nor ineffective in motivating environmental performance among employees ($\mu = 3.98$, s.d. = 1.38). Respondents were neutral about the extent to which their organizations' reward systems motivated employee environmental task performance ($\mu = 3.97$, s.d. = 1.45), environmental innovation ($\mu = 3.93$, s.d. = 1.51) or teamwork for environmental performance (μ = 4.03, s.d. = 1.43).

Table 8.2 MANOVA results for organizational context differences in environmental proactivity and EHRM diffusion

Organizational factor	Environmental proactivity Mean (s.d.)	EHRM diffusion Mean (s.d.)
Organization size		
• 250–499 employees	4.54 (1.28)	1.87 (1.04)
• 500–999 employees	5.06 (0.75)	2.03 (0.75)
• 1000+ employees	5.43 (1.28)	2.23 (1.10)
F (eta²)	0.97 (0.06)	0.64 (0.04)
Environmental organization unit		
• Present	5.30 (0.96)	2.23 (0.83)
• Absent	3.70 (0.96)	1.19 (1.01)
F (eta²)	16.53*** (0.36)	7.67** (0.20)
Labor union		
• Present	5.22 (1.03)	2.09 (0.96)
• Absent	4.57 (1.26)	1.98 (0.91)
F (eta²)	0.32 (0.01)	0.05 (0.01)
Organization size X Environmental unit		
F (eta²)	4.96* (0.14)	0.84 (0.03)

Notes :
† $p < 0.10$
* $p < 0.05$
** $p < 0.01$
*** $p < 0.001$

Subsequent correlation analysis revealed that reward system effectiveness was positively related to the number of organizational levels that received financial rewards ($r = 0.40$, $p < 0.05$) and recognition rewards for their environmental contributions ($r = 0.44$, $p < 0.05$).[2] Further, reward system effectiveness was positively related to the number of different types of environmental recognition rewards (r = 0.68, ρ < 0.001) and their perceived usefulness (r = 0.57, ρ < 0.01). These findings suggest that organizations' provision of a variety of monetary and non-monetary rewards to employees is positively related to reward system effectiveness in promoting employee environmental contributions. Correlation analyses were also conducted to test Ramus and Steger's (2000) finding that the presence of pro-environmental policies are positively related to employee eco-initiatives. Overall environmental proactivity was positively related to overall reward system environmental effectiveness (r = 0.62, ρ < 0.001). Environmental proactivity in respect to corporate strategic policies was found to be positively related to overall reward system environmental effectiveness (r = 0.66, ρ < .001) as well as to motivating employee environmental task performance (r = 0.55, ρ < 0.001), innovation (r = 0.62, ρ < 0.001) and teamwork (r = 0.68, ρ < 0.001).

Environmental proactivity

Proactive environmental management was proposed as requiring a comprehensive approach encompassing strategic, technical or administrative, and human resource organizational systems. The environmental management programs in these manufacturing organizations appear to moderately meet this criterion of environmental proactivity (μ = 5.04, s.d. = 1.12). Although very few organizations evaluated suppliers' environmental practices, respondents indicated that their organization performed to some extent each of the nine best practices associated with environmental proactivity.

Perceived organizational benefits of environmental management practices

Respondents reported that their organizations' environmental practices had resulted in positive organizational outcomes (μ = 4.43, s.d. = 1.15). Increased marketing opportunities, reduced regulatory compliance costs, reduced material costs, higher employee morale and reduced process or production costs were perceived to be the major organizational benefits of environmental management practices (range of means: 4.97 to 4.67). Environmental management practices were not perceived to have resulted in lower insurance premiums (μ = 3.97) or lower employee turnover (μ = 3.30) in these organizations.

Results of Correlation Analysis

The correlation results in Table 8.1 show significant, positive relationships between perceived organizational benefits of environmental practices, environmental proactivity, EHRM diffusion and environmental reward system effectiveness (r = 0.46 to 0.71, all significant at ρ < 0.001 level). These results suggest that the greatest benefits accrued to those organizations that had more developed and effective environmental management programs. Organizations with environmental units were more environmentally proactive (r = 0.54, ρ < 0.001) and had greater EHRM diffusion (r = 0.33, ρ < 0.10) and more effective environmental reward systems (r = 0.37, ρ < 0.05) than those without environmental units. Larger organizations were slightly more proactive (r = 0.31, ρ < 0.10) and reported greater organizational benefits from environmental management practices (r = 0.50, ρ < 0.01) than smaller organizations. Labor unions were more prevalent in larger organizations (r = 0.60, ρ < .001) and their presence had a positive impact on organizational benefits of environmental management practices (r = 0.29, ρ < 0.10).

Results of Hypothesis Tests

We hypothesized that environmental proactivity and EHRM diffusion would be positively related to organization size (respectively, Hypotheses 3(1) and 3(2)), environmental unit presence (Hypotheses 4(1) and 4(2)) and labor union presence (Hypotheses 5(1) and 5(2)). The results of the MANOVA are presented in Table 8.3. As predicted in our hypotheses, the presence of environmental organization units was found to be positively related to environmental proactivity (F = 18.21, ρ < 0.001; Hypothesis 4(1) supported) and EHRM diffusion (F = 7.67, ρ < 0.01; Hypothesis 4(2) supported). Union presence was not a significant factor for either environmental proactivity (Hypothesis 5(1) not supported) or EHRM diffusion (Hypothesis 5(2) not supported). While organization size did not have a significant main effect for either environmental proactivity (Hypothesis 3(1)) or EHRM diffusion (Hypothesis 3(2)), there was a significant interaction between organization size and presence of an environmental organization unit in respect to environmental proactivity (F = 4.96, ρ < 0.05). *Post hoc* analyses revealed that environmental unit presence was a significant factor for large organizations (1000 or more employees) but not for small organizations (250–499 employees). One interesting finding was that all of the medium-sized organizations (500–999 employees) had environmental organization units. These results provide only partial support for Hypothesis 4(1) in that environmental unit presence was found to be positively related to overall environmental proactivity only for large organizations. Hypothesis 4(1) was not supported for small organizations and the hypothesis could not be tested for medium-sized organizations.

Post hoc group comparisons (using the Kruskal-Wallis one-way ANOVA) were also conducted to determine which aspects of organizations' EHRM programs were affected by the presence of an environmental unit. These analyses found that organizations with environmental units had significantly more employee groups attending environmental awareness training programs (χ^2 = 11.48, ρ < 0.001), and had a greater number of EHRM practices affecting their CEO or President (χ^2 = 4.73, ρ < 0.05) and executives (χ^2 = 8.19, ρ < 0.01) than organizations that did not have these units.

We hypothesized that the organizational benefits of environmental management practices would be positively related to environmental proactivity (Hypothesis 1), EHRM diffusion (Hypothesis 2), environmental organization unit presence (Hypothesis 4(3)) and labor union presence (Hypothesis 5(3)). The results of the ANOVA testing of these hypotheses are presented in Table 8.4.

As hypothesized, environmental proactivity (F = 8.25, ρ < 0.01; Hypothesis 1 supported), EHRM diffusion (F = 6.38, ρ < 0.05; Hypothesis 2 supported) and labor union presence (F = 5.20, ρ < 0.05; Hypothesis 5(3) supported) were positively related to perceived organizational benefits of environmental management practices. Although environmental unit presence did not have a significant main effect, there was a significant interaction between environmental unit and organization size (F = 4.39, ρ < 0.05) as well as a significant and positive main effect for organization size (F = 5.03, ρ < 0.05). The environmental effectiveness of reward systems was positively related to perceived organizational benefits of environmental management practices (F = 3.20, ρ < 0.10) and the use of environmental project teams or task forces was not a significant factor.

To determine the nature of the significant organization size and environmental unit interaction, separate *post hoc* organization size group comparisons were conducted. For large organizations, those that had environmental organization units reported greater organizational benefits (t = -2.13, ρ = 0.06). There was no significant difference in this regard for small organizations, and as previously reported, all of the medium-sized organizations had environmental organization units. Thus only partial support was found for Hypothesis 4(3) that proposed that environmental unit presence would enhance the organizational benefits of environmental management practices. Specifically, Hypothesis 4(3) was supported for only large organizations but not for small organizations, with no test possible for medium-sized organizations.

Table 8. 3 Employee groups affected by EHRM practices: percentage of reporting organizations (n = 37) and summary statistics

| EHRM practices | Employee groups | | | | | | | No Employees | Practice depth[a] Mean (s.d.) |
| | Executives | | | Managers | | Salaried employees | Wage employees | | |
	CEO	Senior envir. executive	Other senior executives	Plant managers	Other managers				
1. Recruitment/selection	14%	38%	14%	30%	55%	14%	16%	16	1.89 (1.24)
2. Job objectives	22%	49%	30%	51%	57%	54%	24%	8	2.28 (1.41)
3. Environmental awareness training	35%	57%	54%	73%	78%	76%	54%	8	3.25 (1.54)
4. Performance appraisals	14%	51%	24%	51%	60%	49%	24%	14	2.19 (1.92)
5. Financial rewards	8%	24%	16%	11%	11%	8%	0%	65	0.69 (1.04)
6. Recognition rewards [c]	22%	32%	24%	33%	38%	32%	27%	27	2.05 (1.60)
No EHRM practices	44%	25%	25%	14%	14%	17%	33%		EHRM Diffusion 2.05 (0.93)
EHRM practices breadth [b]									
Mean	1.17	2.58	1.67	2.58	2.97	2.81	1.47		
(s.d.)	(1.32)	(2.08)	(1.59)	(1.86)	(1.87)	(1.89)	(1.40)		

Notes:

[a] EHRM practice depth calculated as follows (coded: 1 = present; 0 = absent): CEO + executives + managers + salaried employees + wage employees
[b] EHRM practices breadth for each employee group calculated as follows (coded: 1 = present; 0 = absent): recruitment/selection + job objectives + training + performance appraisals + financial rewards + recognition rewards
[c] n = 32 (see note 2)

226

Table 8.4 ANOVA results for perceived organizational benefits of environmental management practices

Independent variables [a]	Perceived organizational benefits of environmental practices	
	F	eta [2]
Environmental proactivity	8.25**	0.27
EHRM diffusion	6.38*	0.23
Environmental organization unit	0.95	0.04
Labor union	5.20*	0.19
Organization size	5.03*	0.31
Environmental project teams/task forces	0.45	0.02
Reward system effectiveness	3.20[†]	0.13
Organization size X environmental organization unit	4.39*	0.17

Notes:
[†] $p < 0.10$
* $p < 0.05$
** $p < 0.01$
*** $p < 0.001$

DISCUSSION AND CONCLUSIONS

This study of Canadian manufacturing organizations found that environmental proactivity and the diffusion of EHRM practices were perceived to enhance organizational performance. Further organization contextual factors such as organization size, environmental organization units and labor unions were found to be related to environmental proactivity and/or perceived organizational benefits of environmental management practices. As found in previous studies (Berry and Rondinelli, 1998; Hart, 1995; Klassen, 1993; Montabon et al., 2000; Sharma and Vredenberg, 1998; Shrivastava, 1996), environmental proactivity was perceived to result in important organizational benefits such as increased marketing opportunities, reduced regulatory compliance costs, reduced material and process or production costs and higher employee morale. Environmental proactivity was also found to be positively associated with the effectiveness of an organization's reward system in motivating employee environmental performance (task performance, innovation and teamwork). These findings support Ramus and Steger's (2000) conclusion regarding the importance of corporate environmental policies for employee environmental innovation. In addition, this study extends their findings regarding the motivating potential of environmental proactivity for employee environmental task performance and teamwork.

One major finding of this study was that the diffusion of EHRM practices throughout an organization enhances the perceived organizational benefits of environmental management practices. Specifically, the incorporation of environmental objectives and criteria in a wide range of HRM practices affecting a greater variety of employees was perceived to facilitate the achievement of organizational performance objectives. These findings support the strategic HRM perspective (Bamberger and Meshoulam, 2000; Delaney and Huselid, 1996) that a high degree of both internal and external fit has a synergistic effect on organizational performance. Even so, as also observed by Wehrmeyer (1996), there is much room for change in terms of integrating environmental considerations into organizational HRM systems.

There was considerable variability in the incidence of different EHRM practices within these manufacturing organizations. Environmental awareness training was the most widely used EHRM practice, especially for managerial and salaried employees (in three-quarters of these manufacturing organizations). Approximately one-half of these organizations provided environmental training for their executive and wage employees and only one-third provided such training for their CEOs. The inclusion of environmental objectives in employee job descriptions and using those objectives in performance appraisals were relatively more prevalent than using environmental knowledge, skills or leadership abilities criteria in employee recruitment and selection processes.

In respect to employee rewards for environmental contributions, non-monetary recognition rewards were significantly more prevalent than financial rewards (the least-utilized EHRM practice). The majority of these manufacturing organizations provided a wide variety of recognition rewards for employee environmental contributions with company celebrations for environmental achievements being rated as the most useful. This study also found that diverse and widespread environmental reward systems were regarded as most effective in motivating employee environmental behaviors (task performance, innovation and teamwork). One implication of this finding is that the design of environmental reward systems should be based on the principles of both variety (monetary and non-monetary, individual and group) and inclusiveness (eligibility extended to all types of organizational employees).

This study found considerable variability in the extent that EHRM practices affected different employee groups in manufacturing organizations. EHRM practices were used relatively more frequently for senior environmental executives, managers (including plant managers) and salaried employees than for CEOs or presidents, other senior executives or wage employees. The low incidence of EHRM practices for CEOs and other senior executives is a concern given that their visible leadership and involvement are often viewed as critical to successful environmental management system implementation (Dechant and Altman, 1994; Shrivastava, 1996). Further, the low incidence of EHRM practices for wage employees (primarily limited to environmental awareness training) is also a concern given their importance in implementing environmental management programs on the manufacturing shopfloor (Callenbach et al., 1993; Shrivastava, 1996). In this regard, our findings regarding labor unions as an organizational contextual factor are particularly interesting. Although labor union presence was not significantly related to organizations' environmental proactivity, this study found that organizations with unionized workforces reported greater organizational benefits resulting from environmental management practices. There was a wide variety of responses to the open-ended question regarding the nature of labor union involvement in organizations' environmental management programs. In some manufacturing organizations, labor unions and their members played a very active role in corporate and plant-level joint environmental, health and safety committees, ISO 14000 steering and implementation committees, environmental risk assessment and audit teams and pollution prevention teams. One organization reported that the union local independently conducted environmental training for its members. In other unionized organizations, union member involvement was limited to operational and implementation issues. To date, the role and influence of labor unions has not been investigated in the corporate environmental management literature. This study found that labor union presence was a positive factor and, as such, the nature and implications of labor union involvement in environmental management programs is an important topic for future research.

This study also investigated the influence of organization size and differentiation (for example, establishment of specialized environmental units) on environmental proactivity and the organizational benefits of environmental practices. We found that while organization size was not a significant factor in respect to environmental proactivity or EHRM diffusion, organizations with 500 or more employees reported greater benefits from their environmental management practices than did smaller organizations (250–499 employees). One explanation for this finding can be found in the resource-based perspective on environmental management (Hart, 1995; Russo and Fouts, 1997) which suggests that while resources are not a barrier to environmental proactivity *per se*, larger organizations may have greater tangible resources to develop more effective environmental management systems.

There is some debate in the environmental management literature about whether organizational differentiation in terms of the establishment of a specialized environmental unit is a positive or negative factor in environmental proactivity and environmental management program effectiveness (Berry and Rondinelli, 1998; Henriques and Sadorsky, 1995; Lawrence and Morell, 1995; Shrivastava, 1996; Starik and Rands, 1995). This study found that organizations with environmental units were more environmentally proactive and had higher levels of EHRM diffusion, but did not report greater organizational benefits from their environmental management practices than organizations that did not have these specialized units. One possible explanation is that the influence of environmental organization units on program outcomes may be indirect, through their influence on other aspects of environmental proactivity.

However, the significant interactions between organization size and environmental unit presence in respect to environmental proactivity and perceived organizational benefits provide further insight into the influence of these contextual factors. While environmental unit presence was not a significant factor in environmental proactivity or perceived organizational benefits for smaller organizations, large organizations with environment units were more environmentally proactive and reported greater benefits than those that did not. Although comparisons were not possible for the medium-sized organizations which all had environmental units, these findings suggest that larger organizations benefit from the functional specialization of environmental expertise and centralized coordination of environmental programs (Mintzberg, 1979). Whether the establishment of environmental organization units leads to, is a consequence of, or is synonymous with environmental proactivity and EHRM practices diffusion is a question that cannot be answered with these correlational data.

Limitations of this Study and Directions for Future Research

The relatively small sample size did not allow analysis into some areas of interest such as between manufacturing industry comparisons. The high percentage of responding organizations that had established environmental units suggests that this sample of manufacturing organizations may have been biased in favor of those that are more environmentally proactive than their industry peers. Thus, these findings should be interpreted as what more environmentally proactive companies are doing with regards to EHRM practices. Further research with a larger sample of organizations is needed to determine whether there are significant differences within the manufacturing sector as well as other industrial sectors with regards to EHRM practices and environmental management systems. Our assurances of confidentiality and anonymity to respondents meant that this study was based on self-reported perceptual data which prevented additional tests of organizational and environmental performance (cf. Podsakoff and Organ, 1986). One avenue for future research would be to compare internal evaluations of environmental proactivity and outcomes with external evaluations of corporate environmental practices such as governmental data on environmental performance, environmental professionals' peer ratings and ratings of corporate environmental reputations.

In this study, we investigated the use and effects of a wide range of EHRM practices. However, we were constrained by an already long survey questionnaire (seven pages) from gaining more in-depth knowledge about, for example, the incidence of each EHRM practice within different organizational levels as well as their influence on specific aspects of organizational environmental performance. Future research is needed to fully understand the operation of EHRM practices as well as the design and effect of variable and skill-based pay in SEHRM systems. While this study investigated the diffusion of EHRM practices within an organization, more research is need on the influence of specific types, frequency and timing of EHRM practices on employee and organizational environmental performance. For example, additional research is needed regarding the effectiveness of alternative performance appraisal approaches (for example, multi-rater systems, team-based) in measuring and assessing employee environmental contributions. Research is needed to ascertain the relative impact on organizations' environmental performance of EHRM practice diffusion for organizational executives and managers compared to EHRM practice diffusion for other salaried and wage employees. Another research question concerns the relative efficacy of various EHRM practices in enhancing corporate environmental performance. For example, does the implementation of EHRM financial rewards have a greater impact on corporate environmental performance than the implementation of EHRM recognition rewards?

Another focus of future research could be determining possible interactions between EHRM practices and employee values and preferences. For example, what types of compensation and reward systems are most effective with employees who hold strong pro-environmental values versus those who are less motivated by environmental concerns? Offering a position on a high-profile environmental committee, or the opportunity to attend environmental conferences, may be effective rewards for employees with strong environmental values. However, these environmental rewards may not be as effective for employees who are not strongly motivated by environmental concerns and thus research is needed to identify appropriate behavioral incentives.

And finally, another limitation of this study is the cross-sectional nature of our data (see Lindell and Whitney, 2001). Although disentangling the effects of EHRM practices from other facets of environmental proactivity is challenging, longitudinal research is needed to ascertain the impact of implementing a SEHRM system and various EHRM practices on organizational and environmental performance.

CONCLUSION

In conclusion, the recent literature on corporate environmentalism suggests that a growing number of firms are voluntarily changing their business operations and processes to minimize negative ecological impacts of business operations. The goals and objectives of environmental management systems need to be supported throughout the organization, by all levels of employees. As such, organizations with proactive environmental strategies should have SEHRM systems in place that promote and reward employee values, attitudes and behaviors that help improve environmental performance. Environmentally proactive organizations also need to incorporate continuous feedback mechanisms to determine the efficacy of their SEHRM systems. Although the implementation of SEHRM best practices appears to be relatively under-developed for even environmentally proactive organizations, this study provides preliminary evidence that adopting a SEHRM approach facilitates the achievement of an organization's environmental and corporate objectives.

NOTES

1. As identified in the literature review, variable pay systems (pay for performance, stock options, profitsharing, gainsharing, bonuses) are potential vehicles for rewarding environmental performance. The majority (78 percent) of these manufacturing organizations had variable pay systems. One-third of these organizations had variable pay systems at all organizational levels and an additional 31 percent had variable pay systems for three or four organizational levels. Variable pay systems were widespread for manufacturing organizations'

executive (70 percent CEO, 76 percent executive) and managerial (64 percent) employees. About half (56 percent) had variable pay systems for salaried employees and only 36 percent had these compensation systems for wage employees. In total, there appears to be substantial potential for the inclusion of environmental performance criteria in these organizations' compensation systems.

2. An internal consistency check of responses revealed that while six respondents did not indicate any groups of employees receiving environmental recognition rewards, they indicated that some environmental recognition rewards were used in their organizations in another part of the questionnaire. As a result, these six companies were not included in the analysis of specific employee groups because the number of different groups of employees affected by such rewards could not be determined. However, these six companies were included in the summary analysis of environmental HRM practices as organizations that used recognition rewards for 'nonspecified employees.'

REFERENCES

Agarwal, N.C. (1998), 'Reward systems: emerging trends and issues,' *Canadian Psychology*, **39**(1/2): 60–70.

Anderson, D.R. (1999), 'Incorporating risk management into environmental management systems,' *CPCU Journal*, **52**(2): 115–24.

Aragón-Correa, J.A. (1998), 'Strategic proactivity and firm approach to the natural environment,' *Academy of Management Journal*, **41**(5): 556–67.

Arthur, J.B. (1994), 'Effects of human resource systems on manufacturing performance and turnover,' *Academy of Management Journal*, **37**: 670–87.

Bamberger, P. and I. Meshoulam (2000), *Human Resource Strategy: Formulation, Implementation and Impact*, Thousand Oaks, CA: Sage.

Bansal, P. and K. Roth (2000), 'Why companies go green: a model of ecological responsiveness,' *Academy of Management Journal*, **43**(4): 717–37.

Baruch, Y. (1999), 'Response rate in academic studies – a comparative analysis,' *Human Relations*, **52**(4): 421–38.

Berry, M.A. and D.A. Rondinelli (1998), 'Proactive corporate environmental management: a new industrial revolution,' *Academy of Management Executive*, **12**(2): 38–50.

Brill, H., J.A. Brill and C. Feigenbaum (2000), *Investing with your Values: Making Money and Making a Difference*, Gabriola Island, BC: New Society Publishers.

Buttel, F., C. Geisler and I. Wiswall (1984), *Labor and the Environment*, Westport, CT: Greenwood.

Callenbach, E., F. Capra, L. Goldman, R. Lutz and S. Marburg (1993), *EcoManagement: The Elmwood Guide to Ecological Auditing and Sustainable Business*, San Francisco, CA: Berrett Koehler.

Canadian Business Information Database (1999), *Sales Leads Marketing List by Ontario Postal Code*, Mississauga, Ontario: InfoCanada.

Charter, M. (ed.) (1992), *Greener Marketing: A Responsible Approach to Business*, Sheffield: Greenleaf Publishing.

Christmann, P. (2000), 'Effects of best practices of environmental management on cost advantage: the role of complementary assets,' *Academy of Management Journal*, **43**(4): 663–80.

Cohen-Rosenthal, E. (n.d.), 'Environmental action and social partnership in North America, Work and Environment Initiative, School of Industrial and Labor Relations, Cornell University,' retrieved 14 December 2000, http://www.cfe.cornell.edu/wei/socpart.html

Cooper, M. (1992), 'Jobs vs. the environment,' *CQ Researcher*, **2**(18), 411–31.

Dechant, K. and B. Altman (1994), 'Environmental leadership: from compliance to competitive advantage,' *Academy of Management Executive*, **8**(3): 7–27.

Delaney, J.T. and M.A. Huselid (1996), 'The impact of human resource management practices on perceptions of organizational performance,' *Academy of Management Journal*, **39**(4): 949–85.

Flannery, T.P., D.A. Hofrichter and P.E. Platten (1996), *People, Performance and Pay*, New York: Free Press.

Frankel, C. (1998), *In Earth's Company: Business, Environment and the Challenge of Sustainability*, Gabriola Island, BC: New Society Publishers.

Gibson, R. (ed.) (2000), *Voluntary Initiatives: The New Politics of Corporate Greening*, Peterborough, Ontario: Broadview Press.

Gluck, A.L., D.C. Nanney and W.C. Lusvardi (2000), 'Mitigating factors in appraisal and valuation of contaminated real property,' *Real Estate Issues*, **25**(2): 22–9.

Gottlieb, R. (1993), *Forcing the Spring*, Washington, DC: Island Press.

Hart, S.L. (1995), 'A natural resource-based view of the firm,' *Academy of Management Review*, **20**(4): 986–1014.

Hart, S.L. and G. Ahuja (1996), 'Does it pay to be green? An empirical examination of the relationship between emission reduction and firm performance,' *Business Strategy and the Environment*, **5**(1): 30–7.

Henriques, I. and P. Sadorsky (1995), 'The determinants of firms that formulate environmental plans,' in D. Collins and M. Starik (eds), *Research in Corporate Social Performance and Policy*, Supplement 1, Greenwich, CT: JAI Press.

Henriques, I. and P. Sadorsky (1999), 'The relationship between environmental commitment and managerial perceptions of stakeholder importance,' *Academy of Management Journal*, **42**(1): 87–99.

Hoffman, A. (2000), *Competitive Environmental Strategy*, Washington, DC: Island Press.

Hoffman, A. (2001), 'Linking organizational and field-level analyses: the diffusion of corporate environmental practice,' *Organization and Environment*, **14**(2): 133–56.

Huselid, M. (1995), 'The impact of human resource management practices on turnover, productivity and corporate financial performance,' *Academy of Management Journal*, **38**: 635–72.

Johns, G. (1993), 'Constraints on the adoption of psychology-based personnel practices: lessons from organizational innovation,' *Personnel Psychology*, **46**: 569–92.

Klassen, R.D. (1993), 'The integration of environmental issues into manufacturing,' *Production and Inventory Management Journal*, **34**(1): 82–8.

Klassen, R.D. and C.P. McLaughlin (1996), 'The impact of environmental management on firm performance,' *Management Science*, **42**: 1199–214.

Klassen, R.D. and D.C. Whybark (1999), 'The impact of environmental technologies on manufacturing performance,' *Academy of Management Journal*, **42**(6): 599–615.

Lawrence, A.T. and D. Morell (1995), 'Leading-edge environmental management: motivation, opportunity, resources and processes', in D. Collins and M. Starik (eds), *Research in Corporate Social Performance and Policy*, Supplement 1, Greenwich, CT: JAI Press.

Lindell, M.K. and D.J. Whitney (2001), 'Accounting for common method variance in cross-sectional research designs,' *Journal of Applied Psychology*, **86**(1): 114–21.

Lundy, O. and A. Cowling (1996), *Strategic Human Resource Management*, New York: Routledge.

McElrath, R. (1988), 'Environmental issues and the strategies of the international trade union movement,' *Columbia Journal of World Business*, **23** (3): 63–6.

Menon, A., A. Menon, J. Chowdhury and J. Jankovich (1999), 'Evolving paradigm for environmental sensitivity in marketing programs: a synthesis of theory and practice,' *Journal of Marketing Theory and Practice*, **7**(2): 1–15.

Milliman, J. and J. Clair (1996), 'Best environmental HRM practices in the US,' in W. Wehrmeyer (ed.), *Greening People: Human Resources and Environmental Management*, Sheffield: Greenleaf Publishing.

Mintzberg, H. (1979), *The Structuring of Organizations: A Synthesis of the Research*, Englewood Cliffs, NJ: Prentice-Hall.

Montabon, F., S.A. Melnyk, R. Sroufe and R.J. Calanton (2000), 'ISO 14000: assessing its perceived impact on corporate performance,' *Journal of Supply Chain Management*, **36**(2): 4–16.

Murray, B. and B. Gerhart (1998), 'An empirical analysis of a skill-based pay program and plant performance outcomes,' *Academy of Management Journal*, **41**(1): 68–78.

Obach, B. (1999), 'The Wisconsin labor-environmental network,' *Organization and Environment*, **12**(1), 45–74.

Pfeffer, J. and G.R. Salancik (1978), *The External Control of Organizations: A Resource Dependence Perspective*, New York: Harper and Row.

Podsakoff, P.M. and D.W. Organ (1986), 'Self-reports in organizational research: problems and prospects,' *Journal of Management*, **12**(4): 531–44.

Polonsky, M.J. and A.T. Mintu-Wimsatt (eds) (1995), *Environmental Marketing: Strategies, Practice, Theory and Research*, Binghamton, NY: Haworth.

Post, J.E. and B.W. Altman (1992), 'Models of corporate greening: how corporate social policy and organizational learning inform leading-edge environmental management,' *Research in Corporate Social Performance and Policy*, **3**: 3–29.

Ramus, C.A. and U. Steger (2000), 'The roles of supervisory support behaviors and environmental policy in employee ecoinitiatives at leading-edge European companies,' *Academy of Management Journal*, **43**(4): 604–26.

Russo, M.V. and P.A. Fouts (1997), 'A resource-based perspective on corporate environmental performance and profitability,' *Academy of Management Journal*, **40**: 534–59.

Saari, L.M., T.R. Johnson, S.D. McLaughlin and D.M. Zimmerle (1988), 'A survey of management training and education practices in US companies,' *Personnel Psychology*, **41**: 731–43.

Sarkis, J. (1995), 'Manufacturing strategy and environmental consciousness,' *Technovation*, **15**(2): 79–97.

Schmidheiny, S. and F. Zorraquin (1996), *Financing Change: The Financial Community, Eco-efficiency and Sustainable Development*, Cambridge, MA: MIT Press.

Schonberger, R.J. (1994), 'Human resource management lessons from a decade of total quality management and engineering,' *California Management Review*, 36(4): 109–23.

Schrecker, T. (1993), 'Sustainable development: getting there from here – a handbook for union environment committees and joint labour-management environment committees,' Ottawa: Canadian Labour Congress and the National Round Table on the Environment and the Economy.

Sharma, S. (2000), 'Managerial interpretations and organizational context as predictors of corporate choice of environmental strategy,' *Academy of Management Journal*, 43(4): 681–97.

Sharma, S. and H. Vredenburg (1998), 'Proactive corporate environmental strategy and the development of competitively valuable organizational capabilities,' *Strategic Management Journal*, 19(8): 729–53.

Shrivastava, P. (1995a), 'Ecocentric management for industrial ecosystems: management paradigm for a risk society,' *Academy of Management Review*, 20:118–37.

Shrivastava, P. (1995b), 'Environmental technologies and competitive advantage,' *Strategic Management Journal*, 16: 183–200.

Shrivastava, P. (1996), *Greening Business: Profiting the Corporation and the Environment*, Cincinnati, OH: Thompson Executive Press.

Starik, M. and G.P. Rands (1995), 'Weaving an integrated web: multilevel and multisystem perspectives of ecologically sustainable organizations,' *Academy of Management Review*, 20(4): 908–35.

Taillieu, T. and H.C. Mooren (1990), 'International career orientations of young European graduates: a survey of opinions and aspirations,' Tilberg, Netherlands: University of Tilberg.

Wehrmeyer, W. (ed.) (1996), *Greening People: Human Resources and Environmental Management*, Sheffield: Greenleaf Publishing.

White, M.A. (1995), 'The performance of environmental mutual funds in the United States and Germany: is there economic hope for "green" investors?,' in D. Collins and M. Starik (eds), *Research in Corporate Social Performance and Policy*, Supplement 1, Greenwich, CT: JAI Press.

Willig, J.T. (ed.) (1994), *Environmental TQM*, New York: McGraw-Hill.

Wilson, T.B. (1995), *Innovative Reward Systems for the Changing Workplace*, New York: McGraw-Hill.

Work and Environment Initiative (1997), *Labor, Climate Change and the Environment*, Cornell Centre for the Environment, Ithaca, NY: Cornell University.

Yandle, B. (1985), 'Unions and environmental regulation,' *Journal of Labor Research*, 6(4): 429–36.

Youndt, M.A., S.A. Snell, J.W. Dean Jr. and D.P. Lepak (1996), 'Human resource management, manufacturing strategy and firm performance,' *Academy of Management Journal*, 39(4), 836–66.

Zhang, H.C., T.C. Kuo, H. Lu and S.H. Huang (1997), 'Environmentally conscious design and manufacturing: a state-of-the-art survey,' *Journal of Manufacturing Systems*, 16(5): 352–71.

9. Information disclosure in environmental policy and the development of secretly environmentally-friendly products

Trudy Heller and Jeanne Mroczko

INTRODUCTION

Recent environmental policy has focused on information disclosure, encouraging and sometimes requiring firms to provide public information about the toxic substances that they use and release into the environment. This new policy effort conflicts with traditional organizational behavior characteristics of secrecy, proprietary knowledge and corporate control of information disclosure. Little is known about how these conflicting dynamics actually affect business environmental performance.

This chapter reports on a study of two cases of environment-related product development that illuminate these dynamics. Interviews gathered the stories of these products that were initially criticized on environmental grounds, and then revised to become more 'green.' Interviews also focused on the public presentation of the products, as the products' sustainable features were not only not apparent to consumers but, in one case, were actively kept secret.

Findings suggest that three contextual features serve to shape how these companies understand and present their environmentally-friendly products: skeletons in the closet, strategic identity and the capacity to envision a 'double bottom line.' Implications for policy-makers and management researchers include mechanisms that may mediate information disclosure and corporate greening, and the prospect that a business's actual environmental performance, in some cases, may be better than that which is publicly disclosed. Therefore, in some cases, a company's 'walk' may actually be greener than its 'talk.'

This chapter examines two companies that have responded to pressure to address environmental problems, each created by one of their respective products. Both firms have successfully revamped the criticized products, and corrected their respective product's environmental problems. In both cases, the new more positive and sustainable environmental features of the product remain secret. In one case, the firm wants the new feature of its product to remain secret. In the other case, the environmental features of the product remain unrecognized by consumers in spite of efforts on the part of the firm to publicize these features.

What factors are involved in this seemingly inconsistent practice? What can these cases tell environmental scholars and policy-makers about the use of environmental regulations that rely on information disclosure? This chapter adds some concrete examples to current discussions of disclosure and greening in both management and environmental policy arenas. The result is to refine and add enriching complexity to these conversations.

The chapter is laid out as follows. First, the management and policy conversation about disclosure and greening is introduced. The research methods used in the comparative case studies are then recounted. The cases, Kodak and Giftco, are then briefly described and themes that emerge from these cases are presented. Finally, lessons for environmental policy and management theory and practice are discussed.

THEORETICAL PERSPECTIVES

Information Disclosure as an Instrument of Environmental Policy and Corporate Greening

Policy-makers and regulators who develop strategies for facilitating sustainability have created interventions, or policy instruments, aimed at advancing the goal of sustainable development. Recently, environmental policy strategies have focused on information disclosure. Moving away from an exclusive reliance on 'command and control' regulations of an earlier era, environmental policy-makers in the United States have been supplementing these with policies requiring firms to disclose information about the toxic substances that the firms use and release into the environment (Cohen, 2000; Hoffman, 1999; Outen, 2000). A primary instrument in this effort is the Emergency Planning and Community Right-to-Know Act of 1986:

> This legislation requires manufacturing establishments with 10 or more employees in SIC codes 20 through 39 (with certain threshold sizes of chemical emissions) to publicly disclose the quantity and type of toxic chemicals released

into the environment ... Data from these reports have been referred to as the Toxic Release Inventory (TRI) (Konar and Cohen, 1997: 110).

There are high hopes that this policy will achieve its goals. Fred Krupp, the Executive Director of Environmental Defense, has called the implementation of the Toxic Release Inventory (TRI) the most significant event in the history of the environmental movement since the publication of Rachel Carson's *Silent Spring* in 1962. Entrepreneurial environmental organizations have developed services that help interpret the mass of environmental information now disclosed by firms, for example, Environmental Defense's web-based 'Scorecard.' The interpreted data presumably provides opportunities for wider dissemination and use by consumers and other stakeholders.

The policy assumes that well-informed stakeholders, including consumers, stockholders and financial analysts, are more liable to exert pressure on firms to become more green (Outen, 2000). This 'green pressure' will provide market-based incentives for firms to operate more cleanly. Thus disclosure is assumed to create pressure for firms to become greener in two related ways. First, a threat of exposure will be created if a company's poor environmental performance results in negative publicity. Second, the release of environmental good news may be a reward that companies will strive to achieve. The case for the effectiveness of this environmental information disclosure policy initiative rests firmly on these two assumptions.

Evidence of Effectiveness

Studies have generally supported the idea that disclosure of information, and the resulting visibility of firm activity, creates pressure on firms to become green (Bowen, 2000; Cohen, 2000; Hamilton, 1995; Konar and Cohen, 1997). Using TRI data, one study found that firms with higher pollution levels are more likely to have their toxic releases publicized by print journalists (Hamilton, 1995). These firms are also more likely to have statistically significant, abnormal negative stock returns at the time the environmental information was released (Hamilton, 1995). Furthermore, firms with the greatest stock declines subsequently reduced their emissions more than industry peers (Konar and Cohen, 1997), suggesting evidence that the pressure created by disclosure and media exposure leads to corporate greening. Bowen (2000) reviewed research on corporate environmental visibility and concluded:

One way to improve the environmental performance of firms is to make them, and their activities, more visible by publicizing poor performance, conspicuously rewarding examples of good practice, requiring firms to produce a verified environmental report or encouraging site visits by local constituents (p. 104).

Positive reports of the effectiveness of disclosure programs are, however, qualified. Cohen (2000) noted that 'we cannot assume the success of one program is transferable to another program unless we understand the *mechanism* by which the first program succeeded' (p. 4); (emphasis added). The present study advances this effort by uncovering mechanisms that connect information disclosure policies and corporate greening. It explores a related but broader research question: How do the dynamics of environmental visibility, disclosure and exposure unfold in the context of the normal business activity of product development? What can researchers, practitioners and policy-makers learn about these mechanisms through cases of new product development – an arena of business activity that is traditionally characterized by secrecy?

RESEARCH METHOD

Data Gathering

The research questions were explored through field case studies. This research strategy allowed for the observation of dynamics of disclosure, visibility and secrecy in the course of business activity, rather than posing abstract or hypothetical questions to informants. Originally we planned for multiple case studies. We applied a 'replication logic' (Yin, 1989), and viewed the cases as repeated experiments. The goal was to continue to gather cases until 'saturation' had been achieved, or until the consideration of further cases was unlikely to yield new or surprising results. However, the first two cases that we examined contained such a rich set of similarities and differences that we decided to present our results as a report of work in progress (Ragin, 1987).

Table 9.1 lists the striking similarities and differences of these two cases. Both companies were producers of a product, or products, that was subsequently criticized for environmentally damaging characteristics. Both companies revised their product to become more environmentally friendly. In both cases, consumers were largely unaware of these revisions and the environmental features of the product. The lack of consumer awareness in one case was the result of deliberate efforts to keep the green features of the product secret. In the other case, lack of consumer awareness persisted in spite of the company's interest in making this feature of their product known.

Table 9.1 Similarities and differences between Kodak and Giftco

Similarities	Differences
Both companies' products criticized for environmental problems.	In one case the company tries to get the word out, but consumers remain largely unaware.
Both companies' products revised to correct environmental problem.	In the other case the company wants to keep the product's environmental features secret.
In both cases consumers remain unaware of the product's 'green' features.	

Sources of Data

Each case study included a field visit and workplace interviews with company managers involved with the development of the products in question. Interviews were semi-structured, focusing on the particular product's development, its subsequent revision to become more environmentally friendly and choices about public presentation of the product's environmental revision.

Because of the sensitive nature of the interview material, no tape recordings were made. The researcher used ethnographic methods of writing field notes immediately after the field visits (Lofland and Lofland, 1984; Schatzman and Strauss, 1973). Field notes contained descriptions of the setting and paraphrased and verbatim comments of interviewees, as well as theoretical and methodological notes. While the field notes were not reviewed by the respondents, a copy of the final paper was given to the respondents to review.

A tour of manufacturing facilities was included in field trips to each company. At Kodak, the recycling facility was included in the tour. These tours also afforded the opportunity to talk to employees that were not on the list of official interviewees. Written documents, such as reports posted on the firm's website and company newsletters, supplemented the data contained in the field notes. Table 9.2 lists the sources of data for each case.

Table 9.2 Data sources for Kodak and Giftco

Kodak	Giftco
Individual interviews with worldwide manager of recycling, and manager of recycling facility.	Individual interviews with EHS manager, 2 product development engineers, 1 computer systems engineer, General Manager of the facility.
Group interview of 4 members of recycling team.	Tour of manufacturing facility and factory outlet retail store.
Tour of manufacturing and recycling facilities.	Document review: company newsletter.
Document review: company brochure, article in industry publication, website material.	

Data Analysis

Normally both researchers would have scrutinized the field notes and documents to develop constructs that address our research question. However, one of the researchers is a director of an environmental regulatory enforcement agency. Because it was possible that corporate behaviors in contravention of environmental regulations could be revealed in the interviews, we decided that the director would not conduct the interviews and would not view the raw data of the field notes. Instead we worked with the theoretical notes, using them as discussion points.

With this modification in our method for data analysis, we used techniques developed by Strauss (1987) for creating theoretical constructs from qualitative data, including frequent reference to field notes and comparison of similarities and differences between the two cases. The aim of this method is to develop categories, or themes, that organize and explain the data rather than simply summarizing interviewee's views.

The two cases are briefly described below. The first case concerns Eastman Kodak and its single-use-camera. The second case focuses on Giftco, a manufacturer of high-quality products that are given as gifts and handed down as family heirlooms.

CASE STUDIES

Kodak's Single-use Camera

The single-use camera (SUC) began with the 'Fling,' a camera that would take advantage of Kodak's high-speed film. Kodak is historically and traditionally a film company, and the 'Fling' was originally conceived as a vehicle for selling Kodak film. Some Kodak managers were concerned that the camera might cannibalize the company's film business. The camera and film were conceived as a unified system that would continue to sell Kodak's primary product, high-speed film.

At the time of this study, the SUC program had existed for more than ten years, beginning in 1987–88. At Kodak Park, the corporate headquarters, this project was considered a small side-business. Starting out as a 'skunk works' operation, the product was developed without senior management attention. Product developers had created the design earlier, but had not gained the support to implement it.

Then Fuji entered the market with its single-use camera, and according to Kodak interviewees, 'We weren't ready.' Therefore, Kodak initially bought another company's single-use camera and put Kodak's 110 film into it, rushing the product to market to compete with Fuji. Kodak then took its own design work off the shelf and developed the Fling single-use camera, which was advertised as a 'one-time use camera' (OTUC) was marketed in Europe as the 'Fun Saver.'

The Fling was, indeed, a 'throwaway' camera. Once the film was removed for development, the camera became waste. As the market began to grow, however, the product developers began to realize an underlying issue, that is, the growing amount of waste being generated by the single-use cameras. Environmental groups also noticed the mounting waste from the single-use cameras, and gave Kodak a 'Waste Maker' award (Field, 2000). This motivated the product innovators to begin thinking about recycling:

> Lo and behold, we found ourselves in the recycling business. We put teams around the business, and pulled metrics out.

The cameras were redesigned for easier recycling. Then, Kodak used its well-established relationships with film processors to set up an infrastructure for reclaiming the used cameras. Eventually, single-use cameras were being collected from film processors all over the world, and shipped to manufacturing locations in Rochester, New York; Chalon, France; and Guadalajara, Mexico, where cameras were sorted and recycled.

Throughout this initiative, Kodak did not use the term 'recyclable' or 'recycled' to advertise its camera. Interviewees cited legal restrictions on the use of that term and resistance from the marketing department:

> Marketing has maintained that there are only so many qualities you can convey in a message on the packaging.

The recycled message did not top the list of priorities emphasized on the package and label, though information about the recycling program did appear on the back of the outer cardboard packaging. Although 60 percent of cameras worldwide are recycled (70 percent in the United States), this seemingly valuable green message is not readily apparent to the consumer, and therefore many consumers may still consider the camera a throwaway product.

The Removal of Toxic Ingredient, 'T' at Giftco (a Pseudonym)

Giftco is a producer of fine, quality keepsakes. Their products are often purchased as gifts for special occasions such as weddings, anniversaries and other holidays. Their products are intended to become treasures that stay in a family and are passed down from generation to generation.

Giftco's main manufacturing facility is located in a rural setting – although a new development of homes and a golf course is now located across the road. Aside from this single, new development, trees and country roads surround the plant.

The idea for revising the process for manufacturing Giftco's products originated as a response to pressure by the United States government's Occupational Safety and Health Administration (OSHA) and the Department of Environmental Protection (DEP) of the state in which Giftco's manufacturing plant and headquarters is located. OSHA was concerned about the exposure of employees to toxic ingredient 'T.' The state DEP was concerned about the disposal of sludge containing ingredient T that was left over from the manufacturing process.

According to Giftco's management, 'The writing was on the wall.' If they did not do something voluntarily, they would soon be required to remove T from the manufacturing process. In addition, competitors were introducing T-free products, and consumers now had a choice about whether they wanted T in their products.

Alternatives to ingredient T were available, but T had a technical production advantage over the available substitutes. T was 'forgiving,' and allowed the manufacturing process to be less than perfectly precise. Small amounts of impurities and variations in the manufacturing process did not matter when T was part of the process. Without T, greater precision and quality control was required.

Thus, in order to eliminate T, Giftco's engineers had to revise the entire manufacturing process. The process was computerized, with the result that greater quality control was achieved. The engineers were able to gain the precision they needed to implement a new manufacturing process that eliminated T. Lagoons of T-contaminated sludge behind the plant were also cleaned up.

When the state DEP learned of Giftco's accomplishment, they were eager to tout the company's achievement with a press release and other publicity. Giftco, however, declined, preferring to keep the elimination of T from their products secret. Their stated philosophy was, 'We only want our name in the newspaper when we place an advertisement.'

RESULTS: MANAGEMENT AND POLICY THEMES

A comparison of the above two cases yielded three themes that illuminate differences in the approaches of the two firms to disclosing, or advertising, the green features of their products. These themes, described in the following section, are: 'Skeletons in the Closet,' 'Strategic Integration,' and 'Envisioning the Double Bottom Line.' Table 9.3 lists the themes with quotes from field notes that illustrate the grounding of the themes in the data.

Skeletons in the Closet

Giftco's managers offered two reasons for their preference not to publicize the removal of T from their products. One reason concerned the fact that their products were intended to be enduring and that customers typically did own them for a long period of time. Managers expressed concern that the customers who still owned the products containing ingredient T would be upset. These customers may not even be aware that their products contained T. A public announcement that all Giftco products were now T-free might arouse consumer distrust and concern that the products they owned may not be safe. One skeleton that may come out of the closet is the fact that Giftco had been making products with T for many years.

A second reason for eschewing publicity concerned the T-contaminated sludge lagoons behind the plant. Although present for many years and in the process of being eliminated, these lagoons had never been the subject of negative journalistic reporting. Drawing attention to Giftco's history of using T at the plant might, similarly, bring unwelcomed attention to this facility's undesirable, local environmental impacts. Giftco had enjoyed a certain lack of

Table 9.3 Themes and illustrative quotes from notes on Kodak and Giftco

Theme	Illustrative quotes
Skeletons in the closet	JS said that Kodak Park has tried to clean up the sins of the past … He said they are monitoring the wells around the [previously] contaminated area and are not finding anything. (Kodak) They haven't been able to [produce the product] without ingredient 'U'. So it's not like they are toxin free. To breach the subject of ingredient 'T' would open the door to 'Well, OK, you got rid of the 'T', so do you have other toxins here? OOPS, you've got ingredient 'U''. (Giftco)
Strategic identity	In the selection of new product concepts to develop, they choose no new programs that are unfriendly to recycling … they have a gate requirement for recycling in any new product that comes along. The bottom line is that they cannot go backwards. (Kodak) Their core competence is pictures: superior pictures through better value, and part of the value is the recycling piece. (Kodak) J kept repeating that there had never been a case of poisoning. This 'T' was an emotional scare word issue … There have been people [using Giftco products] for 70 years, and nothing bad has happened. (Giftco)
Envisioning the double bottom line	As for the financials, it [recycling] saves us money. We see recycling as a competitive advantage ... The recycling program 'drives a better business model.' It's not a 'mop up operation.' (Kodak)

Theme	Illustrative quotes
Envisioning the double-bottom line	Another thing we talked about were the process improvements that went along with the elimination of ''T''. I asked them if they would have undertaken this process review anyhow. They replied that they would have gotten around to it at some point, but that the pressure to get rid of ''T'' was a factor [in doing it at that time]. (Giftco)
	On the financials: 'We gained some and lost some so that it washed out.' (Giftco)

scrutiny in their rural location, away from homes and neighbors. Giftco's management felt that they had much to lose and little to gain from an announcement that their products were now T-free.

Kodak also had skeletons in their closet and ghosts from the past. Their facility at Kodak Park in Rochester, New York had been the subject of a great deal of scrutiny by the local community for its use of toxic chemicals and contamination of groundwater (Kodak website, 2000). Unlike Giftco, however, these skeletons had long been out of the closet. The Kodak website contained extensive information about the current status of the historical contamination and clean-up efforts. A Kodak manager explained, 'They are monitoring the wells around the contaminated area and are not finding anything.'

More to the point, however, was the fact that the environmental criticism of the original product was also highly visible. Indeed, the original disposable camera had been the recipient of a 'Waste Maker' award by environmental groups (Field, 2000). The disposable camera had become a symbol of the throwaway culture – an environmental anathema. Kodak had nothing to lose and much to gain by public announcements of the environmental revisions to their product and the new recycling program. In their instance, disclosing the good news would not lead to a disclosure of bad news, since the bad news was already out.

Strategic Identity

The term 'strategic identity,' is used to capture the way interviewees described the core business, or mission, of their organizations in relation to the environmental problems that they faced. The concept includes both the individuals' identification with the mission of their organization and their notions of the image they present to outside stakeholders. The strategic identity of each firm framed their reactions to the criticism of their products. Managers at Giftco viewed their mission as one of making heirlooms and keepsakes, products that would be treasured for a long time. Their products were frequently bought as gifts for life's special moments, for example, weddings, anniversaries, christenings or as hostess gifts for dear friends, which are all happy occasions. Giftco's products are reminders of these pleasant events, and they very much identify with being in the business of commemorating life's significant and pleasant events.

Giftco has a reputation for being customer-oriented. Their policy is to address any problems with their products immediately. Quality customer service is a part of their perceived strategic identity. Any flaw in a product provides grounds for immediate recall or replacement. Extensive packaging protects the fragile products from breakage during shipping. One failed product was a gift that was intended for use as a server for cold liquids. Some customers, however, put hot liquids into the product that caused damage. These items were discontinued, and customers who had bought the products were compensated.

To acknowledge any negative environmental impact would create a stark contrast to the image of Giftco described above. For a company whose products are a part of life's happy occasions, negative environmental issues are anathema. The contrast between the serene beauty and happy images of the product displays at the factory store and the image of the lagoons of T-tainted sludge behind the manufacturing plant is stark. Thus the exposure of environmental issues threatened to dismantle the carefully crafted strategic identity of the firm.

At Kodak, environmental issues also interact with strategy but are more easily integrated. The Kodak strategic identity is that of a quality photographic film and equipment company. A Kodak manager used the analogy of Intel's use of labels on computers that announce 'Intel inside,' to describe Kodak film inside a camera as an assurance of quality that customers understood.

As a photographic film company, Kodak's use of chemicals and pollutants to manufacture their products was common knowledge. Unlike Giftco, Kodak had a tradition of community involvement and concern. They interacted with the community in both positive and confrontational situations. On the one hand, their philanthropy is renowned in their home community of Rochester, New York. On the other hand, they have faced concerned community residents about a possible brain cancer cluster in the community surrounding Kodak Park (Kodak website, 2000).

Regarding the level of community concerns about pollution at Kodak Park at that time, one manager stated that, 'Kodak has tried to clean up the sins of the past, and all of the skeletons are out on the table.' He reported that Kodak was monitoring the wells around the contaminated area and was not finding any indication of concern. At least among insiders, the health, safety and environment (HSE) program at Kodak Park was known for its rigor (Lave et al., 1997). One manager reported, 'There's an incredible level of scrutiny' of all operations. Also, unlike the film business, the facility where the single-use camera was developed is geographically distinct from Kodak Park, and has not been a source of environmental concerns.

Envisioning the 'Double Bottom Line'

The two companies also differ in the extent to which they envision a 'double bottom line,' wherein positive business outcomes (including increased market share and higher profits) are linked to improved environmental performance. Both firms revised and improved their manufacturing processes at the same time that they addressed environmental issues with their respective products. At Giftco, new technology was introduced to the manufacturing process, and the increased computerization improved quality control. At Kodak, automation at the single-use camera manufacturing facility increased the efficiency of the manufacturing process.

However, each firm interpreted these developments differently. At Giftco, improvements to the manufacturing process were not viewed as related to the greening of the product. In other words, Giftco managers did not interpret events as evidence of a double bottom line. The health, safety and environment (HSE) staff instigated the effort to eliminate T from the products and manufacturing processes. The engineering staff had already made plans for the introduction of new technology and quality control improvements. The push to eliminate T, however, provided a catalyst for these changes. When asked if they would have made these changes anyway, Giftco managers replied that they would have got round to it eventually. The HSE initiative to eliminate T prompted Giftco to make these changes sooner.

The technology and quality improvements were driven by the company's emphasis on the quality and enduring nature of their products. The efforts to eliminate T, on the other hand, derived from the pressure by outside regulatory agencies and concerns for worker health and environmental pollution from the waste stream. These two separate pressures were never seen as interrelated. The managers of Giftco continued to view these two developments in the company as separate events. They never concluded that the environmentally-oriented process improvements, coupled with quality and technology advances, created a double bottom line.

In contrast, at Kodak, double bottom line thinking was more widespread through management processes. In the selection of new product development concepts, no new programs were chosen that did not include opportunities for recycling. Kodak's HSE staff was also more active in product development. Kodak also put new incentives in place for its sales and marketing teams to sell more recyclable products: 'They set up this incentive system from scratch. It didn't exist before this [recycling] program.' In the field, Kodak created a training tape to teach film processors how to recycle used cameras, and the value of recycling for the environment. A Kodak manager summed up the double bottom line viewpoint:

> As for the financials, it saves us money. We see recycling as a competitive advantage ... The recycling program drives a better business model.

Concern for the environment was beginning to be integrated into strategy at Kodak. Managers reported that their strategy was to 'Bring photographically superior products to consumers.' They viewed their core competence as superior photos through better value, and recognized that part of the value came from the recycling program.

Why were similar events interpreted differently at these two firms? One answer may lie in the different roles that HSE staff played in the two cases. At Kodak, the same group of product developers planned and implemented the single-use camera and the subsequent recycling program. Thus, recycling was integrated into the product design and business plan, the way any other product feature would be. These innovators were geographically separate from the HSE staff who worked at the headquarters building. They worked from a product development perspective, focusing on creative product design rather than on regulatory requirements that demand the attention of HSE staff. Kodak's product innovators welcomed the challenge of redesigning the single-use camera.

At Giftco, however, the HSE staff instigated the product's redesign under pressure from regulatory agencies. 'The writing was on the wall.' If they didn't eliminate ingredient T voluntarily, they would have been forced to do so. Thus, the redesign efforts were regarded as another unwanted cost of doing business in a regulatory climate, despite the quality improvements in the manufacturing process and the positive environmental benefits.

Belief systems also differed at the two firms. At Kodak organizational actors believed in the value of recycling for addressing environmental problems. One product development team member was known for requiring only one small bag for trash each week for a family of three. At Giftco, however, the HSE officer believed that toxic ingredient T was a 'political and emotional problem, not a scientific problem.' The scientific evidence suggesting that T was harmful to workers and/or consumers did not convince him.

DISCUSSION AND CONCLUSION

Theoretical Contribution: Mechanisms that Mediate Corporate Greening and Information Disclosure

These cases suggest a model that addresses the theoretical research question concerning mechanisms that mediate information disclosure and corporate greening. Rather than looking at how mandated information disclosure may, or may not, lead to corporate greening, this study explored the situation in reverse. In the cases of this study, companies engaged in greening behavior that did or did not lead to disclosure of their green activity.

This study's results support previous findings concerning influences on corporate greening, including: (1) ways in which a firm's history provides a context for understanding environmental issues (Hoffman, 1999; Hoffman and Vantresca, 1999; Jennings and Zandbergen, 1995), (2) how strategic identity organizes perceptions of issues confronting organizations (Dutton and Dukerich, 1991; Heller, 2000) and (3) how individual organizational actors interpret events around environmental issues (Sharma et al., 1999; Sharma, 2000).

At the broadest level of analysis, the firm's history sets the stage concerning how much the firm has to gain or lose by the revelation or disclosure of green activity. A potential first exposure of negative environmental impact was experienced as a great threat at Giftco. As veterans of disclosure and exposure, subsequent disclosures were experienced differently at Kodak. This finding supports King's (2000) suggestion that a firm's initial defensive reaction to environmental regulation may differ from subsequent, more positive reactions.

At the level of organization and strategy, results support observations that strategic identity shapes the importance attached to an issue and that issues or actions that are dissonant with strategic identity will be particularly salient to organizational actors (Dutton and Dukerich, 1991; Heller, 2000). The stark contrast between environmental problems and the identity of Giftco as a high-quality heirloom producer made them especially averse to publicity concerning environmental issues. At Kodak, on the other hand, the identity as a high-value photographic film and equipment company allowed for an easier inclusion of environmental issues, as green features of its product were seen as part of the value that they took pride in offering.

At the level of individual organizational actors, findings of this study support previous research concerning the role that interpretation plays, as managers assess whether environmental issues are threats or opportunities (Sharma et al., 1999; Sharma, 2000). Kodak's managers demonstrated an ability to envision a double bottom line and a new business model. This ability is related to two of the factors identified in previous research as enabling individuals to see opportunity in environmental issues. First, recycling was legitimated by its consonance with corporate identity. In addition, the manager, Worldwide OTUC Recycling had 'discretion to take action at the business–natural environment interface' (Sharma et al., 1999: 104).

The EHS manager at Giftco did not have these organizational supports, and did not see the double bottom line. Furthermore, his organization waited until the last minute in the issue life cycle to act when 'the writing was on the wall' and discretion had all but disappeared.

Implications for Research

Green actions and disclosure are inconsistent in these cases, but not in the way that is often assumed in management research. In the case of Giftco's 'invisible' double bottom line, the operational reality is more advanced, in terms of greening, than the espoused policy of compliance. The walk is greener than the talk. Future researchers should not assume that a firm's reluctance to disclose information necessarily means that negative environmental impacts are being kept secret. These cases suggest that the secret may actually be environmentally friendly products.

These cases also underline the importance of multi-level (Starik and Rands, 1995), context-grounded analysis for understanding these complex phenomena. Future research is needed to explore the dynamics of disclosure and visibility in the context of normal business activity. Only then can we learn how this requirement of current environmental policy interacts with traditional organizational behaviors of secrecy, proprietary knowledge and control of information disclosure.

Policy and Managerial Implications: Dynamics of Exposure, Disclosure, Visibility and Secrecy

The study reported in this chapter began with the broad research question: How do dynamics of information disclosure interact with traditional organizational behaviors of secrecy, proprietary knowledge and corporate control of information? Cases of product development were studied that capture these themes in the context of business activity. We looked at how these themes played out in cases where products were subjected to criticism on environmental grounds, then revised to become more green.

The dynamics of disclosure differed in each case. At Giftco, the unspoiled image created a force for secrecy. The firm saw that its interest was in keeping information private. They reasoned that the revelation of good news may also lead to revelations about the firm's negative environmental impact. Publicity was, therefore, experienced as a threat rather than as reward.

The dynamic at Kodak was the reverse. Current practices were enacted against a backdrop of historic, publicized negative environmental impacts. The drive was to tout activities that represented responsible environmental behavior. Under these circumstances, publicity was experienced as a reward. The 'Waste Maker' award for the original throwaway camera reinforced the effort to develop the recycling system. In other words, making the bad news public contributed to the drive to create a good news story and to make it public as well.

Thus, the model that emerges from these cases is a process in which publicity of positive environmental activity is experienced as rewarding only when it follows after the publicity of negative environmental impact. Without the visibility of negative environmental impact, the prospect of publicizing positive environmental activity is experienced as a threat. The threat is that attention will be drawn to negative aspects of the firm's environmental performance.

The policy question, then, becomes: Under what circumstances is publicity of green activity rewarding to a firm? The answer suggested by these cases is: When there has been previous publicity of negative environmental impact. This finding is consistent with research that suggests that visibility creates pressure for firms to green their activities (Bowen, 2000). Companies who have experienced negative publicity of their environmental impacts are in a position of being motivated to seek publicity for more positive environmental activities. In the words of a Giftco manager, 'They have nothing to lose.'

Finally, for managers pondering a decision to publicize (or not to publicize) a firm's green activity, this study suggests that a longer time horizon may be useful. Establishing a track record of transparency for environmental impacts, good or bad, creates a background of public trust. Hoarding skeletons of environmental bad news in the closet, on the other hand, may create a regrettable situation in which disclosure of good news becomes, understandably, viewed as a threat.

REFERENCES

Bowen, F.E. (2000), *Environmental Visibility: A Trigger of Green Response?*, *Business, Strategy and the Environment*, **9**: 92–107.

Carson, R. (1962), *Silent Spring*, Boston: Houghton Mifflin.

Cohen, M.A. (2000), 'Information as a policy instrument in protecting the environment: what have we learned?', Paper presented at the Business Environment Learning and Leadership (BELL) Conference, Vanderbilt University, Nashville, TN, July.

Dutton, J.E. and J.M. Dukerich (1991), 'Keeping an eye on the mirror: image and identity in organizational adaptation,' *Academy of Management Journal*, **34**(3): 517–54.

Field, K.A. (2000), 'Say Greeeeeeen!,' *Design News*, 15 May: 68–74.

Hamilton, J.T. (1995), 'Pollution as news: media and stock market reactions to the toxics release inventory,' *Journal of Environmental Economics and Management*, **28**: 98–113.

Heller, T. (2000), '"If only we'd known sooner:" developing knowledge of organizational changes earlier in the product development process,' *IEEE Transactions on Engineering Management*, **47**(3): 335–59.

Hoffman, A.J. (1999), ' Institutional evolution and change: environmentalism and the US chemical industry,' *Academy of Management Journal*, **42**(4): 351–71.

Hoffman, A.J. and M.J. Ventresca (1999), 'The institutional framing of policy debates,' *American Behavioral Scientist*, **42**(8):1368–92.

Jennings, D. and P.A. Zandbergen (1995), 'Ecologically sustainable organizations: an institutional approach,' *Academy of Management Review*, **20**(4): 1015–52.

King, A. (2000), 'Organizational response to environmental regulation: punctuated change or autogenesis?,' *Business, Strategy and the Environment*, **9**: 224–38.

Kodakwebsite(2000), *www.kodak.com/US/en/corp/environment/community/involvement/other/* environmental.shtml. 25th September.

Konar, S. and M.A. Cohen (1997) 'Information as regulation: the effect of community right to know laws on toxic emissions,' *Journal of Environmental Economics and Management*, **32**: 109–24.

Lave, L.B., N. Conway-Schempf and A. Horvath (1997), *Eastman Kodak Case – Implementation of TQEM at Kodak Park's Utilities Division*, Washington, DC: Management Institute for Environment and Business, World Resources Institute.

Lofland, J. and L.H. Lofland (1984), *Analyzing Social Settings: A Guide to Qualitative Observation and Analysis*, Belmont, CA: Wadsworth Publishing Company.

Outen R.B. (2000),'Designing information rules to encourage better environmental performance,' Washington, DC: World Resources Institute.

Ragin, C.C. (1987), *The Comparative Method: Moving Beyond Qualitative and Quantitative Strategies*, Berkeley and Los Angeles: University of California Press.

Schatzman, L. and A.L. Strauss, Anselm (1973), *Field Research: Strategies for a Natural Sociology*, Englewood Cliffs, NJ: Prentice-Hall.

Sharma, S. (2000), 'Managerial interpretations and organizational context as predictors of corporate choice of environmental strategy,' *Academy of Management Journal*, **43**: 681–97.

Sharma, S., A. Pablo and H. Vredenburg (1999),'Corporate environmental responsiveness strategies: the importance of issue interpretation and organizational context,' *Journal of Applied Behavioral Science*, **35**(1): 87–108.

Starik, M. and G.P. Rands (1995), 'Weaving an integrated web: multilevel and multisystem perspective of ecologically sustainable organizations,' *Academy of Management Review*, **20**(4): 908–35.

Strauss, A.L. (1987), *Qualitative Analysis for Social Scientists*, Cambridge: Cambridge University Press.

Yin, R.K. (1989), *Case Study Research: Design and Methods*, Newbury Park: Sage
    Publications.

10. Sustainable stakeholder accounting beyond complementarity and towards integration in environmental accounting

W. Richard Sherman, David S. Steingard and Dale E. Fitzgibbons

INTRODUCTION

This chapter explores the possibility of integrating environmental performance measures directly into financial statements in order to assess a company's financial impact on sustainability. In conventional accounting, the environmental costs of doing business are largely invisible, externalized and unrecorded. Current efforts at environmental accounting, in the form of a stand-alone CER (corporate environmental report), provide information about a company's environmental performance. However, these reports typically fail to influence the financial performance of a company as reflected in financial statements. Sustainable stakeholder accounting, on the other hand, directly integrates environmental costs, liabilities, and sustainable investments into the financial statements. Using these re-engineered financial statements, investors, managers, customers and other stakeholders can have a more holistic and accurate picture of a company's contribution (positive or negative) to a sustainable future:

> We not only need new forms of accountability but also new forms of accounting (Shell, 1998).

How do stakeholders know if a company is environmentally responsible? To what extent are investors, consumers, employees, the community and other stakeholders cognizant of the environmental records of the company in question? How is this environmental performance measured? How is a company's environmental impact communicated? What disclosures are required? Are these disclosures subject to external verification?

This chapter seeks answers to these questions – and where no answers currently exist, to propose new forms of accounting for the impact that virtually all companies have on the natural environment. In the process, we examine the 'separate but unequal' status which is given to environmental and other social disclosures which are intended to complement and supplement the financial statements which are prepared and issued in accordance with generally accepted accounting principles (GAAP) and regulatory requirements such as SEC filings. The purpose of this chapter is to explore a more holistic relationship between financial and environmental reporting with the goal of transforming how corporations measure and communicate their environmental performance and are evaluated in terms of their sustainable (or unsustainable) impact on all stakeholders.

Current practice

Extant efforts in the fields of socially responsible investing (SRI), corporate social responsibility (CSR), and green/social accounting assess the environmental and social performance of a corporation using stakeholder audits, corporate social audits, environmental impact statements and corporate environmental reports. From an external reporting perspective, the most common vehicle for communication of a company's environmental performance is a separate corporate environmental report (CER) that stands apart from the company's annual financial reports. Thirty-five percent of the Fortune 250 largest companies published separate environmental or health, safety and environment (HSE) reports, with 18 percent of these CERs being externally verified (KPMG/WIMM, 1999).[1] However, since these disclosures are not required[2] and no standard form for these reports has been developed, the quality, quantity and consistency of the information presented varies greatly among companies and industries (Gamble et al.,1995; Gray et al., 2001).[3]

Furthermore, the information contained in these reports is rarely of a financial nature, nor are the CERs linked directly to the financial statements in the company's annual report. As a result, while these non-financial reports on social and environmental activities are intended to complement conventional financial reports, they do not actually alter the usual key indicators of corporate performance such as profitability, solvency and liquidity. Given their complementary nature, both types of reports (social and environmental, and financial) would be expected to have significant impact on corporate managers, investors and consumers in their decision-making. However, the intended relationship between non-financial reporting and financial analysis provided by traditional corporate reports has not been realized. Social and environmental reports are not weighed commensurately in the market valuation and performance assessment of a firm. Instead, 'financial statements have a dominant place in organizational performance. It is . . . their very primacy as *the* measure of organizational success and the way in which that measure is founded upon fundamental assumptions we accountants make in our calculation of profit that is at the very heart of the causes . . . of environmental degradation' (Gray et al., 2000: 14).

Even with the increasingly sophisticated developments in life cycle assessment (LCA) and 'full' or 'total cost' accounting,[4] a gap exists between the internal use of environmental accounting systems[5] and the information that is being communicated to external stakeholders. The lack of integration between the monetary values reported on the face of the company's financial statements and information contained in the environmental accounting systems prevents a fuller and more accurate picture of corporate performance from being presented to those outside the organization. In addition, such practices tend to ignore the recent and growing organizational literature that recognizes corporations are inextricably connected to the physical and ecological environment.[6] This literature explicitly recognizes that managerial decisions significantly affect the viability and sustainability of the planet and if we ignore these effects, we do so at our own peril (see Starik and Marcus, 2000, for a comprehensive overview as well as Gladwin et al., 1995, and Starik and Rands, 1995). Once the importance of these environmental and ecological issues is acknowledged, accounting practices must also change in order to better reflect them.

THREE ACCOUNTING PARADIGMS

Each organization, depending on its particular market and constituents, is forced to focus on specific environmental issues and contemplate the environmental decisions that accompany those issues. Drivers such as public pressure, regulatory requirements, economic concerns, competition, environmental disasters and corporate values all interact to dictate which environmental issues and decisions receive corporate attention and are ultimately transformed into formal corporate policies and programs, replete with associated risks and costs (Dillon and Fischer, 1992). The way that an organization visualizes itself and responds with respect to the natural environment has been deemed the organization's environmental paradigm (Jennings and Zandbergen, 1995). As evidenced in the conglomeration of rules, routines and initiatives of the organization, the environmental paradigm provides the views and ideas that are used by individual members to bracket or interpret particular environmental issues as they arise (Dutton, 1993; Jennings and Zandbergen, 1995).

Just as an organization operates within an environmental paradigm, accountants, both inside and outside the organization, operate within their own paradigms. These paradigms, in turn, affect the theory and practice of accounting. While seemingly objective and without bias, a company's accounting paradigm may place additional burdens on the organization's environmental initiatives due to the limitations and unintended consequences of the information which is collected, analyzed and reported to decision-makers and other stakeholders.

Figures 10.1 to 10.3 provide a graphical depiction of the relationship between the natural environment, the environmental paradigm which an organization holds and the accounting paradigm which assists or impedes the operation of these corporate environmental paradigms (adapted from Sherman et al., 2000). In Figure 10.1, the company treats environmental issues as being merely 'social issues' – that is, secondary to what is perceived as being the primary corporate purpose of maximizing stockholder wealth in the short term. The conventional accounting paradigm is perfectly suited to supporting this corporate environmental stance, reporting only on those environmental issues that would have a direct impact on the short-term profitability, namely, known or probable environmental liabilities. (See Box 10.1 for an example of conventional accounting's reporting of Exxon's environmental impact.)

Figure 10.2 depicts an increasingly common situation in which the corporation has embraced environmental issues as being an integral piece of its strategic focus. No longer is the natural environment treated as yet another externality that is addressed only when required. Instead, eco-savings, eco-efficiencies and other environmental concerns are treated as strategies to achieve corporate objectives. Despite this shift in corporate environmental stance, the organization's accounting system often lags behind, stuck somewhere between its conventional roots and the development of a more inclusive recording of environmental impacts. The prime motivator in shifting from the top to the bottom of Figure 10.2 is the necessity of having accounting data to support the 'strategic' corporate environmental paradigm. As a result, most of the 'environmental accounting' is done for internal decision-making, not for external reporting purposes. Nevertheless, as previously noted, in order to promote a more transparent communication of its environmental activities, the 'strategic issue' company often issues separate environment reports (CERs) to supplement the conventional financial statements published in the corporate annual report.

The shift from the social issue to the strategic issue paradigm is a major step towards creating a sustainable corporation, but it is not enough. Indeed, natural environmental issues have the potential to revolutionize the way that organizations conduct business and interact with internal and external stakeholders (Post, 1991). This 'ecocentric' view of the relationship between business and the environment, illustrated in Figure 10.3, is in line with Shrivastava's (1995) notion of the natural environment as a 'fundamental transforming force' for managers. In contrast to the traditional 'technocentric' management paradigm emphasizing production, consumption and financial risk, the paradigm of ecocentric management advocates reconceptualizing the activities of business organizations in such a way that the natural environment forms the core around which organizational processes occur (Purser et al.,1995; Shrivastava, 1995). Accordingly, if businesses are to effectively address the environmental degradation occurring in our society, they must seek designs and practices that are ecologically sustainable. These include considerations of the renewability and sustainability of inputs and outputs, alternative energy sources, cyclical systems of production, assessments of the ecological impact of technologies and a re-evaluation of the desirability of growth (Jennings and Zandbergen, 1995; Shrivastava, 1995). This is where both conventional and environmental accounting systems fall short in supporting an ecocentric paradigm. Not only do they not effectively communicate the company's environmental efforts and performance to outsiders, these systems do not and cannot provide the necessary information to support the ecocentric managers who are trying to provide for a sustainable future.

Table 10.1 provides a conceptual framework that outlines three possible paradigms of environmental accounting. Despite a marked increase in the number of companies shifting into the environmental accounting paradigm, conventional accounting continues to predominate in corporate practice (Sherman et al., 2000). Furthermore, the sustainable accounting paradigm exists in theory only. Just as no company is truly sustainable, no company has adopted a system of accounting that truly integrates the financial, environmental and social aspects of its operations.[7]

TOWARDS A NEW ACCOUNTING: SUSTAINABLE STAKEHOLDER ACCOUNTING

Accounting numbers can change corporate and investor behavior. Estes (1996) argues that accounting has the ability to define how the game is being played. If we want to change the rules of the game, then we first need to change accounting. Gray is more emphatic when he considers the impact that accounting has had on the natural environment:

(A)ccounting is the score-keeper. The 'score' takes no account of environmental matters and so, as a result, neither does 'economic' decision-making. Given the importance of accounting information and the way in which we account it seems inevitable therefore that 'economic' decisions must be environmentally malign. The environmental crisis is an inevitable result of the way we accountants do what we do. Accounting bears a serious responsibility for the growing level of environmental devastation (Gray et al., 1993: 22).

Table 10.1 Three accounting paradigms

Paradigm	Conventional accounting	Environmental accounting system	Sustainable stakeholder accounting
Integration of environmental impact	None except for disclosure of liabilities	Complementary	Integrative
Underlying assumption about environment	Secondary issue: reactive, compliance, no strategic importance	Environment as competitive advantage, proactive, beyond compliance	Environment as fundamental, sustainable profit and development, ecocentric
Reporting method	Financial only	Financial and stand-alone environmental	Sustainable stakeholder accounting report
Costs	Internal and historical	Internal and historical	Internal, historical, external, future
Profit	Short-term profit but for unsustainable operations	Short-term profit but for unsustainable operations	Long-term profit for sustainable operations

Given its role as 'scorekeeper', accounting needs to be more creative. Furthermore, in light of the disproportionate attention that monetary values are given by both internal (managers) and external (investors and creditors) users of information, this more creative accounting needs to use monetary values, however difficult to calculate, to give greater transparency to a corporation's efforts and achievements, costs and failures – and to tie those numbers into the face of the financial statements.

Environmental accounting can be seen as one aspect of the broader field of social accounting, auditing and reporting (SAAR or SEAAR: social and environmental accounting, auditing and reporting). As such, it has been of interest to academics,[8] professional accounting bodies,[9] governmental units[10] and, increasingly, non-governmental organizations (NGOs).[11] While valuable contributions have been made and general reporting guidelines have been suggested, few have actually attached monetary units to their models.

Some companies have experimented with attaching dollars and cents to their environmental efforts. For example, since 1996, Baxter International has been preparing and distributing environmental financial statements (EFS) as part of its stand-alone (that is, without being integrated with the company's conventional Annual Report) Sustainability Report (Baxter 1999b). Questions about the methodology used and meaningfulness of the numbers reported in Baxter's 'estimated environmental costs and savings' have been raised:

> It is not difficult to criticize the EFS on grounds of the definitions of terms and of the approximations behind several calculations. However, its stated purpose is not as a problem-solving tool, or even for direct decision support, but for attention-directing, to arouse interest and raise the profile within the company of environmental management (Bennett and James 1998: 309).

The United Nations-sponsored 'case study' by Rubenstein (1992, 1994) provides another example of how accounting can better communicate the environmental issues that face a company. In discussing a variety of possible valuation methods such as abatement *versus* damage costing, remediation cost, non-utilization or subsidy value, capitalized earnings of alternative sustainable uses and compensation value, Rubenstein expands the conventional definitions of assets and liabilities to encompass natural capital, broadens the time frame under consideration from the conventional annual accounting period to 60 years, and creates 'green balance sheets' with 'intergenerational trust accounts.' Using such mixed and creative methodologies to value renewable and non-renewable natural capital, Rubenstein calculates the cost of a Canadian forest for the purpose of both internal and external financial reporting by a lumber company. Despite (or because of) its fresh approach to environmental reporting, Rubenstein's methodology has yet to find its way into any company's published financial reports.

Much less detailed than Rubenstein as to how one would actually arrive at the monetary values is Gray's suggested use of:

> a parallel accounting system which provided calculations of what additional costs must be borne by the organization if the organization activity were not to leave the planet worse off, i.e., what it would cost at the end of the accounting period to return the planet and biosphere to the point it was at the beginning of the accounting period . . .
>
> To be effective, this shadow accounting system would preferably produce numbers which can be deducted from calculated accounting profit and be expanded in the restoration of the biosphere. *This will, thus, lead to a recognition that organization income has been grossly overstated for some considerable time and that current generations have been benefiting at the cost of some future generations. The probability is that no western company has made a sustainable profit for a very long time, if ever* (Gray, 1992: 419–20).

Using this model, a company would calculate its revenues and expenses as it would normally do under conventional GAAP. However, once this calculation of profit or loss was completed, a second computation of additional costs necessary to make the company 'sustainable' (that is, leaving the environment no worse off than it was before the company's operations) would be used to 'adjust' reported earnings. It is this 'sustainable profit' (or, more probably, 'sustainable loss') which would be the true measure of a company's performance for a particular period.[12]

Gray's model is fraught with nightmarish issues concerning the methodology used and consequent validity of the numbers produced.[13] For example, in arriving at a 'sustainable cost,' Gray would include the costs of both the 'sustainable' (that is, substitutable or renewable resources like water, air, timber and so on) and 'critical' (non-replaceable natural resources such as the ozone layer, wetlands and critical habitats) natural capital which a company used in its operations. Left with the unenviable task of arriving at a monetary value for 'priceless' non-replaceable capital, Gray is forced to assign infinity as the cost for the critical natural capital expended.

The problems with sustainable cost calculations do not stop there. Using another definition of external cost – 'a cost imposed by an entity as a by-product of its economic activity on third parties (for example, households)' (Atkinson, 2000) – a company that wishes to accurately account for the total cost or total impact is left with the unenviable task of trying to measure, for example, the cost of the pollution created as a by-product of its operations which has been imposed on employees, consumers, communities and others.[14]

In spite of these seemingly insurmountable obstacles with costing and valuations, the true contribution of Rubenstein's costing methodology for natural resources and Gray's calculation of sustainable profit lies not in the exactness of the numbers produced but in their attempt to make visible that which is currently invisible. Whereas only unsustainable profits are currently being reported using traditional accounting disclosures, 'sustainable' profits reported by Gray's shadow system would provide a more accurate portrayal for stakeholder decision-making. Moreover, by reporting these environmentally adjusted profits and losses, environmental impacts can find their way into the financial ratios and other analytical techniques so widely used in performance evaluation and investment decisions.[15] In sum, the fact that 'the resultant data should be both disruptive and shocking' (Gray, 1992: 417) would effect a change in managerial, investor and stakeholder behavior.

Another conceptual technique, described by Magness (1997), is the use of an experimental balance sheet containing an environmental equity section. This section would contain those environmental costs which have not already been included in the calculation of the company's net income due to their external nature – for example, medical costs arising from reduced air quality, lost wages due to illness, crop damage and declining biodiversity. As the company makes environment-related expenditures, this environmental equity would be reduced on the balance sheet. The resulting decrease of environmental equity as a percentage of total equity would show that 'environmental resources have suffered less damage or depletion while sustaining the operations of this business' (Magness, 1997: 16). On the other hand, if the environmental equity section increases as a percentage of total equity, then the environment is being depleted by the business operations, which in turn affects the company's ability to be profitable on an ongoing basis (Magness, 1997: 18).

Combining Gray's idea of a sustainable income (profit and loss) statement with Magness's environmental equity balance sheet account, new forms of sustainable stakeholder accounting (SSA) statements could be developed. These statements would express environmental impacts using monetary units as a form of common denominator so that a company's environmental performance could be directly tied into the conventional financial statements found in Annual Reports, 10K and 10Q filings, earnings announcements and other financial reports and regulatory disclosures.

An example of these statements – a profit and loss statement for sustainable operations and a statement of sustainable financial position[16] – is presented in Table 10.3. Conventional financial statements – an income statement and a balance sheet – are also presented in order to provide a contrast to the SSA statements. To further clarify the accounting treatment (or non-treatment) of a company's environmental performance, Table 10.2

presents the impact that the company's operations have on the accounting equation under conventional reporting and under our proposed sustainable stakeholder accounting (SSA).

The fact pattern is similar to that provided by Magness (1997). As a starting point, the company's balance sheet is presented at the end of the year 2000 (all numbers in millions). The assets represent the resources owned by the company at the year-end; the equity side shows the sources of these assets – with $400 (or 40 percent) coming from creditors (that is, liabilities) and the remaining $600 (or 60 percent) coming from the owners (the company's stockholders). During 2001, the company reports revenues of $900 and expenses of $500. These expenses include some (in this case, only $25) but not all the environmental costs of doing business. Under conventional accounting, $300 of the external costs (such as medical costs associated with reduced air quality, lost wages due to illness, crop damage, declining biodiversity and so on) have not been internalized by the company and would not be reported – that is, would not be incorporated into the company's income statement, nor in the company's balance sheet, or anywhere else. As a consequence, the net income of $400 reported on the income statement is overstated inasmuch as it does not account for all of the company's environmental costs of doing business. Table 10.2 shows the impact that the $400 of profit has on the accounting equation, with equal increases in the company's assets[17] and in the stockholders' equity section.

On the other hand, SSA does account for these external costs by recognizing an environmental liability and an offsetting environment equity component. As a point of departure from Magness's treatment of this $300 of environmental equity as a positive number, we believe that it makes more sense to treat this as a negative component of the company's equity (a contra-equity account). In essence, the equity which the stockholders have in the company is reduced or compromised by the 'equity' sacrificed by other stakeholders who are worse off as a result of the company's operations. To simplify this example, assume that the entire $300 of additional environmental costs relates to the current period (2001) and as such will be shown as a negative environmental impact on the company's profit and loss statement for sustainable operations. This adjustment to the company's reported income follows Gray's model of a 'parallel' or 'shadow' accounting system. Instead of merely reporting an unsustainable profit of $400, the profit and loss statement for sustainable operations reflects more accurately that the company has only been able to generate a sustainable profit of $100.

As these results from operations flow through to the statement of sustainable financial position, the subtotal for 'income before environmental impact' does indeed increase the 'Stockholders' Equity' section of the balance sheet by $400 (from $600 on 31 December 2000 to $1,000 on 31

December 2001). However, the environmental charge also flows to the statement of sustainable financial position (SSA's version of the balance sheet) in the form of an environmental liability and as a negative component of the company's equity shown as 'Environmental Equity.' Thus, the company's total equities (liabilities plus stakeholder equities) is the same as that reported on a conventional balance sheet – only the composition has changed to highlight the interests of stakeholders (the community, future generations, nature and so on) other than the stockholders or owners. Moreover, this new form of sustainability accounting recognizes and reports the existence of the environmental liability that will have to be satisfied at some point in the future for the company – and the world – to survive.

A further implication of this new SSA system can be seen by looking at its effect on two commonly used financial ratios. The debt to total assets (or the similar debt to equity ratio) measures the relative contribution of creditors to the company's resources. For example, as originally calculated for our company, the debt to total asset ratio of 0.40 indicates that the company has raised 40 percent of its capital by way of debt, with the company's owners or stockholders providing the other 60 percent. From the point of view of creditors (existing or potential), a relatively low debt to total asset ratio is desirable. Indeed, debt covenants frequently set ceilings on how high a company's debt ratio can climb before the loan is technically in default and will be called in. Note that under conventional accounting, this company's debt to total asset ratio is improving (at least, from the perspective of the company's creditors) – falling from 0.40 at the end of 2000 to 0.286 at the end of 2001. However, by recognizing the environmental liability and negative environmental equity, the company's ratio has actually climbed from 0.40 to 0.50 at the end of 2001. Given this new accounting, one which more accurately reflects the true liabilities of the company, creditors would be much less willing to make a loan – or continue to carry an already outstanding loan. In short, in terms of its sustainable financial position, this company is far riskier than conventional accounting would have us believe.

Net profit margin measures how much of each dollar of revenue a company is able to bring down to its 'bottom line.' Under conventional reporting, this company appears to be very profitable with a net profit margin of 44.44 percent (that is, 44 cents of each dollar of revenue showing as profit). However, this profit is reduced dramatically (to 11.11 percent) by the recognition of the company's negative environmental impact – confirming Gray's belief that with the use of a 'shadow' environmentally-adjusted accounting system, 'the resultant data should be both disruptive and shocking' (Gray, 1992: 417).

The workings of this proposed sustainable stakeholder accounting will most often result in a more negative portrayal of a company's operations and financial position than would be presented under conventional accounting. However, it is possible, at least in theory, for a company to have a positive environmental (that is, sustainable) impact during a particular period – and even a positive environmental equity section on its sustainable financial position statement. For example, assume that during year 2002, the company engages in positive contributions to the natural environment it had previously degraded (for example, water clean-up, re-forestation or other environmental remediation). Assume further that the cost of these contributions totals $350, with all other revenues and expenses remaining the same as in year 2001. These contributions not only satisfy the previously recognized environmental liability but also create an environmental 'surplus' (that is, an environmental asset) on the company's sustainable financial position statement. Table 10.5 illustrates this possibility. (Table 10.4 shows the impact of these new facts on the accounting equation under conventional accounting and under SSA.)

While the company's conventional income statement and balance sheet are similar to those for year 2001,[18] the company's profit from sustainable operations and sustainable financial position are dramatically improved. This improvement is captured in its ratios. Profit margin from sustainable operations jumps from 11.11 percent in 2001 to 83.33 percent in 2002. The company's debt to total assets ratios falls from 0.50 in 2001 to 0.216 in 2002, making this a much more attractive (that is, less risky) venture for existing or future creditors.

Clearly, this example is overly simplified for purposes of illustrating the workings of SSA. In any year, a company is likely to have both positive and negative environmental impacts. Whether both should be shown on the face of the SSAS or whether they should be offset against one another, reporting only the net positive or negative impact, would depend on the size and nature of the items. Following the accounting concept of materiality, if the items are such that they would affect the decision of the stakeholder, they should be disclosed separately. Consequently, it would not be unusual for a company's SSAS to show both positive and negative adjustments to arrive at its profit or loss for sustainable operations with a concomitant increase and decrease in its environmental assets, liabilities, and equity. (See Table 10.7 where Baxter's net positive environmental impact is shown on its statement of profit and loss for sustainable operations.)

The primary advantage of implementing a system like sustainable stakeholder accounting is that by being expressed in monetary units, the impact of the company's environmental performance (or, for that matter, of any particular aspect of CSR) can be integrated directly into the financial statements and from there, developed into an index or ratio to facilitate analysis.[19] Just as liquidity, solvency and profitability ratios facilitate the analysis of these aspects of an organization, sustainable stakeholder ratios can facilitate the evaluation of the company's socially responsible activities. Moreover, by embedding the financial impact of corporate environmental performance, both positive (such as cost savings and eco-efficiencies) and negative (such as environmental degradation), in the financial statements, a more comprehensive evaluation of true liquidity, solvency and profitability can be made.

AN UNSUSTAINABLE SITUATION: EXXON AND SUSTAINABLE STAKEHOLDER ACCOUNTING

Due to the fact that broader sustainable impacts, total environmental liabilities and environmental equity are not currently measured or disclosed, it is impossible to take these concepts of SSA and apply them directly to some 'real life' companies. However, given the information available in the notes to the financial statements (that is, the 'footnotes') and from other sources, the financial statements of Exxon can be partially restated in terms of sustainable stakeholder accounting.

As is well known, in 1989, Exxon (now ExxonMobil) was involved in one of the largest environmental disasters in history when its tanker, the Valdez, ran aground in Alaska. In addition to $286.8 million in remediation costs, Exxon was also found liable for punitive damages totaling $5 billion – an amount that is still on appeal. Under conventional accounting,[20] the only required disclosure of this contingent liability can be found in the notes to the financial statements. (See Box 10.1 for the content of these notes from 1993 through 1997.) The $5 billion does not appear on Exxon's balance sheet or on the face of any other of the company's financial statements. Consequently, it has no impact on the financial ratios that creditors, investors and other decision-makers use to evaluate Exxon's creditworthiness, solvency or profitability.[21]

This $5 billion charge should actually refer back to 1989 when the Valdez accident occurred. Not only did Exxon not go back and restate its 1989 results, it did not even attempt to make an estimate of this potential risk – a fact which Rubenstein (1994) characterizes as just plain bad accounting. Perhaps even worse 'bad accounting' is being done in 1996, the year in which the judgment was rendered, inasmuch as none of the $5 billion liability appears on any of Exxon's financial statements for that year. The use of SSA would remedy this. Table 10.6 shows the impact that the $5.058 billion environment charge has on Exxon's profit and loss statement for sustainable operations for the year ended 1996 (which, again, should actually be shown on the company's 1989 statements), reducing the reported profit of $7510 million to $2452 million. This charge finds its way into Exxon's sustainable stakeholder financial position, lowering stockholders' equity of $43 542 million to a stakeholders' equity of $38 484 million. As a consequence of these adjustments, the company's ratios suffer – net profit margin falling from a reported 5.59 percent to a profit margin for sustainable operations of 1.83 percent; Exxon's debt to total asset ratio increases from 0.544 to 0.597.

To put this in perspective, these restatements do not come close to approximating the true nature and degree of Exxon's negative impact on the environment. The $5 billion judgment rendered in 1996 is a result of a single lawsuit on just one incident of environmental degradation. As such, it vastly underestimates the environmental damage caused by a company engaged in what, by its very nature, is an unsustainably extractive industry. It does not and cannot capture the true unrecorded costs absorbed by the other stakeholders (for example, community, natural environment, local industry, future generations) as a result of Exxon's normal business practices. If more advanced methodologies for capturing these external environmental costs were used (for example, those formulated by Rubenstein, 1994), a more accurate calculation of the company's true sustainable profit would almost certainly confirm Gray's suspicion 'that no western company has made a sustainable profit for a very long time, if ever' (Gray, 1992: 419–20). Ultimately, such enormous charges would motivate firms to act more responsibly or suffer the consequences of insolvency.

A Sustainable Impact: Baxter International

As was noted previously, Baxter International has been preparing 'environmental financial statements' since 1996. These EFSs attempt to monetize the company's environmental efforts in order to better communicate Baxter's concern for and commitment to sustainable business activities. Due to the limitations of the current state of environmental accounting, not all of Baxter's environmental impacts are measured or disclosed. However, using the information from Baxter's EFS and including it in the integrative statement of profit for sustainable operations, stakeholders would be able to make better decisions from more holistic communication about Baxter's performance. Table 10.7 presents such a statement. Note that the actual profits reported under conventional and sustainable stakeholder accounting are identical. The essential difference is that under conventional accounting Baxter's environmental cost savings ($98 million as reported in its 1999 EFS) are hidden (invisible) in the income statement whereas the fruits of these efforts would be highlighted (made visible) as a positive 'sustainable impact' in a statement of profit and loss for sustainable operations.

Championing Environmental Transformation with SSA

The financial statements in annual reports and other regulatory filings (such as 10Ks and 10Qs) convey liquidity, solvency, profitability, shareholder return and other measures of corporate performance in financial language. On the other hand, social and environmental reports mostly convey impacts of sustainability in terms of non-financial measures like pounds of pollutants released, regulatory compliance and violations, and tons of recycled material. Only occasionally, social and environmental impacts are reported in financial terms. As a result, these dimensions of corporate performance never enter the sacred realm of financial reporting. However, the purported differentiation between financial and non-financial values is inaccurate.

While the output of financial and social and environmental reporting may ostensibly differ, the underlying values these systems translate into measures are essentially comprised of the same substance – human determinations of what is important and worthy of entry into a system of measurement and report. Financial and non-financial values are constitutionally similar enough because they are human values at their core. By realizing their common origin in human consciousness, the privileging of one type of value over the other in terms of the influence of financial and non-financial value accounting is no longer an incontrovertible reality. The key is to combine both types of values into one integrated system of assessment and documentation.

The preceding example of Exxon demonstrates how the integrative nature of SSA could ultimately reflect and communicate the impending insolvency of companies failing to incorporate genuine sustainability into the core of their operations. Exxon's continued legal maneuvering to evade its liability to injured stakeholders affected by the Valdez disaster will make it a risky investment. Likewise, its unwillingness to disinvest itself from extractive fossil fuel technologies, a fact that would be highlighted under the SSA system, would jeopardize its long-term viability. Eventually, Exxon would either have to evolve into a more environmentally sustainable business or dissolve. It would simply be too costly and risky to carry that much 'environmental debt' with its concomitant increasingly negative environmental equity account. (It also bears noting that even while Baxter would receive a somewhat more favorable financial reporting for its proactive measures toward sustainability, a more comprehensive application of SSA would most probably indicate that Baxter's negative environmental impact would most likely net the company a continuing spiral toward bankruptcy.)

Given the reporting done under a SSA system, a corporation would be forced to work toward the long-term sustainability of person and planet or it would not survive. This system safeguards future generations of people and the environment from exploitative, destructive profits reaped in the short term. Moreover, it provides a more accurate picture of the company's true performance, negating the ability of a company seemingly thriving in the present at the expense of as yet unrecorded future costs.

The SSA approach can also be expanded to include the impact from other social information that would be relevant to particular stakeholders. Indeed, it is our hope that organizations will provide an entire range of social cost – benefit information – stated in monetary terms – that can be used by any particular stakeholder group (different information for different users) to make analytical adjustments to the general purpose financial statements that are devoid of these important items. We have used environmental adjustments to illustrate the workings of our SSA because the methodologies for the costing or pricing of these items are much better developed than in other areas of social responsibility accounting and reporting. It is just a matter of time before better, more advanced, more generally accepted methodologies are developed for other socially responsible activities. For example, human resource accounting is an idea that dates back to the 1960s (Brummet et al., 1968; Flamholtz, 1985), and the recent methodology for the costing of discrimination (Adams and Harte, 2000) reflects the rigor and creativity that accounting can bring to disclosing an organization's social activities.

However, in a clearly value-laden field, we are not proposing the use of a composite index of social responsibility. Such an index would necessarily entail the offsetting or netting of one aspect of social responsibility against another, with the result that a company would, in effect, be imposing its sense as to what constitutes a 'good' trade-off on its stakeholders. Instead, we argue for different (that is, separate) disclosures on each social or stakeholder issue. A company should disclose the benefits it provides for the environmental, community, workforce and other stakeholders as well as the costs it imposes on these stakeholders. It will then be up to the particular stakeholders to pick and choose which costs and benefits are relevant to their own analysis and evaluation of corporate social performance.

Sustainable Stakeholder Accounting as an Inspired Vision of Holistic Success

Given the current state of accounting standard setting, the impetus for a shift to SSA will have to come from within the companies themselves. The Financial Accounting Standards Board (FASB), the private organization which creates new US GAAP, is burdened with political pressure from Corporate America and can not be expected to require the kind of disclosures proposed by our SSA. (See Miller et al., 1997 for an excellent discussion of the political dimensions of the FASB.) A similar forecast of inactivity by the

International Accounting Standards Board (IASB) in improving stakeholder disclosures must also be given. This is particularly troubling in light of the fact that the newly reorganized IASB is working to create a generally accepted set of standards that will, if it is successful, be adopted in 2005 by the European Union and required for financial reporting by listed (publicly traded) companies in any of the EU's member-states. Because of the tremendous potential impact of the IASB's work, one would have hoped that the board would lead the way to a more comprehensive, holistic and sustainable communication of company performance. However, as one consequence of the IASB's primarily investor or shareholder orientation, one IASB member predicts that it will be four or five years before the board even considers requiring environmental disclosures, let alone other information useful to other stakeholder groups (Whittington, 2001).

Unfortunately, environmental issues are still construed as punitive – if you transgress the environment, you will be punished. If a firm moved from mere compliance (for fear of punishment) to one of restoration (embracing sustainability), it might bring about what Ray Anderson, CEO of Interface, calls 'the next industrial revolution' (1998). This paradigm shift would create a variety of differences in organizational structures and processes. For example, we might find environmental champions throughout the organization who would identify, package and sell the issue of environmental importance to top management strategic decision-makers. Ideally, while such champions could come from anywhere in the organization, they are most likely found among those who have a technical interest or passion for environmental issues (Andersson and Bateman, 2000). We would see corporate leaders who are 'more ecocentric, open to change and self-transcendent' than their peers (Egri and Herman, 2000) and thus are better leaders overall. We would most certainly find higher levels of 'eco-innovation,' which would make these firms more flexible and adaptive in turbulent corporate environments (Ramus and Steger, 2000). These might include anything from better waste treatment and cost-efficient packaging to more sensitive managerial compensation packages predicated on the sustainable stakeholder accounting practices discussed earlier. Lastly, we would find firms devising more sophisticated corporate strategies because they would interpret environmental issues not as threats to their existence but as opportunities to prosper and grow (Sharma, 2000). In fact, most aspects of organizational design, structure and process would change as a result of incorporating a more balanced scorecard inherent in these integrative sustainable stakeholder practices (Kaplan and Norton, 1996). Companies like Interface, Patagonia and Ikea who invest in clean technologies, replant forests, follow the Natural Step for business, go beyond OSHA and EPA compliance (Andersson and Bateman, 2000), would reverse the punishment paradigm and be great benefactors. We envision a truly sustainable future through the use of the sustainable stakeholder accounting system.

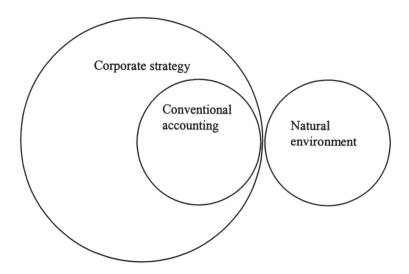

Figure 10.1 Social issues paradigm and conventional accounting paradigm

Source: The Interplay Between Environmental and Accounting Paradigms (Adapted from Sherman et al., 2000)

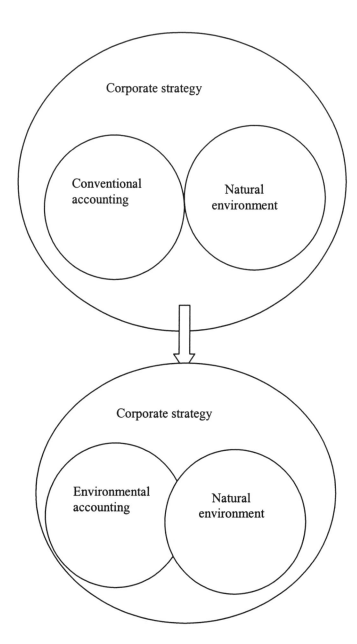

Figure 10.2 Strategic issues paradigm with shift from conventional to environmental accounting paradigm

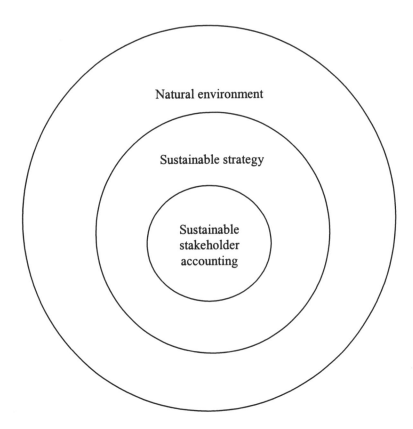

Figure 10.3 Environmental issues as drivers of ecocentrism with shift to sustainable stakeholder accounting

Table 10.2 Impact on the accounting equation

Year 1 - Ending 31 December 2001

Conventional accounting

	Assets			Liabil-ities		Equity	
	Other	Environ-mental		Other	Environ-mental	Stock-holders'	Environ-mental
1 Jan. 2001	1000	0		400	0	600	0
2001 Results	+400	0			0	+900 -500	0
31 Dec. 2001	1400	0		400	0	1000	0

Total assets = 1400   **Total liabilities = 400; Stockholders' equity = 1000**

Sustainable stakeholder accounting

	Assets			Liabil-ities		Equity	
	Other	Environ-mental		Other	Environ-mental	Stock-holders'	Environ-mental
1 Jan., 2001	1000	0		400	0	600	0
2001 Results	+400	0			+300	+900 -500	-300
31Dec. 2001	1400	0		400	300	1000	-300

Total Assets = 1400   **Total Liabilities = 700; Stakeholders' Equity = 700**

Year 1 - Ending 31 December 2001

Conventional accounting

	Assets			Liabil-ities		Equity	
	Other	*Environ-mental*		*Other*	*Environ-mental*	*Stock-holders'*	*Environ-mental*
1 Jan 2001	1000	0		400	0	600	0
2001 Results	+400	0			0	+900 -500	0
31 Dec. 2001	1400	0		400	0	1000	0

Total assets = 1400   Total liabilities = 400; Stockholders' equity = 1000

Sustainable stakeholder accounting

	Assets			Liabil-ities		Equity	
	Other	*Environ-mental*		*Other*	*Environ-mental*	*Stock-holders'*	*Environ-mental*
Jan. 1, 2001	1000	0		400	0	600	0
2001 Results	+400	0			+300	+900 -500	-300
Dec. 31, 2001	1400	0		400	300	1000	-300

Total assets = 1400   Total liabilities = 700; Stakeholders' equity = 700

Table 10.3 Example of conventional vs. sustainable stakeholder accounting - negative environmental impact

Balance sheet
(Beginning)

Assets:		Liabilities	$400
	$1000	Equity:	
		stockholders'	600
Total assets	$1000	Total liabilities and equity	$1000

Ratio: Debt to Total Assets = 0.40

First year's results:		$900
Revenues		
Expenses:		
Regular	$475	
Environmental	25	
Total recorded expenses		$500

Also the company had $300 of unrecorded 'external' environmental costs (negative impact on environment: ozone depletion, increased healthcare costs, etc.) related to this first year.

Conventional accounting income statement (for Year 1)

Revenues	$900
Expenses	(500)*
Net Income	$400

Balance sheet (at end of Year 1)

Assets	$1400	Liabilities	400
(1,000 + 400)		Equity:	
		Stockholders'	
		(600 + 400)	1000
Total assets	$1400	Total liabilities and equity	$1400

Ratios: Net profit margin = 44.4% Debt to Total Assets = 0.286

* Note: Traditional accounting does not take into account $300 of external environmental costs.

Sustainable stakeholder accounting

Statement of profit and loss for sustainable operations (for Year 1)

Revenues	$900
Expenses	(500)
Income before environmental impact	$400
Environmental impact	(300)
Profit (or loss) for sustainable operations	$100

Statement of sustainable financial position (at end of Year 1)

Assets	$1400	Liabilities:	
(1000 + 400)		environmental	$300
		other	400
		Total liabilities	$700
		Equity:	
		stockholders $1000	
		(600 + 400)	
		Environmental (300)*	
		Total equity	700
Total assets	$1400	Total liabilities and equity	$1400

Ratios: Profit margin for sustainable operations = 11.1%
Debt to total assets = 0.50

Note: Sustainable stakeholder accounting does take into account $300 of external environmental costs

Table 10.4 Impact on the accounting equation

Year 2 - Ending 31 December 2002

Conventional accounting

	Assets			Liabil-ities		Equity	
	Other	*Environ-mental*		*Other*	*Environ-mental*	*Stock-holders'*	*Environ-mental*
1 Jan. 2002	1400	0		400	0	1000	0
2002 Results	+400	0			0	+900 -500	0
31 Dec. 2002	1800	0		400	0	1400	0

Total assets = 1800   **Total liabilities = 400; Stockholders' equity = 1400**

Sustainable stakeholder accounting

	Assets			Liabil-ities		Equity	
	Other	*Environ-mental*		*Other*	*Environ-mental*	*Stock-holders'*	*Environ-Mental*
1 Jan. 2002	1400	0		400	300	1000	-300
2002 Results	+400	50			-300	+900 -500	+350
31 Dec. 2002	1400	50		400	0	1400	50

Total assets = 1850   **Total liabilities = 400; Stakeholders' equity = 1450**

Table 10.5 Example of conventional vs. SSA - positive environmental impact

Second Year's Results:

Revenues		$900
Expenses:		
Regular	$475	
Environmental	25	
Total recorded expenses		$500

<u>Also</u> the company had $350 of unrecorded environmental contributions (positive impact on environment: reforestation, waste clean-up, etc.) related to this second year.

Conventional accounting income statement (for Year 2)

Revenues	$900
Expenses	(500)*
Net income	$400

Balance sheet (at end of Year 2)

Assets	$1800	Liabilities	$400
(1,400 + 400)		Equity:	
		Stockholders'	
		(1000 + 400)	1400
Total assets	$1800	Total liabilities and equity	$1800

Ratios: Net profit margin = 44.4%   Debt to total assets = 0.222

* *Note*: Traditional accounting does not take into account $350 of environmental contributions.

Sustainable stakeholder accounting

Statement of profit and loss for sustainable operations (for Year 2)

Revenues	$900
Expenses	(500)
Income before environmental impact	$400
Environmental impact	350*
Profit (or loss) for sustainable operations	$750

Statement of sustainable financial position (at end of Year 1)

Assets:		Liabilities:	
Other	$1800	environmental (300 - 300)	$0
Environmental	50*	other	400
(350 - 300)		Total Liabilities	400
		Equity:	
		stockholders $1400	
		environmental 50*	
		(350-300)	
		Total equity	1450
Total assets	$1850	Total liabilities and equity	$1850

Ratios: Profit margin for sustainable operations= 83.3%
Debt to total assets = 0.216

*Note: Sustainable stakeholder accounting does take into account $350 of environmental contributions.

Table 10.6 Exxon Corporation after Valdez

Conventional accounting **Income statement**		**Sustainable stakeholder** **Profit and loss statement for sustainable operations**	
For year ended 31 December 1996		For year ended 31 December 1996	
Revenues	$134249	Revenues	$134249
Expenses	(126739)	Expenses	(126739)
		Income before environmental impact	$7510
		Less: environmental impact	(5058)
Net income	**$7510**	**Profit for sustainable operations**	**$2452**
Net profit margin	**5.59%**	**Profit margin for sustainable operations**	**1.83%**
Balance sheet		**Sustainable stakeholder financial position**	
31 December 1996		**31 December 1996**	
Assets	$95527	Assets	$95527
Liabilities	**$51985**	**Liabilities**	**$51985**
		+ Environmental liability (Valdez)	5058
		Total liabilities	**$57043**
Equity		**Stakeholders' equity**	
	43542	Stockholders	43542
		Environmental	(5058)
		Total stakeholder equity	**$38484**
Total liabilities and stockholders' equity	**$95527**	**Total liabilities and stockholders' equity**	**$95527**
Debt to total assets	**0.544**	**Debt to total assets**	**0.597**

Box 10.1 Exxon's notes to financial statement reference to the Valdez accident and judgment

FROM 1993 ANNUAL REPORT

A number of lawsuits, including class actions, have been brought in various courts against Exxon Corporation and certain of its subsidiaries relating to the release of crude oil from the tanker Exxon Valdez in 1989. Most of these lawsuits seek unspecified compensatory and punitive damages; several lawsuits seek damages in varying specified amounts. Certain of the lawsuits seek injunctive relief. The claims of many individuals have been dismissed or settled. Most of the remaining actions are scheduled for trial in federal court commending May 2, 1994. Other actions will likely be tried in state court later in 1994. The cost to the corporation from these lawsuits is not possible to predict; however, it is believed that the final outcome will not have a materially adverse effect upon the corporation's operations or financial condition.

FROM 1995 ANNUAL REPORT

14. Litigation and Other Contingencies
A number of lawsuits, including class actions, have been brought in various courts against Exxon Corporation and certain of its subsidiaries relating to the accidental release of crude oil from the tanker Exxon Valdez in 1989. Most of these lawsuits seek unspecified compensatory and punitive damages. Several lawsuits seek damages in varying specified amounts.

A civil trial in the United States District Court for the District of Alaska commenced on May 2, 1994 on punitive damage claims made by a class composed of all persons and entities seeking punitive damages from the corporation as a result of the Exxon Valdez grounding. On September 16, 1994, the jury returned a verdict awarding the class punitive damages of $5 billion. The verdict is not final. The corporation plans to appeal this verdict following entry of a final judgment by the District Court. The corporation believes that this verdict is unjustified and should be set aside or substantially reduced by the District Court or appellate courts.

Many of the claims of individuals have been dismissed by the courts but have been appealed. A number of claims have been settled. With respect to the remaining compensatory damage claims against the corporation arising from the grounding, many of these claims have been or will be addressed in the same federal civil trial proceeding, which is still ongoing. On August 11, 1994, the jury returned a verdict finding that fisher plaintiffs were damaged in the amount of $286.8 million. On August 31, 1995, the District Court issued an order that reduced this verdict to about $70 million to reflect payments already made to the plaintiffs by the corporation and others. The corporation expects this lesser amount to be further reduced. Additional claims for compensatory damages, scheduled for determination in the final phase of the trial, have been settled. The remaining class action claims are included in a $3.5 million settlement of this final phase. The class settlement is subject to approval by the court. The total amount of the settlement will be satisfied by recognition of prior payments made to the plaintiffs by the corporation and others. If the settlement is approved, the federal trial will be concluded. There are a number of additional cases pending in state court in Alaska where the compensatory damages claimed have not been fully specified.

The ultimate cost to the corporation from the lawsuits arising from the Exxon Valdez grounding is not possible to predict and may not be resolved for a number of years.

FROM 1997 ANNUAL REPORT

13. Litigation and Other Contingencies
A number of lawsuits, including class actions, were brought in various courts against Exxon Corporation and certain of its subsidiaries relating to the accidental release of crude oil from the tanker Exxon Valdez in 1989. Essentially all of these lawsuits have now been resolved or are subject to appeal.

On September 24, 1996, the United States District Court for the District of Alaska entered a judgment in the amount of

$5.058 billion in the Exxon Valdez civil trial that began in May 1994. The District Court awarded approximately $19.6 million in compensatory damages to fisher plaintiffs, $38 million in prejudgment interest on the compensatory damages and $5 billion in punitive damages to a class composed of all persons and entities who asserted claims for punitive damages from the corporation as a result of the Exxon Valdez grounding. The District Court also ordered that these awards shall bear interest from and after entry of the judgment. The District Court stayed execution on the judgment pending appeal based on a $6.75 billion letter of credit posted by the corporation. Exxon has appealed the judgment. The corporation continues to believe that the punitive damages in this case are unwarranted and that the judgment should be set aside or substantially reduced by the appellate courts.

The ultimate cost to the corporation from the lawsuits arising from the Exxon Valdez grounding is not possible to predict and may not be resolved for a number of years.

On January 29, 1997, a settlement agreement was concluded resolving all remaining matters between Exxon and various insurers arising from the Valdez accident. Under terms of this settlement, Exxon received $480 million. Final income statement recognition of this settlement will be deferred in view of uncertainty regarding the ultimate cost to the corporation of the Valdez accident.

Table 10.7 Baxter International

<u>Conventional accounting</u>		<u>Sustainable stakeholder accounting</u>	
Income statement		**Profit and loss statement for sustainable operations**	
For year ended 31 Dec. 1999 (millions)		For year ended 31 Dec. 1999 (millions)	
Revenues	$6380	Revenues	$6380
Expenses	(5583)	Expenses	(5681)
		Subtotal	$699
		+ Net environ- mental impact	98
Net Income	**$797**	**Profit for sustainable operations**	**$797**
Net profit margin	**12.49%**	**Profit margin for sustainable operations**	**12.49%**

NOTES

1. In addition to the Fortune 250 companies, the KPMG/WIMM survey included the top 100 companies in 11 countries. Using this total sample of 1100 companies, 24 percent issued some form of environmental report.

2. Under US GAAP, the only environmental disclosure required in a company's financial statements are of the liability (existing or contingent) for past pollution or degradation (FASB, 1975,1976). For an example of this type of disclosure, see the notes to Exxon's financial statements in Table 10.8. International Accounting Standards 5 and 37 parallel the US disclosure requirements. A few European countries (for example, the Netherlands, Norway, Sweden and Denmark) have passed 'Green Account' legislation requiring disclosure of pollution emissions and resource usage. However, these environmental impacts are not required to be expressed in terms of monetary units nor are they linked to the companies' financial statements. Australia and Korea have also recently passed mandatory environmental reporting legislation but the required disclosures suffer from the same shortcomings.

3. While guidelines for a more standardized form of environmental disclosure have been proposed (see, for example, GRI, 2000), these remain developmental and voluntary in nature. See also Ditz and Ranganathan (1977) on environmental performance indicators (EPIs) and a common framework for environmental accounting. Neither proposal would necessarily assign monetary values to the reporting entity's environmental impact.

4. See, also, the concept of 'total impact accounting' (Mathews, 1984, 1997).

5. Although the focus of this chapter is on the external reporting in which companies engage, perhaps the greatest advances in environmental accounting have been made in the internal reporting (the so-called 'managerial accounting systems') which many organizations have developed to capture the environmental costs and savings of their activities. See, for example, CICA (1997), Epstein (1996) and the EPA case studies (1995a, 1995b, 1995c). Indeed, it is precisely because of these advances in 'environmental bookkeeping' that our proposals for improved external disclosures would be feasible.

6. In particular, see *Academy of Management Review* (Jackson, 1995), and *Academy of Management Journal* (Starik et al., 2000) for special issues devoted to these symbiotic relationships.

7. Among others, Royal Dutch/Shell Oil is experimenting with triple bottom line (financial, environmental and social) reporting in its annual reports. Nevertheless, Shell's environmental and social performance measures are expressed in non-monetary terms which prevents a successful integration with its financial statements (Shell, 1998, 2000).

8. See, for example, Bennett and James (1998a), Epstein (1996), Gray (1992), Gray and Bebbington (2000), Gray et al. (1993), Hawken et al. (1999) and Mathews (1984, 1997).

9. Among the professional associations which have provided guidance on SSAR are the Association of Certified and Chartered Accountants (Bebbington and Thomson, 1996, Bennett and James, 1998b, Gonella et al., 1998), the Canadian Institute of Chartered Accountants (1992, 1993a, 1993b, 1997), and the Federation des Experts Comptables Europeens (FEE) (1999).

10. See, for example, the US Environmental Protection Agency (EPA 1995a, 1995b, 1995c) and the European Commission (2001).

11. For example, the United Nations and the Global Reporting Initiative (2000), while possessing no legislative or governmental authority, have been at the forefront of encouraging more complete social and environmental reporting.

12. Throughout this chapter, the term 'sustainable' is used in the context of ecological and social sustainability as opposed to financial sustainability. While Gray uses 'sustainable profit and loss,' we will attempt to remove any potential confusion by describing sustainable stakeholder accounting's profit calculation as 'profit and loss from sustainable operations' and the resulting ratio as 'profit margin for sustainable operations.'

13. Gray acknowledges these problems but also emphasizes that 'as we are trying to move away from mechanistic calculative decision-making, any information which broadly illustrates the sort of magnitude of costs' would encourage better (that is, more environmentally sound) decision-making (1993: 419).

14. Paul Hawken et al. conclude 'While there may be no "right" way to value a forest, a river or a child, the wrong way is to give it no value at all. If there are doubts about how to value a seven hundred year old tree, ask how much it would cost to make a new one' (1999: 321).

15. It would be a gross oversimplification to believe that managerial, investment, and other economic decisions are based exclusively on the information contained in a company's financial statements. However, one should not underestimate the significance of 'reported earnings' and other accounting disclosures. As evidence of the primacy of financial reporting (that is, GAAP reporting), one need look no further than the hue and cry raised by companies whenever a particular disclosure is proposed by a standard-setting organization that would adversely affect these reported results. Given the pressures on publicly traded (that is, listed) companies to meet analysts' earnings forecasts, any effect on the accounting numbers reported will have a concomitant impact on the market price of the company's shares.

16. As noted previously, the term 'sustainable' is used in the context of ecological and social sustainability as opposed to financial sustainability.

17. Whether assets increase, liabilities decrease, or a combination of the two is of no consequence because, in any case, net assets would increase by the $400 profit.

18 Assuming the environmental contribution merely changes the composition, not the dollar amount of the assets, total assets (that is, net total assets) and stockholders' equity increases by the $400 profit earned during 2002.

19. It is this last step that is critical. In its proposed framework for sustainability reporting, the Global Resource Inititative (GRI, 2000) encourages the use of ratios inasmuch as they 'relate two absolute figures to each other and thereby provide a context to both … Ratios help illuminate linkages across economic, environmental, and social dimensions.'

20. *Statement of Financial Accounting Standard No. 5: Accounting for Contingencies* (FASB, 1995).

21. The fact that the $5 billion contingent liability is disclosed in Exxon's footnotes does allow users to make their own analytical adjustments to Exxon's financial statements. As such, the Valdez liability is not the best example of how SSA would provide a more comprehensive presentation. A better example would be seen in the monetization of the massively destructive impact which Exxon's operations have on the environment – and to include those 'environmental liabilities' on the SSA statements.

REFERENCES

Adams, C. and G. Harte (2000), 'Making discrimination visible,' *Accounting Forum*, **24**(1): 56–79.

Anderson, R. (1998), *Mid-Course Correction: Toward a Sustainable Enterprise*, Atlanta GA: Peregrinzilla Press.

Andersson, L.M. and T.S. Bateman (2000), 'Individual environmental initiative: championing natural environmental issue in US business organizations,' *Academy of Management Journal*, **43**(4): 548–70.

Atkinson, G. (2000), 'Measuring corporate sustainability', *Journal of Environmental Planning and Management*, **43**(2): 235–52.

Baxter International (1999a), *Annual Report*, Deerfield, IL: Baxter International.

Baxter International (1999b), *Environmental, Health and Safety Report*, Deerfield, IL: Baxter International.

Bebbington, J. and I. Thomson (1996), *ACCA Research Report No. 48: Business Conceptions of Sustainability and the Implications for Accountancy*, London: Certified Accountants Educational Trust.

Bennett, M. and P. James (1998a), *The Green Bottom Line: Environmental Accounting for Management*, Sheffield: Greenleaf Publishing.

Bennett, M. and P. James (1998b), *ACCA Research Report No. 55: Environment Under The Spotlight: Current Practice and Future Trends in Environment-Related Performance Measurement for Business*, London: ACCA.

Brummet, R.L., E.G. Flamholtz and W.C. Pyle (1968), 'Human resource measurement: a challenge for accounts', *Accounting Review*, April: 217–24.

CICA (Canadian Institute of Chartered Accountants) (1992), *Environmental Auditing and the Role of the Accounting Profession*, Toronto: CICA.

CICA (Canadian Institute of Chartered Accountants) (1993a), *Environmental Stewardship: Managing Accountability and the Role of Chartered Accountants*, Toronto: CICA.

CICA (Canadian Institute of Chartered Accountants) (1993b), *Reporting on Environmental Performance*, Toronto: CICA.

CICA (Canadian Institute of Chartered Accountants) (1997), *Full Cost Accounting from an Environmental Perspective*, Toronto: CICA.

Dillon, P. and K. Fischer (1992), *Environmental Management in Corporations: Methods and Motivations*, Medford: Tufts University.

Ditz, D. and J. Ranganathan (1997), *Measuring Up: Towards A Common Framework For Tracking Corporate Environmental Performance*, Baltimore: World Resources Institute.

Dutton, J. E. (1993), 'The making of organizational opportunities: an interpretive pathway to organizational change,' in B.M. Staw and L.L. Cummings (eds), *Research in Organizational Behavior*, **15**: 195–226, Greenwich: JAI Press.

Egri, C. and S. Herman (2000), 'Leadership in the North American environmental sector: values, leadership styles, and contexts of environmental leaders and their organizations,' *Academy of Management Journal*, **43**(4): 571–604.

EPA [United States Environmental Protection Agency] (1995a), *An Introduction to Environmental Accounting as a Business Management Tool: Key Concepts and Terms*, Washington, DC: USEPA.

EPA [United States Environmental Protection Agency] (1995b), *Environmental Accounting Studies: Green Accounting at AT&T*, Washington, DC: USEPA.

EPA [United States Environmental Protection Agency] (1995c), *Environmental Accounting Case Studies: Full Cost Accounting for Decision Making at Ontario Hydro*, Washington, DC: USEPA.

Epstein, M.J. (1996), *Measuring Corporate Environmental Performance: Best Practices for Costing and Managing an Effective Environmental Strategy*, Chicago, IL: Irwin.

Estes, R. (1996), *Tyranny of the Bottom Line*, San Francisco, CA: Berrett-Koehler Publishers.

European Commission (1992), *The Fifth Action Programme*, Corn (92)23 Final, I–III, Brussels.

European Commission (EC) (2001), 'Commission recommendation of 30 May 2001 on the recognition, measurement and disclosure of environmental issues in the annual accounts and annual reports of companies,' *Official Journal of the European Communities*, C (2001), 1495.

Exxon Corporation (1993), *Annual Report*, Trenton, NJ: Exxon.

Exxon Corporation (1995), *Annual Report*, Trenton, NJ: Exxon.

Exxon Corporation (1997), *Annual Report*, Trenton, NJ: Exxon.

FASB (1975), *Statement of Financial Accounting Standards No. 5: Accounting for Contingencies*, Stamford, CT: FASB.

FASB (1976), *FASB Interpretation No. 14: Reasonable Estimation of the Amount of a Loss*, Stamford, CT: FASB.

Federation des Experts Comptables Europeens (FEE) (1999), *Review of International Accounting Standards for Environmental Issues*, Brussels: FEE.

Flamholtz, E.G. (1985), *Human Resource Accounting*, San Francisco, CA: Jossey-Bass.

Gamble, G.O., K. Hsu, D. Kite and R.R. Radtke (1995), 'Environmental disclosures in annual reports and 10Ks: an examination,' *Accounting Horizons*, 9(3), 34–45.

Gladwin, T.N., J.J. Kennelly and T. Krause (1995), 'Shifting paradigms for sustainable development: implications for management theory and research,' *Academy of Management Review*, 20(4): 874–907.

Global Reporting Initiative (GRI) (2000), *Sustainability Reporting Guidelines on Economic, Environmental, and Social Performance*, Boston, MA: Coalition for Environmentally Responsible Economies.

Gonella, C., A. Pilling, S. Zadek and V. Terry (1998), *Making Values Count: Contemporary Experiences in Social and Ethical Accounting, Auditing, and Reporting*, London: ACCA.

Gray, R. (1992), 'Accounting and environmentalism: an exploration of the challenge of gently accounting for accountability, transparency, and sustainability,' *Accounting Organizations and Society*, 17(5): 399–425.

Gray, R. and J. Bebbington (2000), 'Environmental accounting, managerialism and sustainability: is the planet safe in the hands of business and accounting?,' *Advances in Environmental Accounting and Management*, 1: 1–44.

Gray, R., J. Bebbington and D. Walters (1993), *Accounting for the Environment*, Princeton: Markus Wiener Publishers.

Gray, R., M. Javad, D. Power and C. Sinclair (2001), 'Social and environmental disclosure and corporate characteristics: a research note and extension,' *Journal of Business, Finance and Accounting*, 28(3/4): 327–56.

Hawken, P., A. Lovins and L.H. Lovins (1999), *Natural Capitalism: Creating The Next Industrial Revolution*, Boston: Little, Brown Co.

Jackson, S.E. (ed.) (1995), 'Special topic forum on ecologically sustainable organizations,' *Academy of Management Review*, **20**(4): 873–1115.

Jennings, P.D. and P.A. Zandbergen (1995), 'Ecologically sustainable organizations: an institutional approach,' *Academy of Management Review*, **20**(4): 1015-52.

Kaplan, Robert S. and David P. Norton (1996), *The Balanced Scorecord: Translating Strategy into Action*, Boston: Harvard Business School Press.

KPMG/WIMM (1999), *International Survey of Environmental Reporting 1999*, Amsterdam: KPMG.

Magness, V. (1997), 'Environmental accounting in Canada: new challenges to old theory,' *CMA Magazine*, **71**(1): 15–18.

Mathews, M.R. (1984), 'A suggested classification for social accounting research,' *Journal of Accounting and Public Policy*, **3**(3): 199–222.

Mathews, M.R. (1997), 'Twenty-five years of social and environmental accounting research: is there a silver jubilee to celebrate?,' *Accounting, Auditing and Accountability Journal*, **10**(4): 481–531.

Miller, P.B., R.J. Redding and P.R. Bahnson (1997), *The FASB: The People, the Process and the Politics*, New York: McGraw-Hill Higher Education.

Post, J.E. (1991), 'Managing as if the earth mattered,' *Business Horizons*, July/August: 32–8

Purser, R.E., C. Park and A. Montuori (1995), 'Limits to anthropocentrism: toward an ecocentric environmental paradigm?,' *Academy of Management Review*, **20**(4): 1053–89.

Ramus, C. and U. Steger (2000), 'The roles of supervisory support behaviors and environmental policy in employee "ecoinitiatives" at leading-edge European companies,' *Academy of Management Journal*, **43**(4): 605–26.

Rubenstein, D.B. (1992), 'Bridging the gap between green accounting and black ink,' *Accounting, Organizations and Society*, **17**(5): 501–8.

Rubenstein, D.B. (1994), *Environmental Accounting for the Sustainable Corporation*, Westport, CT and London: Quorum Books.

Sharma, S. (2000), 'Managerial interpretations and organizational context as predictors of corporate choice of environmental strategy,' *Academy of Management Journal*, **43**(4): 681–97.

Shell (1998), *The Shell Report: Profits and Principles–Does There Have to Be a Choice?* London: Shell Group.

Shell (2000), *The Shell Report: Planet, Profits, Principles*, London: Shell Group.

Sherman, W.R., L.M. Andersson and S.W. Davis (2000), 'Shifting the corporate environmental paradigm: implications for green accounting,' *Saint Joseph's University; Erivan K. Haub School of Business Working Paper Series #00-13*.

Shrivastava, P. (1995), 'Ecocentric management for a risk society,' *Academy of Management Review*, **20**(1): 118–37.

Starik, M., and A. Marcus (2000), 'A field emerging from multiple paths, with many challenges ahead', *Academy of Management Journal*, **43**(4): 539–47.

Starik, M., A. Marcus and A. Ilinitch (eds) (2000), 'Special research forum: the management of organizations in the natural environment,' *Academy of Management Journal*, **43**(4): 539–736.

Starik M., and Rands, G. (1995), 'Weaving an integrated web: multilevel and multisystem perspectives of ecologically sustainable organizations,' *Academy of Management Review*, **20**(4): 908–35.

Whittington, G. (2001), 'The IASB and global accounting regulation,' Keynote Address delivered at the European Institute for Advanced Studies in Management's

International Workshop on Accounting and Regulation, Siena, 27–29 September, 2001.

Wicks, A. (1996), 'Overcoming the separation thesis: the need for reconsideration of business and society research,' *Business and Society*, **35**(1): 89–118.

11. Enhancing environmental management teaching through applications of toxic release information[1]

Mark Cordano and Irene Hanson Frieze

ABSTRACT

Business students (n = 466) in the United States were given brief presentations of toxic release information. We examined the impact this few minutes of reading had on their evaluations of pollution problems, attitudes toward environmental regulation and limits on property rights, and behavioral intentions for pro-environmental behavior. Students expressed greater environmental concern when toxic release information included descriptions of potential human health impacts. Based on our findings, we suggest some strategies and activities that instructors can use to incorporate toxic release information into their classes. The intent of our suggestions is to arouse students' interest and develop deeper involvement with real information on industrial pollution, environmental problems and corporate environmental strategies.

INTRODUCTION

The goal of increasing managers' understanding of environmental issues poses a continuing challenge for management researchers (Porter and van der Linde, 1995; Reinhardt, 1999) and management educators alike (Hoffman and Ehrenfeld, 1998; Roome, 1998; Ryland, 1998; Shrivastava, 1994). Management educators must stimulate students' interest before they can expect to increase business students' awareness and understanding of environmental issues (Rands, 1990, 1993). The United States government has provided a potentially powerful teaching tool to assist management educators. The Toxic Release Inventory (TRI) provides a rich resource that educators can use to expose students to 'real-world' information about pollution resulting from industrial activity (Vail, 1995). This resource can help gain the attention of those business students who may be less receptive to environmental topics.

Increasingly, organization and natural environment researchers have recognized that sound corporate environmental performance requires managers at all levels to be aware of and committed to environmental objectives (Andersson and Bateman, 2000; Bansal and Roth, 2000; Cordano and Frieze, 2000; Flannery and May, 2000; Ramus and Steger, 2000; Sharma, 2000). This recognition prompts inquiry as to whether business schools are adequately preparing students to handle environmental responsibilities in their future management positions (Rands, 1993; Roome, 1998). Business schools need to incorporate environmental topics throughout their curricula to properly prepare students for the managerial realities of modern organizations (Hoffman, 1999). Environmental awareness is a critical element for students to be adequately prepared to manage environment, health and safety responsibilities (Shrivastava, 1994). Poor understanding of environmental issues can limit a manager's ability to recognize the business opportunities these issues offer (Reinhardt, 1999).

As management educators attempt to integrate environmental topics into the curriculum of business courses, they are likely to experience resistance from students who are not inclined to see these topics as important or even relevant to management education. Like their real-world counterparts, business students may need some prompting to stimulate their interest in environmental issues. Business students tend to express lower levels of environmental concern and have fewer intentions to engage in pro-environmental behavior, in comparison to other college majors (Benton, 1994). We expected the TRI information to affect students in a manner resembling its impact on managers. The publication of the TRI data prompted managers to focus their attention on waste management practices, and as a result improved corporate environmental performance (Forrest, 1996; Santos et al., 1996). The TRI information should elevate students' interest in environmental problems. We presented TRI information to students to examine whether it would heighten their environmental concerns. Based on our findings, we suggest some methods for educators to introduce and incorporate TRI information into the classroom to arouse interest in environmental topics.

INFORMATION REGULATION AND THE TRI

Since the early 1990s, there has been an increase in the use of information regulation in the United States (Kleindorfer and Orts, 1998). Information regulation (IR) refers to any regulation that requires organizations to make available, to the public, information about operations, plans or products. This requirement can include information communicated directly to the public, such as the consumer confidence reports required by the Safe Drinking Water Act Amendments of 1996 or indirectly to the public via government agencies such as required under the Emergency Planning and Community Right-to-Know Act of 1986 (Appendix C tells readers how to get more information about these and other US federal environmental regulations).

Information regulation serves as a substitute and complement to the existing framework of command and control environmental regulations (Kleindorfer and Orts, 1998). Information regulation enables numerous stakeholders to act as surrogate regulators. Legislators expect concerned stakeholders to use information, made available by IR, to exert pressure on organizations so as to change them to better serve the public interest. Probably the most well-known IR is the Toxic Release Inventory created under the Superfund Amendment and Reauthorization Act (SARA) passed in 1986. The creation of this law was prompted by the tragic events in Bhopal India in 1984. The primary mission of SARA was to require facilities to do thorough emergency planning to prevent tragedies like Bhopal and to inform communities about the use and release of toxic materials by local facilities. To create the TRI, thousands of facilities report their annual releases of over 600 toxic materials. Companies started reporting their toxic releases in 1988.

Numerous stakeholders have benefited by the availability of the TRI information. Hundreds of environmental groups, including grass-roots organizations (Gottlieb et al., 1995), use the TRI to target companies for stakeholder activism (McCauley, 1997). Companies have responded to these information-empowered stakeholders by significantly changing environmental practices to improve environmental performance (Santos et al., 1996).

The TRI offers numerous opportunities for researchers. However, researchers have yet to directly examine how individuals react to the TRI information. Anecdotal reports suggest the TRI reporting requirements tend to heighten managers' attention to environmental issues (Forrest, 1996). We expected a similar reaction among business students. The TRI information should increase their level of environmental concern, and interest them in discussions of corporate practices intended to improve environmental performance.

TOXIC RELEASE INFORMATION AND ENVIRONMENTAL CONCERN

We designed our analysis according to the components of information in the TRI. The TRI contains information about the volume of toxic materials released and the potential impact on human health of these releases. The volume information is contained in the main body of the TRI reports. Media stories in the United States often focus solely on the volume data to rank polluters (for example, Dempsey, 2000a). We wanted to examine the impact of the volume information alone, since it is the most accessible and commonly reported part of the TRI. We hypothesized that:

Hypothesis 1: Individuals receiving toxic release volume information would express higher levels of environmental concern.

Information on the potential human health impacts resulting from toxic releases is presented in a separate section of the TRI reports called the Chemical Fact Data Sheets (in the online format this information is now presented in a variety of websites, see Appendix B for additional discussion about these websites). The Chemical Fact Data Sheets (CFDS) contain information accumulated from numerous health, safety and ecological databases. Within the CFDS, the toxic materials are listed individually. Each CFDS provides a description to identify the toxic material and outlines its common industrial uses, the likely symptoms resulting from human exposure, the necessary worker safety precautions when using the material and the potential negative impacts on flora and fauna. The majority of the materials listed in the TRI are known carcinogens, teratogens (materials that cause abnormal development of the fetus) and/or materials demonstrated to impede or permanently damage human organs as a result of acute or chronic exposure. While the toxicity of each material is not reported using any form of quantitative measure, the CFDS provide a thorough qualitative description of the comparative toxicity of materials. We expected the information in the CFDS, that identifies potential human health impacts, to increase individuals' concern about environmental issues. Based on this expectation, we hypothesized:

Hypothesis 2: Individuals receiving information about the human health impacts that could result from toxic releases would express higher levels of environmental concern.

ENVIRONMENTAL CONCERN, BEHAVIORAL INTENTION AND DECISION-MAKING

In recent empirical studies of the environmental management practices and strategies of organizations, researchers have increasingly recognized the role individuals play in determining corporate environmental performance. Researchers have surveyed and interviewed environmental champions (Andersson and Bateman, 2000), environmental directors (Bansal and Roth, 2000), environmental affairs managers (Cordano and Frieze, 2000), metal-finishing managers (Flannery and May, 2000) and senior management (Sharma, 2000). We chose to examine several potential indicators of environmental concern and behavioral intention, because of their potential relevance to environmental decision-making and behavior in organizations. The areas of environmental concern we selected were evaluations of the seriousness of pollution problems, attitudes involving environmental regulation and property rights and intentions to engage in pro-environmental behaviors. Researchers have found that these aspects of environmental concern are related to individuals' environmental awareness and behavior.

Baldassare and Katz (1992) found that negative perceptions of environmental problems increased the likelihood that someone would engage in personal pro-environmental practices such as recycling and water conservation. Similarly, recent business research has demonstrated that environmental attitudes influence managers' selection and preferences for waste management plans and practices (Cordano and Frieze, 2000; Flannery and May, 1994, 2000). We focused on attitudes involving environmental regulation and property rights because managers in the United States often view environmental issues solely as regulatory issues (Tenbrunsel et al., 1997) and consequently this perspective tends to drive the goals and practices of the environmental management function (Lawrence and Morell, 1995).

Individual commitment can have a significant impact on the environmental performance of a facility or company (Henriques and Sadorsky, 1999). Hanna et al. (2000) demonstrated that employee commitment provides the link between operational and environmental improvement. In community settings, Bullard (1994) found that potential environmental threats increased individual efforts to regulate the behaviors of polluters by actions such as writing letters, protest marches and helping to raise funds for activist organizations. Given the potential impact individual commitment can have on a company or community, and the possibility that environmental threats can stimulate personal commitment, we examined students' behavioral intentions for pro-environmental behavior as an indication of strong personal commitment.

METHOD

Sample and Data Collection

This study surveyed undergraduate business students from a large public university in Ohio, USA. The majority of these students came from a fourteen-county region surrounding the university. Since Ohio recently ranked fourth in the United States in total toxic releases, second in toxic metals released, fourth in reproductive toxins released and fifteenth in carcinogens released (Dempsey, 2000b), there was a high likelihood that many of these students would live or have lived near a facility that releases some toxic materials.

The students were surveyed in required management classes selected to minimize the potential of overlapping participants. A student research assistant distributed the surveys, explained the purpose of the study, collected the completed surveys and disbursed participant remuneration ($2). Students read all of the toxic release information and completed the survey in approximately 15 minutes. This data collection process yielded 466 usable surveys from among 486 distributed and collected. The resulting sample was fairly evenly distributed among females (n = 236, 50.6 percent) and males (n = 230, 49.4 percent). The most common age was 21 years although the average was 23.6 years since age ranged from 19 to 50 years.

Measures

Respondents evaluated all scale items with responses ranging from strongly disagree (1) to strongly agree (7), except for the seriousness of pollution problem items, which ranged from not serious at all (1) to very serious (4). All of the scales were coded so that higher-scale scores indicated greater levels of environmental concern. All scale items are listed in Appendix A.

Seriousness of pollution problems

We created the seriousness of pollution problems scale (labeled pollution) by combining the format of the personal environmental threat items, from a study by Baldassare and Katz (1992), with the format of the pollution problem items used in a study by Dietz et al. (1998). The four items in the pollution scale produced a Cronbach's alpha of 0.82. A sample item is: 'How serious of a threat do you think pollution in rivers, lakes, and streams is to your health and well-being?'

Environmental regulation attitudes

We modified Van Liere and Dunlap's (1981) pollution scale to create an environmental regulation attitudes scale (labeled 'regulation'). An example item is: 'Anti-pollution laws should be enforced more strongly.' The four items in this scale produced a Cronbach's alpha of 0.74.

Property rights attitudes

For this measure, we used Dunlap and Van Liere's (1984) property rights scale (labeled 'property') with a new item added. An example item is: 'Property owners have an inherent right to use their land as they see fit (reverse coded item).' The five property items produced a Cronbach's alpha of 0.75.

Intended pro-environmental behavior

We used items from studies by Séguin et al. (1998) and by Stern et al. (1993), and added two original items to create a five-item scale of intended pro-environmental behavior (labeled 'pro-environmental'). These items produced a Cronbach's alpha of 0.90. An example item is: 'I would participate in a protest against a company that is harming the environment.'

We completed a principal components analysis using an oblique rotation to ensure each of the multi-item scales assessed a separate aspect of environmental concern and behavioral intention. The four multi-item scales loaded onto four separate factors each with eigenvalues greater than 1.0. The four factors explained 62.3 percent of the variance in the data.

Survey Groups

There were three groups in this study. All three of these groups received surveys containing all of the measures of environmental concern. The remainder of the survey contained varying amounts of TRI information. One group (the control group, n = 149) did not receive any information about toxic releases. The volume group's (n = 155) survey included only the toxic release volumes of the largest local polluting facilities. The health group (n = 162) had the toxic release volume information along with added information about the potential health impacts of the toxic materials released by the high volume polluters. The three different versions of the surveys were shuffled prior to each administration so as to distribute grouping assignments non-systematically.

Control group

This version of the survey did not contain any information about toxic releases. Instead, this survey contained some environmental attitude measures, which were not part of this study.   This was done so that individuals receiving different versions of the survey would take approximately the same amount of time to complete the survey.

Table 11.1 Toxic release volume information

Toxic releases in the Dayton area
Below is a list of some Dayton area manufacturing facilities that released toxic materials into the air and water. This list contains the ten facilities that released the largest amounts of toxic materials in 1997. The facilities are ordered by the amount of their toxic releases. The largest toxic polluter is listed first. These Dayton area facilities released a variety of toxic materials into the local environment including xylene, hydrochloric acid, methanol, glycol ethers, toluene and methyl ethyl ketone. These releases were legally permitted by state and federal regulators. The amounts were self-reported by the facilities and published by the United States Environmental Protection Agency.

Top ten toxic polluters listed by total volume of annual releases (based on 1997 US EPA data)		
Facility	*City*	*Releases (lbs)*
1 AK Steel Corp.	Middletown	**978136**
2 GoodYear Tire and Rubber Co.	Saint Marys	**508112**
3 Champion International	Hamilton	**428200**
4 Honda of America Mfg. Inc.	East Liberty	**377565**
5 Appleton Papers Inc.	West Carrollton	**373780**
6 Cargill Inc.	Sidney	**321531**
7 GMC NATP	Moraine	**288018**
8 Brown-Bridge Ind./Spinnaker Coating	Troy	**254205**
9 Delphi Chassis Sys.	Kettering	**193215**
10 Navistar International Trans. Corp.	Springfield	**155182**

Volume information group
The volume survey presented toxic release information in a table on a single page at the start of the survey (see Table 11.1). The table listed the top ten polluters in the Dayton, Ohio area. This presentation format is typical of the manner in which TRI information is often presented in news releases (for example, Dempsey, 2000a).

Table 11.2 Health impact information

These Dayton area facilities released a variety of toxic materials into the local environment including xylene, tetrachloroethylene, toluene, and methyl ethyl ketone. These materials produce a variety of human health effects. Many petroleum-based solvents, such as methyl ethyl ketone, have been shown to cause brain and nerve damage. Other effects include reduced memory and concentration, reduced coordination, and/or effects on nerves supplying internal organs and limbs. Methyl ethyl ketone damages developing fetuses in animals. Until further testing is done methyl ethyl ketone should be handled as potentially having similar effects on human fetuses.

Toluene exposure irritates the eyes, nose, and throat. Higher levels of exposure causes lightheadedness, fainting, headaches, and death. Toluene may cause mutations in living cells and damage developing fetuses. Repeated exposures may cause low blood cell counts and damage to the liver, kidneys, and brain.

Xylene exposure irritates the eyes, nose, and throat, causes headaches, nausea, vomiting, fainting, and death at extremely high levels. Xylene has been found to damage developing fetuses. Long term exposure can damage the eye surface, stomach, bone marrow, liver, and kidneys.

Tetrachloroethylene is a carcinogen. Exposure to tetrachloroethylene can burn the eyes and skin, irritate the nose, throat, and lungs, and cause a build-up of fluid in the lungs. Overexposure can cause an irregular heartbeat, liver and kidney damage, and death.

These releases were legally permitted by state and federal regulators. The amounts were self-reported by the individual facilities. The information on these toxic releases and their potential human health effects are made available by the United States Environmental Protection Agency.

Health information group

The health survey presented the same information as the volume group survey with added descriptions of some potential health impacts that could be produced by a few of the toxic materials released from these facilities (see Table 11.2). Health impact information was provided on four toxic materials that have been released in substantial quantities by the top ten polluters listed. As was done with the volume group survey, the health information was given at the start of the survey accompanying the list of the top ten polluters.

RESULTS

Descriptive Information

Table 11.3 lists the means for the pollution, regulation, property and pro-environmental variables for the entire sample and by each survey group. The average for the pollution scale was 3.01, on a four-point scale ranging from not serious at all (1) to very serious (4). The majority of the sample (53.9 percent) rated pollution problems at or between somewhat serious (2) and serious (3). Over 40 percent (43.1 percent) considered pollution problems to be greater than serious (3). Very few people (3 percent) rated pollution problems as less than somewhat serious (2).

Table 11.3 Group means

Variable	Sample (n = 466)		Control (n = 149)	Volume (n = 155)	Health (n = 123)
	avg.	std. dev.	avg.	avg.	avg.
Pollution	3.01	0.66	2.93	2.98	3.12*
Regulation	5.45	0.91	5.34	5.40	5.59*
Property Rights	4.96	1.02	4.75	4.97	5.14*
Pro-environmental	3.73	1.28	3.80	3.65	3.74

Notes:
Pollution seriousness rated from 1 = Not at all to 4 = Very serious. Other variables rated from 1 = Strongly disagree to 7 = Strongly agree.
* For Pollution, Regulation, and Property Rights, the Health Group differed significantly from the Control group at $p < 0.05$, using a Tukey post hoc test.

The regulation, property and pro-environmental scales all used a response code ranging from strongly disagree (1) to strongly agree (7). The sample averaged 5.45 for the regulation scale. The majority of the sample (53.4 percent) was at or between the slightly agree (5) to agree (6) response with about one in 11 (9.4 percent) opposed to environmental regulation, scoring below the neutral (4) response.

The average for the property scale was 4.96. The majority of the sample (43.0 percent) scored at or between the slightly agree (5) and agree (6) levels with roughly one in five (19.5 percent) scoring at or below the neutral (4) response.

The majority of the sample (58.6 percent) scored at or below the neutral response (4) for the pro-environmental scale, with an average of 3.73. Very few respondents (1.7 percent) had strong intentions for pro-environmental behavior – as indicated by scoring above the agree (6) response. One in 20

(4.7 percent) strongly opposed pro-environmental behavioral intentions responding with a strongly disagree response (1).

Table 11.4 Correlations and scale reliabilities (reliabilities in parentheses)

Variable	1	2	3	4
1. Pollution	(0.82)			
2. Regulation	0.41***	(0.74)		
3. Property	0.25***	0.46***	(75)	
4. Pro-environmental	0.38***	0.44***	0.25***	(0.90)

Note: *** $p < 0.01$

All of the pairwise correlations among the pollution, regulation, property and pro-environmental variables were significant at the $p < 0.001$ level. The strongest correlation was between regulation and property at $r = 0.46$. The weakest among these significant correlations was for the pollution–property and property–pro-environmental correlations which were both at $r = 0.25$. Among the correlations with pro-environmental behavioral intention, the regulation variable produced the strongest correlation at $r = 0.44$.

Tests of the Hypotheses

The two hypotheses were tested with a multivariate analysis of variance for group (the control group and the two information groups) and gender, with the four dependent variables pollution, regulation, property and pro-environmental. Gender was used as a control variable since some studies have found women to differ from men in environmental concern and perceptions of pollution risks (Davidson and Freudenburg, 1996).

As predicted, there was a significant multivariate main effect for the group variable [Multivariate $F(8, 916) = 2.72$, $p < 0.01$]. Univariate analyses and a Tukey *post hoc* analysis indicated that the differences were significant between the control group and the health group for the perceived seriousness of pollution ($p < 0.04$), for attitudes about environmental regulation ($p < 0.04$) and for attitudes about property rights ($p < 0.01$). There were no significant differences across the groups in their intention to engage in pro-environmental behavior ($p > 0.60$). All effects were in the predicted direction such that those students who received the health information viewed pollution as more serious, expressed greater support for environmental regulation and for limiting property rights when necessary to protect the environment. Differences for the volume group were not significantly different from the control group for any of the dependent variables.

DISCUSSION

Our research demonstrates that the health information in the TRI information is critical to stimulating concern among business students in the United States. We were surprised that the volume information alone had no significant impact on students' environmental concerns and intended pro-environmental behavior. We presented the toxic release volume information in a relatively neutral form. No specific threats to personal health were provided in the volume condition. In discussions with participants who wanted to know more about the study, many stated that the volume information did not have any meaning to them. As a result, the toxic release volumes were not perceived as making a direct threat to personal safety or the environment. Given this pattern of results, it appears that toxic release information must be placed in a context that identifies specific potential health impacts if it is to stimulate an arousal of environmental concern. Interestingly, some students who received the health impact information inquired not only about the study itself but also asked where they could look for more information about the toxic releases. In the classroom, such interest in pollution and environmental issues would be a welcome change from the typical response from business students presented with environmental topics.

Overall, we were surprised by the subdued response to the TRI information. Initially, we were hesitant to distribute information about any potential health threats since we believed some students might be alarmed or view such information as inflammatory or defamatory of their community. Consequently, we limited the amount and depth of the information given. More information about the potential health impacts may have produced a stronger impact. Additionally, the design of study did not force students to digest the information. There is the possibility that only a portion of the study participants carefully read the TRI information since students did not seek this information out.

Students might have greater reactions if the TRI information is combined with other information about facility environmental performance. Discussions with the students who participated in the study suggested one possible reason for the subdued response. Some students commented that the releases were described as legal and they assumed that legality implied safety. This context of legality may be important in the absence of actual cases of negative health impacts. The context of legality may serve to alleviate some individuals' concerns since they may believe the government is carefully watching these emissions. Since we were listing actual companies where study participants, along with their family and friends, may have worked we did not want to suggest that any of the releases by local facilities were illegal, even though one facility has a long history of poor compliance. Additionally, the emissions reported in the TRI are not always within the bounds of the law. Some environmental activists use the TRI data as a means to cite companies who are in violation of their air and water permits (Fiero, 2000). Assignments that require students to review regulators' websites listing environmental and safety violations might stimulate even deeper interest and recognition of the importance of the environmental, heath, and safety issues.

Future research is needed to examine whether the reactions we found can be produced in response to data relevant to other environmental problems. We would expect a similar impact whenever data is readily available from government sources and can be linked directly to human health and quality of life impacts. For example, the Safe Drinking Water Act Amendments of 1996 require local facilities to send annual reports to citizens. When incidents of contamination are noted, the reports list the possible sources of contamination. Often agricultural and industrial activities are noted as likely sources of contamination. More complex environmental issues where the human health impact is less evident, such as climate change or the loss of biodiversity, would probably require the presentation of additional information. However, we would expect a similar response if the impact on human health can be tied to the environmental data. In the United States, such data is often accumulated in the monitoring and assessment reports required under the Clean Air Act, the Clean Water Act, the Endangered Species Act and other environmental laws (see Appendix C for instructions how to get additional information about each of these laws).

The results of this study can inform management educators trying to incorporate environmental topics into functional area courses or trying to design a course focusing on environmental topics. The descriptive information provides some insights into business students' environmental views. They see pollution problems as only a somewhat serious threat to human health. They reluctantly accept environmental regulation with a small group, about one in nine, who strongly oppose any regulation. They weakly support any restrictions on property rights with roughly one in five opposing any limits on property rights to protect the environment. On average, they do not intend to engage in pro-environmental behaviors. This study demonstrates that the introduction of TRI information, accompanied by information about possible human health impacts, can increase business students' levels of concern about pollution along with their acceptance of environmental regulation and limits on property rights. Such increased sensitivity should facilitate discussions on environmental issues.

Learning Applications

Information regulation in the United States, and similar laws in other countries, offers management educators a versatile resource to stimulate interest and demonstrate the relevance of environmental topics within the business curriculum. In their review of environmental attitudes and personal pro-environmental behaviors (such as energy conservation and recycling), Gardner and Stern (1996) devoted an entire chapter to educational interventions that attempt to change attitudes by providing information to motivate pro-environmental behavior. They concluded that 'the success of information programs depends less on getting information presented than on getting it used' (p. 90). A striking attribute of our findings is the ease of use to many teaching or training situations. The health information group took a mere five minutes to read the one page of health impact information that heightened their levels of environmental concern. This minimal time requirement, and ease of application, demonstrates how information regulation can be an effective tool for instructors using a wide variety of instructional methods. Researchers should develop and assess more exercises, such as the one in this study, that can be easily added to a wide variety of learning environments. In the United States, educators can incorporate TRI information into the classroom to create learning experiences that are relevant and meaningful to students with limited interest in environmental topics (in Appendix B we suggest a few ways for instructors to access TRI information so as to begin to develop the TRI for use in the classroom).

If an instructor wants to make environmental issues meaningful to business students, then the instructor should introduce TRI data with health impact information as part of any presentation of environmental topics. This will help to establish the legitimacy of environmental problems and the need for managers to address pollution reduction. It is important to present this information to students who contend that industry has addressed all of the United States' environmental problems. The TRI can demonstrate to skeptical students that companies still do release large quantities of pollutants, and environmental problems do persist.

One attractive feature of the TRI is its ability to pinpoint facilities by county, town or zip code. Students will soon discover that toxic materials are being released throughout the United States in varying degrees. They can review the TRI information for facilities that are local to their university, in proximity to their home communities, in industries that they have an interest to work, or just some well-known companies. The TRI information can become local and personally relevant to anyone in the United States. Assignments that expose students to a greater amount of health information would likely stimulate even stronger reactions than we witnessed in our study.

The Chemical Fact Data Sheets (CFDS), along with multiple websites about toxic materials, contain information about the safe usage of hazardous materials. Students can review the TRI and these related sites to complete management tasks such as outlining how to do a plant inspection or a safety audit of a facility. These realistic assignments can be integrated with visits to facilities to see the people and practices described in the TRI.

The unfortunate prevalence of industrial pollutants in the United States enables students to consider toxic releases from multiple stakeholder positions such as community member, parent and employee along with the traditional managerial view examined in business courses. This circumstance can enrich discussions of public policy and stakeholder management along with enhancing the relevance of corporate environmental strategy. To this end, the TRI information can be used to create in-class exercises such as role plays involving multi-stakeholder interactions. Multi-stakeholder role plays can greatly enhance students' understanding of complex environmental issues (Egri, 1999). Students can assume a variety of stakeholder roles such as community residents exposed to a toxic material, a manager responsible for community relations or a politician trying to balance the interests of these different stakeholders. Instead of having discussions about regulating pollution problems, a class can discuss different strategies that a community can use to protect itself against heavy polluting industries, along with the necessary management responses to these problems. Since many environmental affairs managers, particularly at the corporate level, have substantial experience interacting with local communities as a result of the TRI regulations, it would probably be easy for instructors to invite these managers into the classroom to review or engage in these role plays.

Presenting the TRI information early in a course provides some relevant data that can be used to weave together readings that students may not see as related. The TRI can help to establish the links between environmental problems and management tools, and the management tools and corporate environmental performance. For example, an instructor could use the TRI information as a context for readings that outline environmental management practices. The TRI includes information about the pollution prevention practices of facilities and the organizational methods used to select among the different pollution prevention practices. Instead of merely describing practices, instructors can discuss practices in relation to specific industries and toxic materials found in the TRI. Readings about corporate environmental performance also can be tied to the TRI since it is widely used as an indicator of environmental performance by managers and investors (Hamilton, 1995).

Because the TRI contains actual data listed by specific facilities, students can use it to do in-depth preparation for classroom visitors from local facilities or regulatory agencies. Speakers are impressed when students ask questions involving the use of specific toxic materials in their manufacturing processes. Such preparation elevates the interaction between the guest speaker and students so as to build students' confidence in interacting with actual managers. Overall, this level of preparation reflects well of the students and college to the business community.

Applications for Environmental Professionals and Regulators

In our discussion we have emphasized the application of our findings to business education in the United States. However, our findings can be applied to many settings. There are a large number of environmental informants in the media, non-governmental organizations, government agencies and consulting organizations throughout the world. Professionals in all of these fields often make presentations on environmental issues to disinterested audiences. The tools offered by information regulation can be used to establish rapport with an audience. This rapport can provide the foundation for dialogue and learning on many pressing environmental issues. Given our findings, presenters should explicitly identify potential human health impacts whenever possible. Participants in our study did not express any feeling of being personally threatened, so it is not necessary to present potential health threats as an imminent danger. It is possible that overemphasis could be seen as exaggerating the potential threats. Such exaggeration may arouse defensiveness and strong reaction to a discussion of environmental problems. While our study focused on students in the United States, we believe applications of information regulation can be useful in training corporate managers who are unfamiliar with the amount of toxic releases emitted by industry and the potential health impacts of these releases. Research on applications to corporate training is needed to assess whether managers' reactions to the publication of toxic release information in the United States was motivated by their concern about protecting corporate assets and reputation or their concern about the potential health impacts.

Environmental policy-makers in the United States have increasingly used information gathering and reporting legislation to address environmental issues. While United States environmental policy-makers intend for these regulations to empower stakeholders, few policy-makers may have recognized the education benefits these laws provide. Our study demonstrates that accessible information that is easily interpreted can enrich the knowledge and sensitivity of the next generation of managers and concerned citizens.

CONCLUSION

Researchers have discovered that managers hold false assumptions and misconceptions regarding environmental issues (Porter and van der Linde, 1995). These misconceptions can limit a manager's ability to capitalize on business opportunities (Reinhardt, 1999). If managers are to realize the opportunities environmental issues offer, then they must change their environmental views and move beyond framing environmental problems solely as regulatory threats (Sharma et al., 1999). Given this need to inform all managers, we considered the obstacles management educators must overcome to inform students throughout the business curriculum and not just those few students in environmental electives who typically respond enthusiastically to these topics (Ryland, 1998). Our intent was to consider how to assist educators facing a reluctant audience in a required course.

To reach students in required business courses, management educators need some tools that sensitize students, and working managers, to environmental issues. Research has demonstrated that the TRI can motivate managers to improve corporate environmental performance (Forrest, 1996; Hamilton, 1995; Regan, 1993, Santos et al., 1996). Our study demonstrates that the TRI, accompanied by information about potential health impacts, can increase business students' concern about pollution problems and acceptance of environmental regulation. Such changes can foster interest in the growing instructional literature on business and the natural environment intended for the classroom (for example, Reinhardt and Vietor, 1996) and the practicing manager (for example, DeSimone and Popoff, 1997; Hoffman, 2000). In the appropriate context, the TRI information can be used in the classroom to enrich learning and loosen students' existing conceptual framing of environmental issues so as to open up opportunities to introduce sustainable development (Rands, 1993; Roome, 1998) and ecocentric frameworks (Shrivastava, 1994).

APPENDIX A

Measures of Environmental Concern and Behavioral Intention
Respondents evaluated all scale items with responses ranging from strongly disagree (1) to strongly agree (7) except for the seriousness of pollution problem items which ranged from not serious at all (1) to very serious (4).

Regulation

1) Pollution laws have gotten too strict in recent years.
2) Anti-pollution laws should be enforced more strongly.
3) We must take stronger measures to conserve our nation's resources.
4) Environmental regulations have placed unfair burdens on industry.

Property rights

1) Among the fundamental rights in this country is the use of one's property without outside interference.
2) Natural resources should be used for whatever purposes humans desire.
3) Property owners have an inherent right to use their land as they see fit.
4) Where natural resources are privately owned, society should have no control over what the owner does with them.
5) Property owners have the right to abuse their land even if it becomes unfit for use by future generations.

Pro-environmental behavior

1) I would participate in a protest against a company that is harming the environment.
2) I would participate in protests against current environmental conditions.
3) I plan to participate in events organized by environmental groups.
4) I would distribute information published by environmental groups to my family and friends.
5) I plan to write a letter to public officials to increase their support of environmental protection efforts.

Pollution

How serious a threat do you think [.....] is to your health and well-being?
1) air pollution by industry
2) pesticides and chemicals used in farming
3) pollution of rivers, lakes, and streams
4) air pollution caused by cars

APPENDIX B

Useful Websites for Instructors to Begin Using TRI Information

Instructors wishing to use Toxic Release Inventory (TRI) information can access it by a few different means. Nearly every university library in the Unites States carries TRI information stored on compact disk. This format was commonly used before there was widespread use of the Internet. The TRI information is provided in two compact disks with one listing the toxic release volumes and the other disk containing the Chemical Fact Data Sheets.

Today, the easiest means for instructors and students to access TRI information is to go to websites supported by the United States Environmental Protection Agency (EPA) and most state environmental regulation authorities in the United States. The web address for the US EPA's TRI site is www.epa.gov/tri/. This site provides the search capability to access toxic release volumes sorted by county, city, or zip code. In place of the Chemical Fact Data Sheets, the EPA site provides a series of links that describe the potential health impacts of the toxic materials listed. One link, named Toxnet, is widely used to evaluate the toxicity of TRI materials, but there are many other links that provide a thorough evaluation of the human and environmental impacts of toxics along with safety guidelines for using these toxic materials. Additionally, the EPA, and most state agencies, list a contact person or department to enable individuals to better use these resources.

Another useful website is the right-to-know network. Its address is www.rtk.net/. It includes some easy-to-use search capabilities that allow users to examine toxic releases by geographic area, parent company, or industry along with other sorting categories.

For an integrated look at pollution and business organizations, instructors can incorporate the Environmental Defense Fund's Scorecard website (www.scorecard.org) into their courses. This site integrates information sources to present information about toxic releases, air pollutants and water pollutants. It also presents information about environmental quality and the risks posed to communities by polluting organizations. This site includes numerous search and sort capabilities so students can easily examine targeted relevant information such as specific neighborhoods, the multiple facilities of a single firm, an entire industry, the highest cancer risks in an area, or the top producers of a specific pollutant. This site has also integrated the health information with the individual pollutants. One need only to click on a highlighted pollutant to get a summary of the risks it poses. One additional area that may be particularly interesting, given our thinking about polluting firms and the context of legality, is a listing of regulatory inspections and fines. The scorecard site contains so much information that instructors should be able to use in a variety of ways to create relevance and meaning for business and environment issues.

APPENDIX C

Easy Access to United States Environmental Laws

The United States Environmental Protection Agency's website (www.-epa.gov) contains details about all of the major federal environmental regulations. Instructors, and students, can easily find information about specific laws on the EPA website by doing a web search , using any web browser, of the acronym for the regulation they wish to examine. For example, the Safe Drinking Water Act can be found by searching the term SDWA. The Emergency Planning and Community Right-to-know Act can be found by searching EPCRA. Within the EPA website, each of these laws has a detailed page that includes a subdirectory reviewing the reporting requirements of the regulation. These regulation web pages are much more user friendly than law texts or the Federal Register since they are designed to assist compliance at organizations that may not have the resources for a lawyer trained in environmental law.

NOTE

1. The data collection in this study was made possible by a grant from the Office of Research and Sponsored Programs, Wright State University, Dayton, Ohio.

REFERENCES

Andersson, L.M. and T.S. Bateman (2000), 'Individual environmental initiative: championing natural environmental issues in US business organizations,' *Academy of Management Journal*, **43**(4): 548–70.

Baldassare, M. and C. Katz (1992), 'The personal threat of environmental problems as predictor of environmental practices,' *Environment and Behavior*, **24**(5): 602–16.

Bansal, P. and K. Roth (2000), 'Why companies go green: a model of ecological responsiveness,' *Academy of Management Journal*, **43**(4): 717–36.

Benton, R. (1994), 'Environmental knowledge and attitudes of undergraduate business students compared to non-business students,' *Business and Society*, **33** (2): 191–211.

Bullard, R.D. (1994), *Dumping in Dixie*, San Francisco, CA: Westview Press.

Cordano, M. and I.H. Frieze (2000), 'Pollution reduction preferences of US environmental managers: applying Ajzen's theory of planned behavior,' *Academy of Management Journal*, **43**(4).

Davidson, D.J. and W.R. Freudenburg (1996), 'Gender and environmental risk concerns: a review and analysis of available research,' *Environment and Behavior*, **28**(3): 302–39.

Dempsey, D. (2000a), 'Ohio EPA: DP and L plant top polluter,' *Dayton Daily News*, 11 March: 12A.

Dempsey, D. (2000b), 'Ohio ranks among most polluted states,' *Dayton Daily News*, 17 February.

DeSimone, L.D. and F. Popoff (1997), *Eco-efficiency: The Business Link to Sustainable Development*, Cambridge, MA: MIT Press.

Dietz, T., P.C. Stern and G.A. Guagnano (1998), 'Social structural and social psychological bases of environmental concern,' *Environment and Behavior*, **30**: 450–71.

Dunlap, R.E. and K.D. Van Liere (1984), 'Commitment to the dominant social paradigm and concern for environmental quality,' *Social Science Quarterly*, **65**: 1013–28.

Egri, C.P. (1999), 'The environmental round table role-play exercise: the dynamics of multistakeholder decision-making processes,' *Journal of Management Education*, **23**(1): 95–112.

Fiero, J.D. (2000), 'Surviving and thriving ecologically: the story of two regional environmental organizations integrating structuration, autopoietic, and social construction theories,' Unpublished Doctoral Dissertation, The Fielding Institute.

Flannery, B.L. and D.R. May (1994), 'Prominent factors influencing environmental activities: an application of the environmental leadership model,' *Leadership Quarterly*, **5**(3): 201–21.

Flannery, B.L. and D.R. May (2000), 'An empirical study of the effect of moral intensity on environmental ethical decision making,' *Academy of Management Journal*, **43**(4): 642–62.

Forrest, C.J. (1996), 'The TRI, P2, and public dialogue,' *Pollution Prevention Review*, Winter: 1–9.

Gardner, G.T. and P.C. Stern (1996), *Environmental Problems and Human Behavior*, Needham Heights, MA: Allyn and Bacon.

Gottlieb, R., M. Smith, J. Roque and P. Yates (1995), 'New approaches to toxics: production design, right-to-know, and definition debates,' in R. Gottlieb (ed.),

Reducing Toxics: A New Approach to Policy and Industrial Decisionmaking, Washington, DC: Island Press.

Hamilton, J.T. (1995), 'Pollution as news: media and stock market reactions to the Toxics Release Inventory,' *Journal of Environmental Economics and Management*, **28**: 98–113.

Hanna, M.D., W.R. Newman and P. Johnson (2000), 'Linking operational and environmental improvement through employee involvement,' *International Journal of Operations and Production Management*, **20**(2): 148–65.

Henriques, I. and P. Sadorsky (1999), 'The relationship between environmental commitment and managerial perceptions of stakeholder importance,' *Academy of Management Journal*, **42**(1): 87–99.

Hoffman, A. (2000), *Competitive Environmental Strategy: A Guide to the Changing Business Landscape*, Washington, DC: Island Press.

Hoffman, A.J. (1999), 'Environmental education in business school,' *Environment*, **41**(1): 4–5.

Hoffman, A.J. and J.R. Ehrenfeld (1998), 'Corporate environmentalism, sustainability, and management studies,' in N.J. Roome (ed.), *Sustainability Strategies for Industry: The Future of Corporate Practice*, Washington, DC: Island Press.

Kleindorfer, P.R. and E.W. Orts (1998), 'Informational regulation of environmental risks,' *Risk Analysis*, **18**(2): 155–70.

Lawrence, A.T. and D. Morell (1995), 'Leading-edge environmental management: motivation, opportunity, resources, and processes,' in D. Collins and M. Starik (eds.), *Research in Corporate Social Performance and Policy* (Supplement 1), Greenwich, CT: JAI.

McCauley, A. (1997), 'What you don't know can hurt you,' *Sierra*, January/February, 94: 38–43

Porter, M. and C. van der Linde (1995), 'Green and competitive: ending the stalemate,' *Harvard Business Review*, September–October: 120–34.

Ramus, C.A. and U. Steger (2000), 'The roles of supervisory support behaviors and environmental policy in employee "ecoinitiatives" at leading-edge European companies,' *Academy of Management Journal*, **43**(4): 605–26.

Rands, G.P. (1990), 'Environmental attitudes, behaviors, and decision making: implications for management education and development,' in W. Hoffman, R. Frederick and E. Petry (eds) *The Corporation, Ethics, and the Environment*, New York: Quorum Books.

Rands, G.P. (1993), 'Preparing students to work for sustainability: teaching as if the earth's future mattered,' in A.T. Mintu, H.R. Lozada M.J. Polonsky (eds), *Environmental Issues and the Curricula of International Business: The Green Imperative*, New York: Haworth Press.

Regan, M.B. (1993), 'An embarrassment of clean air,' *Business Week*, 31 May: 34.

Reinhardt, F.L. (1999), 'Bringing the environment down to earth,' *Harvard Business Review*, July–August: 149–57.

Reinhardt, F.L. and R.H.K. Vietor (1996), *Business Management and the Natural Environment: Cases and Text*, Cincinnati: South-Western College Publishing.

Roome, N.J. (1998), 'Conclusion: implications for management practice, education, and research,' in N.J. Roome (ed.), *Sustainability Strategies for Industry: The Future of Corporate Practice*, Washington, DC: Island Press.

Ryland, E.K. (1998), '"Greening" business education: teaching the paradigm,' *Journal of Management Education*, **22**(3): 320–43.

Santos, S.L., V.T. Covello and D.B. McCallum (1996), 'Industry response to Sara Title III: pollution prevention, risk reduction, and risk communication,' *Risk Analysis*, **16**(1): 57–66.

Séguin, C., L.G. Pelletier and J. Hunsley (1998), 'Toward a model of environmental activism,' *Environment and Behavior*, **30**(5): 628–52.

Sharma, S. (2000), 'Managerial interpretations and organizational context as predictors of corporate choice of environmental strategy,' *Academy of Management Journal*, **43**(4): 681–97.

Sharma, S., A.L. Pablo and H. Vredenburg (1999), 'Corporate environmental responsiveness strategies: the importance of issue interpretation and organizational context,' *Journal of Applied Behavioral Science*, **35**(1): 87–108.

Shrivastava, P. (1994), 'Greening business education: toward an ecocentric pedagogy,' *Journal of Management Inquiry*, **3**(3): 235–43.

Stern, P.C., T. Dietz and L. Kalof (1993), 'Value orientations, gender, and environmental concern,' *Environment and Behavior*, **25**(3): 322–48.

Tenbrunsel, A.E., K.A.Wade-Benzoni, D.M. Messick and M.H. Bazerman (1997), 'The dysfunctional aspects of environmental standards,' in M.H. Bazerman, D.M. Messick, A. E. Tenbrunsel and K.A. Wade-Benzoni (eds), *Environment, Ethics, and Behavior*, San Francisco, CA: New Lexington Press.

Vail, J.H. (1995), 'The Toxics Release Inventory: A "real world" resource for environmental educators,' Proceedings of 88th Annual Meeting of the Air and Waste Management Association.

Van Liere, K.D. and R.E. Dunlap (1981), 'Environmental concern: does it make a difference how it is measured?,' *Environment and Behavior*, **13**(6): 651–76.

12. Childhood's end? Sustaining and developing the evolving field of organizations and the natural environment

Mark Starik

No utopia can ever give satisfaction to everyone, all the time. As their material conditions improve, men raise their sights and become discontented with power and possessions that once would have seemed beyond their wildest dreams. And even when the external world has granted all it can, there still remain the searchings of the mind and the longings of the heart ...Yet among all the distractions and diversions of a planet which now seemed well on the way to becoming one vast playground, there were some who still found time to repeat an ancient and never-answered question: 'Where do we go from here?'—(Narrative in *Childhood's End* by Arthur C. Clarke, 1953).

The Introductory Chapter to this volume and the chapters that follow illustrate with significant clarity that the field of organizations and the natural environment (O&NE) is a rapidly emerging, increasingly integrated, set of scholarly perspectives and products. Though this research agenda and record had many disparate roots that developed over several decades (Starik and Marcus, 2000), only since the late 1980s or so have topics such as environmental strategy and sustainable development become salient streams of inquiry and practice (Kolk and Mauser, 2002). The present chapter views this brief period as just the beginning, the childhood, of this field, with much more development, including surprises and challenges, expected in the decades ahead.

This chapter presents a number of suggestions about the future of O&NE-related research. None of these outcomes may be quite as dramatic as those in the science fiction classic *Childhood's End*, though some of our colleague-readers may view one or more of these future-views as too far 'out there' to be seriously considered. However, the intent of this chapter does admittedly share one aspect of writer Arthur C. Clarke's work, which is to spark the researcher-reader's imagination into broadening his or her perspectives and, in the academic's case, expanding the research agenda, if not to the cosmic level, then at least to a wider, multi-focused view on much that has yet to be discovered in and about our young, growing field.

WELCOME TO SOME POSSIBLE ORGANIZATION AND NATURAL ENVIRONMENT RESEARCH FUTURES – ENTER AT YOUR OWN RISK

Prospective approaches to academic and other activities have both their rewards and their hazards. On the one hand, the task can be considered a pleasant, even enjoyable, endeavor, providing an opportunity to be creative and constructive in suggesting what could come to pass. In academic research, prospective notions are often presented with the intention of seeding ideas among (especially new) researchers in the hopes of providing direction, lessons learned and connections to and extensions beyond, past and current research efforts. The 'prospectivist's' pay-offs are seeing how close he or she can approach what actually occurs and, perhaps to some limited extent, assisting in the occurrence of these events.

On the other hand, looking ahead in time (and, Arthur C. Clarke might include, space) can be perilous. Making inaccurate predictions or suggesting foolish pathways is a prognosticator's nightmare, at minimum reducing credibility, and, much worse, potentially damaging or destroying valuable directions or opportunities. In academic research, new faculty and doctoral student researchers could be distracted or deterred from developing promising research streams or wasting time heading down conceptual culs-de-sac because of ill-advised predictions or suggestions.

So, it is with great trepidation that this author assumes the important responsibilities of suggesting his views on what corporate sustainability research may be conducted in the mid- and long-term futures of this field. However, as indicated earlier in this volume, the co-editors canvassed nearly three dozen active corporate sustainability researchers on their own perceptions of future academic research in this area and include in this article appropriate attributions to the 21 who responded. Accordingly, the co-editors wish to thank Tima Bansal, Max Bazerman, Mark Cohen, Mark Cordano, Alberto Aragón-Correa, Jonathan Doh, Carolyn Egri, Andy Hoffman, John Jermier, David Levy, Mark Milstein, Jorge Rivera, Mike Russo, Paul Shrivastava, Mark Sharfman, Ed and Jean Stead, Diane Swanson, Marie-France Turcotte, Gurneeta Vasudeva, David Wheeler and Monika Winn. The author of this chapter accepts any and all responsibility in errors of commission or omission regarding the ascription or characterization of any statements attributed to these valued colleagues.

In addition, the last several years of a number of O&NE-related journals and special issues were reviewed and our local university researcher-colleagues and graduate students were asked for their reactions to these recommendations. Hopefully, adopting this external collaborative approach has resulted in enhancing the overall usefulness of this chapter's projections. The suggestions in this chapter are intended to provide both predictions and recommendations for future research in the traditional spirit of suggestions by research publication authors for future researchers. Of course, readers are also advised to seriously consider those research recommendations advanced by this volume's authors in their respective articles.

EXPLORING THE RESEARCH FIELD OF ORGANIZATIONS AND THE NATURAL ENVIRONMENT

Similar to other sets of organizations and natural environment (O&NE) research recommendations, this set groups its suggestions into two well-known categories: research contexts and processes, and research content (Starik, 1995; Starik and Marcus, 2000). Since many O&NE-related researchers (including the co-editors) identify with or are at least familiar with the strategic management field of study, the approach adopted for this chapter in part loosely utilizes a 'research needs and issues' guide that was developed for the strategic management field just as it was being reconceptualized (and renamed) several decades ago (Schendel and Hofer, 1979). While that list was made up of 18 sections, the present effort, employing a different sequencing scheme, combines a number of these into seven groupings, identifying the intersections, respectively, between natural environment topics and: (1) strategy context and research method (or process); (2) strategy concept and process; (3) governance and general management; (4) goal formulation and structure and social responsibility; (5) strategy formulation and environmental analysis; (6) strategy implementation; and (7) strategy performance evaluation and control.

ORGANIZATIONS AND THE NATURAL ENVIRONMENT RESEARCH CONTEXTS AND PROCESSES (METHODS)

A 'Matter' of Emphasis

Most of the scholarship that is O&NE-related has focused primarily on the 'O' part of that acronym, that is, organizations. Given that many of the scholars who conduct research in this area teach in business, and not natural science, schools and affiliate themselves with organization-related professional associations, such as the Academy of Management and the Greening of Industry Network, this organization-dominant focus is understandable. And, since many of these academics have educational backgrounds in university social science and professional schools, both their interests and their knowledge base highlight this organization (rather than environment) focus. However, over time and at various times in this field's development, we may find that, when a number of organizationally-focused topics become saturated, the emphasis might shift a bit toward the 'NE' part of the acronym, that is, the natural environment. So, for example, we might observe some O&NE-related research centering on the organizational aspects of such topics as land-use development, the environmental impacts of violent human conflict, and asteroid impact threats and organizational responses, among many others. While some social scientists and many natural scientists have explored these natural environment phenomena as they affect (or are affected by) our species, few organizational researchers appear to have done so. We apparently are just beginning to examine the businesses, government agencies, and non-profit organizations that have been associated with these and many other natural environmental phenomena, indicating that nature-based contexts are ripe for organizational research opportunities. And, while engineers and other technically-oriented researchers have addressed the multitude of technologies each of these phenomena involve, most organizational researchers have yet to investigate significantly those organizations developing, manufacturing, procuring, marketing, promoting or regulating these technologies (as in, for example, Delmas and Heiman, 2001). In short, it may soon be time for some of us to more fully 'green' our research, that is, to focus as much on natural environment phenomena as on organizational variables.

The Double-Edged Sword (and Sheath) of Technology

Further regarding organizations and technology in the natural environment, many organizations involved in technology streams constitute their own sectors, industries or industry segments and could be explored as such. What are the organization and natural environment aspects of: nuclear fission and fusion technologies; renewable and energy-efficiency technologies; organic and advanced agricultural technologies; and robotics, superconductor, space and genetic engineering technologies (Sharma and Nguan, 1999)? Most O&NE-related research has not examined high-tech organizations and their products and services, and, most has not focused on the technologies, in general, even when low-tech, well-known organizations have been studied. With the ever-quickening pace of technological change in many developed societies, ample opportunity exists for research to more centrally focus on the O&NE-related impacts (and inputs) of these advancements. Conversely, traditional technologies, often found in indigenous cultures in developing countries, such as low-resource consumption techniques, holistic health care and natural construction approaches, are equally available to explore in O&NE-related research. Similar to the previous set of recommendations suggesting that researchers can study the 'bio-physicalness' of their subject organizations and natural environments, those technologies that appear to hold either great promise or potential peril (or both) are associated with organizations which bear some investigation.

Our Environment, Ourselves

Continuing on the theme of research context and process, while a few of our colleague-respondents mentioned that researchers in our field needed to examine many of our assumptions about organizations and the natural environment and to adopt critical perspectives in relation to our research topics and approaches overall, only one (Swanson) hinted that our own environmental values and practices were legitimate or necessary research subjects. The present chapter's author believes that, just as most of us expect researchers to reveal any possible organizational conflicts of interest or other bases for potential bias, those of us who study environmental topics both have an obligation and an opportunity to let our stakeholders know our own attitudes and behaviors regarding the topics we study. A common ethical research perspective is to ensure that when we analyze, we limit our biases; when we advocate, we need to clearly state that intention and to increase the consistency between what we say and what we do, both individually and organizationally. On the latter topic, opportunities to investigate our own respective organizations' environmental phenomena can be welcomed, suggested and assisted. Doing so not only allows us to integrate our research into the rest of our lives, but also potentially provides unique insights into our organizations (and networks), which have their own environmental aspects. Such introspection and integration can enhance both self-respect and stakeholder credibility, as well as provide valuable environmental insights.

NGOs and Public Organizations and Policy

This section is the first in this chapter to employ the 1979 strategy research needs review mentioned earlier. Unlike the subjects above, the topic of NGOs and public organizations and policy were included in that review as the last several in a long list of strategy context areas, perhaps because those authors accorded them lesser importance to the field of strategic management, relative to the other topics it reviewed. However, judging from much of the literature on organizations and the natural environment, exactly the opposite is the case for environmental strategic management. Both non-profit and governmental organizations have been keys to the advancement of environmental principles, policies and practices, especially in developed countries, so both sets of non-business organizations have been given substantial attention by O&NE-related researchers (for example, Collins and Starik, 2001; King and Lenox, 2000; Hoffman, 1999). However, most of the studies conducted by these scholars apparently have considered non-profit and public organizations mainly from the perspective of stakeholders of business environmental activities (Porter and van der Linde, 1995), rather than as legitimate focal points for organizational research in their own right. For instance, while a few case studies have been developed on some Western environmental NGOs, these are often written to highlight the NGO–business linkage, rather than to explore how the NGO operates in its multiple (including natural) environments (Starik and Dyer, 1999).

Similarly, when O&NE-related researchers have incorporated public organizations into their studies, much attention has been directed at how businesses have responded to government regulation, and less at how particular government organizations (and their sub-units) developed and implemented their environmental policies (including the role of business influence in these activities). Therefore, apparently, much work remains on developing understanding about the ways environmental NGOs and public agencies operate, the conditions in which they arise and in which they function (or malfunction), and the impacts that they have on their societies and environments. Further, NGOs which have garnered the most attention from O&NE-related researchers have been the largest, most mainstream environmental organizations, mostly in Northern developed countries. Many smaller, 'edgier' ENGOs, such as the Earth Island Institute (Frooman, 1999) could be interesting focal organizations. In addition, interactions both between organizations in these sectors and between these and businesses on environmental matters also appear needed and useful (Turcotte, 2000). Finally, their involvement with particular environmental public policies (Vig and Kraft, 2000), such as federal, state or local environmental authority distribution, environmental leadership to enhance the building of environmental cultures, the environmental responsibilities of different branches of government and sectors of society, market versus regulatory versus ethical environmental approaches, and environmental justice and sustainable development, could all be more thoroughly studied.

Similar to our research on businesses, which includes those which are environmentally-oriented and those which are not, O&NE-related research can focus not on just those non-profit organizations and governmental units which have environmentally-related missions but also on those which do not. Most developed (and, to a lesser extent, developing) nations have thousands of non-profit organizations in the labor, medical, educational, arts, social services and other sub-sectors, all of which have some level and type of environmental impact, that could be of interest to the organizations and natural environment research community. To the extent that sustainability will connect the social and environmental realms more closely in the future, studies of these social organization environmental impacts appear timely.

A World of Applications

Previous reviews of O&NE-related literature suggested that this field of research needed to expand its various application contexts, especially geographical and cultural, since much of the literature tended to focus on large manufacturing corporations in Western regions of the North. While some expansion in industries and areas has been noted (and in this volume the Branzei and Vertinsky chapter on China and Japan is part of this expansion), this author and a number of our colleague-respondents suggest a continued opening up of O&NE-related geographic research contexts. As in previous reviews, developing countries have been identified as an under-researched context in this field (at least as indicated by the lack of English-language studies) and so this author, Mike Russo, David Wheeler and Jorge Rivera all recommend more attention to multiple levels of economic development, including poor and near-poor countries. One obvious suggestion for North American researchers is to begin internationalizing their research by considering Mexico and the rest of Central America and the Caribbean as potential O&NE-related research contexts. On a related point, several of our colleague-respondents suggested that we address regionalism (Hoffman) and globalization (Wheeler) issues, adopt comparative approaches in doing so (Russo and Doh), and attend to particular international environmental programs, such as greenhouse gas emissions inventorying and private sector sustainable development financing (Vasudeva).

Finally, organizational scale is another context variable that O&NE researchers have only begun to explore fully, in the sense of paying attention to the environmental activities and results of small and medium-sized organizations (de Bruijn and Hofman, 2000). Given that these organizations are much more numerous than larger organizations, researchers can surmise that, at least cumulatively, they have non-negligible impacts (both positive and negative) on the natural environment. O&NE researchers, therefore, could focus more attention on smaller-scale businesses and other organizations, new ventures and other environmentally-oriented entre-preneurship phenomena.

Process, Methods and Theories

Similar to the 1979 strategy research needs review, previous ONE-related reviews have identified that, while a growing number of more sophisticated research methods have been utilized by researchers in this field, several well-known approaches have yet to be extensively employed, including longitudinal and multi-level analyses. Two very promising developments in this field appear to be the wider consideration of 'grounded theory' research methods (for example, Bansal and Roth, 2000) and longitudinal analyses (Hoffman, 1999), but the 1995 review which indicated limited use of several statistical tests (such as multi-dimensional scaling) and research designs (such as verbal protocols) still appears applicable for O&NE-related research. In addition, our colleague-respondents in general suggested both more empirical testing (Cohen and Milstein) and more qualitative approaches (Jermier and Cohen) for research in this field, indicating that Monika Winn's suggestion that we balance rigor with ensuring connectedness to reality and relevance may be a prudent course. Regarding employing particular research theories, cultural theory (Egri and Jermier), transaction cost economics (Russo), decision theory (Bazerman), political economy perspectives (Levy and Hoffman), institution theory (Turcotte), and theory of planned behavior (Jermier) were suggested for future researcher consideration.

ORGANIZATIONS AND NATURAL ENVIRONMENT RESEARCH CONTENT

Strategy Concept and Process

New fields typically proceed through a definitional period and often are segmented into other stages and components in a field's initial organizing. Regarding these first overall strategic management categories, potential O&NE-related research topics are plentiful. For instance, while a number of studies have addressed various aspects of strategy content (for example, Sharma, 2000), questions about the definitions, components and steps of strategy, in general, can be explored more extensively in the strategic environmental management area. Just what are environmental strategies, do they include environmental goals or just the means to achieve these or both, do they have multiple levels (enterprise, corporate, business, functional and individual elements), and, if so, what are the relationships among these? What are the environmental strategy similarities and differences of their respective organizational and environmental performance effects, and can these environmental strategies be changed at will and over time to achieve the desired performance effects?

Governance and General Management

Organizational governance includes organizational leadership, which is often identified with boards of directors and top (or general) management, whereas environmental leadership may emanate from anywhere within or even outside the organization. What roles do official organizational leaders play in relation to unofficial environmental leaders, regarding the development of environmental goals and strategies of their organizations? Leadership was mentioned by several of our colleague-respondents as a promising O&NE-related research issue, and one, Carolyn Egri, a co-author in this volume, has begun conducting research on both organizational and environmental leaders (Egri and Herman, 2000). In addition to research questions raised in that line of research, others may include: What is the environmental make-up (values and attitudes) of corporate boards of directors and top management echelons, and how do these leaders cooperate or conflict with one another in advancing organizational environmental strategies? What are the short-term and long-term risks, responsibilities and rewards of these leaders? How do they balance these for overall organizational and environmental performance? Finally, one of our colleague-respondents, Mark Cordano, suggested that future O&NE research address the environmental perspectives of organizational decision-makers and how best to educate them for more effective incorporation of strategic environmental information into the systems and institutions they design.

Goal Formulation and Social Responsibility

Organizations are said to establish goals and objectives, either explicitly or implicitly, to provide milestones and targets to enhance their success (Richards, 1986). Regarding organizational and environmental performance, environmental goals and objectives are often included in organizational environmental strategies. However, significant research has yet to be conducted on the nature of these goals, whether these appear in organizational slogans, annual reports, or internal performance documents, or do not appear at all, but are simply understood. While many environmental goals can be said to be compliance-oriented, both these and beyond-compliance goals likely exhibit a very wide range of degrees, types and, of course, eventual integration and realization. Therefore, O&NE-related researchers could identify and analyze the structures and functions of environmental goals in organizations of many different types, focusing on those objectives that stand alone, as well as those which are melded with other organizational objectives. Regarding combining environmental and economic goals, a number of our colleague-respondents, including Marie-France Turcotte and David Wheeler, mentioned the popular research topic of environmental–financial performance connections, although not all were supportive of further studies on this topic. While we can probably expect more research to be conducted on this subject in the future, what may be needed are much more micro and more basic approaches that associate particular environmental activities with particular financial measures at the sub-organizational, group, network and even individual levels. This topic will be more fully addressed later in this chapter.

Social responsibility was a topic that was only briefly included in the 1979 strategy research needs guide, but probably plays a much larger role in O&NE-related research, given the traditional inclusion of 'environment' in discussions of social responsibility (though the 'e-word' is not mentioned in that section of the previous strategy topic list). Over the last several decades, environmental responsibility, and, lately, sustainability have at times eclipsed social responsibility as salient strategy research topics. A number of our colleague-respondents, including Mark Milstein and Tima Bansal, indicated that sustainability and sustainable development would be important continuing O&NE-related research topics, and others emphasized the need to integrate environmental, social and economic issues into our research. For instance, Monika Winn, Paul Shrivastava and Jorge Rivera all suggested that organization and natural environment researchers begin to focus on poverty, especially in developing countries. In addition, Paul suggested that our sustainability research needs to include attention to the 'digital divide' and sustainable consumption. On the latter topic, sustainable consumption, which often addresses the question: How much is enough? (Durning, 1992) is one of two business sustainability–social responsibility areas that may be most problematic for business (and business school academics) to tackle, since the topic (question) cuts to the heart of the business enterprise ultimate strategic question – how can we create customers (Drucker, 1954)? Perhaps not coincidentally, the other core business sustainability challenge that was identified in the earlier O&NE-related research reviews also centers on this demand characteristic – human population. Curiously, none of our colleague-respondents identified this issue as an O&NE-related research topic need, though a large number of respected academics and practitioners have raised the issue as one of the world's primary environmental challenges (for example, Wilson, 2002).

Two topics that were particularly salient during the writing of the present chapter can be associated with aspects of O&NE-related social responsibility. The first is the financial and political management scandal of Enron, the major US energy broker that exercised a global (over)reach in its energy project investments. Among many other possibilities, this case may prompt some O&NE researchers to consider examining the business ethics of their organizational research subjects. Regarding the second topic – the 11th September 2001 terrorist attacks – only one of our colleague-respondents, Jonathan Doh, approached the possible research topic of environmental security, though others did mention crisis management as a continuing O&NE-related research area. Given the airliner crashes, as well as the anthrax postal poisonings that occurred a few weeks afterwards, the organization and natural environment aspects related to the vulnerability of nuclear and other energy facilities, transportation systems and a host of other large-scale infrastructure security concerns appear to be salient research topics, especially if our field begins framing personal (or collective) security into its concepts of the natural environment, since sustainability, on a very basic level, certainly involves survival.

Strategy Formulation and Environmental Analysis

Following on the topics of goal formulation and social responsibility, the 1979 strategy research needs review guide addressed strategy formulation and environmental analysis, the latter of which is sometimes categorized (nested) within the former. Overall, strategy formulation, also known as strategic planning, includes identification of strategic issues, the process and content of alternative strategies, and the projected assessment of potential consequences of following these. While many strategic issues have been identified in O&NE-related research on environmental strategic planning processes, including extent, type and occurrence of various air, water and solid waste pollutants, and of various natural resource depletion and deterioration activities and results, others such as sustainable consumption and population have yet to receive significant attention. Still others which have not garnered much O&NE-related researcher interest, but were suggested in the 1995 review, include the organizational aspects of urban sprawl, agricultural loss of topsoil, non-point source pollution, extraction subsidies, bioregionalism, indigenous peoples and Agenda 21, the sustainability plan developed at the Rio conference in 1992. Speaking of the latter, the next World Summit on Sustainable Development is scheduled to occur during the late summer of 2002 in Johannesburg, South Africa, yet a number of issues that are likely to be addressed, including several mentioned above, could be much better represented in O&NE-related research. These include organizational connections to shrinking aquifers, desertification, persistent organic pollutants, effects of internal violent conflicts and the relationships between human rights and environmental quality (Flavin et al., 2002).

Similar to the 1979 strategy research needs guide, the present set of suggestions regarding environmental strategy could also include exhaustive descriptions of strategy formulation processes (Schendel and Hofer, 1979: 521). Though some significant research efforts have been made in understanding individual environmental project champions (Andersson and Bateman, 2000), environmental planning information needs (Henriques and Sadorsky, 1995) and the 'greening' process overall (Winn and Angell, 2000), our field still needs to understand, for a wide variety of organizations, who performs environmental strategy formulation (and who is excluded), how decision-makers in these organizations collect, process and use environmentally-related information (and what information is excluded or devalued). In addition, how do these decision-makers structure this information into a useful environmental plan? And how do they persuade other decision-makers, both inside and outside their organizations, to accept, improve and/or implement their plans? To what extent do these decision-makers use their own environmental values and attitudes in formulating these plans versus those of others in the process? What negotiation strategies, analytical frameworks and information systems, including forecasts, are employed in environmental strategic formulation and with what result? Several of our colleague-respondents suggested similar O&NE-related topics for future researchers, including the need for attention to environmental information (Sharfman), corporate impacts on social and environmental values in their 'communities' (Hoffman), environmental quality trends (Russo and Hoffman) and environmental negotiation (Bazerman and Turcotte).

The one environmental strategic formulation topic that O&NE-related researchers have addressed perhaps more than any other either in this or any other category in this article is that of 'stakeholders'. The 1995 review identified this trend which appears to have continued to the present (for example, Madsen and Ulhoi, 2001; Hartman et al., 1999). However, despite its frequency as a research topic in the past, numerous stakeholders' connections to environmental strategy still appear to warrant some attention, including its linkages to local environmental organizations, environmental consultants, environmental entrepreneurs (also suggested by Doh and Swanson), environmental professional associations and environmental trainers and educators. Other stakeholders mentioned in the 1995 review, including military organizations, neighborhood associations, labor unions and the media, still appear to warrant researcher attention. Further, Jonathan Doh advocated more research on an emerging area of business–government–non-profit environmental networks, and Diane Swanson listed environmental whistleblowers as other under-researched stakeholder groups. Particular groupings of environmental stakeholders, sometimes called industrial ecology (or symbiosis), are contiguous organizations which form networks to exchange material and energy inputs and outputs, and appear to be a very promising O&NE research area (for example, Dunn and Steinemann, 1998). Another environmentally-oriented network example that appears worthy of investigation are various emissions-related consortia, such as the Global CO^2 Capture Project that aims to share information on CO^2 sequestration (a suggestion for which the author thanks Gurneeta Vasudeva).

Finally, related overall to the several strategy formulation sub-topics of environmental decision-makers and environmental scanning, environmental stakeholders and environmental networks, we are still near the front of our research learning curve regarding our knowledge and understanding of the phenomena of multiple environmental and organizational levels (Starik and Rands, 1995). While it has been hypothesized that multiple levels of sustainability entities exist (including ecological, political and economic, sociocultural, interorganizational, organizational and sub-organizational, and individual) more descriptive and inferential studies have yet to be conducted highlighting the linkages between and among these environmental strategy levels, and whether the types or degrees of these linkages have important environmental strategy implications. Connections between and among the various levels of environmental strategy, suggested by several of our colleague-respondents, include international governance regimes and multinational corporations (Levy), international trade participants and ecological economics and policy (Steads), public environmental enforcement agencies (Jermier), certification standards (Aragón), regionalism (Hoffman) and organizational and individual environmental behavior (Bazerman and Hoffman). In addition to these traditional O&NE-related research levels, this author and the Steads suggest that sustainable communities, which of course are largely collections of organizations and the individuals who belong to them, also be studied.

Strategy Implementation

While the 1979 strategy research needs review included several other categories, since many of these have already been addressed in the present chapter, two more remain – strategic implementation, and strategy performance evaluation and control. Typical topics in the first category, and used here, are organizational structure, processes, capabilities and culture. O&NE-related researchers have often included environmental, health and safety (EHS) managers in their survey samples (for example, Cordano and Frieze, 2000), but many EHS structural issues remain to be extensively explored, such as the size, position, resources and responsibilities of EHS departments and the relationship of these variables to organizational influence or environmental performance or industry type and position. Environmental capabilities and behaviors been also appear to need more analysis throughout multiple departments (not just in EHS) in a wide variety of organizations, industries and cultures.

The subject of organizational departments is closely related to the strategy implementation sub-topic of organizational processes or systems. While a number of O&NE-related studies have focused on manufacturing processes, and a more limited number on research and development and on marketing functions, most other organizational departments, processes or systems, including their relationships to one another, to headquarters, and to key external stakeholders, are only beginning to be explored. So, as our colleague-respondents have indicated, management information systems (Mark Sharfman), human resources management systems (Egri), marketing (Russo, Swanson and Wheeler), procurement (Jermier) and legal and public affairs (Swanson) functions are all potential environmental strategy implementation research subjects. Both Mark Cohen and Mike Russo indicated research needs in the organizational structure and greening area.

Very little research has yet been conducted on organizational environmental capabilities, that is, employee resolve, flexibility, enthusiasm, team-orientation, skills, knowledge and other characteristics, with major exceptions being innovation (for example, Blum-Kusterer and Hussain, 2001; Foster and Green, 2000; Ramus and Steger, 2000) and organization-wide strategic capabilities (Sharma and Vredenburg, 1998). Given the attractiveness of a resource-based view of organizations among many O&NE researchers, more attention to these organizational assets seems warranted.

Organizational culture has been one of the few environmental strategy implementation topics that O&NE-related researchers have begun to address much more frequently than others in this category. However, the organizational culture sub-topics of top management and shared environmental values and worldviews seem to have received the bulk of this attention, with many other aspects of organizational culture still relatively unexplored, including the 'greening' of the informal aspects of organization, such as environmentally-oriented workplace or market place aesthetics, morale enhancement, extra-organizational activities, oral histories and visual and auditory cues. While much has been made of organizations 'hitting the green wall' (a topic that may still need more investigation, as suggested by Monika Winn), significantly less has been discovered about 'nurturing green seeds' in organizations. Several of our colleague-respondents (Egri, Jermier and Doh) indicated that the overall environmental aspects of organizational culture could use far more exploration, analysis and evaluation by O&NE-related researchers. In addition to identifying its significant internal characteristics, studies could also be conducted on the many likely relationships between environmental organizational culture features and other interesting variables, such as other aspects of strategy implementation, environmental strategy formulation and, of course, performance (both environmental and organizational).

Strategy Performance Evaluation and Control

The 1979 strategy research needs review next turned to strategy performance evaluation and control as useful categories and, once again, this set of subtopics can also be applied to environmental organizational strategy. As indicated earlier, some O&NE-related research over the past decade has focused some attention on the environmental and financial performance topic (for example, Thomas, 2001). A number of macro (corporate-level) studies have found a generally positive relationship between these two outcome variables sets (for example, Russo and Fouts, 1977). However, studies that highlight why these connections existed, how they evolved, and whether they are evident in organizations below the corporate level (that is, when comparing the fiancial and environmental performance of subsidiaries, product lines or organizational functions), would likely be valuable to researchers and practitioner decision-makers. In addition, information and insights are still needed on how organizational environmental strategies undergo changes over time and, of course, with what effects (both financially and environmentally).

Related to both formulation and implementation, and centered on the concept of goal achievement, is the subject of strategic control. Environmental strategy control would involve the monitoring and adjusting of efforts to attain 'green' or sustainability-oriented organizational objectives, such as pollution prevention and depletion reduction targets, as well as changes in environmentally-related reputation and financial performance associated with these strategies. While a number of O&NE-related studies have often employed environmental and other performance measures in assessing their impacts, quite a number of environmental strategy control research approaches have yet to be attempted at more than a minimal level. These open subtopics are: the short-term or annual environmental objectives that organizations select to reorient their overall long-term environmental strategy; the pace at which organizations either intend to or actually do achieve these targets; the changes in environmental strategy that are attempted or actually implemented based on environmental goal achievement or non-achievement; and the transparency, accuracy and usefulness of both the measures and the actions taken to ensure appropriate progress is being made. One set of documents that are often said to be useful in organizational strategy control are financial statements, but these may be less than helpful in environmental strategy control, since so little environmental data is typically reflected in them. One set of this volume's authors addresses this research and practice deficit (Sherman et al.), but more studies of current and suggested environmental accounting practices could be welcomed by environmental strategy control advocates and analysts. What organizational information is disclosed and to whom and how are topics that have received some attention, such as the Global Reporting Initiative, but given the potential amount, frequency and importance of such disclosures, these subjects may receive continuing researcher attention in the future (Turcotte).

OTHER PROSPECTS?

Regarding the future-oriented O&NE-related research overall, scholars are encouraged to make their own projections about which issues, areas and approaches will be most salient in some relevant time frame. Environmental trends appear to point in the direction of increasing numbers of potential pollutants that may generate regulatory and ENGO interest, more attention to environmental problems of the elderly in developed countries and young adults in developing countries, and of children worldwide, continued pressures on many world ecosystems, including endangered and threatened species and habitats (WRI, 2000). With the popular media focused on globalization, human rights of many varieties may become more salient in environmental research. Regarding individuals of species, non-human species may receive more attention in the future, given the increasing number of personal pets and greater sensitivity to animal testing, humane animal treatment and human health-related non-animal food substitutes (Gaines and Jermier, 2000). And, O&NE researchers could more fully explore their own and their culture's environmental ethics and philosophies (Egri, 1997; Stead and Stead, 2000; Flannery and May, 2000), including controversial topics such as environmental justice (Shibley and Prosterman, 1998; Hampton, 1999). Along these lines, we invite our reader-researchers to join us in taking a few more prudent, measured risks (or, depending on one's perspective, pursue more exciting opportunities and challenges) in exploring a wider variety of topics, pushing the boundaries of acceptable subjects, and utilizing a full range of methodologies, including a few needing further development, modification and adaptation.

Just Getting Started

This view through the looking glass of organizations and the natural environment possible futures is by no means meant to be a definitive survey of even a modest percentage of the possibilities that researchers may explore in the next few years of this field's development. Rather, this chapter is a subjective assessment of at least a small number of O&NE-related sub-fields, suggesting a few potential directions in each. Undoubtedly, this volume's co-editors, authors, colleague-respondents and readers can and will (and should) identify and assess more O&NE sub-fields and more directions. This author's hope is that we all will continue to unleash our imaginations in the scholarly service of our field, an endeavor that is now ready to move beyond the safety of its childhood, toward a full blossoming into a vital and energized community of organizations and natural environment scholars.

REFERENCES

Andersson, L.M. and T.S. Bateman (2000), 'Individual environmental initiative: championing natural environmental issues in US business organizations,' *Academy of Management Journal*, **43**(4): 548–70.

Bansal, P. and K. Roth (2000), 'Why companies go green: a model of ecological responsiveness,' *Academy of Management Journal*, **43**(4): 717–36.

Blum-Kusterer, M. and S. Hussain (2001), 'Innovation and corporate sustainability: an investigation into the process of change in the pharmaceuticals industry,' *Business Strategy and the Environment*, **10**(5): 300–16.

Christmann, P. (2000), 'Effects of "best practices" of environmental management on cost advantage: the role of complementary assets,' *Academy of Management Journal*, **43**(4): 663–80.

Clarke, A.C. (1953), *Childhood's End*, New York: Harcourt, Brace and World.

Collins, E. and M. Starik (2001), 'Do voluntary environmental programs work? A multi-stakeholder perspective of the US Environmental Protection Agency's Project XL,' Presented at the Academy of Management Meetings, Washington, DC, August.

Cordono, M. and I.H. Frieze (2000), 'Pollution reduction preferences of US environmental managers: applying Ajzen's theory of planned behavior,' *Academy of Management*, **43**(4): 627–41.

De Bruijn, T.N.M. and P.S. Hofman (2000), 'Pollution prevention in small and medium-sized enterprises: evoking structural changes through partnerships,' *Greener Management International*, **30**: 61–9.

Delmas, M. and B. Heiman (2001), 'Government credible commitment in the French and American nuclear industry,' *Journal of Policy Analysis and Management*, **20**(3): 433–56.

Drucker, P. (1954), *The Practice of Management*, New York: Harper and Row.

Dunn, B.G. and A. Steinemann (1998), 'Industrial ecology for sustainable communities,' *Journal of Environmental Planning and Management*, **41**(6): 661–72.

Durning, A. (1992), *How Much is Enough?* New York: W.W. Norton.

Egri, C.P. (1997), 'Spiritual connections with the natural environment: pathways for global change,' *Organizations and Environment*, **10**(4): 407–31.

Egri, C.R. and S. Herman (2000), 'Leadership in the North American environmental sector: values, leadership styles, and contexts of environmental leaders and their organizations,' *Academy of Management Journal*, **43**(4): 571–604.

Flannery, B.L. and D.R. May (2000), 'Environmental decision making in the US metal finishing industry,' *Academy of Management Journal*, **43**(4): 642–62.

Flavin, C., H. French and G. Gardner (2002), *State of the World, 2002*, New York: W.W. Norton.

Foster, C. and K. Green (2000), 'Greening the innovation process,' *Business Strategy and the Environment*, **9**(5): 287–303.

Frooman, J. (1999), 'Stakeholder influence strategies,' *Academy of Management Review*, **24**(2): 191–205.

Gaines, J. and J.M. Jermier (2000), 'Animal inequality and organizations: introduction,' *Organizations and Environment*, **13**(4): 426–8.

Hampton, G. (1999), 'Environmental equity and public participation,' *Policy Sciences*, **32**(2): 163–74.

Hartman, C.L., P.S. Hofman and E.R. Stafford (1999), 'Partnership: a path to sustainability,' *Business Strategy and the Environment*, **8**(5): 255–66.

Henriques, I. and P. Sadorsky (1995), 'The determinants of firms that formulate environmental plans,' in D. Collins and M. Starik, *Research in Corporate Social Policy and Performance*, Greenwich, CT: JAI Press.

Hoffman, A. (1999), 'Institutional evolution and change: environmentalism and the US chemical industry,' *Academy of Management Journal*, **42**(4): 351–71.

King, A.A. and M.J. Lenox (2000), 'Industry self-regulation without sanctions: the chemical industry's Responsible Care Program,' *Academy of Management Journal*, **43**(4): 698–716.

Kolk, A. and A. Mauser (2002), 'The evolution of environmental management: from stage models to performance evaluation,' *Business Strategy and the Environment*, **11**(1): 14–31.

Madsen, H. and J.P. Ulhoi (2001), 'Integrating environmental and stakeholder management,' *Business Strategy and the Environment*, **10**(2): 77–88.

Porter, M.E. and C. van der Linde (1995), 'Green and competitive: ending the stalemate,' *Harvard Business Review*, September–October: 120–34.

Ramus, C.A. and U. Steger (2000), 'The roles of supervisory support behaviors and environmental policy in employee "ecoinitiatives" at leading-edge European companies,' *Academy of Management Journal*, **43**(4): 605–26.

Richards, M.D. (1986), *Setting Strategic Goals and Objectives*, St Paul, MN: West.

Russo, M.V. and P.A. Fouts (1997), 'A resource-based perspective on corporate environmental performance and profitability,' *Academy of Management Journal*, **40**(3): 534–9.

Schendel, D. and C.W. Hofer (1979), *Strategic Management: A New View of Business Policy*, Boston: Little-Brown.

Sharma, S. (2000), 'Managerial interpretations and organizational context as predictors of corporate choice of environmental strategy,' *Academy of Management Journal*, **43**(4): 681–97.

Sharma, S. and O. Nguan (1999), 'The biotechnology industry and biodiversity conservation strategies: the influence of managerial interpretations and risk propensity,' *Business Strategy and the Environment*, **8**(1): 46–61.

Sharma, S. and H. Vredenburg (1998), 'Proactive corporate environmental strategy and the development of competitively valuable organizational capabilities,' *Strategic Management Journal*, **19**: 729–53.

Shibley, M.A. and A. Prosterman (1998), 'Silent epidemic, environmental injustice, or exaggerated concern?' *Organizations and Environment*, **11**(1): 33–58.

Starik, M. (1995), 'Research on organizations and the natural environment: some paths we have traveled, the "field" ahead,' in D. Collins and M. Starik *Research in Corporate Social Performance and Policy – Sustaining the Natural Environment: Empirical Studies on the Interface Between Nature and Organizations*, Greenwich, CT: JAI Press.

Starik, M. and R.E. Dyer (1999), *World Resources Institute: Moving to Engage Business*, Washington, DC: World Resources Institute.

Starik, M. and A.A. Marcus (2000), 'Special research forum on the management of organizations in the natural environment: a field emerging from multiple paths, with many challenges ahead,' *Academy of Management*,

Starik, M. and G.P. Rands (1995), 'Weaving an integrated web: multilevel and multisystem perspectives of ecologically sustainable organizations,' *Academy of Management Review*, **20**(4): 908-35.

Stead, J.G. and W.E. Stead (2000), 'Eco-enterprise strategy: standing for sustainability,' *Journal of Business Ethics*, **24**(4): 313–29.

Thomas, A. (2001), 'Corporate environmental policy and abnormal stock price returns: an empirical investigation,' *Business Strategy and the Environment*, **10** (3): 125–34.

Turcotte, M.F. (2000), 'Working non-"STOP" for sustainable development: case study of a Canadian environmental NGO's relationship with businesses since 1970,' in J. Bendell (ed.), *Terms for Endearment: Business, NGOs, and Sustainable Development*, Aizlewood's Mill: Greenleaf Publishing.

Vig, N. and M. Kraft (2000), *Environmental Policy in the 21st Century*, Washington, DC: CQ Press.

Wilson, E.O. (2002), 'The bottleneck,' *Scientific American*, **286**(2): 84–8.

Winn, M.I. and L.C. Angell (2000), 'Toward a process model of corporate greening,' *Organization Studies*, **21**(6): 1119–47.

World Resources Institute (2000), *A Guide to World Resources 2000–2001; People and Ecosystems: The Fraying Web of Life*, Washington, DC: World Resources Institute.

Index